Singapore

"All you've got to do is decide to go
and the hardest part is over.

So go!"

TONY WHEELER, COFOUNDER – LONELY PLANET

THIS EDITION WRITTEN AND RESEARCHED BY
Cristian Bonetto

Contents

Plan Your Trip 4

Explore Singapore 44

Understand Singapore 163

Survival Guide 181

Singapore Maps 200

(left) **Noodles p31** Food is a Singapore highlight

(above) **Chinatown p67** Colourful architecture and festivals

(right) **Esplanade Bridge p56** Great views of the city skyline

WITHDRAWN

Welcome to Singapore

Long dismissed as little more than a sterile stopover, Singapore has reinvented itself as one of the world's hotlist destinations.

Asian 'It' Kid

Asia's perennial geek has finally found its groove. More than just satay and malls, new-school Singapore is all about sci-fi architecture in billion-dollar gardens, contemporary art in converted colonial barracks, and single-origin coffee in heritage shophouses. There's a deepening self-confidence and it's driving everything, from Singapore's striking new hotels to its modern menus and expertly curated cocktails. Beyond these bold new thrills is a nation with history and depth, recounted in museums as enlightened as they are engaging. Singapore, boring? Pah-*lease*.

Food, Glorious Food

From chilli crab to fragrant laksa, *rendang* (spicy coconut curry) and biryani, Singapore is a mouthwatering feast of flavours. Singaporeans are obsessed with food, and you'll find it steaming, sizzling and simmering almost everywhere you look. Indeed, food is the greatest unifier across ethnic divides, and the country's celebrated hawker centres are a heady mix of Chinese, Malaysian and Indian spices. Centuries of cultural exchange shine through in the region's unique Nonya cuisine, while modern Singapore's global status is reflected in a booming restaurant scene that covers all bases.

Shop Until You Drop

Dirt-cheap prices may be a thing of the past but Singapore remains a retail joyride. Its malls are the stuff of legend – ambitious consumer temples packed with catwalk couture, on-trend street brands and just-released electronics. Beyond the malls is a scene that's deliciously eclectic and increasingly idiosyncratic: hunt down Chinese medicines, dusty antiques or local art in heritage Chinatown shophouses; bag bespoke fragrances to the Islamic call to prayer in Kampong Glam; or pick up local frocks, bling and books in the deco buildings of Tiong Bahru.

The Wild Side

The world's aspiring 'City in a Garden' is an unexpected wonderland for fans of all things green and natural. Catch a city bus and end up in ancient rainforests rustling with monkeys and greater racket-tailed drongos, muddy wetlands teeming with lobsters and giant lizards, or sleepy farms heaving with bananas, papayas and jackfruit. Alternatively, hop on a bumboat and then cycle your way around a rustic island paradise. Or just stay central and escape to Singapore's soothing Botanic Gardens. Welcome to the wild side, in an oh-so-Singaporean, user-friendly package.

Why I Love Singapore

By Cristian Bonetto, Author

What I love most about Singapore are the sharp and constant contrasts: smoky temples in the shadow of skyscrapers, luxe condos backing onto jungle, old-school shophouses housing secret cocktail dens. I can travel the world without ever leaving the island. One minute I'm in the 'Hong Kong' wet markets and malls of Chinatown, the next the 'Mumbai' street scenes of Little India, and later the red-light 'Patpong, Bangkok' district of Geylang. Dig deeper than the 'sterile' cliches and you'll find a place more complex, contradictory and addictive than you might imagine. Asia's little red dot never fails to make me swoon.

For more about our author, see p224.

Top: Chinese New Year market in Chinatown (p67)

Singapore's
Top 10

1

Hawker Food (p30)

1 Fragrant chicken rice, rich and nutty satay, sweet and sour *rojak*, spicy BBQ *sambal* stingray: Singapore's hawker food is the stuff of legend, and celebrity chefs from Anthony Bourdain to the late *New York Times* writer Johnny Apple have raved about the dazzling array of cheap, lip-smacking dishes available. There's no better way to get into Singapore's psyche than through its cuisine, so get ready to sweat it out over steaming plates of tried, tested and perfected local favourites.

BELOW LEFT: NIGHT MARKET, CHINATOWN

✕ *Eating*

Gardens by the Bay (p52)

2 Spanning 101 hectares, Gardens by the Bay is Singapore's hottest new horticultural asset. The $1 billion 'super park' is home to almost 400,000 plants, not to mention awe-inspiring contemporary architecture. Two giant conservatories rise beside Marina Bay like futuristic shells, one home to ancient olive trees, the other to a towering, tropical mountain. To the north are the Supertrees; futuristic, botanical giants connected by a commanding Skyway and glowing hypnotically each night.

◉ *Colonial District, Marina Bay & the Quays*

Singapore Zoo & Night Safari (p115)

3 We're calling it: this is possibly the world's best zoo. The open-air enclosures allow for both freedom for the animals to roam and unobstructed visitor views. Singapore Zoo is one of the few places outside of Borneo or Sumatra where you can stand under trees with orang-utans a few feet above your head, or where mouse deer and lemurs scamper across your path. As evening closes in, the Night Safari next door uses open-concept enclosures to get visitors up close and personal with nocturnal creatures such as leopards, free-ranging deer and handsome Malay tigers.

⦿ *Northern & Central Singapore*

Asian Civilisations Museum (p50)

4 Travel east to west across the continent at this engrossing ode to Asia's cultures, traditions and crafts. It's like a sprawling, glittering attic, heaving with ancient pottery, instruments and sculptures, mystical weaponry, whimsical puppets and precious royal jewels. You'll find anything and everything from gleaming Javanese headdresses and delicate batik textiles, to rare Qurans and manuscripts, centuries-old Chinese calligraphy, porcelain and statuary; there's even a Tibetan ritual apron made of human and animal bones.

⦿ *Colonial District, Marina Bay & the Quays*

4

5

Botanic Gardens

(p122)

5 Singapore's Garden of Eden is the perfect antidote to the city's rat-race tendencies. At the tail end of Orchard Rd, it's a sprawling oasis laced with elegant lakes and themed gardens, and no shortage of perfect spots for picnics and people-watching. Stroll through the orchid gardens, looking out for Vanda Miss Joaquim, Singapore's national flower, or cool down in a rare slice of ancient rainforest. The Botanic Gardens are also home to a dedicated Children's Garden, free guided tours and free opera performances at the Shaw Foundation Symphony Stage.

⊙ *Holland Village, Dempsey Hill & the Botanic Gardens*

Orchard Road

(p100)

6 What was once a dusty road lined with spice plantations and orchards is now a 2.5km torrent of magnificent malls, department stores and speciality shops. You'll find every brand imaginable, from emerging local designers to global high-street heavyweights and coveted European couture. Indeed, you can shop until you drop, pick yourself up, and continue spending some more. When you've stashed your purchases back at the hotel, duck out to Emerald Hill for Peranakan architecture and happy-hour bar specials.

TOP LEFT: ION ORCHARD MALL (P100)

🛍 **Orchard Road**

Bukit Timah Nature Reserve

(p117)

7 Hiking in sunny, humid Singapore? Why not? After all, the country's British forefathers, Sir Stamford Raffles and William Farquhar, were great naturalists. And Singapore has a surprising number of green pockets. One must-do is to hike the trails at Bukit Timah Nature Reserve. A cacophony of roving monkeys, rare birds and lush canopy hark back to a time when Singapore was mostly thick, wet wilderness.

👁 **Northern & Central Singapore**

Sentosa Island

(p134)

8 Sentosa is Singapore's carefully planned, all-ages playground, a world-class sprawl of theme parks and amusements, evening spectaculars, luxe resorts and a subterranean casino. There's something for everyone, from blockbuster rides and shows at Universal Studios to giant tanks peppered with marine life at SEA Aquarium and man-made surf at Wave House. Palm-fringed beach bars flank stretches of sand, while top-notch restaurants look out over million-dollar yachts.

⭐ **Sentosa Island**

Little India (p81)

9 The most atmospheric of Singapore's historic quarters is as close as it gets to the Singapore of the old chaotic days. Experience it with the masses on the weekends when it gets packed to the gills with Indian workers wanting a slice of home. The five-foot walkways of colourful shophouses spill over with aromatic spices and Bollywood magazines. Backpackers and coolhunters swill beers at laidback bars, and insomniacs head to Mustafa Centre to buy iPads at 3am before tucking into *teh tarik* and *roti prata*.

◉ *Little India & Kampong Glam*

Pulau Ubin (p141)

10 Singapore's very own rustic island getaway offers a glimpse at the *kampong* (village) life that was a big part of Singapore as recently as the 1960s. By hopping aboard a chugging bumboat from Changi, visitors can explore Pulau Ubin's old-growth mangrove swamps and silent, lotus-peppered lakes; cycle past tin-roof shacks and ramshackle shrines; rampage along a cross-country mountain-bike trail; and end the day by digging into seafood by the sea.

◉ *Islands & Day Trips*

What's New

National Gallery Singapore

Singapore's determination to shake off its (inaccurate) 'no culture' reputation takes another step forward with the National Gallery Singapore. A showcase for Singaporean and Southeast Asian art from the 19th century to modern times, its collection includes works by major homegrown talent including Georgette Chen and Chen Chong Swee. The gallery also breathes new life into two of Singapore's heritage buildings, City Hall and the Old Supreme Court. (p54)

Gardens by the Bay

The future has landed. Singapore's futuristic Gardens by the Bay propels botany into the 21st century with high-tech design and innovation. (p52)

S.E.A. Aquarium

The world's largest aquarium delivers a spectacular, insightful journey through the region's diverse marine habitats; its cast of curious creatures include giant spider crabs and freaky anglerfish. (p137)

River Safari

Singapore Zoo and Night Safari have a new neighbour: River Safari recreates the habitats of seven major river systems, though the real draw is its adorable panda duo, Kai Kai and Jia Jia. (p118)

Green Corridor

Running south to north across the island, the Green Corridor has become Singapore's untamed version of New York's High Line, a disused rail route turned verdant urban escape. (p118)

Gillman Barracks

Colonial military barracks get a cultural makeover at Gillman Barracks, a collection of world-class private art galleries set in calming, green surrounds. (p131)

Jalan Besar

Trend oracles have proclaimed it the 'new Tiong Bahru', a historic neighbourhood swept up in a wave of hip cafes, eateries and design-savvy boutiques. (p90)

The Coffee Evolution

The Third Wave coffee evolution continues to gather pace, with specialist cafes such as Nylon Coffee Roasters sourcing, roasting and brewing superlative coffee. (p76)

Craft Cocktails

Good riddance to average mojitos. New-breed cocktail bars like Bitters & Love are raising the bar with their fresh ingredients, expertly researched recipes, and arresting twists on classic libations. (p61)

Indian Heritage Centre

Opening in 2015, this state-of-the-art centre puts the spotlight on Singapore's Indian culture in a shimmering building that stands in sharp contrast to Little India's trademark raffishness. (p83)

Jurong East Malls

Jurong East may not yet be Orchard Rd, but it's hoped that a cluster of new malls such as Jem will help relieve the congestion on Singapore's most famous shopping strip. (p132)

For more recommendations and reviews, see **lonelyplanet. com/Singapore**

Need to Know

For more information, see Survival Guide (p181)

Currency
Singapore dollar ($)

Languages
English (primary), Mandarin, Bahasa Malay, Tamil

Visas
Generally issued upon entry for stays of up to 90 days.

Money
ATMs and moneychangers widely available. Credit cards accepted in most shops and restaurants. Bitcoin accepted in some bars.

Mobile Phones
Local SIM cards, purchased from convenience stores, can be used in unlocked GSM phones.

Time
GMT/UTC plus eight hours

Tourist Information
Singapore Visitors Centre @ Orchard (☎1800 736 2000; www.yoursingapore.com; cnr Orchard & Cairnhill Rds; ⊙9.30am-10.30pm; MSomerset) offers a wealth of information, brochures, maps and helpful staff.

Daily Costs

Budget:
Less than $200
➡ Dorm bed: $20-40

➡ Hawker centres and food courts: around $6 per meal

➡ 30-minute foot reflexology at People's Park Complex: $15

➡ Ticket to a major museum: $6-10

Midrange:
$200-350
➡ Double room in midrange hotel: $140-250

➡ Singapore Ducktour: $33

➡ Two-course dinner with wine: $60

➡ Cocktails at a decent bar: $15-20 per drink

Top end:
More than $350
➡ Four- or five-star double room: $250-700

➡ Food Playground cooking course: $99

➡ Degustation in top restaurant: $250 or more

➡ Theatre ticket: $150

Advance Planning
Two months before Book tickets if you plan on watching short-run, West End-style shows or big-ticket events such as the Formula One race. Reserve a table at hot top-end restaurants.

One month before Book a bed if you are planning on staying at a dorm over the weekend. Subscribe to Groupon Singapore (www.groupon.sg) for regular deals on hotels, restaurants, shopping and spa treatments.

One week before Look for last-minute deals on Singapore accommodation and check for any events or festivals. Book a posh hotel afternoon tea.

Useful Websites
➡ **Lonely Planet** (lonelyplanet.com/singapore) Destination information, hotel bookings, traveller forum and more.

➡ **Your Singapore** (www.yoursingapore.com) Official tourism board website.

➡ **Honeycombers** (www.thehoneycombers.com) A good online guide to Singapore, covering events, eating, drinking and shopping.

➡ **City Nomads** (www.citynomads.com) Another handy website, with reviews and event listings.

➡ **Sistic** (www.sistic.com.sg) One-stop shop for tickets to concerts and shows in Singapore.

WHEN TO GO

Singapore is tropical and humid year-round. School holidays fall in June and July, the hottest time, so try to avoid travelling in these months if possible.

Singapore

°C/°F **Temp**

Rainfall inches/mm

Arriving in Singapore

Changi Airport MRT train/public bus into town, 5.30am/6am to midnight, from $1.85; airport shuttle bus, 6am to midnight, $9 (children $6); taxi ride $18 to $38, 50% more between midnight and 6am, plus airport surcharges; four-seater limousine taxi $55, plus $15 surcharge per additional stop.

HarbourFront Ferry Terminal MRT train into town from $1.40; taxi ride $6 to $13, plus any surcharges.

Woodlands Train Checkpoint Taxi into town $19 to $22, plus any surcharges.

For much more on **arrival**, see p182

Getting Around

➡ **EZ-Link card** Get this credit-card-sized electronic travel card to use on MRT trains and local buses. Just tap on and off at the sensors. You can buy one, and top up your card's credit, at all MRT stations.

➡ **MRT** Local subway, most convenient way to get around between 5.30am and midnight.

➡ **Bus** Goes everywhere the trains do and more. Great for views. From 6am till midnight, plus some night buses from the city.

➡ **Taxis** Fairly cheap if you're used to Sydney or London prices. Flag one on the street or at taxi stands. Good luck getting one on rainy days. Don't be surprised by hefty surcharges during peak hours and from midnight to 6am.

For much more on **getting around**, see p183

Sleeping

Singapore has some of the priciest beds in Southeast Asia. You'll need to book well in advance during major events such as Chinese New Year and the Formula One night race. Booking online and visiting during low season (February to May and August to October) will save money. Hostels and pod hotels are your cheapest option, but you'll be hard-pressed to find a private room with an attached bathroom. There's no shortage of midrange to high-end options, including idiosyncratic, artist-designed boutique hotels, elegant colonial pads and ostentatious chains.

Useful Websites

➡ **Lonely Planet** (lonelyplanet.com/singapore/hotels) Book rooms on Lonely Planet's website.

➡ **Booking.com** (www.booking.com) User-friendly hotel booking site.

For more on **sleeping** see p151

HOW LONG TO STAY FOR?

Singapore is stopover central for long-haul flights and most people stay a day or two. That may be enough to scratch the surface, but if you want to get beyond mall-trawling Orchard Rd, spend at least four days here. This way, you'll get to see all the top sights, eat at some of the best hawker places, be surprised by the nature reserves and have time to properly explore Singapore's booming cafe and bar scenes.

First Time Singapore

For more information, see Survival Guide (p181)

Checklist

➡ Ensure your passport is valid for at least six months past your arrival date

➡ Check airline baggage restrictions

➡ Organise travel insurance

➡ Inform your credit-/debit-card company of your travels

➡ Book your accommodation and any big-ticketed events or hotlist restaurants

➡ Check you can use your mobile (cell) phone

What to Pack

➡ Hat, sunglasses and sunscreen

➡ Mosquito repellent, especially if planning to explore nature reserves

➡ Electrical adaptor

➡ Swimsuit (for the hotel, public pool or water theme parks)

➡ A smart outfit and decent pair of shoes for higher-end restaurants and bars

➡ A photocopy of your passport photo page, stored separately from your passport

Top Tips for Your Trip

➡ Buy an EZ-Link card, an electronic travel card accepted on MRT trains, local buses, the Sentosa Express monorail and by most taxis. Options include one-, two- or three-day 'Singapore Tourist Pass' cards, which offer unlimited travel on buses and trains.

➡ Combination tickets for some sights (eg Singapore Zoo and Night Safari) can save you money.

➡ Leave rigorous outdoor activities for early morning or late afternoon to avoid the peak midday heat.

➡ Party early: there's no shortage of bars offering good-value happy-hour deals, mostly between 5pm and 8pm or 9pm.

➡ Carry a packet of tissues as you won't find serviettes (napkins) at hawker centres.

What to Wear

Singapore is hot and humid, so pack clothes that are light and comfortable. Shorts, T-shirts and flip-flops are acceptable almost everywhere, though higher-end restaurants and bars call for more stylish attire, so consider bringing at least one evening frock or long-sleeved shirt and trousers, and dress shoes. You'll need a pair of trainers or hiking boots if tackling the nature reserves, and it's always a good idea to carry a small, portable umbrella for those sudden tropical downpours, especially during the monsoon season (November to January).

Be Forewarned

Singapore is one of the world's safest and easiest travel destinations, but be aware of the following.

➡ **Drugs** Penalties for the illegal import or export of drugs are severe and include the death penalty.

➡ **Mosquitoes** Outbreaks of mosquito-borne illnesses, such as dengue fever do occur, especially during the wet season. Wear mosquito repellent, especially if visiting nature reserves.

➡ **Public transport** Eating and drinking is prohibited on public transport.

Money

Credit cards are widely accepted, except at local hawker centres and food courts. Cirrus-enabled ATMs are plentiful at malls, banks, MRT stations and commercial areas, but be aware of transaction fees.

For more information, see p187.

Taxes & Refunds

Tourists are entitled to claim a refund of the 7% Goods and Services Tax (GST) paid on purchases made at participating retail stores before leaving the country. This refund is applicable for purchases above $100. See p188 for details.

Tipping

Generally speaking, tipping is not customary in Singapore. Tipping at Changi Airport is prohibited.

➡ **Restaurants** Many add a 10% service charge, in which case tipping is discouraged. That said, a small tip is greatly appreciated when a staff member has gone out of their way to help you. Do not tip at hawker centres and food courts.

➡ **Hotels** Unnecessary at budget places. At higher-end establishments, consider tipping porters around $2 to $5 for helping you with your bags and housekeeping $2 for cleaning your room.

➡ **Taxis** Not expected, although it's courteous to round up or tell the driver to keep the change.

Making offerings at Leong San See Temple (p83)

Etiquette

➡ **Loss of Face** Singaporeans are sensitive to retaining face in all aspects of their lives. Being confrontational or angry with a local makes them lose face and you look rude.

➡ **Uncles & Aunties** It is common to address middle-aged and elderly people as 'Uncle' or 'Auntie' as a sign of respect, even if they are not related or known to you.

➡ **Chopsticks** Do not stick chopsticks upright in a bowl of rice. It is reminiscent of funeral rites and considered bad luck.

➡ **Hands** Use your right hand to greet, wave, eat or interact with someone of Malay, Indonesian or Indian descent as the left hand is associated with restroom use.

➡ **Head & Feet** The head is considered sacred by many so avoid touching someone else's. In contrast, the feet are considered dirty and directly pointing them at someone may cause offense.

Language

Singapore has no less than four official languages: English, Malay, Mandarin and Tamil. English is the first language of instruction in the majority of schools and English speakers will generally find it very easy to communicate with locals. Exceptions to the rule include some older Singaporeans and some newer arrivals, especially people from mainland China.

See p179 for more information on language and Singapore's unique brand of English.

Top Itineraries

Day One

Colonial District, Marina Bay & the Quays (p48)

A stroll around this area offers visitors a glimpse of the colonial influence left on the city. Get museumed out at the **National Museum of Singapore**, the **Asian Civilisations Museum**, or the **Peranakan Museum**. Take your pick – they're all worth your time.

> **Lunch** Maxwell Road Hawker Centre (p73): cheap and cheerful street food.

Chinatown & the CBD (p67)

While the whole area has a touristy feel about it, the **Sri Mariamman Temple**, **Buddha Tooth Relic Temple** and **Thian Hock Keng Temple** offer genuine glimpses into everyday neighbourhood life. Head up **Pinnacle@Duxton** for a bird's-eye view of the city skyline and beyond, or de-stress with super-cheap reflexology at **People's Park Complex**. Either way, follow up with a pre-dinner tipple on **Club St** or **Ann Siang Rd**.

> **Dinner** Ding Dong (p74): contemporary Southeast Asian knockouts.

Northern & Central Singapore (p113)

Early dinner done, catch a taxi to the fantastic **Night Safari**, where you have a date with a cast of majestic and curious creatures. Ride the quiet tram through the park and hop off for atmospheric walks past tigers, leopards and swooping bats.

Day Two

Little India & Kampong Glam (p81)

Little India will erase every preconceived notion of Singapore as a sterile, OCD metropolis. Weathered tailors stitch and sew by the side of the road, and the air is thick with cumin and Bollywood soundtracks. Take in the colours and chanting of **Sri Veeramakaliamman Temple** and buy a sari at **Tekka Centre**.

> **Lunch** Lagnaa Barefoot Dining (p87): a choose-your-own-spice-level adventure.

Orchard Road (p94)

Escape the afternoon heat in the air-conditioned comfort of **Orchard Road**. This is one of the world's most famous shopping meccas, with over 20 malls peddling everything from high-end Euro flagships and discerning local boutiques, to glossy department stores and retro, discount malls.

> **Dinner** Satay by the Bay (p58): breezy, bayside hawker grub.

Colonial District, Marina Bay & the Quays (p48)

If you're dining at Satay by the Bay, you're already at **Gardens by the Bay**. Give yourself plenty of time to explore Singapore's incredible new botanic gardens, including the Flower Dome and Cloud Forest conservatories. The gardens' Supertrees are especially spectacular during the nightly light show (7.45pm and 8.45pm).

Day Three

Little India & Kampong Glam (p81)

The golden-domed **Sultan Mosque** in Kampong Glam is the centre-piece of Singapore's historic Malay district. Radiating out around it is an eclectic mix of restored shophouses, sheesha-scented cafes and buzzing restaurants. Explore the area's fascinating backstory at the re-vamped **Malay Heritage Centre**, housed in a former sultan's palace.

> **Lunch** Cicheti (p87): beautiful, bubbling, woodfired pizzas.

Sentosa Island (p134)

Cultured out, it's time for some pure, unadulterated fun on Singapore's pleasure island, **Sentosa**. Tackle rides both heart-racing and sedate at movie theme park **Universal Studios**, or eye-up creatures great and small at the spectacular **SEA Aquarium**. Alternatively, ride some artificial waves at **Wave House** or book an indoor skydive at **iFly**.

> **Dinner** Mykonos on the Bay (p137): authentic Greek on the marina.

Sentosa Island (p134)

Slow down the pace with evening drinks on a palm-fringed Sentosa beach. Options include family-friendly **Coastes** or the more secluded **Tanjong Beach Club**. If you're travelling with kids, consider catching the popular **Songs of the Sea** show, a multimillion-dollar sound, light and laser extravaganza.

Day Four

Islands & Day Trips (p140)

For a taste of 1950s Singapore, head to Changi to catch a bumboat across to **Pulau Ubin**. Rent a bicycle and cycle the island's peaceful, jungle-fringed roads, passing tin-shacked houses and quirky shrines, or walk along a mangrove boardwalk. There's even a mountain-bike park with trails for varying skill levels.

> **Lunch** Pick a seafood restaurant around Pulau Ubin pier (p142).

Eastern Singapore (p103)

Once you've finished exploring sleepy Pulau Ubin, catch a bumboat back to Singapore. If it's not too late, pay a visit to the moving **Changi Museum and Chapel**, which recounts the suffering and resilience of those who endured Singapore's Japanese occupation. If it is too late, wander the shops at **Changi Village**, stopping for a beer at **Changi Village Hawker Centre**.

> **Dinner** No Signboard Seafood (p108): The best white pepper crab.

Eastern Singapore (p103)

Come evening, swap tranquil nostalgia for neon-lit excess in **Geylang**, a red-light district juxtaposed against temples, mosques and some of the best food in Singapore. Dive into action-packed **Sims Ave** and **Geylang Rd** for a very different take on Singapore street life.

If You Like...

History

Peranakan Museum Get the lowdown on Straits Chinese culture through colourful historic artefacts and multimedia displays. (p53)

National Museum of Singapore Explore centuries of Singaporean highs and lows, from exiled Sumatran princes to modern independence. (p55)

Asian Civilisations Museum Packed to the gills with priceless treasures from across Asia, this museum is one of the region's best and most varied. (p50)

Changi Museum & Chapel Reflect on human nature at its best and worst at this moving tribute to Singapore's grimmest chapter. (p106)

Chinatown Heritage Centre Relive the dangerous, chaotic and overcrowded Chinatown of an era long gone. (p69)

Baba House Experience old-style Peranakan life at one of Singapore's most beautiful heritage homes. (p72)

Art

Singapore Art Museum An inspired showcase of contemporary Singaporean and Asian art. The **8Q** wing across the road has an even sharper edge. (p53 and p53)

National Gallery Singapore Singapore's newest cultural asset explores both 19th-century and modern regional creativity. (p54)

Gillman Barracks A rambling artillery of international galleries

THANK YOU / GETTY IMAGES ©

Ferry boats at Pulau Ubin (p141)

exhibiting revered names in modern and contemporary art. (p131)

NUS Museum Ancient pottery, modern art and the work of sculptor Ng Eng Teng fill this three-in-one gallery at Singapore's national university. (p128)

Local Life

Tiong Bahru Cool cafes, independent bookshops and It-status boutiques dot streets lined with coveted deco abodes. (p78)

Jalan Besar Singapore's newest epicentre of cool, where gritty old workshops schmooze with local design shops and killer coffee. (p90)

Little India It mightn't be off-the-radar, but no other neighbourhood delivers the colours, scents and gritty authenticity of Singapore's slice of subcontinental life. (p81)

Everton Park Cult-status roaster, curated design store and other new-school enterprises: Everton Park is no average HDB complex. (p76)

People's Park Complex Kick back and treat yourself to some wallet-friendly reflexology while catching up on the local soaps. (p80)

Kranji Farms Swap bar-hopping for farm-hopping in Singapore's far northwest, home to a string of rustic enterprises peddling everything from mangoes to goat's milk and frog meat. (p130)

The Great Outdoors

Southern Ridges Start from Kent Ridge, Mt Faber or Hort-Park but, whatever you do, don't miss a stroll along this chain of verdant oases. (p128)

MacRitchie Reservoir Lace up those boots and hike the trail towards the Treetop Walk, a 250m-long suspension bridge. (p116)

Gardens by the Bay Singapore's 'City in a Garden' ambitions take another leap forward with this show-stopping city park. (p52)

Singapore Botanic Gardens Preened lawns, glassy lakes and a pocket of rare rainforest make for one very civilised natural escape. (p122)

East Coast Park A long, soothing stretch of beachfront parkland that sets an ideal scene for ambling, cycling, rollerblading, watersports and long, lazy barbecues. (p106)

Temples, Mosques & Churches

Sultan Mosque The golden-domed hub that holds Kampong Glam together, Sultan Mosque is the stuff of storybook illustrations. (p83)

Sri Mariamman Temple Lose yourself in the Technicolor drama of the *gopuram* (tower), and wander round the back for dramatic temple-meets-skyscraper views. (p70)

For more top Singapore spots, see the following:
➡ Eating (p30)
➡ Drinking & Nightlife (p36)
➡ Entertainment (p39)
➡ Shopping (p41

Thian Hock Keng Temple Singapore's famous Chinese temple stands proud with its stone lions and elaborately carved wooden beams. (p70)

St Andrew's Cathedral Explore the white-washed elegance of Singapore's most famous church, built by Indian convict labour. (p54)

Abdul Gafoor Mosque Moorish, Indian and English architecture meet a one-of-a-kind sundial at Little India's most whimsical mosque. (p84)

Island Escapes

Pulau Ubin Sail across on a bumboat, hire a bike and pedal around this charming, retro island. (p141)

St John's & Kusu Islands Join worshippers on a pilgrimage to Kusu Island, and don't forget to pack your swimsuit for a dip at St John's. (p143)

Sentosa Island An island dedicated to fun, from movie and water theme parks, to indoor skydives and man-made surf. (p134)

Pulau Bintan Sail into a slice of raffish, dusty Indonesian island life. (p144)

Month by Month

January

After the New Year's Eve parties and overpriced drinks, the year kicks off with extreme Hindu devotion and indie music.

⭐ Thaipusam

Hindus head from Sri Srinivasa Perumal Temple on Serangoon Rd to the Chettiar Hindu Temple on Tank Rd carrying *kavadis* (heavy metal frames decorated with peacock feathers, fruit and flowers).

☆ Laneway Festival

A popular one-day music festival (http://singapore. lanewayfestival.com) serving up top-tier indie acts from across the world at Gardens by the Bay. Acts span rock, folk and electronica.

February

Chinese New Year is a big deal in a country where the majority of the people are Chinese. The celebration coincides with a two-day holiday and loud, intense, colourful festivity.

⭐ Chinese New Year

Dragon dances, parades and wishes of *'Gung hei faat choi'* (I hope that you gain lots of money) mark the start of the Chinese New Year. Chinatown lights up, especially Eu Tong Sen St and New Bridge Rd, and the 'Hong-bao Special' at Marina Bay features *pasar malam* (night market) stalls, shows and fireworks.

⭐ Chingay

On the 22nd day after Chinese New Year, Chingay (www.chingay.org.sg) delivers Singapore's biggest street parade. It's a flamboyant multicultural affair featuring lion dancers, floats and other cultural performers. Buy tickets in advance for a seat in the viewing galleries, or battle the crowds for a place at the roadside barriers.

☆ Singapore International Jazz Festival

Held at Marina Bay Sands, the four-day Sing Jazz (www.sing-jazz.com) delivers established and emerging jazz talent from around the world.

March

The northeast monsoon peters out and the mercury starts rising.

☆ Mosaic Music Festival

A 10-day feast of world music, jazz and indie music at the Esplanade, Mosaic (www.mosaicmusicfestival. com) features acts local and international, renowned and obscure.

May

It's the quiet month leading towards the peak of the 'summer' heat and the busy school holidays. A good time to visit Singapore.

⭐ Vesak Day

Buddha's birth, enlightenment and death are celebrated with various events, including the release of caged birds to symbolise the setting free of captive souls. The centre of the activity is the Buddha Tooth Relic Temple on South Bridge Rd.

Affordable Art Fair

A three-day expo (www. affordableartfair.com/singapore) with over 80 local and international galleries showcasing art priced between $100 and $10,000 from 600-plus artists. Held at the F1 Pit Building, the event also takes place in November.

June

School holidays coupled with blockbuster sales equal big crowds. It's one of the hottest months on the calendar, so get ready to sweat.

Great Singapore Sale

The Great Singapore Sale (www.greatsingaporesale. com.sg) runs from the end of May to the end of July. Retailers around the island cut prices (and wheel out the stuff they couldn't sell earlier in the year). There are bargains to be had if you can stomach the crowds.

Beerfest Asia

Asia's biggest beer event (www.beerfestasia.com) pours around 300 types of brews, from both international heavyweights and craft microbreweries. Events include workshops and live music.

July

The dry months continue, and so do the school holidays.

Singapore Food Festival

A 10-day celebration of all things edible and Singaporean (www.yoursingapore. com). Events include tastings, special dinners and food-themed tours. Events take place across the city.

Hari Raya Puasa

Also known as Hari Raya Aidilfitri, this festival celebrates the end of the Ramadan fasting month (dates change annually). Head to Kampong Glam for nightly feasts during Ramadan.

August

National Day, Singapore's best known event, is held every August. Even the unpatriotic love it because it's a public holiday.

Singapore National Day

Held on 9 August, Singapore National Day (www. ndp.org.sg) is a hugely popular spectacle of military parades, civilian processions, air-force fly-bys and fireworks. Tickets are snapped up well in advance.

Hungry Ghost Festival

Marks the day when the souls of the dead are released to walk the earth for feasting and entertainment. The Chinese place offerings of food on the street and light fires. Chinese operas and other events are laid on.

Singapore International Festival of Arts

A small, world-class offering of dance, drama and music (www.sifa.sg) curated by Ong Keng Sen, one of Singapore's most respected theatre practitioners. Runs from mid-August to late September.

September

While the Formula One night race is the hottest ticket on the annual calendar, it does mean that local hotels jack up prices. And beds are still hard to find, especially in the Colonial District where the action happens.

Formula One Grand Prix

The F1 night race (www. singaporegp.sg) screams around Marina Bay. Off-track events include international music acts. Book accommodation months in advance.

Mooncake Festival

Also known as the Lantern Festival, with lanterns in Chinatown and locals nibbling on mooncakes. Takes place on the full moon of the eighth lunar month.

Navarathri

Dedicated to the wives of Siva, Vishnu and Brahma, the Hindu festival of 'Nine Nights' includes traditional Indian dancing. The Chettiar Hindu Temple, Sri Mariamman Temple and Sri Srinivasa Perumal Temple are the main activity hubs.

October

October is an inter-monsoon period. Thunderstorms are frequent but extreme weather is rare.

✨ Deepavali

Rama's victory over the demon king Ravana is celebrated during the 'Festival of Lights'. Little India is ablaze with lights for a month, culminating in a huge street party on the eve of the holiday.

November

As always, Singapore's cultural calendar is packed with religious events.

✨ Thimithi

At this eye-opener of a fire-walking ceremony, Hindu devotees prove their faith by walking across glowing coals at the Sri Mariamman Temple.

December

A sense of festivity (and monsoon rains) permeates the air as the year winds down. The rainy season means that you'll need an umbrella to avoid getting drenched, though the weather is mercifully cool.

☆ ZoukOut

ZoukOut (www.zoukout. com) is Singapore's biggest outdoor dance party, held over two nights on Siloso Beach, Sentosa. Expect A-list international DJs.

☆ Singapore International Film Festival

An 11-day feast of independent and arthouse movies from around the world (www.sgiff.com), plus master classes and fringe events.

Top: Mooncake
Bottom: Chingay

IMAGEMORE CO LTD / GETTY IMAGES ©

ANDREW JK TAN / GETTY IMAGES ©

With Kids

Singapore is one of the easiest Asian countries in which to travel with children – it's safe and clean, with efficient public transport. Kids are welcome everywhere, and there are facilities and amenities catering to children of all ages. Oh, and don't be surprised if locals fawn over your little ones!

Animal Kingdoms

Singapore Zoo, Night Safari, River Safari & Jurong Bird Park

Kids can get up close and personal with orang-utans and cheeky proboscis at Singapore Zoo, watch antelopes trot past at Night Safari, press up against giant manatees at River Safari, or feed technicolour parrots at Jurong Bird Park. Interactive shows at all venues (except River Safari) crank up the excitement.

Island Thrills

Sentosa Island

Whole days in the sun is what you get at attraction-packed Sentosa. Older kids will get a kick out of the rides at Universal Studios, while young tikes can frolic on the beach or get splash happy at Adventure Cove Waterpark.

Pulau Ubin

Bring out your little ones' inner Robinson Crusoe with a trip to old-fashioned Pulau Ubin. Getting there is half the fun: you take a bus to the eastern tip of Singapore and switch to a rickety bumboat for a short jaunt to Pulau Ubin. The island itself is bucolic bliss – rent bikes and go exploring.

Kid-Friendly Culture

National Museum of Singapore

Audio-visual displays, artefacts and child-friendly signs make this museum an engaging place for slightly older children (six and up). It's a highly evocative place, encouraging interaction and bringing Singapore's multifaceted past back to vivid life.

Botanic Blockbuster

Gardens by the Bay

As if the space-age bio domes, crazy Supertrees and bird's-eye Skyway weren't enthralling enough, Singapore's jaw-dropping botanical masterpiece is home to a 1-hectare Children's Garden, complete with motion-sensor wet play zones and giant tree houses.

Rainy-Day Mall Trawls

Orchard Road

Where do you go when it's pouring down with rain? Mall-packed Orchard Rd, of course. You'll find cinemas, IMAX screens and, of course, Toys 'R' Us. There's no shortage of quality food courts, cafes and underground walkways to keep you dry.

Ride a Duck

Singapore Ducktours

The embarrassingly fun Ducktours transports visitors on a brightly coloured amphibious former military vehicle. The tour is loud, informative and over the top, especially when the vehicle drives off-road into Marina Bay!

Like a Local

From taking the MRT out into the 'heartlands', to knowing where to go for cheap beer or a bargain foot rub, you don't have to look too hard for an authentic local experience.

Cheap Beer

Coffeeshops

When Singaporean says 'coffeeshop', they aren't referring to a place for cappuccinos, but rather a food court. Peppered throughout the island are these large collections of food stalls under one roof. Many run late into the night, and some are open 24 hours. While the ambience isn't flashy, you'll get a large bottle of Tiger for $6, alfresco seating and decent food. Each MRT station has a neighbouring coffeeshop. You won't go wrong if you head to Geylang – there's always somewhere to plonk yourself for beer, grub and hyperactive street life.

Happy Hour

Travellers bemoan the expensive drinks in Singapore. While it's true, you can have cheap drinks if you know where and when to go. Most bars offer a happy hour, starting anywhere from noon to 9pm. Deals range from 'one-for-one' (two for the price of one) drinks to $10 cocktails and pints.

Local Obsessions

Foot Reflexology

This Chinese form of relaxation involves lying in a chair and letting the masseur knead and press all the pressure points on your feet. In theory, the different bits of your foot are connected to vital organs, and getting the circulation going is good for you. In reality, it can be bloody painful. Most malls have a foot reflexology place. One Chinatown favourite is People's Park Complex, a mall packed with cheap, no-frills reflexology stalls open late.

Brunch

Given Singapore's work-hard attitude, it's natural that weekend brunch has evolved into such a local passion (not to mention the coolest place to be seen in daylight hours). Whether it's black caviar Mexican eggs at Sentosa's Kith Cafe or free-flow Domaine Chandon at Ann Siang Hill's PS Cafe, any nosh spot worth its hotlist credentials peddles a dedicated brunch menu – usually a pick of dishes off the standard breakfast and lunch menus. Sessions normally run from 11am to between 3pm and 5pm. The golden rule: if you can't book a table, go early.

The Heartlands

Orchard Rd and the CBD area offer plenty for the tourist, but the city's residential neighbourhoods proffer a stronger dose of local culture. Pick any MRT station to stop at and you'll usually emerge in a local mall. Wander away from the mall and you'll see local life in a big way: wet markets, local coffeeshops, tailors, barbers, Chinese medical halls and the like. Lively neighbourhoods include Tampines, Jurong, Bishan, Toa Payoh and Ang Mo Kio.

Shopping 24/7

Bored at 2am? Jump into a taxi and head to the Mustafa Centre in Little India. This popular complex sells everything: cameras, diamonds, Bollywood DVDs, underwear, toys, spices, food and more.

For Free

It's possible to savour some of Singapore's top offerings without reaching for your wallet, from evocative artefacts to million-dollar lightshows. And then there's always the simple pleasure of hitting the city's diverse neighbourhoods, where daily life is the best show in town.

Museums & Galleries

National Museum of Singapore

The National Museum of Singapore's Living Galleries, free from 6pm to 8pm daily, offer a fresh perspective on Singaporean history and culture through fashion, food, photography, film, theatre and opera.

Baba House

You'll need to book ahead, but the reward for your effort is a free, engrossing tour of one of Singapore's most elegantly restored Peranakan homes. Once the domain of a wealthy Straits Chinese family, its ornate architecture and furnishings offer an intimate glimpse into old Singaporean life.

Natural Highs

Exploring Singapore's swath of nature reserves and parks is both free and invigorating. Singapore's Botanic Gardens is one of the country's greatest attractions and, not only is it free, it also hosts free tours and seasonal opera performances. The Southern Ridges is another winner, with forest-canopy strolling, striking architectural features and breathtaking views.

Street Life

Chinatown

Chinatown is a visceral jungle of heady temples, medicinal curiosities, heritage shophouses and still-wriggling market produce. It costs nothing to explore the architecture of places such as the Sri Mariamman Temple and Buddha Tooth Relic Temple, the gut-rumbling Chinatown Complex wet market, or the contemporary exhibitions at pocket-sized Utterly Art.

Little India

Singapore's most refreshingly unruly inner neighbourhood offers an intense dose of colours, sounds and scents. Soak up the hypnotic energy of Sri Veeramakaliamman Temple, the fairytale architecture of Abdul Gafoor Mosque, and the riotously colourful shops and stalls of Dunlop and Buffalo Sts.

Entertainment

Esplanade – Theatres on the Bay

Singapore's iconic arts centre has no shortage of free events, from live-music gigs to art exhibitions and film screenings. Don't miss the million-dollar view from the rooftop garden.

Gardens by the Bay

While the domed conservatories and OCBC Skyway come at a cost, the rest of Singapore's showpiece city-centre gardens are free, from the Heritage Gardens to Marc Quinn's 'floating' sculpture, *Planet*. Topping it off is the twice-nightly Garden Rhapsody sound-and-light show.

Marina Bay Sands

Like Gardens by the Bay, MBS razzle dazzles with its own twice-nightly spectacular, Wonder Full, a light, laser and water show choreographed to a stirring score. The best view is from the CBD side of Marina Bay.

Guided Tours & River Cruises

Although Singapore is one of the world's easiest cities for self-navigation, guided tours can open up the city and its history in unexpected ways. The following list of tours and cruises span everything from fun, family-friendly overviews to specialised themed adventures.

Singapore River after dusk

Neighbourhood Tours

Original Singapore Walks (☎6325 1631; www.singaporewalks.com; adult $35-55, child $15-30) These popular tours deliver irreverent, knowledgeable on-foot excursions through Chinatown, Little India, Kampong Glam, the Colonial District, Boat Quay, Haw Par Villa and war-related sites. Rain-or-shine tours last from 2½ to 3½ hours. Most tours do not require booking; simply check the website for meeting times and places.

Chinatown Trishaw Night Tour (www.viator.com; adult/child $72/47) Commencing at 6pm, this atmospheric, four-hour tour of Chinatown includes dinner, on-foot exploration of Chinatown's streets, a trishaw ride through the neighbourhood's night market, and a bumboat cruise along the Singapore River. Hotel pick-ups and drop-offs are provided.

Trishaw Uncle Hop on a trishaw for an old-fashioned ride through Bugis and Little India. The 45-minute tour also takes in the Singapore River. You'll find the trishaw terminal on Queen St, between the Fu Lu Shou Complex and Albert Centre Market and Food Centre.

Hop-On, Hop-Off Tours

City Sightseeing Singapore (☎6338 6877; www.city-sightseeing.com/tours/singapore/singapore.htm; 24hr ticket adult/child $27/19, combo ticket incl river cruise $33/23) Tickets for these double-decker, hop-on, hop-off buses are valid for 24 hours. There are two routes, both with commentary: the yellow route takes in the Colonial District, Marina Bay Sands, Clarke Quay, Botanic Gardens and Orchard Rd, while the red route reaches Little India, Kampong Glam, Boat Quay, Chinatown and Marina Bay Sands.

SIA Hop-On (☎6338 6877; www.siahopon.com; 24hr ticket for SIA passengers adult/child $8/4, nonpassengers $25/15) Singapore Airlines' hop-on, hop-off bus service traverses the main tourist arteries, passing on its way the Colonial District, the Quays, Chinatown, Botanic Gardens, Orchard Rd and Little India. Buses depart every 20 minutes, starting at Singapore Flyer at 9am, with the last bus leaving at 7.40pm and arriving back at 9.10pm. Buy tickets from the driver.

/ GETTY IMAGES ©

River Tours

Singapore Ducktours (☎6338 6877; www.ducktours.com.sg; 01-330 Suntec City Mall, Nicoll Hwy; adult/child $33/23; ☺10am-6pm; ⓜEsplanade) Jump into a remodelled WWII amphibious Vietnamese war craft for a surprisingly informative and engaging one-hour tour that traverses land and water. The route focuses on Marina Bay and the Colonial District. You'll find the ticket kiosk and departure point in Tower 5 of Suntec City, directly facing the Nicoll Hwy.

Singapore River Cruises (☎6336 6111; www.rivercruise.com.sg; adult/child $22/12; ☺9am-11pm; ⓜClarke Quay) The 40-minute bumboat cruises that ply the stretch between the Quays and Marina Bay depart from several places along the Singapore River including Clarke Quay, Raffles Landing and Boat Quay. The running commentary is a little cringe-inducing, but the trip itself is relaxing, with spectacular views of the skyline and Marina Bay.

Themed Tours

Real Singapore Tours (☎6247 7340; www.betelbox.com/singapore-tours.htm; 200 Joo Chiat Rd; tours $80-100) These insider tours are led by Tony Tan and the team at Betel Box hostel. Choose from nature walks, coastline cycling or a Joo Chiat neighbourhood food odyssey (usually 6pm on Thursday), which will have you chomping on more than 20 authentic dishes from across Southeast Asia.

East West Planners (☎6336 6811; www.eastwestplanners.com) This tour company offers a string of themed tours such as 'Culture & Heritage' and 'Gourmet & Culinary'. Aimed at the more affluent visitor, prices are available on request.

Chef preparing noodles at a food court in Marina Bay Sands (p54)

Eating

Singaporeans are obsessed with makan (food), from talking incessantly about their last meal, to feverishly photographing, critiquing and posting about it online. It's hardly surprising – food is one of Singapore's greatest drawcards, the nation's melting pot of cultures creating one of the world's most diverse, drool-inducing culinary landscapes.

Hawker Centre, Kopitiam or Food Court

Singapore's celebrated hawker centres, *kopitiams* and food courts serve up knockout street food at wallet-friendly prices.

Hawker centres are usually standalone, open-air (or at least open-sided) structures with a raucous vibe and rows of food stalls peddling any number of different local cuisines.

Often found in air-conditioned shopping malls, food courts are basically air-conditioned hawker centres with marginally higher prices, while coffeeshops, also called *kopitiams* (*tiam* is Hokkien for 'shop'), are open shopfront cafes, usually with a handful of stalls and roaming 'aunties' or 'uncles' taking drinks orders.

Hawker Centre Etiquette

➡ Bag a seat first, especially if it's busy. Sit a member of your group at a table, or lay a packet of tissues on a seat. Don't worry if there are no free tables; it's normal to share with strangers.

⇒ If there's a table number, note it as the stall owner uses it as reference for food delivery.

⇒ If the stall has a 'self service' sign, you'll have to carry the food to the table yourself. Otherwise, the vendor brings your order to you.

⇒ Ignore wandering touts who try to sit you down and plonk menus in front of you.

Beyond Hawker

Singapore's restaurant scene is booming. From London chef Jason Atherton's Pollen to fellow Brit Ryan Clift's Tippling Club, the city has an ever-expanding legion of top-notch, celebrity-chef nosheries. Iggy's remains one of Asia's most coveted destination restaurants, with French chef Julien Royer's Jaan providing lofty competition.

Most exciting is Singapore's new breed of lively, midrange eateries, which, alongside trailblazers like Kilo, deliver sharp, produce-driven menus in an altogether more relaxed setting. Among the best are Southeast Asian Ding Dong and Mexican Lucha Loco, two of a string of newcomers that have transformed Chinatown and Tanjong Pagar into dining 'It' spots.

Singapore Specialities

CHINESE

Cantonese is the best known of regional Chinese cuisines, with typical dishes including *xiao long bao* (pork dumplings filled with a piping hot sauce) and dim sum – also known as yum cha – snack-type dishes usually eaten at lunchtime or as a Sunday brunch in large, noisy restaurants. Practically Singapore's national dish, Hainanese chicken rice is a soulful mix of steamed fowl and rice cooked in chicken stock, and served with a clear soup, slices of cucumber and ginger, chilli and soy dips.

Many of Singapore's Chinese are Hokkien, infamously coarse-tongued folk whose hearty noodle dishes include *char kway teow* (noodles, clams and eggs fried in chilli and black bean sauce), *bak chor mee* (noodles with pork, meat balls and fried scallops) and *hokkien mee* (yellow Hokkien noodles with prawns, served either fried or in a rich prawn-based stock).

Seafood is a speciality of delicate Teochew cuisine, with fish *maw* (a fish's swim bladder) cropping up alarmingly often. The classic Teochew comfort food is rice porridge, served with fish, pork or frog (the latter a Geylang favourite).

NEED TO KNOW

Price Range

Bear in mind that most restaurant prices will have 17% added to them at the end: a 10% service charge plus 7% for GST. You'll see this indicated by ++ on menus. In our listings, we've used the following price codes to represent the all-inclusive price of a single dish or a main course.

$ less than $10

$$ $10 to $30

$$$ over $30

Opening Hours

⇒ Hawker centres, food courts, coffeeshops: 7am to 10/11pm, sometimes 24 hours.

⇒ Midrange restaurants: 11am to 11pm.

⇒ Top-end restaurants: noon to 2.30pm and 6pm to 11pm.

Reservations

⇒ Book a table for expensive and 'hot' restaurants.

⇒ Book a table for midrange restaurants for Friday to Sunday nights.

Tipping

Tipping is unnecessary in Singapore, as most restaurants impose a 10% service charge – and nobody ever tips in hawker centres. That said, many do leave a discretionary tip for superlative service at higher-end restaurants.

INDIAN

Spicy, South Indian food dominates Singapore, with a typical dish being thali (rice plate), often a large mound of rice served with various vegetable curries, *rasam* (hot, sour soup) and a dessert. Local Chinese love Indian *roti prata* – a flat bread cooked with oil on a hotplate and served with a curry sauce. Try a *roti telur* (*prata* cooked with an egg) or a *roti tissue* (ultrathin *prata* cooked with margarine and sugar and served in a cone shape).

Other South Indian vegetarian dishes include *masala dosa*, a thin pancake rolled around spiced vegetables with some chutney and *rasam* on the side. Its carnivorous, halal (Muslim) equivalent is *murtabak*, paper-thin dough filled with egg and minced mutton.

MENU DECODER

CHINESE

ah balling	glutinous rice balls filled with a sweet paste of peanut, black sesame or red bean and usually served in a peanut- or ginger-flavoured soup
bak chang	local rice dumpling filled with savoury or sweet meat and wrapped in leaves
bak chor mee	noodles with pork, meatballs and fried scallops
bak choy	Chinese cabbage that grows like celery, with long white stalks and dark-green leaves
bak kutteh	local pork-rib soup with hints of garlic and Chinese five spice
char kway teow	Hokkien dish of broad noodles, clams and eggs fried in chilli and black-bean sauce
char siew	sweet roast-pork fillet
cheng ting	dessert consisting of a bowl of sugar syrup with pieces of herbal jelly, barley and dates
choi sum	popular Chinese green vegetable, served steamed with oyster sauce
congee	Chinese porridge
Hainanese chicken rice	chicken dish served with spring onions and ginger dressing accompanied by soup, rice and chilli sauce; a local speciality
hoisin sauce	thick seasoning sauce made from soya beans, red beans, sugar, vinegar, salt, garlic, sesame, chillies and spices; sweet-spicy and tangy in flavour
kang kong	water convolvulus, a thick-stemmed type of spinach
kway chap	pig intestines cooked in soy sauce; served with flat rice noodles
kway teow	broad rice noodles
lor mee	noodles served with slices of meat, eggs and a dash of vinegar in a dark-brown sauce
mee pok	flat noodles made with egg and wheat
spring roll	vegetables, peanuts, egg and bean sprouts rolled up inside a thin pancake and fried
won ton	dumpling filled with spiced minced pork
won ton mee	soup dish with shredded chicken or braised beef
yu char kueh	deep-fried dough; eaten with congee
yu tiao	deep-fried pastry eaten for breakfast or as a dessert
yusheng	salad of raw fish, grated vegetables, candied melon and lime, pickled ginger, sesame seeds, jellyfish and peanuts tossed in sweet dressing; eaten at Chinese New Year

INDIAN

achar	vegetable pickle
fish-head curry	red snapper head in curry sauce; a famous Singapore-Indian dish
gulab jamun	fried milk balls in sugar syrup
idli	steamed rice cake served with thin chutneys
keema	spicy minced meat
kofta	minced meat or vegetable ball
korma	mild curry with yoghurt sauce
lassi	yoghurt-based drink, either sweet or salted
mulligatawny	spicy beef soup
pakora	vegetable fritter
paratha	flat bread made with ghee and cooked on a hotplate; also called *roti prata*
pilau	rice fried in ghee and mixed with nuts, then cooked in stock
raita	side dish of cucumber, yoghurt and mint; used to cool the palate
rasam	spicy soup
roti john	fried roti with chilli
saag	spicy chopped-spinach side dish

sambar	fiery mixture of vegetables, lentils and split peas
samosa	fried pastry triangle stuffed with spiced vegetables or meat
soup tulang	meaty bones in a rich, spicy, blood-red tomato gravy
tikka	small pieces of baked meat and fish served off the bone and marinated in yoghurt
vadai	fried, spicy lentil patty, served with a savoury lentil sauce or yoghurt

MALAY & INDONESIAN

ais kacang	similar to *cendol* but made with evaporated milk; also spelt 'ice kacang'
attap	sweet gelatinous fruit of the attap palm
belacan	fermented prawn paste used as a condiment
belacan kang kong	green vegetables stir-fried in prawn paste
cendol	local dessert made from a cone of ice shavings filled with red beans, *attap* and jelly, then topped with coloured syrups, brown-sugar syrup and coconut milk
gado gado	cold dish of bean sprouts, potatoes, long beans, *tempeh*, bean curd, rice cakes and prawn crackers, topped with a spicy peanut sauce
itek manis	duck simmered in ginger and black-bean sauce
itek tim	a classic soup of simmered duck, tomatoes, green peppers, salted vegetables and preserved sour plums
kari ayam	curried chicken
kaya	jam made from coconut and egg, served on toast
kecap	soy sauce, pronounced 'ketchup' (we got the word from them)
kepala ikan	fish head, usually in a curry or grilled
kueh mueh	Malay cakes
lontong	rice cakes in a spicy coconut-milk gravy topped with grated coconut and sometimes bean curd and egg
mee siam	white thin noodles in a sourish and sweet gravy made with tamarind
mee soto	noodle soup with shredded chicken
nasi biryani	saffron rice flavoured with spices and garnished with cashew nuts, almonds and raisins
nasi minyak	spicy rice
pulut kuning	sticky saffron rice
o-chien	oyster omelette
rojak	salad made from cucumber, pineapple, yam bean, star fruit, green mango and guava, with a dressing of shrimp paste, chillies, palm sugar and fresh lime juice
sambal	sauce of fried chilli, onions and prawn paste
soto ayam	spicy chicken soup with vegetables, including potatoes
tempeh	preserved soya beans, deep-fried

PERANAKAN

ayam buah keluak	chicken in a rich, spicy sauce served with *buah keluak* (an unusually flavoured black paste-like nut)
carrot cake	steamed radish cake stir-fried with egg, garlic and chilli; also known as *chye tow kway*
kueh pie ti	deep-fried flour cup filled with prawn, chilli sauce and steamed turnip
otak	spicy fish paste cooked in banana leaves; a classic snack, also called *otak-otak*
papaya titek	type of curry stew
popiah	similar to a spring roll, but not fried
satay bee hoon	peanut-sauce-flavoured noodles
shui kueh	steamed radish cakes with fried preserved-radish topping

MALAY & INDONESIAN

The cuisines of Malaysia and Indonesia are similar, with star staples including satay – grilled kebabs of chicken, mutton or beef dipped in a spicy peanut sauce. Both *ayam goreng* (fried chicken) and *rendang* (spicy coconut curry) are popular staples, as are *nasi goreng* (fried rice) and *nasi lemak* (coconut rice served with *ikan bilis,* peanuts and a curry dish).

The Sumatran style of Indonesian food bends much more towards curries and chillies. *Nasi padang,* from the Minangkabau region of West Sumatra, consists of a wide variety of spicy curries and other smaller dishes served with rice. Simply pick and choose what you want and it's dolloped on a plate.

PERANAKAN

Peranakan food is a unique fusion of Chinese ingredients and Malay sauces and spices. It's commonly flavoured with shallots, chillies, *belacan* (Malay fermented prawn paste), peanuts, preserved soybeans and galangal (a gingerlike root). Thick coconut milk is used to create the sauce that flavours the prime ingredients.

Typical dishes include *otak-otak* (a paste-like combo of fish, coconut milk, chilli, galangal and herbs, wrapped and grilled in a banana leaf) and *ayam buah keluak* (chicken stewed with dark, earthy nuts imported from Indonesia to produce a rich sauce). Equally scrumptious is the distinctive Peranakan laksa (noodles in a savoury coconut-milk gravy with fried tofu and bean sprouts).

VEGETARIAN & VEGAN

Little India teems with vegetarian food, and most food courts and hawker centres across the island offer at least some vegetarian options.

Be aware that interpretations of 'vegetarian' food can vary. 'Vegetable soup' can contain both chicken and prawn (the reasoning being that because it contains vegetables, it's a vegetable soup!). Be highly specific when ordering food – don't just say 'vegetarian', but stress that you eat 'no meat, no seafood'.

Vegans may find life a little more difficult, though since the consumption of dairy and other animal by-products is relatively limited, usually all you have to do is ensure there are no eggs.

Cooking Courses

A highly recommended cooking school exploring Singapore's classic dishes is Food Playground (p80). Courses usually run for three hours and can be tailored for budding cooks with dietary restrictions.

Top Guides & Blogs

Start with KF Seetoh's superb *Makansutra,* the bible of hawker centre food; visit www.sg.dining.asiatatler.com for high-end restaurant news and reviews; and check out the following respected food blogs.

ieatishootipost.sg On-the-ball foodie Leslie Tay reviews mainly hawker food around the island.

www.ladyironchef.com Psst, Lady Ironchef is actually a bloke, offering highly respected opinions and helpful 'best' lists.

www.bibikgourmand.blogspot.com Evelyn Chen's reviews focus mainly on buzz-creating restaurants around town.

Eating by Neighbourhood

➡ **Colonial District, Marina Bay & the Quays** Covers all bases, from celebrity fine-diners to food courts and tucked-away foodie gems. (p58)

➡ **Chinatown & the CBD** Old-school hawker centres and trendy, of-the-moment eateries. (p72)

➡ **Little India & Kampong Glam** Cheap, authentic Indian in Little India, old-school Malay and trendy global eats in Kampong Glam. (p86)

➡ **Orchard Road** Superlative food courts, trendy brunch cafes and high-end destination restaurants. (p96)

➡ **Eastern Singapore** Home to local food hubs Katong/Joo Chiat and Geylang. (p108)

➡ **Northern & Central Singapore** Local dining experiences, from chilli crab at a HDB (public housing) complex, to a trendy gourmet market. (p118)

➡ **Holland Village, Dempsey Hill & the Botanic Gardens** Chic bistros and leafy garden restaurants. (p123)

➡ **West & Southwest Singapore** Lush settings and top-notch Thai and Peranakan. (p131)

➡ **Sentosa** Everything from fine-dining hideaways to fish and chips on the beach. (p137)

Lonely Planet's Top Choices

Kilo (p60) Vibrant East-meets-West flavours, competent service and an in-the-know address

Gluttons Bay (p58) Lip-smacking hawker fare and a festive vibe on Marina Bay

Momma Kong's (p72) A tiny Chinatown marvel peddling the island's best chilli crab

Jaan (p60) Clever French creations with dramatic presentation and sky-high views to match

Best by Budget

$

Gluttons Bay (p58) Hawker classics in an easy-to-navigate setting on Marina Bay

Song Fa Bak Kut Teh (p58) Free-flow broth and butter-soft ribs off Boat Quay

Gandhi Restaurant (p86) Quick, authentic Indian in Little India

$$

Momma Kong's (p72) Delicious crab from a family of chilli crab geeks

Lucha Loco (p72) Sucker-punch Mexican on trendy Duxton Hill

Tim Ho Wan (p96) Hong Kong's most famous dumpling peddler, on Orchard Rd

$$$

Kilo (p60) Flavourful fusion fare and a dinner-club vibe

Ding Dong (p74) Competent revamps and cocktails on fashionable Ann Siang Rd

Iggy's (p98) Orchard Rd's most desirable culinary address

Best by Cuisine

Chinese & Peranakan

Paradise Dynasty (p97) Superlative dumplings and hand-pulled noodles

PeraMakan (p131) Spicy Peranakan flavours in a resort-like locale

Song Fa Bak Kut Teh (p58) Steamy pork-rib soul soup

Indian

Lagnaa Barefoot Dining (p87) Flexible spice levels in Little India

Gandhi Restaurant (p86) Flavour-packed *thali*, *dosa* and *uttapam* bites

StraitsKitchen (p98) A high-end regional buffet off Orchard Rd

Malay & Indonesian

Tambuah Mas (p97) Made-from-scratch Indonesian on Orchard Rd

Zam Zam (p87) Old-school *murtabak* in the shadow of Sultan Mosque

Warong Nasi Pariaman (p87) A legendary *nasi padang* joint in Kampong Glam

Western & Fusion

Kilo (p60) Strictly seasonal Italian-Japanese and a killer upstairs lounge

Cicheti (p87) Market-fresh produce and woodfired pizza perfection in Kampong Glam

Smokey's (p110) Authentic, American-style BBQ in laid-back Katong

Best Hawker Centres & Food Courts

Maxwell Road Hawker Centre (p73) Chinatown's most tourist-friendly hawker centre

Chinatown Complex (p73) The hardcore hawker experience

Takashimaya Food Village (p97) A fabulous basement food hall on Orchard Rd

Lau Pa Sat (p73) Worth a visit for its magnificent wrought-iron architecture alone

Best for Crab

Momma Kong's (p72) Good deals, huge buns and Singapore's freshest Sri Lankan crabs

No Signboard Seafood (p108) Superlative white-pepper crab in red-light Geylang

Eng Seng Restaurant (p110) Sweet, sticky black-pepper brilliance in Katong

Best Brunch

Tamarind Hill (p131) Extraordinary Sunday Thai in a jungle-fringed setting

Symmetry (p88) Decadent dishes and winning coffee in a boho Kampong Glam locale

Kith Cafe (p138) Lazy, see-and-be-seen brunching on the Sentosa waterfront

Best for Romance

Cliff (p138) Fine dining with a chic, enchanting backdrop

Jaan (p60) Cutting-edge French high above the Colonial District

Halia (p124) Ginger-spiked menus in a tropical garden wonderland

Best Old-School Singapore

Red Star (p74) Retro yum cha on the edge of Chinatown

Colbar (p132) Hainanese-style Western classics in a former officers' mess in western Singapore

Fireworks over Marina Bay Sands (p54)

Drinking & Nightlife

From speakeasy cocktail bars to boutique beer stalls to artisan coffee roasters, Singapore is discovering the finer points of drinking. The clubbing scene is no less competent, with newcomers including a futuristic club in the clouds and a basement hot spot fit for the streets of Tokyo.

Cocktail Bars & Lounges

Forget the sling. From pea-infused Jolly Green Giants at Tippling Club, to classic Penicillins at Bitters & Love, Singapore's new breed of cocktail bars are shaking and stirring bold and thrilling libations. Locavore tendencies shine through in the likes of Jekyll & Hyde's Mr Bean (vodka, Lao Ban beancurd and kaya), while the meticulous dating of drinks at speakeasy 28 HongKong Street is testament to a deepening reverence for the history and craft of cocktail making.

Pubs & Microbreweries

Singapore's beer scene is also coming of age, with more bars, cafes and restaurants jumping on the craft brew bandwagon. Even Chinatown Complex is in on the act, home to Singapore's first hawker-centre craft-beer stalls Good Beer Company and Smith Street Taps. In stock is Singapore's own award-winning Jungle Beer (www.junglebeer.com), kickstarted by four college friends determined to make beer with flavours that reflect local geography. It's not the only microbrewery in town either, with brewery-bar hybrids Level 33 and RedDot Brewhouse keeping things nuanced and local.

Cafes & Coffee Roasters

While old-school *kopitiams* (coffeeshops) have been serving *kopi* (local coffee) for generations, Singapore's speciality coffee scene is a more recent phenomenon. Inspired by Australia's artisanal coffee culture, contemporary cafes such as Plain, Artisan and Maison Ikkoku are brewing ethically sourced, seasonal beans, using either espresso machines or 'Third Wave' brewing techniques such as Japanese syphons and AeroPress. Also on the increase are cafes sourcing and roasting their own beans, the best of which include Chye Seng Huat Hardware and Nylon Coffee Roasters.

Clubbing

Zouk remains the city's best-known club, and its annual Zoukout – a massive dance party held each December – attracts 40,000 revellers and A-list DJs. Newer hot spots include Japanese-inspired club-lounge Kyō and Altimate, an ambitious, high-tech play-pen giving luxe club **Pangaea** (www.pangaea.sg) a run for its money. Dance clubs proliferate the Clarke Quay area, among them Attica and uni-crowd favourite Home Club. Beyond these, check out **Super 0** (www.super0.sg), which runs top-notch pop-up dance parties, usually towards the end of the year. For updated listings, hit www.timeoutsingapore.com/clubs or www.e-clubbing.com.

Deals & Discounts

Singapore is an expensive city to drink in; a fact not helped by a 25% alcohol tax hike in 2014. A beer at most city bars will set you back between $10 and $18, with cocktails commonly ringing in between $20 and $30.

That said, many bars offer decent happy-hour deals, typically stretching from around 5pm to 8pm, sometimes starting earlier and finishing later. Most deals offer two drinks for the price of one or cheaper 'housepours'. Some – such as Bar on 5 – might offer extra perks, like martinis for under $10. On Wednesday, ladies' night promotions offer cheaper (sometimes free) drinks to women.

Some credit cards and banks also run promotions. MasterCard's Priceless programme (www.pricelesssingapore.com), for example, offers modest discounts at various eateries and bars around town.

NEED TO KNOW

Prices

Regular bars add 17% to your bill: 10% for service charge, 7% for GST. You'll see this indicated by ++ on drink lists.

Opening Hours

Bars 3pm to 1am or 3am

Clubs 10pm to 3am or 5am

Cafes 10am to 7pm

Entry Fees

Unless you know someone at the door or get signed in by a member, at the hottest clubs you'll have to join the queue. You can avoid the cover charge for some bars and clubs if you go early.

Of course, those who don't mind plastic tables and fluorescent lights can always hang out with the locals at hawker centres and coffeeshops, swilling $6 bottles of Tiger.

Drinking & Nightlife by Neighbourhood

➜ **Colonial District, Marina Bay & the Quays** Skyscraper bars and clubs, colonial legends, and party-people bars, pubs and clubs at the Quays. (p60)

➜ **Chinatown & the CBD** Hip cafes, slinky cocktail lounges, hawker beer stalls, Neil St gay bars, and after-work drinks hub Club St. (p74)

➜ **Little India & Kampong Glam** Raffish pubs, artisan coffee and hidden cocktail dens. (p88)

➜ **Orchard Road** Mall-bound tea purveyors and cafes, hotel bars and bar-lined heritage street. (p98)

➜ **Eastern Singapore** Local beer and cider hangouts and relaxed beach-side bars. (p111)

➜ **Northern & Central Singapore** Old-school coffeeshops, a far-flung biker bar and a secret garden oasis. (p119)

➜ **Holland Village, Dempsey Hill & the Botanic Gardens** Cafe-bistro hybrids in Dempsey Hill, raucous expat bars in Holland Village. (p124)

➜ **West & Southwest Singapore** Languid, old-school drinking in a veteran military mess. (p132)

➜ **Sentosa** Beach bars with palms, sand and the odd pool. (p138)

Lonely Planet's Top Choices

Lantern (p61) Stylish rooftop sipping with million-dollar views of Marina Bay

Tippling Club (p74) Spectacular cocktails in booming Tanjong Pagar

Bitters & Love (p61) Custom-made libations in a backroom bar minutes from Boat Quay

Level 33 (p61) A skyscraping microbrewery on the edge of Marina Bay

Chye Seng Huat Hardware (p90) Hardware store turned coffee roaster in hip Jalan Besar

Best Cocktails

Tippling Club (p74) Boundary-pushing libations from the bar that raised the bar

Bitters & Love (p61) Clever surprises from top-tier barkeeps

28 HongKong Street (p61) Chronological cocktails in an unmarked lounge off Boat Quay

Jekyll & Hyde (p75) Surprising ingredients and clever twists in up-and-coming Tras St

Jigger & Pony (p74) A dark, svelte temple to classic cocktails in Amoy St

Best Clubs

Zouk (p63) A multivenue classic west of Robertson Quay

Kyō (p77) Japanese-inspired club in a one-time bank in the CBD

Altimate (p77) High-tech clubbing atop a downtown skyscraper

Taboo (p79) Hot bods and themed nights at Singapore's classic gay club

Best for Views

Level 33 (p61) Spectacular views over Marina Bay, the city and Strait of Singapore

1-Altitude (p76) The world's tallest alfresco bar in the heart of the CBD

Ku Dé Tah (p60) A seamless city and island panorama from Marina Bay Sands' cantilevered rooftop

Orgo (p62) Romantic skyscraper views and a rooftop garden at Esplanade – Theatres on the Bay

Breeze (p75) Gaze out over Chinatown rooftops and CBD towers

Best for Beers

Level 33 (p61) Slurp made-on-site beers 33 floors above the city

The Good Beer Company (p75) A rotating cast of craft suds in a Chinatown hawker centre

Cider Pit (p111) Craft beers and ciders in a down-to-earth Katong pub

RedDot Brewhouse (p125) Local microbrews in a lush Dempsey setting

Tiger Brewery (p130) Pay homage to the national beer at its very home in Singapore's west

Best for Coffee

Chye Seng Huat Hardware (p90) Superlative espresso, filter coffee, on-site roasting and classes

Nylon Coffee Roasters (p76) A small, mighty espresso bar and roaster in up-and-coming Everton Park

Common Man Coffee (p58) An Oz-style cafe and roaster with top-notch grub just off Robertson Quay

Plain (p77) A cafe-scene trailblazer in the Duxton Hill area

Artistry (p89) Kicking coffee meets art and culture in eclectic Kampong Glam

Best for Lingering

Tanjong Beach Club (p138) Sand, palms and lap pool at Sentosa's more tranquil end

Middle Rock (p119) A secluded tropical oasis in the middle of Bishan Park

Handlebar (p119) Open sky, bikers and blues on the Strait of Johor

Coastal Settlement (p111) A lush, green hideaway cafe-bar-restaurant in sleepy Changi

Best Heritage Settings

Raffles Hotel (p62) Sip a sling (if only for the novelty value) where Somerset Maugham once slumbered

Colbar (p132) Knock back beers at a nostalgic colonial mess

Black Swan (p62) Swill martinis in a deco-licious CBD bar-cum-lounge

Emerald Hill Road (p99) Post-shopping drinks on a heritage street off Orchard Rd

Best Wine Bars

Wine Connection (p63) Diverse and interesting wines at affordable prices in Robertson Quay

Ô Batignolles (p75) French flair and a rotating selection of boutique wines on see-and-be-seen Club St

☆ Entertainment

You're never short of a hot night out in Singapore. There's live music, theatre and adrenalin-pumping activities year-round, while at certain times of the year the Little Red Dot explodes into a flurry of car racing, cultural festivals and hot-ticket music events. And if it all gets too much, Singapore's spas are always waiting in the wings.

Theatre

Esplanade – Theatres on the Bay is one of the brightest spots in Singapore's vibrant theatre and dance scene. Visiting Broadway musicals take to the stage at Marina Bay Sands, and local theatre groups such as Wild Rice and the Singapore Repertory Theatre regularly put up local plays as well as the occasional adaptation. Shakespeare in the Park, anyone?

Live Music

Sure, a lot of average Pinoy cover bands grace hotel bars, but an enthusiastic local music scene also thrives (to a point). Esplanade – Theatres on the Bay hosts regular free performances, and is home to the Singapore Symphony Orchestra.

Singapore is on the map for a growing number of international acts, with top-tier talent showcased at both the Singapore International Jazz Festival and indie music favourite Laneway Festival.

Chinese Opera

Also known by the Malay term *wayang* (performance), Chinese opera includes indoor performances and street opera, the latter usually staged during religious events like the Hungry Ghost Festival. Although its popularity has decreased over time, groups such as the Chinese Theatre Circle, Kreta Ayer People's Theatre, and Bian's Cafe keep the tradition alive, with both performances and talks about this centuries-old art form.

Film

Singaporeans love to watch movies and, at around $10 per ticket, it's great value. Multiplex cinemas abound, with many located in larger malls. Beyond them, the historic Rex Cinemas runs Bollywood films, while the annual Singapore International Film Festival screens independent and arthouse films. Singapore's cinemas are notoriously chilly, so remember to wear something warm.

Thrills & Spills

Each September, the Formula One night race roars into town, while hands-on sporting events include December's increasingly popular Marathon Singapore. Around the year, there's no shortage of options for thrill seekers, whether it's indoor skydiving, (artificial) surfing or zip-lining on Sentosa, inner-tubing in Jurong East, wakeboarding in East Coast Park, or cycling the rustic island Pulau Ubin.

Spas & Massage

Pampering is big business in Singapore, from hole-in-the-wall reflexology stalls to luxe day spas. Midrange to high-end spas can be found in most malls and five-star hotels, with **Spa Esprit** (www.spa-esprit.com) a popular beauty empire. At the other end of the scale, People's Park Complex has no shortage of places offering very affordable reflexology, shiatsu, even feet-nibbling fish. Rates vary from around $25 for a foot massage to over $200 for a full-day package.

NEED TO KNOW

Prices

→ $20 to $70 will get you a ticket to a local theatre production.

→ It's often free to watch local bands at local nightspots; some places have a small cover charge.

→ International music acts are expensive and tickets often average $90 to $200.

→ Big-budget musical tickets cost $65 to $200.

→ Expect to pay through the nose during the Singapore Airshow in February and the Formula One season in September – hotel prices often triple. Decent grandstand tickets to the F1 start at $298, but if you're on a budget you can get walkabout tickets from $68.

Tickets

Tickets and an events calendar can be found on the Sistic website (www.sistic.com.sg).

Lonely Planet's Top Choices

Universal Studios (p136) Gold-standard rides for the young and young at heart

BluJaz Café (p89) Swinging sax in a bohemian pub

Pulau Ubin Time-warped Pulau Ubin is a cycling paradise

Home Club (p64) Side-splitting laughs at Tuesday classic 'Comedy Masala' nights

People's Park Complex (p80) Satisfying, bargain massage in an old-school mall

Best for Theatre

Singapore Repertory Theatre (p64) A world-class repertoire that includes seasonal Shakespeare at Fort Canning Park

Wild Rice (p89) Reinterpreted classics, new works and striking sets

TheatreWorks (p64) New commissions and international collaborations

Necessary Stage (p111) Locally flavoured, thought-provoking theatre

Best for Live Music

BluJaz Café (p89) Consistently good jazz and blues in Kampong Glam

Timbrè @ The Substation (p64) Local bands and singer-songwriters in the Colonial District

Crazy Elephant (p64) Rock and blues in party-central Clarke Quay

Esplanade – Theatres on the Bay (p63) Polished performances spanning classical to rock

Best for Film

Golden Village VivoCity (p132) State-of-the-art setup, Gold Class seating, and Hollywood and independent flicks

Screening Room (p77) Cult classics in an intimate suite in Chinatown

Rex Cinemas (p89) Hip-shaking Bollywood hits on the edge of Little India

Best for Pampering

Remède Spa (p101) Luxe treatments just off Orchard Rd

People's Park Complex (p80) Low-cost rubs in atmospheric Chinatown

Spa Esprit (p101) Oil-based therapies in an Orchard Rd apothecary

Willow Stream (p66) Day spa luxury in the Colonial District

Best for Hikes

Southern Ridges (p128) User-friendly trails with panoramic views

MacRitchie Reservoir (p116) Monkeys, monitor lizards and a canopy walk

Bukit Timah Nature Reserve (p117) Walking and bike trails through wild, primary rainforest

Green Corridor Old stations and bridges on a former railway corridor

Best for Kicks

iFly (p139) Freefall 2750m without the need for a plane

G-Max Reverse Bungy (p66) Is it a bird or a plane? It's you, hurled into the air at 200km/h

Universal Studios (p136) Brave the world's tallest duelling rollercoasters

Ultimate Drive (p66) Tear through Singapore in a fast and sexy Italian

Wave House (p139) Surf some waves in a Sentosa pool

Best for Cycling

East Coast Park (p106) Dedicated bike paths, flat terrain, and soothing sea breezes

Pulau Ubin A rustic island getaway made for bikes

Bukit Timah Nature Reserve (p117) Primary forest laced with a mountain-bike trail

Rug stalls on Arab St, Kampong Glam (p92)

Shopping

While its shopping scene mightn't match the edge of Hong Kong's or Bangkok's, Singapore is no retail slouch. Look beyond the malls and you'll find everything from sharply curated local boutiques, to vintage map peddlers and clued-in contemporary galleries.

Malls & Boutiques

Singapore's iconic malls come in all styles and sizes, from shiny, high-tech temples like ION Orchard to budget throwbacks like Far East Plaza. Orchard Rd is Singapore's mall epicentre, with the greatest breadth and depth of stores, from high-street chains to decadent couture. While luxury brands are generally more expensive in Singapore than they are in Hong Kong or in the UK and Europe, some stores offer 10% to 15% discounts for big spenders, so it's always worth asking.

For a more idiosyncratic experience, hit the city's independent boutiques, which stock anything from lesser-known and emerging fashion labels, to inspired design objects and harder-to-find books. You'll find small but thriving scenes in Tiong Bahru and Jalan Besar, as well as on Haji Lane in Kampong Glam.

Electronics

While Singapore is not the cut-price electronics nirvana it used to be, it can offer a few savings for those who do their homework and bargain successfully. Know the price of things before you

NEED TO KNOW

Opening Hours

➡ Retail stores: 11am to 9pm or 10pm.

➡ Mustafa Centre: 24 hours.

Bargaining & Returns

Prices are usually fixed in all shops, except at markets and in some shops in touristy areas. It pays to know the prices of gear back home in case you get over-quoted at independent stores. If you do have to haggle, stay good-humoured and don't get petty – this causes everyone to lose face. Shops in Singapore don't accept returns. Exchanges are accepted if the item has its original tags and packaging.

Taxes & Refunds

Departing visitors can get a refund of the 7% GST on their purchases, under the following conditions:

➡ Minimum spend of $100 at one retailer on the same day for no more than three purchases.

➡ You have a copy of the eTRS (Electronic Tourist Refund Scheme) ticket issued by the shop.

➡ You scan your eTRS ticket at the self-help kiosks at the airport or cruise terminal. If physical inspection of the goods is required as indicated by the eTRS self-help kiosk, you will have to present the goods, together with the original receipt and your boarding pass, at the Customs Inspection Counter.

Smaller stores may not participate in the GST refund scheme.

start shopping around, then browse and compare. Always ask vendors what they can do to sweeten the deal; they should be able to throw in a camera case or some memory cards.

Electronics mall Sim Lim Square is known for its range and negotiable prices, though it's also known for taking the uninitiated for a ride, not to mention for occasionally selling 'new' equipment that isn't quite new: a Google search will bring up blacklisted businesses. Rival Funan DigitaLife Mall has similar prices, but the businesses are generally considered more trustworthy. Never agree to getting the warranty online – the vendor must supply you with a warranty in store.

At both Funan DigitaLife and Sim Lim Square the best deals are on computers and cameras, with prices often 20% lower than major stores. During sale periods, it's not unusual to score a computer or camera at around half the recommended retail price.

Art & Antiques

If you're after art or antiques, it pays to know your original piece from your cheap copy. For Asian antiques, the best places to head are Chinatown, Dempsey Rd or Tanglin Shopping Centre. Deep-pocketed collectors of contemporary Asian art should scour Cham Hampe Galleries, as well as gallery hubs Gillman Barracks and the MICA Building. For more affordable art by local and regional artists, check out Utterly Art and the annual Affordable Art Fair, the latter showcasing the work of local creatives like Billy Ma.

Crafts & Fabrics

Little India is a good spot to pick up spices, decorative items and vibrant saris – you'll find a large choice of the latter at Tekka Centre, with finer options at nearby Nalli. Kampong Glam is the place to go for for Persian rugs. You'll find no shortage of vendors on Arab St, where you'll also find Sifr Aromatics, a modern take on the area's old-school perfume merchants. For colourful Peranakan garments and traditional batik fabrics, head east to the neighbourhood of Katong.

Shopping by Neighbourhood

➡ **Colonial District, Marina Bay & the Quays** Interconnected malls, discount electronics and in-the-know fashion, books and art. (p64)

➡ **Chinatown & the CBD** Chinese antiques, foodstuffs and medicines; local art; and a fashionista bolthole. (p79)

➡ **Little India & Kampong Glam** Spices, incense and sarisa in Little India, rugs, perfumes and indie boutiques in Kampong Glam. (p92)

➡ **Orchard Rd** Singapore's mall-lined shopping epicentre. (p100)

➡ **Eastern Singapore** Traditional wares, from Peranakan clothing, slippers and porcelain, to batik and Malaysian and Indonesian food. (p111)

➡ **Holland Village, Dempsey Hill & the Botanic Gardens** High-end art, antiques in ex-military Dempsey Hill. (p125)

➡ **West & Southwest Singapore** MRT-connected megamalls at HarbourFront and Jurong East. (p132)

Lonely Planet's Top Choices

Orchard Road (p100) You'll find *everything* on Singapore's world-famous retail strip

Raffles Hotel (p64) One-stop souvenir shopping in an iconic locale

Tyrwhitt General Company (p91) Hip, unique objects designed and made by locals

Little India (p92) Five-foot ways redolent of spices and dripping with atmosphere

Antiques of the Orient (p100) Take home a little slice of Singapore history

Best Luxury Malls

ION Orchard (p100) High-end labels in Singapore's most striking mall

Shoppes at Marina Bay Sands (p65) Bayside luxury and the world's first floating Louis Vuitton store

Paragon (p100) Coveted brands and a dedicated children's floor

Hilton Shopping Gallery (p102) Harder-to-find A-listers in a tranquil setting

Best Midrange Malls

313@Somerset (p101) High-street staples and an upbeat vibe right above Somerset MRT

ION Orchard (p100) Everything from H&M to Uniqlo and Zara in the heart of Orchard Rd

VivoCity (p132) Midrange labels galore at Singapore's biggest mall

Jem (p132) One of Singapore's newest players, in suburban Jurong East

Best for Local & Independent Designers

Front Row, Raffles Hotel Arcade (p64) Cult local and foreign threads and accessories at Raffles Hotel

Raoul, Paragon (p100) Sharp, chic threads for discerning men and women

Reckless Shop (p100) Affordable and avant-garde threads by young, talented Afton Chan

Nana & Bird (p78) Feminine fabulousness from local and emerging foreign designers

Willow and Huxley (p80) A small boutique with an epic reputation for clued-in local and foreign pieces

Club 21b, Forum (p102) Cult-status, multilabel threads from street to chic

i.t (p101) Hip designers in a Hong Kong concept store at Wisma Atria

Best for Souvenirs

Raffles Hotel Gift Shop (p64) Everything from vintage poster prints to tea and tomes

Antiques of the Orient (p100) Beautiful old maps, prints and photos of Singapore and the region

Rumah Bebe (p112) Peranakan fashion, accessories and craft in Katong

Sifr Aromatics (p92) Bespoke fragrances from a third-generation artisan in Kampong Glam

Tea Chapter (p77) Beautiful loose-leaf teas and tea sets in Chinatown

Nalli (p92) Splendid saris in the heart of Little India

Best for Art & Antiques

Tanglin Shopping Centre (p100) Quality Asian antiques and art in an old-school mall

Chan Hampe Galleries (p64) Coveted local and Malaysian contemporary art at Raffles Hotel

Utterly Art (p79) Affordable regional art in a tiny Chinatown gallery

Far East Legend (p80) Pan-Asian homewares and objets d'art in Chinatown

Shang Antiques (p125) Evocative temple artefacts and vintage Asian knickknacks in salubrious Dempsey Hill

Best for Tech

Funan DigitaLife Mall (p64) Your best bet for discount and good-deal computers, cameras and other electronic gadgetry

Sim Lim Square (p92) Six levels of electronics at Singapore's biggest tech mall

Mustafa Centre (p92) No shortage of electronic gizmos, available 24 hours a day

Best for Design

Tyrwhitt General Company (p91) A funky store-cum-workshop peddling local bags, jewellery and designer objects

Strangelets (p78) Eclectic lifestyle objects from Singapore and beyond

Konzepp (p90) A Hong Komg import showcasing top local design, fashion and accessories

The Redundant Shop (p76) A sneaky HDB boutique with hand-picked objects and accessories, from wallets to sunglasses

Explore Singapore

SINGAPORE'S
TOP SIGHTS

Neighbourhoods at a Glance

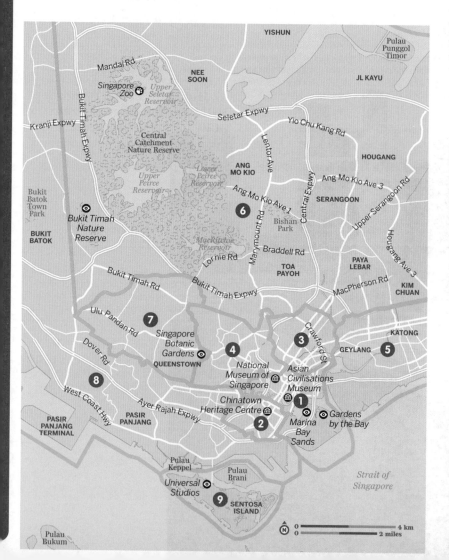

❶ Colonial District, Marina Bay & the Quays p48

The former British administrative enclave is home to a swath of colonial architecture, museums and the track for the Formula One night race. High rollers try their luck at Marina Bay. Bisecting it all, the Singapore River also connects the three quays – home to restaurants, clubs and bars.

❷ Chinatown & the CBD p67

While Singapore's Chinatown may be a tamer version of its former self, its temples, heritage centre and booming restaurant and bar scene make the trip there worthwhile. The CBD is best known for its stunning, ever-evolving skyline: rooftop bars jostle with old-school temples, all set against the financial heart that funds Singapore.

❸ Little India & Kampong Glam p81

Little India is Singapore trapped in its gritty past – it's frenetic, messy and fun. Spice traders spill their wares across its five-foot walkways and Indian labourers swarm into the area each weekend. Kampong Glam, the former home of the local Sultan, is an eclectic mix of Islamic stores and eateries, hipster bars and boutiques.

❹ Orchard Road p94

If you worship the gods of retail, pay your respects at this seemingly endless row of malls. For a slice of history, take a stroll along Emerald Hill Rd, a heritage strip lined with pretty Peranakan houses.

❺ Eastern Singapore p103

Geylang is an incongruous combination of temples, mosques, brothels and cult-status local eateries. East Coast Park is perfect for cycling and picnics by the beach, while nearby Katong and Joo Chiat are steeped in Peranakan culture. At the extreme tip of the island, you'll find moving exhibits at Changi Museum & Chapel and bumboats to Pulau Ubin.

❻ Northern & Central Singapore p113

From treetop walks in MacRitchie to the wetlands of Sungei Buloh, there's plenty to keep lovers of the outdoors busy. If hiking isn't your thing, seek out grand temples and the unmissable Singapore Zoo and Night Safari.

❼ Holland Village, Dempsey Hill & the Botanic Gardens p120

Expats and the well-heeled flock here for good food and drinks after a massage and pedicure at a spa. The entire area is bookended by the gorgeous, lush Botanic Gardens and the Bukit Timah Nature Reserve.

❽ West & Southwest Singapore p126

Walk the stunning Southern Ridges, and drop into the National University of Singapore for fabulous free art. Further west are the family-friendly attractions of the Jurong Bird Park and the Science Centre.

❾ Sentosa Island p134

Singapore's good-time island is dedicated to unabashed fun, from ambitious theme parks and a breathtaking aquarium, to ziplines, fake surf and cool beach bars.

Colonial District, Marina Bay & the Quays

Neighbourhood Top Five

1 Admiring regal jewels, temple carvings and ancient pottery at the world-class **Asian Civilisations Museum** (p50), home to Southeast Asia's finest collection of pan-Asian artefacts.

2 Leaping into a sci-fi future at **Gardens by the Bay** (p52), Singapore's spectacular new botanic garden.

3 Pondering Singaporean ambition from the top of one of the world's greatest engineering feats, **Marina Bay Sands** (p54).

4 Time travelling through Singapore's history at the engrossing **National Museum of Singapore** (p55).

5 Exploring the colour-saturated culture of the Peranakans at the **Peranakan Museum** (p53).

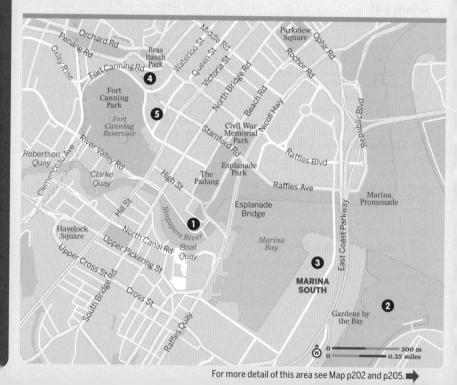

For more detail of this area see Map p202 and p205.

Explore Colonial District, Marina Bay & the Quays

This is the heart of Singapore: grand colonial buildings, modern architectural marvels, superlative museums and parks, and pulsating riverside restaurants, bars and clubs.

The City Hall MRT station bolts the neighbourhood together and is a perfect starting point. Wander northwest along Stamford Rd towards the museums. Head in the opposite direction for booming Marina Bay, home of Marina Bay Sands, Gardens by the Bay and Esplanade – Theatres by the Bay. Around City Hall MRT itself are the iconic edifices of colonialism, among them Raffles Hotel and St Andrew's Cathedral.

Further south are the three riverside quays, best saved for night time. You'll find a few quality drinking dens among the touristy bars at Boat Quay, no shortage of party people at raucous Clarke Quay, and a more grown-up crowd at Roberston Quay. Rising behind Clarke Quay is idyllic Fort Canning Park.

Local Life

➡**Foreign enclaves** Eat, drink and shop Yangon-style at Peninsula Plaza, Singapore's unofficial Little Burma and hub frequented by the city-state's influx of migrant workers.

➡**Artists' Market** Trawl the stalls at the bi-monthly Sunday Artists Market, a showcase for Singapore's oft-underestimated pool of creative talent.

➡**Marina Barrage** The 'green roof' of Marina Barrage is a popular hangout for Singaporean families, love-struck couples and kite enthusiasts. The curvaceous strip of lawn offers breathtaking views of the city skyline and the Strait of Singapore. For the full effect, head here just before sunset.

Getting There & Away

➡**MRT** The efficient subway service is centred on City Hall, an interchange station which is also connected via underground malls towards the Esplanade, from where you can cut across to Marina Bay. Raffles Place (East–West Line) is the next stop for the Quays. The Bayfront MRT station (Downtown Line) serves Marina Bay Sands and Gardens by the Bay.

➡**Bus** The area is well connected by bus to other parts of the island. Key stops are just outside the Raffles Hotel and outside St Andrew's Cathedral along North Bridge Rd. Bus 2 takes you down Victoria St and Hill St. Buses 51, 61, 63 and 80 go along North Bridge Rd. For Beach Rd, hop on buses 100, 107 or 961. Along Bras Basah Rd, get on buses 12, 14, 16, 77 or 111.

Lonely Planet's Top Tip

The Singapore Art Museum offers free entry from 6pm to 9pm every Friday, and some museums offer combined tickets that save you a few bucks. Most bars in the area have 'happy hour' specials from 5pm to 8pm or 9pm. During these hours, drinks are either one-for-one or heavily discounted. Several bars and clubs run weekly Ladies' Nights – usually on Wednesday – where women enjoy free entry and, sometimes, free booze (sorry boys).

◉ Best Sights

➡ Asian Civilisations Museum (p50)
➡ Gardens by the Bay (p52)
➡ National Museum of Singapore (p55)

For reviews, see p50.➡

✕ Best Places to Eat

➡ Kilo (p60)
➡ Jaan (p60)
➡ Gluttons Bay (p58)
➡ Song Fa Bak Kut Teh (p58)
➡ Jumbo Seafood (p60)

For reviews, see p58.➡

☕ Best Places to Drink

➡ Bitters & Love (p61)
➡ Lantern (p61)
➡ 28 HongKong Street (p61)
➡ Kinki (p61)

For reviews, see p60.➡

COLONIAL DISTRICT, MARINA BAY & THE QUAYS

TOP SIGHT
ASIAN CIVILISATIONS MUSEUM

The remarkable Asian Civilisations Museum houses the region's most comprehensive collection of pan-Asian treasures. Set over three levels, its beautifully curated galleries explore the history, cultures and religions of Southeast Asia, China, the Asian subcontinent and Islamic West Asia. Prepare to lose yourself in millennia of ancient carvings, glittering weaponry, jewels and textiles. Add to this a revealing exploration of the Singapore River and top-notch temporary exhibitions, and you have yourself one seriously satisfying cultural date.

Southeast Asia Galleries

Spanning everything from Hindu Buddhist kingdoms to hillside tribes and Javanese performing arts, highlights here include a beautifully illustrated *parabaik* (folded book), its whimsically colourful scenes a rare porthole into 19th-century Burmese life and architecture. The collection of gold decorative arts is especially strong, with spectacular examples of Sumatran and Javanese ceremonial jewellery in the Mary and Philbert Chin Gallery. Also impressive are the Southeast Asian textiles, among them a striking headdress, bag and apron ensemble from northern Thailand's Akha tribe, and a set of boldly geometric, appliquéd garments from northern Vietnam's Lolo community. Upstairs, the collection focuses on the performing arts, with some intriguing examples of puppetry and masks.

DON'T MISS...

➡ Southeast Asia Galleries textiles and jewellery
➡ West Asia Gallery Chinese Quran
➡ China Gallery *Eight Immortals* silk tapestry
➡ South Asia Gallery ritual bone apron

PRACTICALITIES

➡ Map p202
➡ ☎6332 7798
➡ www.acm.org.sg
➡ 1 Empress Pl
➡ adult/child $8/4, half-price 7-9pm Fri, incl Peranakan Museum $11/5.50
➡ ◷10am-7pm Sat-Thu, to 9pm Fri
➡ Ⓜ Raffles Place

West Asia Galleries

The West Asia collection offers exquisite examples of calligraphy, one of the richest, most esteemed artistic legacies of Asia's predominantly Islamic west. Much of it is in the form of Qurans, among which is a fascinating Chinese version that fuses Middle Eastern and Chinese aesthetics. Also noteworthy are the fragments from a 12th- or 13th-century Quran from southern Spain or North Africa, written in cursive Maghribi script. An 18th-century Quran stand from Ottoman Turkey exemplifies the region's renowned decorative arts, its entire surface adorned with tortoiseshell and mother of pearl inlay to form a striking geometric pattern. The West Asia collection continues on level three, where you'll find astronomical treatises from 14th-century Iran and 16th-century Egypt, and a 14th-century Dictionary of Medicine.

China Gallery

Look out for the richly hued *Three Votive Paintings of Luohan,* 18th-century silk panels portraying three sages who have realised the Buddhist doctrine (or dharmas). Equally colourful but more action-packed are the *Eight Immortals,* a 17th-century silk *kesi* (Chinese tapestry) filled with auspicious symbols, from the cranes and *shou* (longevity) character in the top centre, to the immortals themselves. The China Gallery houses one of the world's most comprehensive collections of *blanc de Chine* porcelain from Dehua in Fujian, as well as objects from the Belitung shipwreck, the oldest shipwreck found in Southeast Asian waters to date. Among these objects is some rather contemporary-looking stoneware from the early 9th century.

South Asia Gallery

The museum's subcontinental booty includes beautifully carved temple reliefs, as well as textiles and other decorative arts. Highlights include an extraordinary 17th-century gameboard made of teak and veneered with exotic woods, ivory and metals. In the same display case is a very distinguished-looking 17th-century cabinet made of tortoiseshell, ivory and wood, with a silver lock. Other notable pieces include a gold 19th-century *kazhuththu uru,* an ornate wedding necklace. For something a little more macabre, look out for the 17th- or 18th-century Tibetan ritual bone apron, made using human and animal bones.

EMPRESS PLACE BUILDING

The Asian Civilisations Museum's handsome home is the Empress Place Building. Designed by British architect John Frederick Adolphus McNair and built using Indian convict labour in 1865, it originally housed the colonial government offices. Architecture buffs will appreciate its elegant fusion of neo-Palladian classicism and tropical touches like timber louvered shutters and wide shaded porch.

The National Heritage Board's good-value 3-Day Museum Pass (adult/family $20/50) offers admission to six city museums, including the Asian Civilisations Museum, Peranakan Museum and Singapore Art Museum. The pass can be purchased at the museum, and includes entry to its often excellent temporary exhibitions, which usually incur a supplement. Past shows have included recently discovered treasures from China's Famen Temple. Check the museum website for upcoming displays.

 TOP SIGHT
GARDENS BY THE BAY

Welcome to the botanic gardens of the future, a fantasyland of space-age bio-domes, high-tech Supertrees and whimsical sculptures. Costing $1 billion and sprawling across 101 hectares of reclaimed land, Gardens by the Bay is more than just a mind-clearing patch of green. It's a masterpiece of urban planning, as thrilling to architecture buffs as it is to nature lovers.

The Conservatories

Housing 217,000 plants from 800 species, the Gardens' asymmetrical conservatories rise like giant paper nautilus shells beside Marina Bay. The Flower Dome replicates a dry, Mediterranean climate and includes ancient olive trees. It's also home to sophisticated restaurant Pollen (p60), which sources ingredients from the Gardens. Cloud Forest Dome's a steamy affair, recreating the tropical montane climate. Its centrepiece is a 35m mountain complete with waterfall.

Supertrees & Sculptures

Sci-fi meets botany at the Supertrees, 18 steel-clad concrete structures adorned with over 162,900 plants. Actually massive exhausts for the Gardens' biomass steam turbines, they're used to generate electricity to cool the conservatories. For a sweeping view, walk across the 22m-high **OCBC Skyway**, connecting six Supertrees at Supertree Grove, where tickets ($5, cash only) are purchased. Each night at 7.45pm and 8.45pm, the Supertrees become the glowing protagonists of *Garden Rhapsody,* a light-and-sound spectacular.

The most visually arresting of the Gardens' numerous artworks is Mark Quinn's colossal *Planet* (2008), a giant sleeping infant, seemingly floating above the ground. This illusion is brilliant, especially considering the bronze bubba comes in at a hefty 7 tonnes. The work was modelled on Quinn's own son.

DON'T MISS...

- ➡ Flower Dome & Cloud Forest Dome
- ➡ Supertree Grove
- ➡ *Planet* sculpture

PRACTICALITIES

- ➡ Map p205
- ➡ ☑6420 6848
- ➡ www.gardensbythebay.com.sg
- ➡ 18 Marina Gardens Dr
- ➡ gardens free, conservatories adult/child $28/15
- ➡ ⊙5am-2am, conservatories & OCBC Skyway 9am-9pm
- ➡ Ⓜ Bayfront

👁 SIGHTS

ASIAN CIVILISATIONS MUSEUM   MUSEUM
See p50

GARDENS BY THE BAY   GARDEN
See p52

⭐PERANAKAN MUSEUM   MUSEUM
Map p202 (📞6332 7591; www.peranakanmuseum.
sg; 39 Armenian St; adult/child $6/3, 7-9pm Fri
half-price, incl Asian Civilisations Museum $11/5.50;
☺10am-7pm, to 9pm Fri; Ⓜ City Hall) Explore the
rich, fusion heritage of the Peranakans at
this superlative museum. Thematic galleries
cover aspects of Peranakan culture, from the
traditional 12-day wedding ceremony, to Peranakan crafts, spirituality and feasting. Look
out for detailed ceremonial costumes and
beadwork, beautifully carved wedding beds,
and rare dining porcelain. A curious example
of the Peranakans' fusion culture is a pair of
Victorian bell jars, in which statues of Christ
and the Madonna are adorned with Chinese-
style flowers and vines.

The museum shop stocks embroidered
and leather bags, Peranakan-style fans and
ceramics, and books on Peranakan history,
food and architecture.

SINGAPORE ART MUSEUM   MUSEUM
Map p202 (SAM; 📞6332 3222; www.singapore-
artmuseum.sg; 71 Bras Basah Rd; adult/student
& senior $10/5, 6-9pm Fri free; ☺10am-7pm Sat-
Thu, to 9pm Fri; Ⓜ Bras Basah) SAM houses an
engaging collection of Southeast Asian art,
with a strong emphasis on modern and contemporary art from Singapore and the Asian
region. Expect anything, from painting and
sculpture to site-specific installations and
video art. One highlight is the Wu Guang-
zhong gallery, which features a rotating exhibition of $70 million worth of art donated by
the father of modern Chinese painting.

SAM occupies a former Catholic boys'
school and is a gracious example of 19th-
century colonial architecture.

ARTSCIENCE MUSEUM   MUSEUM
Map p205 (www.marinabaysands.com/museum.
html; Marina Bay Sands; adult/child $28/16;
☺10am-7pm; Ⓜ Bayfront) Looking like a giant
white lotus, the lily-pond-framed ArtSci-
ence Museum is well known for hosting
major international travelling exhibitions
in fields as varied as art, design, media,
science and technology. Past shows have included retrospectives of American designers Charles and Ray Eames, and photogra-
pher Annie Leibovitz.

8Q SAM   MUSEUM
Map p202 (www.singaporeartmuseum.sg; 8
Queen St; admission with SAM ticket free; ☺10am-
7pm Sat-Thu, to 9pm Fri; Ⓜ Bras Basah, City
Hall) Round the corner from the Singapore
Art Museum (SAM) is its younger sibling,
named after its address and free with your
SAM ticket. Snoop around four floors of
contemporary art, from quirky installations
and video art to mixed media statements.

RAFFLES HOTEL   HISTORICAL BUILDING
Map p202 (www.raffleshotel.com; 1 Beach Rd;
Ⓜ City Hall) Yes, it's a cliché, but try resist-
ing the allure of that magnificent ivory
frontage, the famous Sikh doorman, and
the echoes of days when Singapore was a
swampy, tiger-tempered outpost of the British Empire. Starting life in 1887 as a modest
10-room bungalow fronting the beach (long
gone thanks to land reclamation), Raffles
is today one of Singapore's most beautiful
heritage sites, laced with quiet tropical gardens, nostalgia-inducing bars and a string
of high-quality art galleries and boutiques.

The Sarkies brothers, proprietors of two
other grand colonial hotels – the Strand in
Yangon (Rangoon) and the Eastern & Oriental in Penang – opened the Raffles in 1899
with the main building, the same one that
guests stay in today. Raffles soon became a
byword for oriental luxury and was featured
in novels by Joseph Conrad and Somerset
Maugham. The famous Singapore sling was
first concocted here by bartender Ngiam
Tong Boon in 1915; far less gloriously, the
last Singaporean tiger, which escaped from a
travelling circus nearby, was shot beneath the
Billiard Room in 1902. By the 1970s, Raffles
was a shabby relic, dodging the wrecking ball
in 1987 with National Monument designa-
tion. In 1991 it reopened after a $160 million
facelift. The hotel lobby is open to the public, and is a popular tourist attraction. Dress
standards apply: no shorts or sandals.

FORT CANNING PARK   PARK
Map p202 (www.nparks.gov.sg; Ⓜ Dhoby Ghaut)
FREE When Raffles rolled into Singapore
and claimed it for the mother country, locals steered clear of Fort Canning Hill, then
called Bukit Larangan (Forbidden Hill) out
of respect for the sacred shrine of Sultan Iskandar Shah, ancient Singapura's last ruler.
These days, the hill is better known as Fort

COLONIAL DISTRICT, MARINA BAY & THE QUAYS SIGHTS

TOP SIGHT
MARINA BAY SANDS

Love it or hate it, it's hard not to admire the sheer audacity of Singapore's $5.7 billion Marina Bay Sands. Perched on the southern bank of Marina Bay, the sprawling hotel, casino, theatre, exhibition centre, mall and museum is the work of Israeli-Canadian architect Moshe Safdie. Star of the show is Marina Bay Sands Hotel, its three 55-storey towers inspired by propped-up playing cards and connected by a cantilevered, 2 hectare 'SkyPark'.

Marina Bay Sands' attention-seeking tendencies extend to the nightly **Wonder Full** (⊙8pm & 9.30pm Sun-Thu, 8pm, 9.30pm & 11pm Fri & Sat), a 13-minute sound-and-light extravaganza which sees Marina Bay transformed into a video art screen of sorts. Best views are from the city side of Marina Bay, such as the Merlion and lofty bars like Lantern, Kinki and Level 33.

The cantilevered Sands SkyPark offers a gobsmacking panorama. Its world-famous infinity pool is off-limits to nonhotel guests, but the **Observation Deck** (adult/child $23/17; ⊙9.30am-10pm Mon-Thu, to 11pm Fri-Sun) is open to all. The deck is completely exposed, so use sunscreen and a hat, and avoid heading up on wet days.

DON'T MISS

➜ Wonder Full sound-and-light show

➜ View from the Sands SkyPark

PRACTICALITIES

➜ Map p205

➜ www.marinabay-sands.com

➜ 10 Bayfront Ave

➜ Ⓜ Bayfront

Canning Park, a wonderfully lush, cool retreat from the hot streets below. Stop at the spice garden and take in the scents of tamarind and cinnamon, or ponder Singapore's wartime defeat at the **Battle Box Museum** (Map p202; www.thebattlebox.com; 2 Cox Tce; adult/child $8/5; ⊙10am-6pm, last entry 5pm; Ⓜ Dhoby Ghaut).

The former command post of the British during WWII, the museum's eerie subterranean rooms use life-sized models to re-enact the fateful surrender to the Japanese on 15 February 1942. Japanese Morse codes are still etched on the walls. Fort Canning Park hosts several outdoor events and concerts throughout the year, including Shakespeare in the Park (April/May), Ballet under the Stars (July) and Films at the Fort (August).

NATIONAL GALLERY SINGAPORE
ART GALLERY

Map p202 (www.nationalgallery.sg; St Andrew's Rd; Ⓜ City Hall) When it opens in late 2015, the National Gallery Singapore will become the latest major player on the cultural circuit, not to mention the country's largest visual arts venue at 64,000 sq metres. Occupying both the former City Hall and Old Supreme Court building, the complex plans to showcase the work of Singaporean and Southeast Asian artists from the 19th century to today, as well as hosting international exhibitions. See the website for updates on the gallery's opening and upcoming exhibitions.

ST ANDREW'S CATHEDRAL
CHURCH

Map p202 (www.livingstreams.org.sg; 11 St Andrew's Rd; ⊙9am-5pm Mon-Sat; Ⓜ City Hall) Funded by Scottish merchants and built by Indian convicts, this wedding cake of a cathedral stands in stark contrast to the glass and steel surrounding it. Completed in 1838 but torn down and rebuilt in its present form in 1862 after lightning damage, it's one of Singapore's finest surviving examples of English Gothic architecture. Interesting details include the tropics-friendly *porte-cochère* (carriage porch) entrance – designed to shelter passengers – and the splendid stained glass adorning the western wall.

ARMENIAN CHURCH
CHURCH

Map p202 (www.armeniansinasia.org; 60 Hill St; ⊙9am-6pm; Ⓜ City Hall) The Armenians were the first Christian community to build a permanent place of worship in Singapore – this handsome, neoclassical number was designed by eminent colonial architect George Coleman. Consecrated in 1836 and dedicated to St Gregory the Illuminator, the building features a Greek cruciform plan and elegant Roman Doric columns and pilasters. The tower and spire were added in the 1850s. Pushing up orchids in the graveyard is Agnes Joaquim, discoverer of Singapore's national flower – the Vanda Miss Joaquim orchid.

SINGAPORE FLYER
OBSERVATION WHEEL

Map p205 (www.singaporeflyer.com.sg; 30 Raffles Ave; adult/senior/child $33/24/21; ⊙ticket booth 8am-10pm, wheel 8.30am-10.15pm; ⓂPromenade) Las Vegas' High Roller may have since stolen its 'World's Biggest Observation Wheel' title, but Singapore's 165m-tall ferris wheel continues to serve up a gob-smacking panorama. On a clear day, the 30-minute ride will have you peering out over the Colonial District, CBD and Marina Bay, the high-rise housing sprawl to the east and out to the ship-clogged South China Sea. Purchase tickets online for a modest discount.

SINGAPORE TYLER PRINT INSTITUTE
ART GALLERY

(STPI; ☑6336 3663; www.stpi.com.sg; 41 Robertson Quay; ⊙10am-6pm Tue-Sat; ⓂClarke Quay) Established by the American master printmaker Kenneth E Tyler, the STPI collaborates with both established and emerging artists to create contemporary, often surprising art based on printmaking and paper. Both local and international names are showcased in the gallery, with past exhibitors including Singaporean sculptor Han Sai Por and celebrated Australian painter and printmaker Brent Harris.

HONG SAN SEE TEMPLE
TEMPLE

(31 Mohamed Sultan Rd; ⊙6am-7pm; ☐32, 54, 139, 195) Perched on a hill, this imposing Chinese temple dates back to 1913. Its sloping tiled roofs and ornamented columns are southern Chinese in style, while the gilded woodcarvings adorning the inner doors are particularly impressive. In the main hall are an altar dedicated to patron deity Guangze Zunwang, and secondary altars to Chenghuang (the City God), Xuantian Shangdi and Guanyin (the Goddess of Mercy). The verses penned on the rear columns are by the late Chinese poet and calligrapher Pan Shou.

COLONIAL DISTRICT, MARINA BAY & THE QUAYS SIGHTS

TOP SIGHT
NATIONAL MUSEUM OF SINGAPORE

Singapore's brilliantly designed National Museum is good enough to warrant two visits. Staid exhibits are eschewed for engaging multimedia galleries bringing Singapore's jam-packed bio to life.

The History Gallery will have you peering into opium dens, eavesdropping on lunching colonial ladies, and confronting harrowing tales of Japanese occupation. The colourful Living Galleries explore Singaporean culture through four themes (Food, Fashion, Film and Wayang, and Photography), while the Goh Seng Choo Gallery showcases exquisite 19th-century botanical watercolours. Adding further layers of enlightenment are the museum's top-notch temporary exhibitions, which cover subjects as diverse as post-independence art to the history of Singapore's islands.

Last but not least is the museum's outstanding architecture. The superb neoclassical wing, built in 1887 as the Raffles Library and Museum, boasts a breathtaking rotunda, lavished with 50 panels of stained glass. A sleek extension features a Glass Passage, with revealing views of the dome's exterior, as well as its own dramatic, 16m-high Glass Rotunda.

DON'T MISS
➜ History, Living and Goh Seng Choo Galleries
➜ Permanent sculptures
➜ Architecture

PRACTICALITIES
➜ Map p202
➜ www.nationalmuseum.sg
➜ 93 Stamford Rd
➜ adult/child $10/5, Living Galleries 6-8pm free
➜ ⊙History Gallery 10am-6pm, Living Galleries 10am-8pm
➜ ⓂDhoby Ghaut

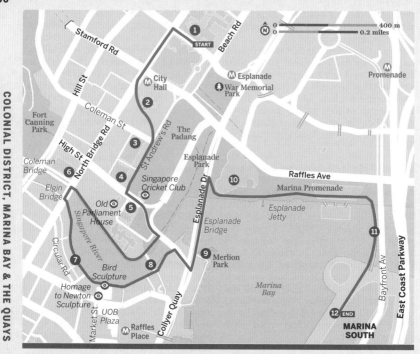

Neighbourhood Walk
Singapore: Colonial to Cutting Edge

START RAFFLES HOTEL
END MARINA BAY SANDS
LENGTH 4KM; FOUR TO FIVE HOURS

Start at **1 Raffles Hotel** (p53), taking in the colonial arcades, tropical gardens and commercial galleries exhibiting Southeast Asian art. Head out along North Bridge Rd and turn left into elegant **2 St Andrew's Cathedral** (p54), used as an emergency hospital during WWII. Heading south down St Andrew's Rd you'll pass City Hall and the Old Supreme Court, two colonial dames that, from late 2015, will house the **3 National Gallery Singapore** (p54). Nearby is the **4 New Supreme Court** (p57), a sci-fi statement co-designed by Sir Norman Foster's firm Foster + Partners. Below where St Andrew's Rd curves to the left stands the **5 Victoria Theatre & Concert Hall** (p57), one of Singapore's first Victorian Revivalist buildings. Before it is the original Raffles statue. Hang a right to walk along the northern bank of the Singapore River, one of the best spots to take

in the CBD's powerhouse towers. They're significantly taller than the multicoloured **6 Old Hill St police station** on the corner of Hill St, proclaimed a 'skyscraper' when completed in 1934. The building houses several high-end art galleries. Cross Elgin Bridge and head down to **7 Boat Quay** (p61), its riverfront shophouses now home to bars and restaurants. Look out for the area's great sculptures, including Fernando Botero's Bird and Salvador Dalí's Homage to Newton. Following the river further east you'll pass **8 Cavenagh Bridge**, constructed in Scotland and reassembled in Singapore in 1869. Soaring beside it is the mighty Fullerton Hotel, Singapore's general post office until 1996. Take a 'wacky' photo with the famous **9 Merlion statue** (p57), then head north along the Esplanade Bridge towards **10 Esplanade – Theatres on the Bay** (p63). Continue east along Marina Promenade to the **11 Helix Bridge**, whose impressive views of the Singapore skyline are upstaged by those from the Sands SkyPark atop **12 Marina Bay Sands** (p54).

CRICKET, COURTS & CULTURE: THE PADANG & AROUND

The field of the **Padang** (Map p202) is where flannelled fools play cricket in the tropical heat, cheered on by members of the Singapore Cricket Club in the pavilion. At the opposite end of the field is the Singapore Recreation Club. Cricket is still played on weekends.

This rather prosaic spot has darker historical significance, as it was to here that the invading Japanese herded the European community before marching them off to Changi Prison. Apart from the reconstructed monstrosity that is the Singapore Recreation Club, the Padang is flanked by a handsome collection of colonial buildings and assorted monuments, all of which can be taken in on a leisurely stroll.

At the Padang's southern end is the recently restored 1862 **Victoria Theatre & Concert Hall** (Map p202; ☑6338 1230; www.vch.org.sg; 11 Empress Pl; Ⓜ City Hall). The 1827 **Old Parliament House** (The Arts House; Map p202; ☑6332 6900; www.theartshouse.com.sg) is Singapore's oldest government building. Originally a private mansion, it became a courthouse, then the Assembly House of the colonial government and, finally, the Parliament House for independent Singapore. It's now an arts centre.

Along St Andrew's Rd, the **Old Supreme Court** (1939) is a relatively new addition and was the last classical building to be erected in Singapore. It replaced the Grand Hotel de L'Europe, which once outshone the Raffles as Singapore's premier hotel. Situated next door, and even newer, is the **New Supreme Court** (Map p202), its disc-shaped crown a new-millennium answer to its older sibling's dome.

City Hall (1929), with its classical facade of Corinthian columns, is located next to the Supreme Court. It was here that Lord Louis Mountbatten announced Japanese surrender in 1945 and Lee Kwan Yew declared Singapore's independence in 1965. Looking on quite reverently is neo-Gothic St Andrew's Cathedral (p54), last but not least of the Padang area's colonial beauties.

MERLION
MONUMENT

Map p202 (1 Fullerton Rd; Ⓜ Raffles Place) Back in the 1980s, someone at the tourism board created a myth about a half-fish, half-lion, and the gawking tourists helped seal its status as an iconic (nobody said it was pretty) Singapore sight. While visiting the $165,000 concrete creature isn't in itself worth your time, the Marina Bay views make the trip worthwhile, especially during Marina Bay Sands' twice-nightly light-and-laser show. Don't forget to jump on a boat cruise for a complete circuit of Singapore's changing waterways.

MARINA BARRAGE
PARK

Map p205 (☑6514 5959; www.pub.gov.sg/marina; 8 Marina Gardens Dr; ☺9am-9pm daily, Sustainable Singapore Gallery closed Tue; ☐400; Ⓜ Marina Bay) Singaporean ingenuity in action, Marina Barrage is both a flood-control dam of the Marina Channel and a gorgeous public park with commanding skyline views. The onsite Sustainable Singapore Gallery includes fascinating photos and archival footage of the Singapore River before its extreme makeover, as well as a nifty working model of the Marina Barrage itself. The highlight, however, is the actual park, its lawn dotted with locals flying their colourful kites.

MINT MUSEUM OF TOYS
MUSEUM

Map p202 (www.emint.com; 26 Seah St; adult/child $15/7.50; ☺9.30am-6.30pm; Ⓜ City Hall, Bugis) Nostalgia rulz at this slinky ode to playtime, its four skinny floors home to over 50,000 vintage toys. You'll see everything from rare Flash Gordon comics and supersonic toy guns to original Mickey Mouse dolls and oh-so-wrong golliwogs from 1930s Japan. Stock up on whimsical toys at the lobby shop or celebrate adulthood with a stiff drink at the adjacent **Mr Punch Rooftop Bar** (Map p202; ☑6334 5155; 26 Seah St; ☺6pm-2am Mon-Thu, to 3am Fri & Sat; Ⓜ City Hall or Bugis).

NATIONAL LIBRARY
LIBRARY

Map p202 (☑6332 3255; www.nl.sg; 100 Victoria St; ☺10am-9pm; Ⓜ Bugis, Bras Basah) FREE Designed by Malaysian architect and ecologist Ken Yeang, this white, curvaceous brains trust is home to numerous facilities, including a reference library, lending library and drama centre. For visitors, the real draws are the display of beautiful maps of Asia on level 10 (some dating back to the 16th century), and the library's program of free exhibitions. If you have little ones in tow, head to the forest-themed children's library in the basement for some storytime R&R.

MICA BUILDING ART GALLERIES
Map p202 An architectural pin-up famed for its Technicolor shutters and neo-Renaissance design, the MICA Building houses a string of well-known commercial art galleries representing successful regional artists. While the most famous of these is **Gajah Gallery** (Map p202; www.gajahgallery.com; ☉11am-7pm Mon-Fri, noon-6pm Sat & Sun), make sure to also pop into **Art-2 Gallery** (Map p202; www.art2.com.sg; ☉11am-7pm Mon-Sat) and **Cape of Good Hope** (Map p202; ☑6733 3822; www.capeofgoodhope.com.sg; 140 Hill St; ☉11am-7pm Mon-Sat, noon-6pm Sun; Ⓜ Clarke Quay).

EATING

⭐**GLUTTONS BAY** HAWKER CENTRE $
Map p202 (www.makansutra.com; 01-15 Esplanade Mall; dishes from $4; ☉3pm-1am Mon-Thu, to 2am Fri & Sat, to midnight Sun; Ⓜ Esplanade) Selected by the *Makansutra Food Guide,* this row of alfresco hawker stalls is a great place to start your Singapore food odyssey. Get indecisive over classics like oyster omelette, satay, barbecue stingray and carrot cake (opt for the black version). Its central, bayside location makes it a huge hit, so head in early or late to avoid the frustrating hunt for a table.

SATAY BY THE BAY HAWKER CENTRE $
Map p205 (www.gardensbythebay.com.sg; 18 Marina Gardens Dr, Gardens by the Bay; dishes from $4; ☉food stalls 8am-10pm, drinks stall 24hr; Ⓜ Marina Bay, then bus 400) Gardens by the Bay's own hawker centre has an enviable location, alongside Marina Bay and far from the roar of city traffic. Especially evocative at night, it's known for its satay, best devoured under open skies on the spacious wooden deck. Expectantly, prices are a little higher than at more local hawker centres, with most dishes between $8 and $10.

SONG FA BAK KUT TEH CHINESE $
Map p202 (www.songfa.com.sg; 11 New Bridge Rd; dishes $3.50-9; ☉7am-9.15pm Tue-Sun; Ⓜ Clarke Quay) If you need a hug, with its *bak kut teh* (pork rib soup). Literally 'meat bone tea', it's a sooth-ing concoction of fleshy pork ribs simmered in a peppery broth of herbs, spices and whole garlic cloves. The ribs are sublimely soft, sweet and melt-in-the-mouth, and staff will happily refill your bowl with broth.

Be in by 11.45am at lunch or before 7pm at dinner or head to the back of the queue.

YET CON CHINESE $
Map p202 (25 Purvis St; chicken rice $5.50; ☉10am-10pm; Ⓜ City Hall) Retro Yet Con has been serving up superlative Hainanese chicken rice since 1940. Don't come expecting designer decor or charming service. Just come for the chicken, which is tender, packed with flavour and served to faithful suits, old-timers and geeky, 20-something food nerds by stern-looking aunties. Don't be put off by the crowds either – turn over is usually fast.

RASAPURA MASTERS FOOD COURT $
Map p205 (www.rasapura.com.sg; 2 Bayfront Ave, Level B2, The Shoppes at Marina Bay Sands; dishes from $5; Ⓜ Bayfront) If you prefer your hawker grub with air-con and a flanking ice-skating rink, head down to this slick, sprawling food court in the basement of the Marina Bay Sands mall. Its stalls cover most bases, from Japanese ramen and Korean kimchi, to Hong Kong roast meats and local Bak Kut Teh pork-rib soup.

Dishes average around $8 to $10 – more expensive than local hawker centres but still a bargain in this corner of town.

KOPITIAM HAWKER CENTRE $
Map p202 (www.kopitiam.biz; cnr Bras Basah Rd & Bencoolen St; dishes around $7; ☉24hr; Ⓜ City Hall, Bras Basah) A sound spot in the district for a late-night feed, this branch of the Kopitiam chain is just the ticket after a long and boozy night. The food is uniformly good and you won't pay much more than $7 for a meal.

COMMON MAN COFFEE CAFE $$
(www.commonmancoffeeroasters.com; 22 Martin Rd, Robertson Quay; dishes $14-34; ☉8am-6.30pm; ☑; ☐64, 123, 186) While this airy, industrial-cool cafe roasts and serves top-class coffee, it also serves seriously scrumptious grub. Produce is super fresh and the combinations simple yet inspired, from all-day brekkie winners like green-pea fritters with crispy pancetta and balsamic syrup, to a lunchtime tortilla of grilled asparagus, spiced aubergine and goat's cheese.

THE BURMESE PENINSULA

Burma by MRT? Hop off at City Hall station, cross North Bridge Rd, and you might just think you've hit a vertical Yangon. In truth, you're in **Peninsula Plaza** (Map p202; 111 North Bridge Rd; MCity Hall) mall, unofficially known as Singapore's 'Little Burma'. Among the moneychangers, camera shops and sprawling Bata shoe shop is a legion of Burmese businesses, from visa and travel agencies to cluttered tailors and stalls selling sweet Burmese tea, and even betel nut stands.

Yet this is more than just a hub of Burmese enterprise. It's a hub for Singapore's estimated 100,000-strong Burmese community, a place to connect with fellow expats, catch up on news from home, and even rally community support. In the wake of 2008's Cyclone Nargis, the mall became the nerve centre of grassroots action, with no shortage of donation drives and people dropping off aid to assist those affected.

The air is heady with the smell of fish sauce and *ngapi* (fish or shrimp paste), wafting from the string of simple eateries serving up authentic Burmese grub. The most accessible of these is basement restaurant **Inle Myanmar** (Map p202; www.inlemyanmar.com.sg; B1-07 (A/B), Peninsula Plaza, 111 North Bridge Rd; ⊙11am-10pm; MCity Hall), a bright, upbeat space serving classics like *mohinga*, a delicate, sweet-and-sour noodle soup of fish broth, hard-boiled eggs, fishcake, and crunchy chickpea fritters. Order a bowl and pair it with some pickled tealeaf salad, an earthy, sesame-sprinkled concoction of fermented and pickled tea leaves, crisp chickpeas, tomato, cabbage, roasted peanuts, dried shrimp and chillies. If there is more than one of you, the restaurant also offers a Burmese dinner buffet ($22.90 Monday to Thursday, $24.90 weekends), available from 5.30pm to 9.30pm.

There's a small, palatable selection of wines by the glass, and a choice of house blend or single origin coffee.

PIZZERIA MOZZA
ITALIAN $$
Map p205 (The Shoppes at Marina Bay Sands; pizzas $20-30, salads $10-22; ⊙noon-11pm; MBayfront) This dough-kneading favourite is co-owned by New York super chef Mario Batali, and it's one of the few celebrity chef eateries at Marina Bay Sands that won't have you mortgaging your house. While both the antipasti and pasta dishes should appease the pickiest nonnas, the star turn is the woodfired pizzas, with big, crispy crusts to die for.

INDOCHINE WATERFRONT
SOUTHEAST ASIAN $$
Map p202 (☑6339 1720; www.indochine.com.sg; Asian Civilisations Museum, 1 Empress Pl; salads $17-26, mains from $18; ⊙noon-3pm & 6.30-11.30pm Mon-Thu, noon-3pm & 6.30pm-12.30am Fri, 6.30pm-12.30am Sat, 6.30-11.30pm Sun; ☑; MRaffles Place) In the same building as the Asian Civilisations Museum, the IndoChine cartel's riverside operation comes with Boat Quay views and sumptuous surrounds, from Ming Dynasty–inspired chairs to glittering chandeliers. The menu is a long, sophisticated tri-nation affair of Vietnamese-, Cambodian- and Laotian-inspired dishes, with no shortage of vegetarian options. Best of all, your food comes sans MSG, colourings or preservatives.

ARTICHOKE
MEDITERRANEAN $$
(☑6336 6949; www.artichoke.com.sg; 161 Middle Rd; mains $16-30; ⊙6.30-9.30pm Tue-Fri, 11.30am-2.30pm & 6.30-9.30pm Sat, 11.30am-2.30pm Sun; MBugis, Bras Basah) Sequestered in a cosy little building behind an old church, cafe-style Artichoke is the stamping ground of street-smart chef Bjorn Shen. His schtik is Middle Eastern grub with radical twists, whether it's seared scallops paired with miso and mint, fried chicken served with spiced fries, or dark chocolate brownies jammed with chunky dates. Sharing plates make it a good spot for foodie friends.

CHIN CHIN EATING HOUSE
CHINESE $$
Map p202 (19 Purvis St; dishes $6-25; ⊙7am-9pm; MCity Hall) For a no-fuss Chinese comfort feed, step into Chin Chin's halogen glow. Top billing goes to the Hainanese specialities, from the celebrated chicken rice and claypot mutton, to the golden pork chop. Breaded and fried, the chop is crunchy and surprisingly light, served with homestyle roast potatoes and a vinegary,

HP dipping sauce. The only thing missing is your Chinese mama serving up seconds.

JAI THAI
THAI $$

Map p202 (www.jai-thai.com; 27 Purvis St; dishes $5-16; ⊙11.30am-3pm & 6-9.30pm; MCity Hall) On a street studded with reputable eateries, lo-fi Jai Thai peddles cheap, tasty Thai under the gaze of Siamese royalty. Grab a pavement table and channel Bangkok with fragrant green curry chicken or mouthwatering fried prawns in a sweet and sour tamarind sauce. Like it hot? Slurp a bowl of fiery tom yum soup (order the shrimp version). Cash only.

★KILO
FUSION $$$

(☑6467 3987; www.kilokitchen.com; 66 Kampong Bugis; sharing plates $15-24, mains $27-39; ⊙restaurant 6-10.30pm Mon-Sat, bar 6pm-1am Wed-Sat; MLavender) Its location might be slightly off the radar (the 2nd floor of an industrial riverside building), but gastro geeks know exactly how to reach this cool and swinging legend. Book ahead to swoon over modern, beautifully textured dishes like salmon sushi with crunchy chicken skin, an earthy wasabi tuna tartare, or sublime Italo-Japanese black and white prawn ravioli with sake butter.

Unusually for Singapore, service is efficient, professional and personable. Fed and satisfied, head up to the 8th floor and the effortless cool of the Kilo Lounge (p62). Simplify life by taking a taxi.

★JAAN
FRENCH $$$

Map p202 (☑6837 3322; www.jaan.com.sg; Swissôtel The Stamford, 2 Stamford Rd; lunch/dinner set menus from $68/198; ⊙noon-2pm & 7-10pm Mon-Sat, 7-10pm Sun; ⊿; MCity Hall) Perched 70 floors above the city, chic and intimate Jaan is home to French chef Julien Royer and his show-stopping, contemporary Gallic creations. From *amuse-bouches* appetisers like *cèpes sabayon* and mushroom tea, to protagonists like hay-roasted Bresse pigeon, flavours are revelatory and the presentation utterly theatrical. Always book ahead, and request a window seat overlooking Marina Bay Sands for a bird's-eye view of the nightly laser-and-light show.

JUMBO SEAFOOD
CHINESE $$$

Map p202 (☑6532 3435; www.jumboseafood. com.sg; 01-01/02 Riverside Point, 30 Merchant Rd; dishes from $12, chilli crab around $55 per kg; ⊙noon-2.15pm & 6-11.15pm; MClarke Quay) If you're lusting for chilli crab – and you should be – this is a good place to indulge. The gravy is sublimely sweet and nutty, with just the right amount of chilli. Make sure to order some yeasty *mantou* (fried buns) to soak up the gravy. While all of Jumbo's outlets have the dish down to an art, this one has the best riverside location.

One kilo of crab (or 1.5kg if you're especially hungry) should be enough for two.

POLLEN
EUROPEAN $$$

Map p205 (☑6604 9988; www.pollen.com.sg; Flower Dome, Gardens by the Bay, 18 Marina Gardens Dr; mains $58-68; ⊙noon-2.30pm & 6-10pm Tue-Sun, afternoon tea 3-5pm; ⊿; MBayfront) Set right inside Garden by the Bay's Flower Dome, Pollen is the Singapore spin-off of Pollen Street Social, London's Michelin-starred darling. While the fine-dining restaurant delivers gorgeous, contemporary European dishes like lobster with fennel cream and sea urchin, more fun and accessible is afternoon tea in the cafe; the scones and macarons are worth the trip alone. Book ahead (up to a week ahead on weekends).

🍷 DRINKING & NIGHTLIFE

You'll find no shortage of touristy bars and pubs on Boat Quay and Clarke Quay, with a small handful of more discerning cocktail bars behind Boat Quay. There's no shortage of rooftop options either, with many of the best skirting Marina Bay.

★BITTERS & LOVE
COCKTAIL BAR

Map p202 (www.bittersandlove.com; 36 North Canal Rd; ⊙6pm-midnight Mon-Thu, to 2am Fri & Sat; MClarke Quay) When the drinks are this good, you don't need signage to draw the crowds. Lurking behind top-notch eatery Shoebox Canteen, this intimate cocktail den is home to some of the city's top barkeeps, who stir, shake and slurp local-twist libations like the rum-based, tea-infused Kaya Toast. Peckish? Swoon over buttery Wagyu Beef Cubes or get decadent with seasonal live oysters.

KU DÉ TA
ROOFTOP BAR

Map p202 (www.kudeta.com; Marina Bay Sands; ⊙11am-late; MBayfront) While we don't think much of the drinks, this tourist trap atop

QUAYS OF THE CITY

The stretch of riverfront that separates the Colonial District from the CBD is known as the Quays. A walk along them offers a glimpse into the changes that have impacted Singapore's trade through the years. To get a rundown on the area's history, visit the Asian Civilisations Museum (p50).

Boat Quay (Map p202; MRaffles Place) This was once Singapore's centre of commerce. By the mid-1980s, many of the shophouses were in ruins, business having shifted to high-tech cargo centres. Declared a conservation zone, the area became a major entertainment district of touristy bars, shops and menu-clutching touts luring the masses into their waterside restaurants. Discerning punters ditch these for the growing number of cafes and drinking dens dotting the streets behind the main strip, among them coffee peddler Ronin (p63) and 'speakeasy' cocktail bars 28 Hong-Kong Street and Bitters & Love.

Clarke Quay (Map p202; www.clarkequay.com.sg; MClarke Quay) This is the busiest and most popular of the three quays, its plethora of bars, restaurants and clubs pulling in crowds every night. How much time you spend here depends upon your taste in aesthetics. If pastel hues, Dr Seuss–style design, and lad-and-ladette hangouts are your schtick, you'll be well in your element.

Robertson Quay (🚌64, 123, 143, MClarke Quay) Robertson Quay is at the furthest reach of the river. Some of the old *godown* (warehouses) have found new purposes as bars and members-only party places. The vibe here is more 'grown up' than Clarke Quay, attracting a 30-plus crowd. In recent years, a handful of notable riverside hangouts have popped up further west of Saiboo St, among them Australian roastery-cafe Toby's Estate and a branch of Singapore's highly regarded Kith Cafe.

---

the Marina Bay Sands Hotel is worth a one-off visit for its jaw-dropping panorama of Singapore. Snap away at Marina Bay, the city sprawl, and busy South China Sea. From 6pm, the club lounge enforces a 'no shorts, no singlets, no flip flops' dress code, though the place is best avoided after dark.

★ LANTERN   ROOFTOP BAR

Map p202 (☏6597 5299; Fullerton Bay Hotel, 80 Collyer Quay; ⊙8am-1am Sun-Thu, 8am-2am Fri & Sat; MRaffles Place) It may be lacking in height (it's dwarfed by the surrounding CBD buildings) and serves its drinks in plasticware (scanadalous!), but Lantern remains a magical spot for a sophisticated evening toast. Why? There's the flickering lanterns, the shimmering, glass-sided pool (for Fullerton Bay Hotel guests only), and the romantic views over Marina Bay. To avoid disappointment, consider booking a table two to three days ahead, especially on weekends.

28 HONGKONG STREET   COCKTAIL BAR

Map p202 (28HKS; ☏6533 2001; www.28hks. com; 28 Hongkong St; ⊙5.30pm-1am Mon-Wed, to 2am Thu, to 3am Fri & Sat; MClarke Quay) Softly lit 28HKS plays hide and seek inside an unmarked '60s shophouse. Slip inside and into a slinky scene of cosy booths and passionate mixologists turning grog into greatness. Marked with their date of origin, cocktails are seamless and sublime, among them an award-winning Whore's Bath, pimped with Baby's Breath. House-barreled classics, hard-to-find beers and lip-smacking comfort grub seal the deal.

KINKI   BAR

Map p202 (www.kinki.com.sg; 02-02 Customs House, 70 Collyer Quay; MRaffles Place) While Kinki's restaurant is justifiably known for its sushi, it's the rooftop bar one floor up that takes the cake. Pimped with graffiti panels and video projections, its sweep takes in Marina Bay Sands and its twice-nightly light-and-laser spectacular. Music levels allow for conversation (though it does get packed later in the week) and, despite the knockout location, the vibe is rarely obnoxious.

If you're feeling peckish, fill up on Nippon-esque nosh like temaki bites, spiced meatballs and Ebi fries.

LEVEL 33   MICROBREWERY

Map p205 (www.level33.com.sg; Level 33, Marina Bay Financial Tower 1, 8 Marina Blvd; ⊙noon-midnight Sun-Thu, noon-2am Fri & Sat; 🛜; MDowntown)

In a country obsessed with unique selling points, this one takes the cake. Laying claim to being the world's highest 'urban craft-brewery', Level 33 brews its own lager, pale ale, stout, porter and wheat beer. But we can live with the hype as long as the views are this good and the beer crisp and cold.

THE BLACK SWAN   BAR

Map p208 (☑8181 3305; www.theblackswan.com.sg; 19 Cecil St; ⊘11am-1am Mon-Thu, to 2am Fri & Sat; ⓂRaffles Place) Was that Rita Hayworth? You'll be mistaken for thinking so at this art-deco marvel, set inside a former 1930s bank building. While we adore the bustling downstairs bar – complete with inlaid wood, geometric windows and centrepiece U-shaped bar – it's the upstairs Powder Room that takes the breath away – a dark, decadent, plush lounge perfect for top-tier whiskies or classic with-a-twist cocktails.

ORGO   ROOFTOP BAR

Map p202 (☑6336 9366; www.orgo.sg; 4th fl Esplanade Roof Terrace, 8 Raffles Ave, ; ⊘6pm-1.30am; ⓂEsplanade) ✐ It's hard not to feel like the star of a Hollywood rom-com at rooftop Orgo, with its commanding view of the skyline. Slip into a wicker armchair, order a glass of vino (hell, order a cigar as well!) and Instagram the view to the sound of soft conversation and sultry tunes.

KILO LOUNGE   BAR

(66 Kampong Bugis; ⊘7pm-1am Wed & Thu, to 3am Fri & Sat; ⓂLavender) Six floors above cult-status restaurant Kilo, Kilo Lounge is one of Singapore's hottest new drinking spots. Polished concrete, recycled wood and handsome leather sofas set a slinky mood, cranked up by live music and lush DJ sets on Friday and Saturday night. At the time of writing, the venue was considering the introduction of a happy hour, so consider calling ahead to confirm opening times.

RAFFLES HOTEL   BAR

Map p202 (www.raffles.com; 1 Beach Rd; ⊘11am-11pm; ⓂCity Hall) Drink prices are exorbitant, but there's something undeniably fabulous about an afternoon cocktail at Singapore's most iconic hotel. Ditch the gloomy, cliched **Long Bar** (⊘11am-12.30am Sun-Thu, 11am-1.30am Fri & Sat) for the fountain-graced **Raffles Courtyard** (⊘11am-10.30pm) or sip Raj-style on the verandah at the **Bar & Billiard Room** (☑6412 1816; ⊘11am-11pm Thu-Sat). Tip: pass on the sickly sweet Singapore sling for something more palatable, like the Autumn Sling.

THE ART OF HIGH TEA

For a little afternoon delight, it's hard to beat a long, slow session of high tea. Not only is it a civilised antidote to Singapore's high speed and higher temperatures, it's the perfect mid-afternoon recharge. While most luxury hotels are in on the act, not all high teas are created equal. Pick the right spots and you practically have yourself a late lunch.

Singapore's best high tea is arguably at the **Landing Point** (Map p202; www.fullertonbayhotel.com; Fullerton Bay Hotel, 80 Collyer Quay; high tea adult/child $45/22, with glass of champagne $65; ⊘7am-midnight Sun-Thu, to 1am Fri & Sat, high tea 3-5.30pm; ⓂRaffles Place), the plush, waterfront lounge inside the Fullerton Bay Hotel. Book ahead (one day for weekdays, two weeks for weekends), style up, and head in on an empty stomach. Blue-ribbon TWG teas are a fine match for luxe bites like truffled egg sandwiches, melt-in-your-mouth quiche, brioche buns topped with duck and blueberries, and scandalously rich, caramel-filled dark-chocolate tarts. You won't be able to stop at one, which is just as well, as your three-tier stand will be gladly replenished.

The Landing Point's most serious competitor is the Ritz-Carlton's **Chihuly Lounge** (Map p202; ☑6434 5288; Ritz-Carlton Millenia Singapore, 7 Raffles Ave; high tea from $49; ⊘9.30am-1am, high tea 2.30-5pm; ☎; ⓂPromenade), whose eight-course version includes an equally sublime array of bites, from moreish smoked salmon pastry to juicy macarons. Less appealing is the scandalous use of tea bags, an unworthy match for the beautiful French Bernardaud porcelain. Aptly, the light-filled lounge is graced with an original Dale Chihuly glass sculpture. It forms part of the hotel's renowned collection of modern art, valued at around $5 million and including works from Andy Warhol, David Hockney and Frank Serra. After tea, head to the concierge desk to borrow an iPod guide (bring photo ID) and tour the works for free. High tea at the Ritz-Carlton should also be booked ahead (two days for weekdays, a week or two for weekends).

WINE CONNECTION
WINE BAR

(www.wineconnection.com.sg; 01-05 Robertson Walk, 11 Unity St; ⊗11am-2am Mon-Thu, to 3am Fri & Sat, to midnight Sun; 🚇64, 123, 143) Oenophiles love this contemporary, spacious wine bar at Robertson Quay. The team works closely with winemakers across the world, which means no 'middle man', an interesting wine list, and very palatable prices; we're talking glasses from $7 and bottles as low as $25. If you're a cheese fiend, dive into its neighbouring Cheese Bar, where you can also kick back with a decent drop.

RONIN
CAFE

Map p202 (17 Hongkong St; ⊗8am-8pm Tue-Sun; ⓜClarke Quay) Ronin hides its talents behind a dark, tinted glass door. Walk through and the brutalist combo of grey concrete, exposed plumbing and low-slung lamps might leave you expecting some tough-talking interrogation. Thankfully, the only thing you'll get slapped with is sucker-punch Genovese coffee, T2 speciality teas and simple, solid cafe grub like fantastic French toast and gourmet panini. Cash only.

NEW ASIA
BAR, CLUB

Map p202 (Swissôtel The Stamford, 2 Stamford Rd; admission $25; ⊗5pm-1am Sun-Tue, to 2am Wed & Thu, to 3am Fri & Sat; ⓜCity Hall) Martinis demand dizzying skyline views and few deliver like this sleek bar-club hybrid, perched 71 floors above street level. A classic go-to for the cabin-crew crowd, it's worth heading in early for sundowners before shaking your booty on the dance floor. Smart casual dress.

LOOF
ROOFTOP BAR

Map p202 (📞9773 9304; www.loof.com.sg; 03-07 Odeon Towers Bldg, 331 North Bridge Rd; ⊗5pm-1am Mon-Thu, to 3am Fri & Sat; 🛜; ⓜCity Hall) Red neon warmly declares 'Glad you came up' at revamped Loof, its name the Singlish mangling of the word 'roof'. Sit at the edge of the leafy rooftop deck and look out over Raffles Hotel and Marina Bay Sands with a calamansi-spiked Singapore sour in hand. Weekday happy hour lasts from 5pm to 8pm, with the cheapest drinks early on.

ACTORS
BAR

Map p202 (📞6535 3270; www.actorsthejambar.com; 13A-15A South Bridge Rd; ⊗6pm-2am Mon-Sat; ⓜClarke Quay) Every night is open-mic night at Actors, where customers are given the chance to get up and play music on one of the instruments laid out for jamming.

AH SAM COLD DRINK STALL
COCKTAIL BAR

Map p202 (60A Boat Quay; ⊗6pm-midnight Mon-Thu, to 3am Fri & Sat; ⓜClarke Quay) Get that in-the-know glow at this sneaky cocktail den perched above the tacky Boat Quay pubs. Adorned with vintage Hong Kong posters and feeling more like a party than a bar, it's the domain of five young mates with a passion for mixology. Tell them your preferences, and watch them twist, shake and torch them into clever creations.

They mightn't be the strongest drinks in town, but they beat the tourist dross downstairs hands down.

☆ ENTERTAINMENT

ZOUK
CLUB

(www.zoukclub.com; 17 Jiak Kim St; ⊗Zouk 10pm-late Wed, Fri & Sat, Phuture & Velvet Underground 9pm-late Wed, Fri & Sat, Wine Bar 6pm-2am Tue, 6pm-3am Wed & Thu, 6pm-4am Fri & Sat; 🚇5, 16, 64, 75, 123, 175, 186, 195) Ibiza-inspired Zouk is still one of Singapore's favourite clubs, with five bars, a multi-level dance floor, and no shortage of coveted, globe-trotting DJs manning the decks. You'll also find alfresco **Zouk Wine Bar**, hip-hop-centric club **Phuture** and plush club-meets-lounge **Velvet Underground**, pimped with original artworks from Andy Warhol, Frank Stella and Takashi Murakami. Take a taxi, and be prepared to queue.

ATTICA
CLUB

Map p202 (www.attica.com.sg; 01-03 Clarke Quay, 3A River Valley Rd; ⊗Attica 10.30pm-4am Wed, Fri & Sat, to 3am Thu; Attica Too 11pm-5am Wed, 11pm-5.30am Fri & Sat; ⓜClarke Quay) Attica has secured a loyal following among Singapore's fickle clubbers, modelling itself on New York's hippest clubs but losing the attitude somewhere over the Pacific. Locals will tell you it's where the expats go to pick up on the weekends, mostly in the courtyard. Beats span chart hits, house, electro and R&B; check the website for themed nights.

ESPLANADE –
THEATRES ON THE BAY
ARTS CENTRE

Map p202 (📞6828 8377; www.esplanade.com; 1 Esplanade Dr; ⊗10am-6pm; ⓜEsplanade, City Hall) Home of the esteemed Singapore Symphony Orchestra (SSO), Singapore's architecturally striking arts centre includes an 1800-seater state-of-the-art concert hall, a

1940-seater theatre, and an action-packed programme spanning music, theatre and dance, including performances by the Singapore Dance Theatre (p91). Check the website for upcoming events, which include regular free concerts, and don't miss an evening tipple at sultry rooftop bar Orgo (p62).

SINGAPORE REPERTORY THEATRE THEATRE

(✆6733 8166; www.srt.com.sg; DBS Arts Centre, 20 Merbau Rd; 🚌64, 123, 143, Ⓜ Clarke Quay) Based at the DBS Arts Centre, but also performing at other venues, the SRT produces international repertory standards, as well as modern Singaporean plays. The company's Shakespeare in the Park series, enchantingly set in Fort Canning Park, is deservedly popular. Check the website for upcoming productions.

THEATREWORKS THEATRE

(✆6737 7213; www.theatreworks.org.sg; 72-13 Mohamed Sultan Rd; 🚌32, 54, 139, 195) One of the more experimental theatre companies in Singapore, TheatreWorks is led by enigmatic artistic director Ong Keng Sen. A mix of fresh local work and international collaborations, performances are housed in the company's headquarters, a former rice warehouse just off Robertson Quay. See the website for updates.

TIMBRÈ @ THE SUBSTATION LIVE MUSIC

Map p202 (www.timbre.com.sg; 45 Armenian St; ⏰6pm-1am Sun-Thu, to 2.30am Fri & Sat; Ⓜ City Hall) Young ones are content to queue for seats at this popular live-music venue, whose daily rotating roster features local bands and singer-songwriters playing anything from pop and rock to folk. Hungry punters can fill up on soups, salads, tapas and passable fried standbys like buffalo wings and truffle fries.

CRAZY ELEPHANT LIVE MUSIC

Map p202 (www.crazyelephant.com; 01-03/04 Clarke Quay; ⏰5pm-2am Sun-Thu, to 3am Fri & Sat; Ⓜ Clarke Quay) Anywhere that bills itself as 'crazy' should set the alarm bells ringing, but you won't hear them once you're inside. This touristy rock bar is beery, blokey, loud, graffiti covered and testosterone heavy!

HOME CLUB COMEDY

Map p202 (homeclub.com.sg; B1-1/06 The Riverwalk, 20 Upper Circular Rd; ⏰6pm-2am Tue-Thu, to 3am Fri, to 4am Sun; Ⓜ Clarke Quay) While hardly the top club in town, the Tuesday night **Comedy Masala** (comedymasala.com; adult/student incl one drink \$10/6) is a blast. Running from 9pm to 11.30pm, the open-mic event showcases some of the sharpest stand-up acts in town.

CAPITOL THEATRE THEATRE, CINEMA

Map p202 (www.capitolsingapore.com; cnr North Bridge & Stamford Rds; Ⓜ City Hall) After years of neglect, the freshly restored Capitol Theatre is set to take centre stage again in 2015. Built in 1929 and locally dubbed 'the Grande Dame', the former movie palace will host both film screenings and live theatre. It forms part of Capitol Singapore, a major redevelopment project incoporating a luxury hotel, high-end retail and apartments.

🛍 SHOPPING

While the area has no shortage of malls – from luxury to electronics – it's also home to a handful of inspired options, selling everything from local art and design, to independent fashion and retro frocks.

RAFFLES HOTEL ARCADE MALL

Map p202 (www.raffles.com; 328 North Bridge Rd; Ⓜ City Hall) Part of the hotel complex, Raffles Hotel Arcade is home to some rather notable retailers. You'll find quality, affordable souvenirs at **Raffles Hotel Gift Shop** (www.raffleshotelgifts.com; 01-01/03 Raffles Hotel Arcade; ⏰8.30am-9pm; Ⓜ City Hall) – the vintage hotel posters are great buys – high-end Singaporean and Malaysian art at **Chan Hampe** (www.chanhampegalleries. com; 01-20/21, Raffles Hotel Arcade; ⏰11am-7pm Tue-Sun); and inspired, independent fashion labels and accessories for men and women at **Front Row** (www.frontrowsingapore.com; 02-09 Raffles Hotel Arcade; ⏰noon-8pm Mon-Sat, noon-5pm Sun).

And even if you can't afford its cameras, the **Leica** (www.leica-store.sg; 01-18 Raffles Hotel Arcade; ⏰10am-8pm) store usually has a free, high-quality photographic exhibition.

FUNAN DIGITALIFE MALL ELECTRONICS

Map p202 (www.funan.com.sg; 109 North Bridge Rd; Ⓜ City Hall) Hardwire yourself across six floors of electronics, camera and computer stores. Funan is a better bet than Sim Lim Sq if you don't know exactly what you're doing. Occupying the 6th floor, you can find almost anything at the massive **Challenger**

Superstore (www.challenger.com.sg; Level 6; ☺10am-10pm). For cameras, visit family-run **John 3:16** (☑6337 2877; www.john316photo. com; 04-27 Funan DigitaLife Mall; ☺12:30-9:30pm Mon-Sat).

GRANNY'S DAY OUT   FASHION
Map p202 (☑6336 9774; www.grannysdayout. com; 03-25 Peninsula Shopping Centre, 3 Coleman St; ☺noon-8pm Mon-Fri, noon-6.30pm Sun; Ⓜ City Hall) Aptly set inside très-retro Peninsula Shopping Centre, Granny's Day Out peddles a fabulous, ever-changing booty of vintage clothes, shoes and accessories from the '50s to the '80s. Sorry guys, unless you're into cross-dressing, these goods are just for the ladies.

ROXY DISC HOUSE   MUSIC STORE
Map p202 (☑6336 6192; 03-42 The Adelphi, 1 Coleman St; ☺1-8pm Mon-Sat, 2-8pm Sun; Ⓜ City Hall) Squeeze into Roxy's skinny aisles and scan the shelves for top-notch vinyl, both new and used, as well as CDs. Jazz and blues make up the bulk of the offerings, with both English- and Chinese-language collectors' editions thrown into the mix. You'll find the shop on the 3rd floor of the Adelphi, a lo-fi mall packed with audio equipment shops.

RAFFLES CITY   MALL
Map p202 (www.rafflescity.com.sg; 252 North Bridge Rd; Ⓜ City Hall) Raffles City is one of Singapore's best malls, complete with a three-level branch of fashion-savvy **Robinsons** department store and high-street fashion brands like **Topshop**. Level 1 is handbag heaven, while Level 3 offers a handful of kids' boutiques. Seek culture at **Ode to Art** (☑6250 1901; 01-36 Raffles City Shopping Centre) gallery or a bite to eat at the top-floor food court or basement food outlets.

SUNTEC CITY   MALL
Map p202 (www.sunteccity.com.sg; 3 Temasek Blvd; Ⓜ Promenade, Esplanade) Vast, bewildering and often frustratingly inaccessible, Suntec has no shortage of retail hits, including **Uniqlo**, **Fossil**, **Kiehl's** and **Aesop**, not to mention over 50 restaurants, cafes, food courts and a sprawling branch of supermarket **Giant Hyper**. The star turn is the **Fountain of Wealth** (Map p202), declared the World's Largest Fountain (though not Most Attractive) in the *Guinness Book of Records*. Touch the water for good luck, or at least for a quirky pic.

MARINA SQUARE   MALL
Map p202 (www.marinasquare.com.sg; 6 Raffles Blvd; ☺10am-10pm; Ⓜ Esplanade) Over 250 outlets, including loads of global brands like **Desigual**, **Zara** and **Muji**, are packed into this massive shopping space. Centrally located in the Marina Centre area, it has easy access to and from CityLink Mall, Suntec City, Millenia Walk and the Esplanade.

CITY LINK MALL   MALL
Map p202 (1 Raffles Link; ☺10am-10pm; Ⓜ City Hall) Designed by New York's Kohn Pederson Fox, this seemingly endless tunnel of retail and food outlets links City Hall MRT station with Suntec City and the Esplanade. It's a handy means to escape searing sun or teeming rain, and a comfortable way of getting into the city from the Marina Bay hotels.

BASHEER GRAPHIC BOOKS   BOOKSTORE
Map p202 (www.facebook.com/BasheerGraphic; 04-19, Bras Basah Complex, 231 Bain St; ☺10am-8pm Mon-Sat, 11am-6pm Sun; Ⓜ Bugis, City Hall) Spruce up your coffee table at this cornucopia of graphic books and magazines. Located inside the Bras Basah Complex (locally dubbed 'Book City'), it has everything from fashion and design tomes to titles on art, architecture and urban planning. The shop also does a brisk mail-order business, so if you're mid-travel and want to have something mailed to you, staff are happy to help.

CAT SOCRATES   GIFTS
Map p202 (☑6333 0870; www.catsocrates. com.sg; 02-25, Bras Basah Complex, 231 Bain St; ☺noon-8pm Mon-Sat, 1-7pm Sun; Ⓜ Bugis) Can't find that Mao alarm clock? What about that Pan-Am–themed wrapping paper? Chances are you'll find them at this quirky shop, inside the bookworm mecca that is Bras Basah Complex. Expect anything from Japanese design magazines and Korean rucksacks, to supercool Singapore souvenirs like city-themed graphic postcards and playing cards.

SHOPPES AT MARINA BAY SANDS   MALL
Map p205 (www.marinabaysands.com; 10 Bayfront Ave; Ⓜ Bayfront) You'll find all the 'it' brands at this sprawling temple of aspiration, including runway royalty like Prada, Miu Miu and Fendi. Many people visiting cloister themselves in the dungeonlike

SUNDAY ARTISTS MARKET

Tap into Singapore's creative side at the bimonthly **Sunday Artists Market** (Map p202; 6222 5001; www.thevault.com.sg; The Vault, 23 Circular Rd; 1-6pm Sun, bimonthly; Clarke Quay). Held at the Vault, a bar-club behind Boat Quay, it's a showcase for over 20 local artists and craftspeople, selling the likes of handmade jewellery, totes and shoes, skincare, stationery and more. Extra perks include cold beer, DJs and the odd hairstylist ready to hipsterfy your mop. Not only is it a great spot to pick up some one-off local art and design, it's a fantastic opportunity to support Singapore's burgeoning creative scene. For details and dates, check the Vault's website or Facebook page. The market is one of several around town, with other notables including the monthly **MAAD** (Market of Artists and Designers; www.facebook.com/goMAAD; Red Dot Design Museum, 28 Maxwell Rd), held at the Red Dot Design Museum, and the regular **Every Little Thing** (www.public-garden.com); its rotating locations have included the National Museum of Singapore.

casino, leaving the mall relatively thin on crowds – good news if you're not a fan of the Orchard Rd pandemonium.

On-site quirks include boat rides on an artificial canal, an ice-free ice-skating rink, and the world's first floating Louis Vuitton store, right on Marina Bay.

ROYAL SELANGOR
GIFTS

Map p202 (www.royalselangor.com.sg; 01-01 Clarke Quay; Clarke Quay) Malaysia's pewter specialists mightn't rank high on the hip list – think the kind of personalised tankards your uncle uses for his real ale – but don't discount their jewellery, some items of which might even suit painfully fashionable teens.

The best bit is the School of Hard Knocks (SOHN), at which groups of 12 bash pewter into malleable masterpieces. Thirty-minute courses cost $30 and you get to keep your inscribed dish.

🏃 SPORTS & ACTIVITIES

G-MAX REVERSE BUNGY
THRILL RIDE

Map p202 (www.gmax.com.sg; 3E River Valley Rd; per ride $45; 2pm-late; Clarke Quay) Prepare to be strapped into padded chairs inside a metal cage and propelled to a height of 60m at speeds of up to 200km/h before being pulled back down by gravity. Though the ride offers spectacular views to those who can keep their eyes open, it's best avoided by people prone to velocity-induced vomiting.

GX-5 EXTREME SWING
THRILL RIDE

Map p202 (www.gmax.com.sg; 3E River Valley Rd; per ride $45; 3pm-late Mon-Fri, noon-late Sat & Sun; Clarke Quay) A relatively gentle high ('relatively' is the key here) is offered right next door to the G-Max Bungy. Whereas the G-Max offers a straight-up face-peeling vertical trip, the GX5 swings riders up and over the Singapore River with somewhat less nauseating velocity. The trip also lasts longer, though which one provides more bang for your buck is utterly subjective.

ULTIMATE DRIVE
SPORTS CAR RIDE

Map p205 (6688 7997; www.ultimatedrive.com; Marina Bay Sands Hotel Tower 3, 1 Bayfront Ave; ride as driver/passenger from $298/238; 9am-10pm; Bayfront) Dress to kill, then make a show of getting into a Ferrari F430 F1 Spider (red!) or Lamborghini Gallardo Spyder (yellow!) before tearing out for a spin. A taste of luxury can be yours, if only for 15 to 60 minutes. One can dream, right? Rides also depart from the Singapore Flyer (p55).

WILLOW STREAM
SPA

Map p202 (6431 5600; www.willowstream.com/ singapore; Level 6, Fairmont Hotel, 80 Bras Basah Rd; massage treatments from $149; 7am-10pm, treatments from 9am; City Hall) Spoil yourself silly at this lavish spa, complete with jacuzzis, plunge pools, rooms that puff aromatic steam and staff that will slather good stuff on your face before pushing, prodding and kneading the kinks out of your jetlagged (or shopped-out) body. There's also an in-house salon, covering everything from hair and waxing to manicures and pedicures.

Chinatown & the CBD

Neighbourhood Top Five

❶ Visiting the evocative **Chinatown Heritage Centre** (p69) and delving into the unspeakable hardships, destructive temptations and ultimate resilience of the immigrants who gave this part of town its name.

❷ Meeting the stars of the show in the unusually informal **Chinese Theatre Circle** (p77).

❸ Skipping your hotel brekkie and heading to **Ya Kun Kaya Toast** (p72) for a traditional morning slap-up.

❹ Giving the chopsticks a rest and tackling showstopping Mexican at hot, hot, hot **Lucha Loco** (p72).

❺ Toasting, chatting and flirting the night away on hedonistic **Club St**, the city's bar-scene heartland.

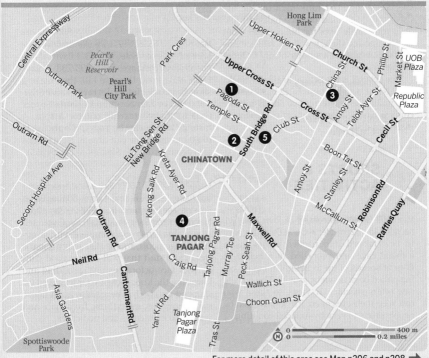

For more detail of this area see Map p206 and p208. ➡

Lonely Planet's Top Tip

As with anywhere in Singapore, it's worth taking advantage of happy hours (usually until 8pm or 9pm) at the hotlist bars around Chinatown. If it's still too pricey for you, neck a few beers at a hawker centre instead.

✖ Best Places to Eat

➡ Ding Dong (p74)

➡ Momma Kong's (p72)

➡ Lucha Loco (p72)

➡ Chinatown Complex (p73)

For reviews, see p72.➡

🍷 Best Places to Drink

➡ Tippling Club (p74)

➡ Breeze (p75)

➡ Nylon Coffee Roasters (p76)

➡ The Good Beer Company (p75)

For reviews, see p74.➡

👁 Best for History & Culture

➡ Chinatown Heritage Centre (p69)

➡ Baba House (p72)

➡ Sri Mariamman Temple (p70)

For reviews, see p70.➡

Explore Chinatown

With the possible exception of the Chinatown Heritage Centre, sights here are interesting rather than must-see, but that's a good thing. It leaves more time to focus on Chinatown's star attraction – food. Start early with a traditional Singaporean breakfast in a *kopitiam* (coffeeshop). For lunch, join the crowds at one of Chinatown's bustling hawker centres. Come evening, take your pick of Singapore's hotlist eateries, serving anything from real-deal Mexican to punchy Southeast Asian.

In between meals, poke your head into an antiques shop, gallery or a heady temple or two. Savour beautifully renovated shophouses and superlative lattes on the gentrified streets of the Duxton Hill area (south of Chinatown).

Once the sun's gone down, catch the breeze and the city skyline from a rooftop bar on Ann Siang Rd or Club St.

Local Life

➡**Hawker Centres** It's a wonder any of Singapore's high-end restaurants stay in business given that hawker centre food is dirt cheap and so damn good. Chinatown is no exception. Eat at as many hawker centres as you can while you're here, but if you've only time for one, make it Maxwell Rd.

➡**Coffee versus kopi** While hip, Third Wave cafes and roasteries are making big waves in the Duxton Hill area, don't miss the chance to slurp old-school *kopi* (pronounced 'koh-pee') at a traditional *kopitiam*. Try Ya Kun Kaya Toast (p72) but read our *kopi* primer before you go (p75).

➡**Souvenirs** Skip the tourist tat in the lanes around Trengganu St and hunt down an antiques shop or a local art gallery for a souvenir with a story. Our favourites are Tong Mern Sern Antiques (p80) and Utterly Art (p79).

Getting There & Away

➡**MRT** The heart of Chinatown is served by Chinatown MRT station, which spits you out onto Pagoda St. Telok Ayer station is handy for eateries and bars around Amoy St and Club St. Further south, Outram Park and Tanjong Pagar stations are best for Duxton Hill. Raffles Place station is best for the CBD.

➡**Bus** From the Colonial District, hop on buses 61, 145 or 166, which take you from North Bridge Rd to South Bridge Rd. From Hill St, buses 2, 12 and 147 run down New Bridge Rd. It's easy to walk from the river and the CBD to Chinatown.

PHOTOLIBRARY / GETTY IMAGES ©

TOP SIGHT
CHINATOWN HERITAGE CENTRE

The **Chinatown Heritage Centre** lifts the lid of Chinatown's chaotic, colourful and often scandalous past. Its endearing jumble of old photographs, personal anecdotes and recreated environments deliver an evocative stroll through the neighbourhood's highs and lows. Spend some time in here and you'll see Chinatown's now tourist-conscious streets in a much more intriguing light.

Roots Exhibition

Although Chinatown was allocated to all Chinese traders in the Raffles Plan of 1828, the area was further divided along ethnic lines: Hokkien on Havelock Rd and Telok Ayer, China and Chulia Sts; Teochew on Circular Rd, Boat Quay and Upper South Bridge Rd; and Cantonese on Upper Cross St, Lower South Bridge Rd and New Bridge Rd. The Roots exhibition explores the experiences of these migrants, from their first impressions to the role played by clan associations.

Living Quarters & Tailor Shop

Faithfully designed according to the memories and stories of former residents, a row of cubicles will have you peering into the ramshackle living quarters of opium-addicted coolies, stoic Samsui women, and even a painter and his family of 10! It's a powerful sight, vividly evoking the tough, grim lives that many of the area's residents endured right up to the mid-20th century.

The time travel continues one floor down, with a recreated tailor shopfront, workshop and living quarters. By the early 1950s, Pagoda St was heaving with tailor shops and this is an incredibly detailed replica of what was once a common neighbourhood fixture. Compared with the cubicles upstairs, the tailor's living quarters appear relatively luxurious, with separate quarters for the apprentices.

DON'T MISS

➡ Historical anecdotes of life in Chinatown
➡ Recreated cubicles
➡ Tailor shop

PRACTICALITIES

➡ Map p206
➡ 6221 9556
➡ www.singaporechina-town.com.sg
➡ 48 Pagoda St
➡ adult/child $10/6
➡ 9am-8pm
➡ Chinatown

👁 SIGHTS

CHINATOWN HERITAGE CENTRE   MUSEUM

See p69

SRI MARIAMMAN TEMPLE   HINDU TEMPLE

Map p206 (244 South Bridge Rd; ⊙7am-noon & 6-9pm; MChinatown) Paradoxically in the middle of Chinatown, this is the oldest Hindu temple in Singapore, originally built in 1823, then rebuilt in 1843. You can't miss the fabulously animated, Technicolor 1930s *gopuram* (tower) above the entrance, the key to the temple's South Indian Dravidian style. Sacred cow sculptures graze the boundary walls, while the *gopuram* is covered in kitsch plasterwork images of Brahma the creator, Vishnu the preserver and Shiva the destroyer.

Every October, the temple hosts the Thimithi festival; devotees queue along South Bridge Rd to hotfoot it over burning coals!

BUDDHA TOOTH RELIC TEMPLE   BUDDHIST TEMPLE

Map p206 (www.btrts.org.sg; 288 South Bridge Rd; ⊙7am-7pm, relic viewing 9am-6pm; MChinatown) Consecrated in 2008, this hulking, five-storey Buddhist temple is home to what is reputedly the left canine tooth of the Buddha, recovered from its funeral pyre in Kushinagar, northern India. While its authenticity is debated, the relic enjoys VIP status inside a 420kg solid-gold stupa in a dazzlingly ornate 4th-floor room. More religious relics await at the 3rd-floor museum, while the peaceful rooftop garden features a huge prayer wheel inside a 10,000 Buddha Pavilion.

THIAN HOCK KENG TEMPLE   TAOIST TEMPLE

Map p206 (www.thianhockkeng.com.sg; 158 Telok Ayer St; ⊙7.30am-5.30pm; MTelok Ayer) Oddly, while Chinatown's most famous Hindu temple is swamped, its oldest and most important Hokkien temple is often a haven of tranquillity. Built between 1839 and 1842, it's a beautiful place, and once the favourite landing point of Chinese sailors, before land reclamation pushed the sea far down the road. Curiously, the gates are Scottish and the tiles Dutch.

PINNACLE@DUXTON   OBSERVATION DECK

Map p208 (www.pinnacleduxton.com.sg; Block 1G, 1 Cantonment Rd; rooftop $5; ⊙9am-10pm; MOutram Park, Tanjong Pagar) For killer city views at a bargain price of $5, head to the 50th-floor rooftop of Pinnacle@Duxton, the world's largest public housing complex. There are skybridges connecting the seven towers, which provide a gobsmacking, 360-degree sweep of the city, port and sea. Chilling out is encouraged, and patches of lawn, modular furniture and sunlounges are provided. Payment is by EZ-Link card only (you can purchase one for $10 at the 7-Eleven store beside the ticket machine on level 1 of Block G). Rest the card on the ticket machine and $5 will be automatically deducted.

SINGAPORE CITY GALLERY   MUSEUM

Map p206 (www.ura.gov.sg/gallery; URA Bldg, 45 Maxwell Rd; ⊙9am-5pm Mon-Sat; MTanjong Pagar) Get a glimpse into Singapore's future at this interactive city-planning exhibition, which provides surprisingly compelling insight into the government's resolute policies of land reclamation, high-rise housing and meticulous urban planning. The highlight is an 11m-by-11m scale model of the central city, which shows just how different Singapore will look once all the projects currently under development join the skyline.

WAK HAI CHENG BIO TEMPLE   TAOIST TEMPLE

Map p208 (cnr Phillip & Church Sts; MRaffles Place) The name of this Taoist temple translates as Calm Sea Temple, which serves as a reminder that this area was once lapped by waves. Upon reaching dry land, Teochew Chinese immigrants would head here to give thanks for the safe journey, first at a smaller shrine built in 1826, and then at the present temple, which dates back to the 1850s. It's an atmospheric place, with giant incense coils smoking over the empty forecourt and sculptural reliefs depicting scenes of Chinese opera inside.

SENG WONG BEO TEMPLE   TAOIST TEMPLE

Map p208 (113 Peck Seah St; ⊙8am-5:30pm; MTanjong Pagar) Tucked behind red gates next to the Tanjong Pagar MRT station, this temple, seldom visited by tourists, is dedicated to the Chinese City God, who is not only responsible for the well-being of the metropolis but also for guiding the souls of the dead to the underworld. It's also notable as the only temple in Singapore that still performs ghost marriages, helping parents of children who died young arrange a marriage for their deceased loved one in the afterlife.

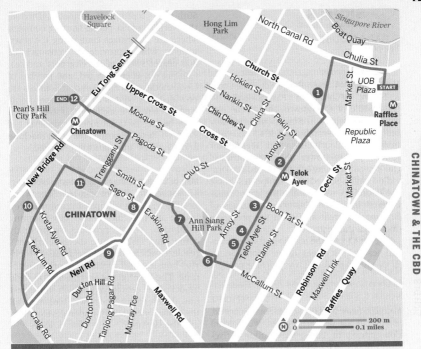

🏃 Neighbourhood Walk
Chinatown

START RAFFLES PLACE MRT STATION
END PEOPLE'S PARK PLAZA
LENGTH 2.5KM; 2½ HOURS

From Raffles Place MRT station head west along Chulia St then south down Phillip St to **①Wak Hai Cheng Bio Temple** (p70). Cross over Church St to Telok Ayer St until you reach **②Ying Fo Fui Kun**, a two-storey building established in 1822 for the Ying Fo Clan Association. It serves Singapore's Hakka Chinese to this day. At the junction with Boon Tat St is the **③Nagore Durgha Shrine**, a mosque built between 1828 and 1830 by Chulia Muslims from South India. A little further on is the beautifully restored **④Thian Hock Keng Temple** (p70) and the **⑤Al-Abrar Mosque**, built in the 1850s.

Turn right and walk one block to Amoy St where at No 66 you'll see **⑥Siang Cho Keong Temple**. Left of the entrance is a small 'dragon well' into which you can drop a coin and make a wish. Close by is a small archway marked Ann Siang Hill Park. Go

through and follow the walkway upwards to what is Chinatown's highest point and entry point to **⑦Ann Siang Rd**. Some of the terraces here once housed Chinese guilds and clubs – note the art-deco buildings at Nos 15, 17 and 21. At the end of the street, turn left into South Bridge Rd and drop into the epic **⑧Buddha Tooth Relic Temple** (p70). Where South Bridge Rd meets Neil Rd and Tanjong Pagar Rd is the triangular **⑨Jinriksha station**, once the depot for hand-pulled rickshaws. Walk along Neil Rd to Keong Saik Rd, a curving street of ornate old terraces. At the junction with Kreta Ayer Rd is the Hindu **⑩Layar Sithi Vinygar Temple**, built in 1925. The five-tier *gopuram* over the entrance was added in 2007.

Continuing along Keong Saik Rd, you'll hit the back of the **⑪Chinatown Complex** (p73), where you can stop for a cheap feed, or carry on through kitschy Trengganu St, turning left at Pagoda St and using the pedestrian bridge at the end to reach **⑫People's Park Complex** (p80) for some reflexology.

WORTH A DETOUR

BABA HOUSE

A short walk west of Chinatown, along Neil Rd, is **Baba House** (Map p208; ☑6227 5731; www.nus.edu.sg//cfa/museum; 157 Neil Rd; ☻1hr tours 2pm Mon, 6.30pm Tue, 10am Thu, 11am Sat; Ⓜ Outram Park) **FREE**, one of the best-preserved Peranakan heritage homes found anywhere in Singapore. This beautiful blue three-storey building was donated to the National University of Singapore (NUS) by a member of the family that used to live here. The NUS then set about renovating it so that it best matched how it would have looked in 1928 when, according to the family, Baba House was at its most resplendent. Period furniture has been added to original family photos and artefacts to create a wonderful window on the life of a wealthy Peranakan family living in Singapore a century ago. Baba House can only be visited on a one-hour guided tour, held every Monday, Tuesday, Thursday and Saturday, but the tour is excellent and costs absolutely nothing. Call ahead – bookings are essential and, frustratingly, emails do not always receive replies.

✖️ EATING

★ YA KUN KAYA TOAST   CAFE $
Map p206 (www.yakun.com; 01-01 Far East Sq, 18 China St; kaya toast set $4.20; ☻7.30am-7pm Mon-Fri, 8.30am-5.30pm Sat & Sun; Ⓜ Telok Ayer) Though it's now part of a chain, this airy, retro coffeeshop is an institution, and the best way to start the day the Singaporean way. The speciality is buttery *kaya* (coconut jam) toast, dipped in runny egg (add black pepper and a few drops of soya sauce) and washed down with strong *kopi* (coffee).

The outdoor seating is a good spot for rush-hour people-watching.

JING HUA   CHINESE $
Map p206 (☑6221 3060; 21-23 Neil Rd; dishes $3-10; ☻11.30am-3pm & 5.30-9.30pm Thu-Tue; Ⓜ Chinatown) Locals outnumber out-of-towners at halogen-and-laminex Jing Hua. Tuck into a limited yet satisfying repertoire of northern Chinese classics, among them plump pork dumplings, noodles with minced pork and soyabean paste, and red-bean paste pancake. Best of the lot is the Chinese pizza, a hearty, deep-fried pastry packed with minced prawn, pork and crab, and spring onion. Cash only.

TONG HENG   BAKERY $
Map p206 (285 South Bridge Rd; snacks from $1.40; ☻9am-10pm; Ⓜ Chinatown) Hit the spot at this veteran pastry shop, specialising in pastries, tarts and cakes from the southern Chinese province of Guangdong. While locals flock here for the egg tarts, leave room for the slightly charred perfection of the *char siew su* (barbecue pork puff).

LIM CHEE GUAN   SNACKS $
Map p206 (www.limcheeguan.com.sg; 203 New Bridge Rd; pork bak kwa 300g $13.20; ☻9am-10pm; Ⓜ Chinatown) When food snobs hanker for *bak kwa* (barbecued preserved pork), they snack at this veteran. Around since 1938, Lim Chee Guan grills like no other, turning thin slices of jerky-like pork into wonderfully smokey, caramelised snacks with just the right balance of sweetness, saltiness and chewiness. Come Lunar New Year and the waiting time here can reach eight hours. Yes, it's *that* good.

There are another two branches in town, including one across the street at **People's Park Complex** (Map p206; 01-25 People's Park Complex; pork bak kwa 500g $25; Ⓜ Chinatown).

★ LUCHA LOCO   MEXICAN $$
Map p206 (www.luchaloco.com; 15 Duxton Hill; 4-10.15pm Tue-Thu, 4-11pm Fri, 6-11pm Sat; ☻dishes $8-20; Ⓜ Outram Park, Tanjong Pagar) Packed nightly with eye candy, flirtatious barkeeps and succulent Mexican street food, this pumping *taquería* cum garden bar explodes with X-factor. While we adore the ceviche, tostaditas and addictive *elotes* (corn rolled in mayonnaise and Cotija cheese), it's the tacos that leave us loco, generously topped with fresh, beautiful produce. No reservations, so head in early or late, or grab a Mezcal and wait.

★ MOMMA KONG'S   SEAFOOD $$
Map p206 (☑6225 2722; www.mommakongs.com; 34 Mosque St; mains from $20; ☻5-10pm Tue-Sun; 🛜; Ⓜ Chinatown) Small, funky Momma Kong's is run by two young brothers and a cousin obsessed with crab. While the

compact menu features numerous finger-licking, MSG-free crab classics, opt for the phenomenal chilli crab, its kick and non-gelatinous gravy unmatched in this town. One serve of crab and four giant, fresh *mantou* (Chinese bread buns) should happily feed two stomachs.

Unlike many other chilli crab joints, it has fixed prices, good-value combo deals, and a one-for-one happy hour (5pm to 7.30pm) with decent beers. Book two days ahead (three days for Friday and Saturday).

SARNIES CAFE $$

Map p206 (⌨6224 6091; www.sarniescafe.com; 136 Telok Ayer St; sandwiches & salads $13.50-16.50, weekend brunch $15.90-25.90; ⊘7.30am-9.30pm Mon-Fri, 9am-4pm Sat & Sun; MTelok Ayer) Luscious, epic sarnies (British slang for sandwiches) bust the jaws of suits and hipsters at this new-school Aussie cafe. Farm-to-table produce shows off in sandwich combos like grilled aubergine and hummus, or blokey grass-fed steak with mushrooms and caramelised onions. Gourmet soups and salads pack an equal punch, while the weekend brunch includes house-cured bacon. Coffee snobs will appreciate the on-site roasting, best sampled in Sarnie's impressive espresso martini.

PS CAFE INTERNATIONAL $$

Map p206 (www.pscafe.com; 45 Ann Siang Rd; mains $19-36; ⊘restaurant 11.30am-10.30pm Mon-Fri, 9.30am-10.30pm Sat & Sun; bar open to 12.30am Mon-Thu & Sun, to 2am Fri & Sat; MChinatown) From the ground-floor black marble bar to the upstairs sweep of crisp linen, Chesterfield banquettes and Dior-clad ladies, colonial glamour is always in vogue at this leafy, heavenly scented hideaway. Compare notes on husband and maid over vibrant, seductive bistro fare like the soy-cured salmon Big Nihon Salad, or delicate miso cod.

HAWKER CENTRE MUSTS

If you're new to Singapore, brush up on your hawker centre etiquette, then dive into one of the following for a cheap, delicious feed. Expect to pay around $3 to $6 for a dish.

Maxwell Road Hawker Centre (Map p206; cnr Maxwell & South Bridge Rds; dishes from $2.50; ⊘individual stalls vary; ✍; MChinatown) Chinatown's most touristy hawker centre is a good spot for the uninitiated, and best frequented at lunch. Top choices here include rice porridge from **Zhen Zhen Porridge** (Stall 54; dishes from $2.50; ⊘5.30am-2.30pm), and fragrant chicken rice from **Tian Tian Hainanese Chicken Rice** (Stall 10; chicken rice $3; ⊘11am-8pm Tue-Sun).

Chinatown Complex (Map p206; 11 New Bridge Rd; dishes from $2.50; ⊘individual stalls vary; MChinatown) Leave Smith St's revamped 'Chinatown Food Street' to the out-of-towners and join old-timers and foodies at this nearby labyrinth. The 25-minute wait for mixed claypot rice at **Lian He Ben Ji Claypot Rice** (Stall 02-198/199; dishes $2.50-20, claypot rice $15-20; ⊘4-10pm Fri-Wed) is worth it, while the rich and nutty satay at **Shi Xiang Satay** (Stall 02-79; satay from $5; ⊘4-8.30pm Fri-Tue) is insane. For a little TLC, opt for Ten Tonic Ginseng Chicken Soup at **Soup Master** (Stall 02-05; soups $3.20-11; ⊘10am-8.30pm).

Hong Lim Food Centre (Map p208; cnr South Bridge Rd & Upper Cross St; dishes from $3; ⊘Individual stalls vary; MChinatown) Musts include *char kway teow* (stir-fried rice noodles) from **Outram Park Fried Kway Teow** (Block 531A, Stall 02-18; dishes $3; ⊘6am-4.30pm Mon-Sat) and the Hokkien *chang* (pork dumpling with mushroom, chestnut and salted egg) from **Hiong Kee Dumplings** (Block 531A, Stall 02-37; dumplings $1.30-3.30; ⊘8.30am-7.30pm Mon-Sat). Seafood lovers queue at **Tuck Kee Ipoh Sah Hor Fun** (Stall 02-40; dishes $3-6; ⊘11am-3pm Mon-Sat) for the crayfish and prawn *hor fun* (stir-fried ribbon rice noodles with shellfish).

Lau Pa Sat (Map p208; 18 Raffles Quay; dishes from $4, satay from $0.60; ⊘24hr, individual stalls vary; MTelok Ayer, Raffles Place) *Lau pa sat* means 'old market' in Hokkien, which is appropriate since the handsome iron structure shipped out from Glasgow in 1894 remains intact. The real magic happens on the facing street, when Boon Tat St transforms into **Satay Street** (Map p208; Boon Tat St; satay around $0.60 per stick; ⊘7pm-1am Mon-Fri, 3pm-1am Sat & Sun), a KL-style sprawl of tables, beer-peddling aunties and smoky satay stalls.

The popular weekend brunch cranks up the decadence, with free-flow Domaine Chandon or house wine options. *Cin cin, darlink.*

BLUE GINGER
PERANAKAN $$

Map p208 (☑6222 3928; www.theblueginger.com; 97 Tanjong Pagar Rd; mains $12-38; ⊗noon-2.15pm & 6.30-9.45pm; Ⓜ Tanjong Pagar) Elegant Blue Ginger is one of the few places in Singapore showcasing the spicy, sour flavours of Peranakan food; a unique fusion of Chinese and Malay influences. Mouthwatering musts include *kueh pie tee* (shredded bamboo shoots and turnips garnished with shrimp in fried *pie tee* cups), *sambal terong goreng* (spicy fried eggplant), and a sublimely delicate Nonya fish-head curry. Bookings recommended.

RED STAR
CHINESE $$

(54 Chin Swee Rd; yum cha items $3-8; ⊗7am-3pm & 6-10.30pm; Ⓜ Chinatown) Armed with trolley-clutching aunties who swoop like fighter jets, classic Red Star is perfect for a Hong Kong–style yum cha breakfast or lunch. Keep your ears pricked for the pork bao and the mango salad, the latter a deep-fried pastry packed with sweet crab meat and runny mango. The restaurant is tucked away inside an old HDB block; look for the old neon sign on the street.

DEPARTMENT OF CAFFEINE
CAFE $$

Map p206 (DOC; ☑6223 3426; www.deptof-caffeine.com; 15 Duxton Rd; meals $15-18; ⊗10.30am-7.30pm Mon & Tue, 10.30am-10.30pm Thu & Fri, 9.30am-7.30pm Sat & Sun; Ⓜ Tanjong Pagar) The coffee cognoscenti don't just hang here for the smooth, nutty brews. They fill their bellies from an ever-changing menu of ridiculously fresh grub. Start the day with homemade granola, feel virtuous over chilli and garlic-spiked char-grilled broccoli, or fill up on comfort mains like succulent chicken with lemon sumac and za'atar. If you're feeling naughty, seek out the honey and lavender tea cake.

THE FLYING SQUIRREL
JAPANESE $$

Map p206 (www.theflyingsquirrel.com.sg; Stall 01-02, 92 Amoy St; lunch $16-38, dinner mains $13-36; ⊗11am-10pm Mon-Thu, to 11pm Fri & Sat; 🛜; Ⓜ Telok Ayer) This sneaky squirrel lurks down a laneway off Amoy St. Find it and your reward is fresh, delicious Japanese in a cool but cosy combo of brickwork, filament bulbs and designer chairs. Bento boxes are the lunchtime hit, while the more elaborate dinner menu includes a 're-invented' Wagyu Burger, in which bread and beef are minced together and pan-fried in a moreish red wine sauce.

Between 2.30pm and 6pm it's drinks (including great coffee) and sweet treats only. Book ahead for dinner.

★ DING DONG
SOUTHEAST ASIAN $$$

Map p206 (www.dingdong.com.sg; 23 Ann Siang Rd; dishes $12-25, set menus $55 & $79; ⊗noon-2.30pm & 6pm-10.30pm Mon-Thu, noon-2.30pm & 6-11.30pm Fri, 6-11.30pm Sat) From the graphic bar tiles, to the meticulous cocktails, to the wow-oh-wow modern takes on Southeast Asian flavours, it's all about attention to detail at this sucker-punch champ. Book a table and drool over zingtastic scallop ceviche with fresh coconut, sultry hay-smoked pork bao, or tart-and-crunchy red curry Wagyu short rib. Can't decide? Opt for the good-value 'Feed Me' menus.

🍷 DRINKING & NIGHTLIFE

Club St and adjacent Ann Siang Rd are the heart of Singapore's booming bar scene, with both streets closed to traffic from 7pm on Friday and Saturday. South of Chinatown, Tanjong Pagar and the Duxton Hill area offer an ever-expanding number of in-the-know cafes and drinking spots, while Chinatown's hawker centers are always a good standby for a no-frills beer.

★ TIPPLING CLUB
COCKTAIL BAR

Map p206 (☑6475 2217; www.tipplingclub.com; 38 Tanjong Pagar Rd; ⊗noon-midnight Mon-Fri, 6pm-midnight Sat) Tippling Club propels mixology to dizzying heights, with a technique and creativity that could turn a teetotaler into a born-again soak. The best seats are at the bar, where under a ceiling of hanging bottles, passionate pros turn rare and precious spirits into wonders like the 'Smoky Old Bastard', a mellow concoction of whisky, sweet tobacco and citrus smoke.

The adjoining restaurant is highly regarded, though painfully priced.

JIGGER & PONY
COCKTAIL BAR

Map p206 (101 Amoy St; ⊗6pm-1am Mon-Thu, 6pm-3am Fri & Sat; Ⓜ Telok Ayer) Once an art gallery,

KOPI CULTURE

There are few things more Singaporean than kicking back at a *kopitiam* (coffeeshop) with a thick-rimmed cup of old-school *kopi* (coffee). Its distinctive taste comes from the way the beans are prepared. Roasted with sugar and margarine, the result is a coffee that's dark and strong, with the smooth caramel and butter character of its roasting companions. *Kopi* is either drunk black or mixed with condensed or evaporated milk. To help you get your head round the terminology, try this *kopi* primer. Note that these terms can also be applied to *teh* (tea).

Kopi Coffee with condensed milk. No sugar, but the condensed milk makes it sweet.

Kopi-O Black coffee with sugar.

Kopi-O kosong Black coffee without sugar (*kosong* is Malay for nothing or zero).

Kopi-C Coffee with evaporated milk and sugar (the C is for Carnation, a popular evaporated milk brand).

Kopi-C kosong Coffee with evaporated milk, but no sugar.

Kopi peng Iced coffee with condensed milk.

Kopi gao Literally, 'thick' coffee (think double espresso).

Kopi poh A 'light' coffee.

now a dark and slinky cocktail bar, Jigger & Pony is well known for honouring classic and long-forgotten libations. Japanese-style meticulousness steers the barkeeps, whose tricks include rare *aperitivi* like crisp Cocchi Cooler (Cocchi Americano, soda water and flambéed orange peel) and one of the smoothest Negronis this side of Turin.

From the crispy bruschettas to the silky tarines, the food options are also worthy accompaniments.

JEKYLL & HYDE
COCKTAIL BAR

Map p208 (www.49tras.st; 49 Tras St; ⊘6pm-midnight Mon-Thu, 6pm-1am Fri & Sat; MTanjong Pagar) By day a respectable nail salon, by night a killer cocktail lounge, Jekyll & Hyde splits itself into two distinct spaces – buzzing back bar and mild-mannered front space. Whichever you choose, you'll be sipping on smooth, inspired libations like the Mr Bean, a strangely seductive blend of bean curd, vodka, kaya, butterscotch liqueur and Frangelico.

CUFFLINK CLUB
COCKTAIL BAR

Map p206 (http://thecufflinkclub.com; 6 Jiak Chuan Rd; ⊘5pm-1am Mon-Thu, 5pm-2am Fri, 6pm-2am Sat; MOutram Park) The master of this handsome, laddish cocktail den is Brit Joel Fraser, who cut his teeth at Melbourne's lauded Der Raum and Singapore's trailblazing Tippling Club. It's a blue ribbon pedigree that shines through in confident, playful drinks like the deliciously tart

Whom The Bell Tolls, a twist on the Hemingway daiquiri, complete with a plane-shaped page from the Ernest Hemingway novel which inspired it. And did we mention the restrooms?

BREEZE
ROOFTOP BAR

Map p206 (www.thescarlethotel.com; Scarlet Hotel, 33 Erskine Rd; ⊘5pm-1am Mon-Thu, to 2am Fri & Sat, to 11pm Sun; ☎; MChinatown) For rooftop sipping without the raucous crowds, take the lift to this seductive hideaway, above the Scarlet Hotel. Splashed with bold tropical fabrics and lush heliconia, it's a sensible spot for quiet conversations, romantic gazing or simply catching a late-night breeze while scanning a sea of rooftops and skyscrapers.

Ô BATIGNOLLES
WINE BAR

Map p206 (2 Gemmill Lane; ⊘noon-midnight Mon-Fri, 11am-midnight Sat, 11am-9pm Sun; ☎; MTelok Ayer) Don those Breton strips and retreat to this corner bistro for a little joie de vivre. Run by a French couple and never short of unwinding lawyers and hopeless Francophiles, it's a fine choice for a well-priced glass (or bottle) of boutique wine; an *assiette de charcuterie;* and a little Club St people-watching.

THE GOOD BEER COMPANY
BEER STALL

Map p206 (11 New Bridge Rd, 02-58 Chinatown Complex; ⊘6-10pm Mon-Sat; MChinatown) Injecting Chinatown Complex with a dose of new-school cool, this hawker-centre beer

EVERTON PARK: THE CREATIVE HDB

Singapore's void decks – the ground-floor space of its public housing blocks (HDBs) – are usually scattered with gossipy uncles and aunties and shrieking kids. At Everton Park, a housing complex skirting trendy Tanjong Pagar, you're just as likely to find Third Wave coffee bloggers and design hunters. Lured by cheaper rents, a handful of young enterprises have set up shop here in recent years, turning the estate into an unlikely nexus of cool.

Top billing goes to **Nylon Coffee Roasters** (Map p208; ☑6220 2330; www.nylon-coffee.sg; 01-40, 4 Everton Park; ☺8.30am-5.30pm Mon & Wed-Fri, 9am-6pm Sat & Sun; Ⓜ Outram Park, Tanjong Pagar), a small, standing-room-only cafe and roastery with an epic reputation for phenomenal seasonal blends and impressive single origins. At the helm is a personable crew of coffee fanatics, chatting away with customers about their latest coffee-sourcing trip (they deal directly with the farmers) or the virtues of French press. Venture beyond espresso with Clever Dripper, a brewing method that shows off the more subtle notes in your cup of coffee.

Our runner-up is **The Redundant Shop** (Map p208; redundantshop.com; Block 5, 01-22A Everton Park; ☺11am-8pm Tue-Sat, to 5pm Sun; Ⓜ Outram Park, Tanjong Pagar), a catchment for design-literate curios from homegrown and international indie labels. Scan the store and you might score svelte leather wallets and funky watches from Singaporean designers, funtastic socks from California, or a sparkly helmet for that vintage Vespa.

Everton Park is an easy 500m walk south of Outram Park MRT. Enter from Cantonment Rd, directly opposite the seven-tower Pinnacle@Duxton housing complex.

stall peddles an impressive booty of bottled craft suds, from homegrown Jungle to Belgian Trappistes Rochefort. A few stalls down is **Smith Street Taps** (Map p206; 02-062, Chinatown Complex, 11 New Bridge Rd; ☺6.30-10.30pm Tue-Sat), run by a friendly dude and offering a rotating selection of craft and premium beers on tap.

FRY BISTRO
ROOFTOP BAR

Map p206 (☑8418 5995; www.facebook.com/FryBistro; 96B Club St; ☺5pm-1am Mon-Wed, to 3am Thu-Sat; Ⓜ Chinatown) Unceremoniously stacked with beer cartons, DIY, rooftop Fry flies under the radar with the Club St hordes. This is why it's so appealing for long, lazy drinking sessions and late-night conversation. The vibe is chilled, the music good and the skyline view just as bewitching as that of its louder, better-known neighbour.

OXWELL & CO
BAR

Map p206 (www.oxwellandco.com; 5 Ann Siang Rd; ☺10am-late Tue-Sat; Ⓜ Chinatown) Laced with cockfighting posters, frontier-style benches and exposed copper pipes, it seems the only thing missing at jumping Oxwell & Co are some wagons out the front. What's not missing is a nightly crowd of tie-loosening suits downing lesser-known beers, solid wines, and sophisticated grub like graze-friendly marinated olives and revamped Brit dude food like Yorkshire pudding.

A neon 'Nosh' points up the stairs, where Gordon Ramsay protégé Mark Sargeant serves produce-driven modern British dishes. Book the restaurant a few days in advance.

TANTRIC BAR
LGBT

Map p206 (78 Neil Rd; ☺8pm-3am Sun-Fri, 8pm-4am Sat; Ⓜ Outram Park, Chinatown) Two indoor bars and two alfresco palm-fringed courtyards is what you get at Singapore's best-loved gay drinking hole. Especially heaving on Friday and Saturday nights, it's a hit with preened locals and eager expats and out-of-towners, who schmooze and cruise to Kylie, Gaga and Katy Perry chart toppers. Lushes shouldn't miss Wednesday night, when $20 gets you two martinis.

1-ALTITUDE
ROOFTOP BAR

Map p202 (www.1-altitude.com; Level 63, 1 Raffles Pl; admission incl 1 drink $30; ☺6pm-late; Ⓜ Raffles Place) Extreme Altitude might be a better name for the world's highest alfresco bar, perched 282m above street level. Its view of Singapore is unmatched, though the quality of the drinks fail to reach such lofty heights. Dress up, snap away, then continue your evening at one of Singapore's better-quality drinking establishments.

LA TERRAZA ROOFTOP BAR

Map p206 (www.screeningroom.com.sg; Level 4, Screening Room, 12 Ann Siang Rd; ⊙6pm-1am Mon-Thu, to 3am Fri & Sat; MChinatown) Perched atop mini cinema the Screening Room, La Terraza is a mixed bag of arresting city views, tipsy expats, and so-so cocktails. For audible conversation, head up early in the night or earlier in the week. If crowds and a buzzing vibe are your thing, Friday and Saturday nights will have you purring. To reserve a table, call or email two days ahead.

TEA CHAPTER TEAHOUSE

Map p206 (www.teachapter.com; 9-11 Neil Rd; ⊙tea house 11am-10.30pm Sun-Thu, to 11pm Fri & Sat; ☎; MChinatown) Queen Elizabeth and Prince Philip dropped by here for a cuppa in 1989, and for a $10 fee you can sit at the table they sipped at. Otherwise, the charge is $8 per person, which includes tea of your choice up to that value. The selection is excellent, and staff is on hand to demonstrate how to properly prepare and savour your tea.

There's a wonderful collection of souvenir tea sets (around $120) at the adjoining store. Tip: buy seperate pieces and create a set for two for under $60.

PLAIN CAFE

Map p208 (www.theplain.com.sg; 50 Craig Rd; ⊙7.30am-5.30pm Mon-Fri, to 7.30pm Sat & Sun; MTanjong Pagar) A combo of stark interiors, neatly piled design magazines, and Scandi-style communal table, the Plain keeps hipsters purring with Australian Genovese coffee, decent all-day breakfasts (from $4) and sweet treats like lemon and lime tarts. Service is friendly and the vibe relaxed.

YIXING XUAN TEAHOUSE TEAHOUSE

Map p206 (www.yixingxuan-teahouse.com; 30/32 Tanjong Pagar Rd; ⊙10am-9pm Mon-Sat, to 7pm Sun; MTanjong Pagar) Banker-turned-tea purveyor Vincent Low is the man behind this venture, happily educating visitors about Chinese tea and the art of tea drinking. For a fuller experience, book a tea-ceremony demonstration with tastings ($20, 45 minutes).

# ⭐ ENTERTAINMENT

CHINESE THEATRE CIRCLE CHINESE OPERA

Map p206 (☑6323 4862; www.ctcopera.com; 5 Smith St; show & snacks $25, show & dinner $40; ⊙7-9pm Fri & Sat; MChinatown) Teahouse evenings organised by this nonprofit opera company are a wonderful, informal introduction to Chinese opera. Every Friday and Saturday at 8pm there is a brief talk on Chinese opera, followed by a 45-minute excerpt from an opera classic, performed by actors in full costume. You can also opt for a pre-show Chinese meal at 7pm. Book ahead.

KYŌ CLUB

Map p208 (www.clubkyo.com; B1-02, Keck Seng Tower, 133 Cecil St; ⊙9pm-3am Wed & Thu, to 5am Fri & Sat; MTelok Ayer, Raffles Place) From boring bank to thumping hot spot, this sprawling, Japanese-inspired playpen is home to the world's longest bar (expect the odd bar-top booty shake), suited eye-candy, and sharp DJs spinning credible electro, house, funk or disco. If you're itching for a little midweek hedonism, you know where to go.

ALTIMATE CLUB

Map p202 (☑6438 0410; Level 61, 1 Raffles Pl; admission $45; ⊙10pm-4am Wed-Sat; MRaffles Place) Party like it's 2099 at Singapore's new A-lister. Two floors below rooftop bar 1-Altitude (p76), the club is a mind-blowing, futuristic mix of digital installations, 3-D projection mapping and virtual avatars, not to mention top DJ talent. Such high-tech hotness comes at a price: you'll need to book ahead, look sharp, cough up a $45 cover charge (which includes two drinks), and, if you reserve a table, bear the minimum-spend policy.

SCREENING ROOM CINEMA

Map p206 (www.screeningroom.com.sg; 12 Ann Siang Rd; MChinatown, Telok Ayer) If your idea of a good night involves sinking into a sofa and watching classic flicks, make some time for Screening Room. Expect anything from *On the Town* to *Sex, Lies and Videotape*, projected onto a pull-down screen. Best of all, people who purchase $15 (plus service charge and GST) of drinks or food at the cinema's Theatre Bar can watch for free.

When the end credits roll, head upstairs to the rooftop bar, La Terraza, for a post-show drink with a silver-screen view.

SINGAPORE CHINESE ORCHESTRA CLASSICAL MUSIC

Map p208 (☑6557 4034; www.sco.com.sg; Singapore Conference Hall, 7 Shenton Way; MTanjong Pagar) Using traditional instruments such as the *liuqin, ruan* and *sanxian*, the SCO treats ears to classical Chinese

Local Life
A Lazy Morning in Tiong Bahru

Spend a late weekend morning in Tiong Bahru, three stops from Raffles Place on the East–West (green) MRT line. More than just hip boutiques, bars and cafes, this low-rise neighbourhood was Singapore's first public housing estate, and its walk-up, art-deco apartments now make for unexpected architectural treats.

❶ To Market

The **Tiong Bahru Market & Food Centre** (83 Seng Poh Rd; ⊘8am-late, individual stalls vary; MTiong Bahru) remains staunchly old-school, down to its orange-hued exterior, the neighbourhood's original shade. Whet your appetite exploring the wet market, then head upstairs to the hawker centre for *shui kueh* (steamed rice cake with diced preserved radish) at **Jan Bo Shui Kueh** (02-05 Tiong Bahru Market & Food Centre; shui $1.20-3.30; ⊘6.30am-10.30pm).

❷ Book Hunting

BooksActually (www.booksactually.com; 9 Yong Siak St; ⊘11am-6pm Mon, 11am-9pm Tue-Fri, 10am-9pm Sat, 10am-6pm Sun; MTiong Bahru) is one of Singapore's coolest independent bookstores, with often unexpected choices of fiction and nonfiction, including some interesting titles on Singapore. For beautiful children's books, check out **Woods in the Books** (www.woodsinthebooks.sg; 3

Yong Siak St; ⊘11am-8pm Tue-Sat, 11am-6pm Sun; MTiong Bahru), three doors down.

❸ The Bold, the Beautiful

Design store **Strangelets** (www.strangelets. sg; 7 Yong Siak St; ⊘11am-8pm Mon-Fri, 10am-8pm Sat & Sun; MTiong Bahru) showcases beautiful and quirky objects from around the world. Cast your eye on anything from intriguing sculptural jewellery, lamps and tables, to retro-inspired radios, heavenly soaps and '70s-inspired rucksacks.

❹ A Good-Looking Bird

Originally a pop-up concept store, **Nana & Bird** (www.nanaandbird.com; 01-02, 79 Chay Yan St; ⊘noon-7pm Tue-Fri, 11am-7pm Sat & Sun; MTiong Bahru) is known across the island for fresh independent fashion and accessories for women, including Singapore labels Aijek and By Invite Only, as well as far-flung up-and-comers like Hungary's Dori Tomssanyi. The newer **flagship store**

Display at Books Actually

(01-65, 59 Eng Hoon St; ☺noon-7pm Tue-Fri, 11am-7pm Sat & Sun; ⓜTiong Bahru) includes kidswear.

❺ Vibrant Vintage

At the helm of cult-status vintage store **Fleas & Trees** (01-10, 68 Seng Poh Lane; ☺6-10pm Tue-Thu, 10am-10pm Fri-Sun; ⓜTiong Bahru) is husband-and-wife team Terrence Yeung and Bella Koh, who scour the world for eclectic homewares, whimsical fashion and jewellery, not to mention supercool books and magazines guaranteed to sass-up the dullest coffee table.

❻ A French Affair

The quintessential Frenchman, baker Gontran Cherrier has all and sundry itching for a little French lovin'. You too can get some at his cool, contemporary **Tiong Bahru Bakery** (☑6220 3430; www.tiong-bahrubakery.com; Stall 01-07, 56 Eng Hoon St; pastries from $3, sandwiches & focaccias from $8; ☺8am-10pm; ⓜTiong Bahru). Faultless pastries include buttery almond brioche, while savouries include salubrious sandwiches exploding with prime ingredients. Topping it off is luscious coffee from Common Man Roasters.

concerts throughout the year. Concerts are held in various venues around the city, with occasional collaborations showcasing Japanese, jazz and Malay musicians.

TABOO
LGBT

Map p206 (www.taboo.sg; 65 Neil Rd; ☺8pm-2am Wed & Thu, 10pm-3am Fri, 10pm-4am Sat; ⓜOutram Park, Chinatown) After drinks at Tantric, cross the street and conquer the dancefloor and what remains the favourite gay dance club in town. Expect the requisite line-up of shirtless gyrators, doting straight women and regular racy themed nights. Note: only the chillout lounge is open on Wednesday and Thursday nights.

TOY FACTORY PRODUCTIONS
THEATRE

Map p206 (☑6222 1526; www.toyfactory.com. sg; 15A Smith St; ⓜChinatown) Originally focussed on puppetry, this bilingual (English and Mandarin) theatre company is now best known for its intercultural collaborations and envelope-pushing local work, performed in various venues across town. Past productions have included a play about Singapore's most famous transsexual and a wicked satire about Singaporean men called *The Penis Society*. Singapore, sterile? Ha!

🛍 SHOPPING

Pagoda St and its immediate surroundings have become a byword for tourist tat, but behind and beyond the stalls crammed with souvenir T-shirts and two-minute calligraphers is a more inspiring selection of shops and galleries selling everything from contemporary local artwork, antique furniture and traditional Chinese remedies, to cognoscenti fashion labels from Singapore, Sydney and Copenhagen.

★UTTERLY ART
ART

Map p206 (☑9487 2006; www.utterlyart.com.sg; Level 3, 20B Mosque St; ☺varies, usually noon-8pm Mon-Sat, to 5.30pm Sun; ⓜChinatown) Head upstairs to this tiny, welcoming gallery for works by contemporary Singaporean, Filipino and Cambodian artists. While painting is the gallery's main focus, there are sculpture and ceramics on occasion, with artworks priced from $50 to around $1400 (depending on the exhibition). Opening times can be erratic, so call ahead.

CHINATOWN & THE CBD ACTIVITIES

TONG MERN SERN ANTIQUES ANTIQUES

Map p208 (51 Craig Rd; ☺9am-5.30pm Mon-Sat, 1.30-5.30pm Sun; ⓜOutram Park) An Aladdin's cave of dusty furniture, books, records, wood carvings, porcelain and other bits and bobs, Tong Mern Sern is a curious hunting ground for Singapore nostalgia. A banner hung above the front door proclaims: 'We buy junk and sell antiques. Some fools buy. Some fools sell.' Better have your wits about you.

WILLOW AND HUXLEY FASHION, ACCESSORIES

Map p206 (www.willowandhuxley.com; 20 Amoy St; ☺9am-8pm Mon-Fri, 11am-3pm Sat; ⓜTelok Ayer) Willow and Huxley peddles a sharp, vibrant edit of smaller independent labels like Australia's Finders Keepers and Bec & Bridge, Denmark's quirky Baum und Pferdgarten, and Sienna Miller's very own Twenty8Twelve. There's jewellery and a small selection of casual, beach-friendly threads for men courtesy of Australia's TCSS and New York's Onia and Psycho Bunny.

FAR EAST LEGEND ANTIQUES, HANDICRAFTS

Map p206 (233 South Bridge Rd; ☺11.30am-6.30pm; ⓜChinatown) This small, charmingly cluttered shop has an intriguing collection of furniture, lamps, handicrafts, statues and objets d'art from all over Asia. You'll find anything from dainty porcelain snuff boxes to ceramic busts of Chairman Mao. The owner is usually willing to 'discuss the price'.

EU YAN SANG CHINESE MEDICINE

Map p206 (www.euyansang.com.sg; 269 South Bridge Rd; ☺shop 8.30am-7pm Mon-Sat, clinic 8.30am-6pm Mon, Tue, Thu & Fri, 9am-6pm Wed, 8.30am-7.30pm Sat; ⓜChinatown) Get your *qi* back in order at Singapore's most famous and user-friendly Chinese medicine store. Pick up some Monkey Bezoar powder to relieve excess phlegm, or Liu Jun Zi pills to dispel dampness. You'll find herbal teas, soups and oils, and you can even consult a practitioner of Chinese medicine at the clinic next door (bring your passport).

YONG GALLERY ANTIQUES

Map p206 (260 South Bridge Rd; ☺10am-7pm; ⓜChinatown) The owner here is a calligrapher, and much of his artwork is on sale. You'll also find jewellery, genuine jade products and antiques as well as more affordable gifts such as decorative bookmarks, Chinese fans and clocks. The shop is stuffed with goodies so it's fun browsing even if you're not in a buying mood.

YUE HWA CHINESE PRODUCTS DEPARTMENT STORE

Map p208 (www.yuehwa.com.sg; 70 Eu Tong Sen St; ☺11am-9pm Sun-Fri, to 10pm Sat; ⓜChinatown) With a deco facade paging Shanghai, this six-storey department store specialises in all things Chinese. Downstairs you'll find medicine and herbs, clothes and cushions. Moving to level 5, you'll pass through silks, food and tea, arts and crafts and household goods, before ending up in a large, cluttered sea of furniture.

🏃 ACTIVITIES

PEOPLE'S PARK COMPLEX SPA

Map p206 (1 Park Rd; ☺9am-11pm, individual stalls vary; ⓜChinatown) The only reason to dive into this old-school Chinatown mall is for the cheap massage (opt for the busier ones). Our favourite is **Mr Lim Foot Reflexology** (Map p206; 03-53 & 03-78 People's Park Complex; 30min foot reflexology $15; ☺10am-11pm; ⓜChinatown), where your rubdown comes with televised local and Taiwanese soaps.

Feeling adventurous? Try one of the fishpond foot spas, where schools of fish nibble the dead skin right off your feet.

FOOD PLAYGROUND COOKING COURSE

Map p208 (☏9452 3669; www.foodplayground.com.sg; 4A Craig Rd; 3hr class from $99; ☺9.30am-12.30pm Mon-Sat; ⓜTanjong Pagar) You've been gorging on Singapore's famous food, so why not learn to make it? This fantastic hands-on cooking school delves into both the cultural and the practical, exploring Singapore's multicultural make-up and seeing you cook up classic dishes like laksa, *nasi lemak* and fried *kway teow*. Courses usually run for three hours and can be tailored for budding cooks with dietary restrictions.

OJAK LALI MASSAGE

Map p208 (☏9489 3799, 6341 1875; 02-79 People's Park Centre 101 Upper Cross St; 1hr body massage $38; ☺10am-7.30pm; ⓜChinatown) Tucked away into retro People's Park Centre (not to be confused with neighbouring People's Park Complex), this small, no-frills massage joint specialises in Javanese massage. It's cheap and justifiably popular, so it's always a good idea to call ahead, especially if you're planning on an afternoon rubdown.

Little India & Kampong Glam

LITTLE INDIA | KAMPONG GLAM | BUGIS

Neighbourhood Top Five

1 Kicking off your flip-flops and braving the infamous chilli challenge at mouthwatering **Lagnaa Barefoot Dining** (p87), one of Little India's tastiest nosh spots.

2 Customising the perfect fragrance at **Sifr Aromatics** (p92), one of a string of one-off shops in eclectic Kampong Glam.

3 Shopping for saris at the **Tekka Centre** (p92), then heading downstairs for lip-smacking street eats at Little India's liveliest hawker centre.

4 Taking a back seat during *puja* (prayers) at **Sri Veeramakaliamman Temple** (p83), Little India's most atmospheric Hindu temple.

5 Kickstarting your night with bolshy margaritas at **Piedra Negra** (p89), slap bang on buzzing Haji Lane.

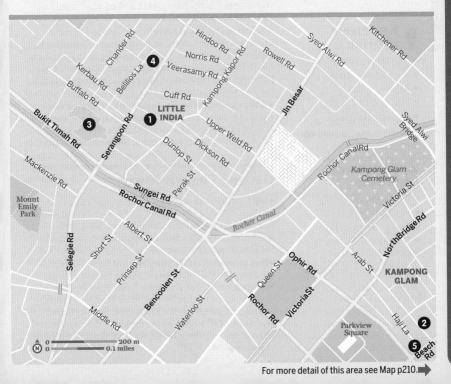

For more detail of this area see Map p210.

Lonely Planet's Top Tip

If you want to experience Little India at its busiest, subcontinental best, come on a Sunday. This is the only day off for many workers, particularly Indian labourers, and at times it feels like you're sharing the streets with half of Mumbai.

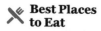

Best Places to Eat

➡ Lagnaa Barefoot Dining (p87)

➡ Cicheti (p87)

➡ Zam Zam (p87)

➡ Gandhi Restaurant (p86)

➡ Nan Hwa Chong Fish-Head Steamboat Corner (p88)

For reviews, see p86.➡

Best Places to Drink

➡ Bar Stories (p89)

➡ Piedra Negra (p89)

➡ Artistry (p89)

➡ BluJaz Café (p89)

➡ Bellwethers (p88)

For reviews, see p88.➡

Best Places to Shop

➡ Sifr Aromatics (p92)

➡ Haji Lane (p92)

➡ Tekka Centre (p92)

➡ Tuckshop & Sundry Supplies (p92)

For reviews, see p92.➡

Explore Little India & Kampong Glam

The heart of Little India lies in the colourful, incense-scented lanes between Serangoon Rd and Jln Besar, stretching from Campbell Lane in the south to Syed Alwi Rd in the north. The best way to take in this area is to simply wander the lanes on foot. Shopping and temple-hopping rank highly, but the main attraction is authentic Indian food.

From Malay and Middle Eastern to Italian and Chinese, scrumptious flavours also await in Kampong Glam, an area sometimes referred to as Arab St. It's an intriguing blend of the Islamic and the hipster, a place of storybook mosques, Third Wave cafes and trendy boutiques dotted around brightly painted laneways. For fun drinking options, Kampong Glam is where it's at, with notable cocktail dens, fragrant sheesha cafes, live music gigs, and a bustling, back-alley vibe.

Local Life

➡**Connect with your food** Using your fingers rather than cutlery is an integral part of the Indian eating experience. Wash your hands before and after (all Indian restaurants have sinks), and be sure to only use your right hand (the left is for toilet duties).

➡**South Indian breakfasts** You'll soon tire of toast-and-tea hotel breakfasts, so head to one of Little India's plethora of canteen restaurants and dig into a scrummy South Indian breakfast of *dosa* (paper-thin lentil-flour pancake), *idly* (fermented rice cakes) or *uttapam* (thick, savoury rice pancake).

➡**Bollywood movies** The colour and rhythm of Little India may just leave you itching for some Bollywood. Head straight to the historic Rex Cinemas (p89) to catch an all-singing, all-dancing Indian blockbuster.

Getting There & Away

➡**MRT** Little India station is right by the Tekka Centre. You can walk here from Bugis and Farrer Park stations. Bugis is best for Kampong Glam. As of 2016, Little India and Bugis stations will be directly connected by the Downtown Line 2 extension.

➡**Bus** Number 65 runs from Orchard Rd to Serangoon Rd. From the Colonial District, catch buses 131 or 147 on Stamford Rd. For Kampong Glam, take bus 7 from Orchard Rd to Victoria St (get off at Stamford Primary School, just past Arab St). From the Colonial District, buses 130, 133, 145 and 197 go up Victoria St, and buses 100 and 107 run along Beach Rd from the Raffles Hotel to Bussorah St.

👁 SIGHTS

👁 Little India

SRI VEERAMAKALIAMMAN
TEMPLE   HINDU TEMPLE

Map p210 (141 Serangoon Rd; ⏱5.15am-12.15pm & 4-9.15pm; Ⓜ Little India) Little India's most colourful temple is dedicated to the ferocious goddess Kali, depicted wearing a garland of skulls, ripping out the insides of her victims, and sharing some family moments with her sons Ganesh and Murugan. The bloodthirsty consort of Shiva has always been popular in Bengal, the birthplace of the labourers who built the structure in 1881. The temple is at its most evocative during each of the four daily *puja* (prayer) sessions.

SRI SRINIVASA
PERUMAL TEMPLE   HINDU TEMPLE

(397 Serangoon Rd; ⏱5.45am-noon & 5-9pm; Ⓜ Farrer Park) Dedicated to Vishnu, this temple dates from 1855 but the striking, 20m-tall *gopuram* (tower) is a 1966 add-on. Inside is a statue of Vishnu, his sidekicks Lakshmi and Andal, and his bird-mount Garuda. The temple is the starting point for a wince-inducing street parade during the Thaipusam festival.

SRI VADAPATHIRA
KALIAMMAN TEMPLE   HINDU TEMPLE

(555 Serangoon Rd; ⏱6am-noon & 4.30-9pm Sun-Thu, 6am-12.30pm & 4.30-9.30pm Fri & Sat; Ⓜ Farrer Park, Boon King) Dedicated to Kaliamman, the Destroyer of Evil, this South Indian temple began in 1870 as a modest shrine, but underwent a facelift in 1969 to transform it into the beauty standing today. The carvings here – particularly on the domed *vimana* inside – are among the best temple artwork you'll see anywhere in Singapore.

LEONG SAN SEE TEMPLE   BUDDHIST TEMPLE

(371 Race Course Rd; ⏱7.30am-5pm; Ⓜ Farrer Park) Dating from 1917 and dedicated to Kuan Yin (Guanyin), this relatively modest temple often swells with more religious fervour than many larger Taoist temples in Singapore. The name translates as Dragon Mountain Temple and its tiled roof ridge is decorated with animated chimera, dragons, flowers and human figures. To get here, walk north up Serangoon Rd then,

INDIAN HERITAGE CENTRE

When its doors finally swing open in 2015, the $12 million, state-of-the-art **Indian Heritage Centre** (Map p210; www.indianheritage.org.sg; cnr Campbell Lane & Clive St; Ⓜ Little India) will spotlight the origins and heritage of Singapore's Indian community through artefacts, maps, archival footage and multimedia displays. Aside from five permanent exhibition galleries, the centre will also house a visitor centre, rooftop garden, and activity spaces. The building itself is a striking contemporary statement. Iridescent during the day, its translucent facade becomes transparent at night, revealing a suitably colour-packed mural.

opposite Beatty Rd, turn left through a decorative archway emblazoned with the Chinese characters for the temple (寺山龍) and you'll find it at the end of the lane.

SAKYA MUNI
BUDDHA GAYA TEMPLE   BUDDHIST TEMPLE

(Temple of 1000 Lights; 366 Race Course Rd; ⏱8am-4.30pm; Ⓜ Farrer Park) Dominating this temple – also known as the Temple of 1000 Lights – is a 15m-tall, 300-tonne Buddha. Keeping him company is an eclectic cast of deities, including Kuan Yin (Guanyin), the Chinese goddess of mercy and, interestingly, the Hindu deities Brahma and Ganesh. The yellow tigers flanking the entrance symbolise protection and vitality, while the huge mother-of-pearl Buddha footprint to your left as you enter is reputedly a replica of the footprint on top of Adam's Peak in Sri Lanka.

The footprint's 108 auspicious marks distinguish a Buddha foot from any other 2m-long foot. The temple was founded by a Thai monk in 1927 and stands opposite the Taoist Leong San See Temple,

👁 Kampong Glam

SULTAN MOSQUE   MOSQUE

Map p210 (www.sultanmosque.org.sg; 3 Muscat St; ⏱9am-noon & 2-4pm Sat-Thu, 2.30-4pm Fri; Ⓜ Bugis) Seemingly pulled from the pages of the *Arabian Nights,* Singapore's largest mosque is nothing short of enchanting,

LITTLE INDIA & KAMPONG GLAM SIGHTS

Neighbourhood Walk
Little India

START FARRER PARK MRT STATION
END TEKKA CENTRE
LENGTH 2.7KM; 1½ HOURS

From Farrer Park MRT, head north along Race Course Rd to ❶**Sakya Muni Buddha Gaya Temple** (p83). Peek inside at its 15m-tall Buddha, then cross the street to appreciate the colourful detailing of Taoist ❷**Leong San See Temple** (p83). The alleyway opposite leads to bustling Serangoon Rd. Head south along it to the striking ❸**Sri Srinivasa Perumal Temple** (p83), Singapore's first temple for worshippers of Lord Vishnu (aka Perumal). Blessings give way to bargains further south at the ❹**Mustafa Centre** (p92), Little India's 24-hour shopping complex. The domed ❺**Angullia Mosque** across the street is popular with Singapore's Bangladeshi foreign workers. Further south, pop into ❻**Sri Veeramakaliamman Temple** (p83), Little India's main Hindu Temple, then head along Veerasamy Rd. Turn right down Kampong Kapor Rd to find the whitewashed 1929 ❼**Kampong Kapor Methodist Church**, then left along Upper Weld Rd and right into Perak Rd. At Dunlop St, turn left to admire the whimsical ❽**Abdul Gafoor Mosque**, a storybook fusion of Arab and Victorian architecture. Above the main entrance is a unique sundial, its 25 rays decorated with Arabic calligraphy denoting the 25 names of the prophets. Backtrack west along ❾**Dunlop St** to soak up the colourful jumble of shophouses, then cross over Serangoon Rd and head down Kerbau Rd to eye up the kaleidoscopic ❿**Tan House**. Pick your jaw up off the ground and walk down the side alley to Buffalo Rd, a thoroughfare lined with buxom produce, colourful garlands, and the airbrushed stares of Bollywood divas. Both Buffalo Rd and Kerbau Rd (*kerbau* means 'buffalo' in Malay) echo a time when this area was awash with the cattle sheds of North Indian farmers. Weary and perhaps a little hungry, slip into the cheap and scumptious ⓫**Tekka Centre** (p92).

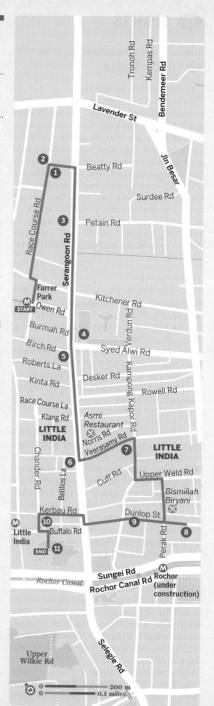

BANKSY, ASIAN-STYLE

Street artist **Ernest Zacharevic** (www.zachas.com) has been dubbed the Malaysian Banksy. Born in Lithuania and based in Penang, the 20-something artist has garnered a global following for his fantastically playful, interactive street art. From Stavanger to Singapore, his murals often incorporate real-life props, whether old bicycles, wooden chairs, even the moss growing out of cracks. In one small work opposite the Malabar Muslim Jama-Ath Mosque, two exhilarated kids freewheel it on a pair of 3D supermarket trolleys. To the right, a young boy somersaults out of a box, while further south on the corner of Victoria St and Jln Pisang, a giant girl caresses a snoozing lion cub. These three Zacharevic creations are not the only ones in town either. Head to the corner of Joo Chiat Tce and Everitt Rd in the eastern neighbourhood of Katong and you'll stumble upon his **Jousting Painters** (Map p214; cnr Everitt Rd & Joo Chiat Tce), a giant mural featuring two very real-looking boys prepared for battle on brightly painted horses. Bursting with joy and whimsy, the mural is just to the right of Zacharevic's trio of minion banditos, painted on three stout bollards.

designed in the Saracenic style and topped by a golden dome. It was originally built in 1825 with the aid of a grant from Raffles and the East India Company, after Raffles' treaty with the Sultan of Singapore allowed the Malay leader to retain sovereignty over the area. In 1928, the original mosque was replaced by the present magnificent building, designed by an Irish architect.

Non-Muslims are asked to refrain from entering the prayer hall at any time, and all visitors are expected to be dressed appropriately (cloaks are available at the entrance). Pointing cameras at people during prayer time is never appropriate.

MALAY HERITAGE CENTRE MUSEUM
Map p210 (☏6391 0450; www.malayheritage. org.sg; 85 Sultan Gate; adult/child under 6yr $4/ free; ◷10am-6pm Tue-Sun; Ⓜ Bugis) The Kampong Glam area is the historic seat of Malay royalty, and the *istana* (palace) on this site was built for the last sultan of Singapore, Ali Iskander Shah, between 1836 and 1843. It's now a museum, its recently revamped galleries exploring Malay-Singaporean culture and history, from the early migration of traders to Kampong Glam, to the development of Malay-Singaporean film, theatre, music and publishing.

Free guided tours run at 11am Tuesday to Friday, while special events include free Malay film nights under the stars – check the museum website for upcoming events.

**MALABAR MUSLIM
JAMA-ATH MOSQUE** MOSQUE
Map p210 (www.malabar.org.sg; 471 Victoria St; ◷2.30-4pm & 5-6.30pm; Ⓜ Lavender) The

golden-domed Malabar Muslim Jama-Ath Mosque is a curious creation clad entirely in striking blue geometric tiles. This is the only mosque on the island dedicated to Malabar Muslims from the South Indian state of Kerala, and though the building was commenced in 1956, it wasn't officially opened until 1963 due to cash-flow problems. This 'better late than never' motif continues with the tiling, only completed in 1995.

HAJJAH FATIMAH MOSQUE MOSQUE
Map p210 (4001 Beach Rd; Ⓜ Nicoll Highway, Lavender) Singapore's 'Leaning Tower of Pisa' is the minaret at this curious mosque, sloping about six degrees off centre due to sandy soil. The mosque itself is intriguing for its idiosyncratic architecture, which blends Middle Eastern and British styles. Among its features is a stained-glass dome roof. Constructed in 1846, the building is named after Melaka-born Singaporean philanthropist, Hajjah Fatimah, whose home once stood on the site.

⊙ Bugis

**KUAN IM THONG
HOOD CHO TEMPLE** BUDDHIST TEMPLE
Map p210 (178 Waterloo St; ◷6am-6.30pm; Ⓜ Bugis) Awash with the frenetic click of *chien tung* (Chinese fortune sticks), this is one of Singapore's busiest (and according to devotees, luckiest) temples. It's dedicated to the goddess of mercy Kuan Yin (Guanyin), a much-loved peddler of good fortune. Flower sellers and fortune tellers swarm around

the entrance, while further up the street, believers rub the belly of a large bronze Buddha Maitreya for extra luck. In a very Singaporean case of religious pragmatism, worshippers also offer prayers at the polychromatic **Sri Krishnan Hindu Temple** (Map p210; 152 Waterloo St) next door.

EATING

Little India

GANDHI RESTAURANT SOUTH INDIAN $
Map p210 (29 Chander Rd; dishes from $2, set meals from $4; ⊙11am-11pm; ⓜLittle India) It might be a canteen-style joint with shabby service and cheap decor, but who cares when the food is this good? Wash your hands by the sink at the back, and tuck into delicious set-meal thali, *dosa* (paper-thin lentil-flour pancake) or *uttapam* (thick, savoury South Indian rice pancake with finely chopped onions, green chillies, coriander and coconut).

SANKRANTI INDIAN $
Map p210 (100 Sayed Alwi Rd; mains from $8; ⊙11.30am-4pm & 6pm-midnight Mon-Thu, 11.30am-midnight Fri-Sun; ⓜLittle India) Arguably the best of a cluster of good restaurants in and around Little India's 24-hour shopping hub, the Mustafa Centre, Sankrati serves specialities from the South Indian state of Andhra Pradesh. The extensive menu includes a number of North Indian dishes, too, and has an enticing choice of set-meal thalis. The pick of the bunch is the Sankrati Special, a 10-piece culinary extravaganza.

ANANDA BHAVAN INDIAN, VEGETARIAN $
Map p210 (www.anandabhavan.com; Block 663, 01-10 Buffalo Rd; set meals $6-9; ⊙7am-10.30pm; ⚲; ⓜLittle India) This supercheap chain restaurant is a top spot to sample South Indian breakfast staples like *idly* and *dosa* (spelt 'thosai' on the menu). It also does great-value thali, some of which are served on banana leaves. You'll find other Little India outlets at 58 Serangoon Rd and 95 Syed Alwi Rd, as well as an outlet at Changi Airport's Terminal 2.

JAGGI'S INDIAN PUNJABI $
Map p210 (34-36 Race Course Rd; dishes $2.50-5; ⊙11.30am-3.30pm & 5.30-10.30pm Mon-Thu, to 10.45pm Fri, 11am-4pm & 5.30-10.45pm Sat & Sun; ⚲; ⓜLittle India) One of the few authentic, no-nonsense outfits in a string of otherwise touristy, overpriced Indian restaurants on Race Course Rd, canteen-style Jaggi's peddles delicious Punjabi food to loyal locals. Point and choose, and mix and match until you have a meal's worth of dishes, then pay the boss and take your tray of goodies to your table.

AZMI RESTAURANT INDIAN MUSLIM $
Map p210 (Norris Rd Chapati; 1 Norris Rd; dishes $1-5, chapati $0.80; ⊙7.30am-10.30pm; ⓜLittle India) This no-frills corner eatery is arguably the best place in Little India to sample freshly baked chapati. Choose from a string of curries, displayed buffet-style, then decide how many chapatis you need to mop up your curry with. Seating is of the plastic-stool variety, so don't bother wearing your Sunday best. Purchase drinks from the separate Chinese-run stall in the corner.

USMAN PAKISTANI $
Map p210 (cnr Serangoon & Desker Rds; dishes $1-16; ⊙11am-2am; ⓜLittle India) Cluttered with sacks of flour and onions, tiny Usman whips up seriously fine paneer (soft, unfermented cheese made from milk curd); the *pulak paneer* (paneer with a creamy spinach gravy) is especially good. Dhal is a dirt-cheap $1, while the tandoori chicken bursts with flavour. Whatever you choose, mop it up with soft, freshly baked naan (tandoor-cooked flatbread).

AZMI RESTAURANT INDIAN MUSLIM $
Map p210 (43 Dunlop St; snacks from $0.50; ⊙8am-8pm; ⓜLittle India) Right beside Abdul Gaffoor Mosque, this pocket-sized Muslim snack shop fills up around prayer time, its customers spilling out onto the street. Tuck into hits-the-spot samosa (deep-fried pastry triangles filled with vegetable or meat) and pakora (bite-sized pieces of vegetable dipped in chickpea-flour batter and deep fried), best washed down with a cup of sweet tea or coffee.

MOGHUL SWEET SHOP SWEETS $
Map p210 (48 Serangoon Rd; sweets from $1; ⊙9.30am-9.30pm; ⓜLittle India) If you're after a subcontinental sugar rush, tiny Moghul is the place to get it. Sink your teeth into luscious *gulab jamun* (syrup-soaked fried dough balls), harder-to-find *rasmalai* (paneer cheese soaked in cardamom-infused clotted cream) and *barfi* (condensed milk

TEKKA CENTRE

Little India's most famous hawker centre, the **Tekka Centre** (Map p210; cnr Serangoon & Buffalo Rds; dishes $2-10; ⊘7am-11pm; 🍴; ⓂLittle India) has stalls serving the Hainanese chicken rice and *nasi goreng* (Indonesian fried rice) you can find in other food centres across Singapore, but it focuses on Indian food too, which means plenty of biryani and tandoor offerings and mutton curries galore. Well worth seeking out is **Ah-Rahman Royal Prata** (Map p210; Stall 01-248; murtabak $4-8; ⊘7am-10pm, closed alternative Mon), which serves even better *murtabak* (stuffed savoury pancake) than those you'll find at Zam Zam – really, they are impossibly good – and watching the chef mould, flip and fill them is like watching an artist at work.

and sugar slice) in flavours including pistachio, chocolate...and carrot.

★ LAGNAA BAREFOOT DINING   INDIAN $$

Map p210 (📞6296 1215; www.lagnaa.com; 6 Upper Dickson Rd; dishes $6-20; ⊘11.30am-10pm; 🍴; ⓂLittle India) You can choose your level of spice at friendly Lagnaa: level three denotes standard spiciness, level four significant spiciness, and anything above admirable bravery. Whatever level you opt for, you're in for finger-licking good homestyle cooking from both ends of Mother India, devoured at either Western seating downstairs, or on floor cushions upstairs. If you're indecisive, order chef Kaesavan's famous Threadfin fish curry.

Those who eat a level-three dish without the aid of yoghurt-based drinks or dishes get their own peg on Lagnaa's string of chilli fame. Devour a level-six dish and expect an invitation to Lagnaa's monthly Full Moon Chilli Challenge. Survive *that* and the meal is on the house.

ANDHRA CURRY   SOUTH INDIAN $$

Map p210 (41 Kerbau Rd; dishes $5.50-24.50; ⊘11.30am-3.30pm & 6-10.30pm Mon-Fri, 11.30am-10.30pm Sat & Sun; 🍴; ⓂLittle India) Dive into this Technicolor shophouse for tasty grub from southern India's Andhra Pradesh state. It's a clean, efficient restaurant, bridging the gap between Little India's salt-of-the-earth, canteen-style boltholes and its sanitised, slightly overpriced tourist favourites. Biryanis are popular – the Hyderabadhi biryani is a speciality – while the tandoor meat dishes are also tasty. The large vegetarian set-meal thalis are good value.

COCOTTE   FRENCH $$$

Map p210 (📞6298 1188; www.restaurantcocotte.com; 2 Dickson Rd; mains from $34; ⊘noon-2pm & 6-9.30pm Sun, Mon, Wed & Thu, noon-2.30pm & 6-10pm Fri & Sat; ⓂLittle India, Bugis) Never mind the Little India address, hip Cocotte is red, white and blue down to its succulent French jus. Try garlicky *escargot gougeres* (snails wrapped in cheese pastry), tender pork, veal and sage *crepinettes,* or the signature *poulet rôti,* a whole roasted chicken served with seasonal vegetables and rich pan juices.

✗ Kampong Glam

★ ZAM ZAM   MALAYSIAN $

Map p210 (699 North Bridge Rd; murtabak from $5, dishes $6-20; ⊘7am-11pm; 🍴; ⓂBugis) These guys have been here since 1908 so they know what they're doing. Tenure hasn't bred complacency, though – the frenetic chefs whip up delicious *murtabak,* the restaurant's speciality savoury pancakes, filled with succulent mutton, chicken, beef, venison, or even sardine.

Servings are epic, so order a medium between two.

WARONG NASI PARIAMAN   MALAYSIAN, INDONESIAN $

Map p210 (📞6292 2374; 738 North Bridge Rd; dishes $2.60-5; ⊘7.30am-2.30pm Mon-Sat; ⓂBugis) It mightn't be much to look at, but this corner *nasi padang* stall is the stuff of legend. Do not miss the *belado* (fried mackerel in a slow-cooked chilli, onion and vinegar sauce), delicate *rendang* beef or *ayam bakar* (grilled chicken with coconut sauce). Get here by 11am to avoid the hordes. And be warned: most of it sells out by 1pm.

★ CICHETI   ITALIAN $$

Map p210 (📞6292 5012; www.cicheti.com; 52 Kandahar St; pizzas $17-25, mains $25-38; ⊘noon-3pm & 6.30-11pm Mon-Fri, 6.30-11pm Sat;

Ⓜ Bugis) Cool-kid Cicheti is a slick, friendly, buzzing scene of young-gun *pizzaioli*, trendy diners and seductive, contemporary Italian dishes made with hand-picked market produce. Tuck into beautifully charred woodfired pizzas, made-from-scratch pasta, and evening standouts like *polpette di carne grana* (slow-cooked meatballs topped with shaved Grana Padana). Book early in the week if heading in on a Friday or Saturday night.

And always leave room for the inspired desserts, whether it's the frozen crème brûlée pimped with candied bacon, or a jar of light and zesty herb-jelly grappa.

NAN HWA CHONG FISH-HEAD
STEAMBOAT CORNER   CHINESE $$
Map p210 (812-816 North Bridge Rd; fish steamboats around $20; ⊙4.30pm-12.30am; Ⓜ Lavender) If you only try fish-head steamboat once, do it at this noisy, open-fronted veteran. Cooked on charcoal, the large pot of fish head is brought to you in steaming, *tee po* (dried flat sole fish) spiked broth. One pot is enough for three or four people, and can stretch to more with rice and side dishes.

There are several fish types to choose from; the red snapper usually has less bone and more meat than the others.

SYMMETRY   CAFE $$
Map p210 (www.symmetry.com.sg; 9 Jalan Kubor; brunch $16-24; ⊙10.30am-9pm Mon, 10.30am-11pm Tue-Thu, 10.30am-midnight Fri, 9am-midnight Sat, 9am-9pm Sun; ☏; Ⓜ Bugis) With its clutter of rusty beams, random lamps and indie tunes, Symmetry feels like a garage made for band jams. But it's all about the grub, coffee and suds. Book ahead for the weekend brunch, its wickedly good offerings including wild mushroom duxelle beignets, pork collar-stuffed croissants, and a satisfying Eggs Sur Le Plat (with pork sausage, smoked paprika, cherry tomato coulis and creamed baby spinach).

Guzzle down full-bodied espresso, nutty cold brew, fresh juices or suds and ciders from as far afield as Norway.

✕ Bugis

QS269 FOOD HOUSE   HAWKER $
Map p210 (Block 269B Queen St; ⊙individual stalls vary; Ⓜ Bugis) This is not so much a 'food house' as a loud, crowded undercover laneway lined with cult-status food stalls.

Work up a sweat with a bowl of award-winning coconut curry noodle soup from **Ah Heng Curry Chicken Bee Hoon Mee** (Map p210; Stall 01-236; dishes from $4; ⊙8am-5pm Sat-Thu) or join the queue at the equally cultish **New Rong Liang Ge Cantonese Roast Duck Boiled Soup** (Map p210; Stall 01-235; dishes from $2.50; ⊙7am-8pm), with succulent roast duck dishes that draw foodies from across the city.

🍷 DRINKING & NIGHTLIFE

When it comes to knocking back a few, Kampong Glam trumps Little India. The scene is focussed on and around pedestrianised Haji Lane, with everything from hipster boltholes serving single-origin brew, to band-jamming bars and the odd bespoke cocktail den. For a cheap, no-frills swill, you can always grab a beer at one of the hawker centres.

🍸 Little India

BELLWETHERS   BAR
Map p210 (www.bellwethers.com.sg; 120 Desker Rd; ⊙5-11.30pm Tue-Thu, 5pm-1am Fri, 11am-1am Sat, 11am-11pm Sun; ☏; Ⓜ Farrer Park) Breezy Bellwethers brings a little hipster cool to the raffish streets of Little India. Grab an oil-drum table on the alleyway and neck a craft beer, whisky, or just a decent cup of Joe. The grub is also good, whether it's snack-friendly *jamón*-wrapped grilled eggplant, or bigger, mostly meaty mains. Happy hour rocks on till 9pm.

ZSOFI TAPAS BAR   ROOFTOP BAR
Map p210 (www.tapasbar.com.sg; 68 Dunlop St; ⊙10am-1am Mon-Thu, to 2am Fri & Sat, 4pm-midnight Sun; Ⓜ Little India) She may no longer be an 'It kid', but Zsofi still draws the punters with her spacious rooftop – a highly unusual offering in this part of town. And while the drinks mightn't be cheap for Little India, every one of them comes with free tapas, which goes some way to softening the blow when you get the bill.

PRINCE OF WALES   PUB
Map p210 (www.facebook.com/POW.Little.India; 101 Dunlop St; ⊙8.30am-1am Sun-Thu, to 2am

Fri & Sat; MLittle India) The closest thing to a pub in Little India, this grungy Aussie hangout doubles as a backpacker hostel. It's an affable, popular spot, with a small beer garden, pool table, sports screens and live music several times a week. Weekly staples include Wednesday Quiz Night (from 8pm) and the Sunday Session, complete with barbecue (3.30pm to 7.30pm) and music jams (from 4pm).

🍺 Kampong Glam

BAR STORIES
COCKTAIL BAR

Map p210 (☑6298 0838; www.barstories.com.sg; 55/57A Haji Lane; ⊙3pm-1am Sun-Thu, to 2am Fri & Sat; MBugis) Call ahead if you're heading in later in the week – this upstairs cocktail den is as small as it is hugely popular. If you're lucky enough you'll be sitting at the bar, where gung-ho barkeeps keep it freestyle, turning whatever spirit or flavour turns you on into a smashing libation. Creative, whimsical and often brilliant.

PIEDRA NEGRA
BAR

Map p210 (www.piedra-negra.com; cnr Beach Rd & Haji Lane; ⊙noon-midnight Mon-Thu, to 2am Fri, 5pm-2am Sat; MBugis) Sexy Latin beats, bombastic murals and tables right on free-spirited Haji Lane, this electric Mexican joint is a brilliant spot for a little evening people-watching, any night of the week. Frozen or shaken, the margaritas pack a punch, and the joint's burritos, quesadillas, tacos and other Tex-Mex staples are filling and delish.

ARTISTRY
CAFE

Map p210 (☑6298 2420; www.artistryspace.com; 17 Jln Pinang; ⊙10am-7pm Tue-Sun; 🛜; MBugis) Killer coffee, rotating art exhibitions and frequent after-hours events – spanning live music and dance, to themed cocktail soirées – Artistry is a hipster version of the cultural salon. Swig on interesting artisanal beers and ciders, or tuck into fresh, delicious grub (served till 5pm) like the sublime BRB (blueberry, ricotta and bacon) pancakes.

Offbeat tidbit: the cafe bar, stools and communal table were custom made using recycled wood from Geylang Serang, a recreated Malay village that once stood on Geylang Rd.

MAISON IKKOKU
CAFE, COCKTAIL BAR

Map p210 (www.maison-ikkoku.net; 20 Kandahar St; ⊙cafe 9am-9pm Mon-Thu, to 11pm Fri & Sat, to 7pm Sun, bar 4pm-1am Sun-Thu, to 2am Fri & Sat; 🛜; MBugis) Pimped with Chesterfield banquettes and suspended dressers, Maison Ikkoku flies the flag for Third Wave coffee, its brewing techniques including Chemex, Syphon, Woodneck, French press, Aeropress and old-school espresso. Edibles include decent sandwiches, salads, cakes, and *mi musubi,* a sushilike Hawaiian snack topped with seasoned spam. Upstairs is the well-regarded cocktail bar, where crafty libations come with a view of Sultan Mosque's golden dome.

⭐ ENTERTAINMENT

☆ Little India

WILD RICE
THEATRE

Map p210 (☑6292 2695; www.wildrice.com.sg; 65 Kerbau Rd; MLittle India) Singapore's sexiest theatre group is based in Kerbau Rd, but performs shows elsewhere in the city (as well as abroad). Productions range from farce to serious politics, and fearlessly wade into issues not commonly on the agenda in Singapore.

REX CINEMAS
CINEMA

Map p210 (http://tickets.rexcinema.com.sg; 2 Mackenzie Rd; tickets $15; MLittle India) Where can you catch the Bollywood blockbusters advertised all over Little India? Why at the Rex, of course. This historic theatre screens films from around the subcontinent, most subtitled in English.

☆ Kampong Glam

BLUJAZ CAFÉ
LIVE MUSIC

Map p210 (www.blujaz.net; 11 Bali Lane; from $6; ⊙noon-1am Mon-Thu, noon-2am Fri, 4pm-2am Sat; MBugis) Bohemian pub BluJaz is one of your best options for live music in town, with regular jazz jams, and other acts playing anything from blues to rockabilly. Check the website for the list of rotating events, which include DJ-spun funk, R&B and retro nights and Wednesday's 'Talk Cock' open-mic comedy night.

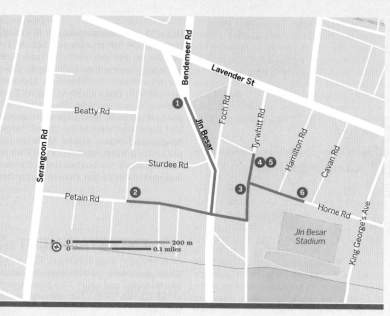

🏃 Local Life
An Afternoon in Jalan Besar

Once better known for hardware stores and boxing matches, Jalan Besar is metamorphising into an area where heritage architecture meets new-school Singapore cool. Just northeast of Little India, this compact district, centred around Jln Besar itself, is studded with artisan cafes and independent shops peddling edgy local design.

❶ Lunching at Suprette

Munch happily at **Suprette** (☎6298 8962; www.suprette.com; 383 Jln Besar; dishes $10-45; ⊙7.30am-3pm & 6-10.30pm Mon, Wed & Thu, 7.30am-3pm Tue, 7.30am-3pm & 6pm-midnight Fri, 7.30am-4pm & 6pm-midnight Sat, 7.30am-4pm & 6-10.30pm Sun; 🛜; 🚍65, 145, 857, Ⓜ Farrer Park), a diner-meets-shophouse space serving insanely delicious comfort grub. Breakfast is served till 2.30pm on weekdays and 3.30pm on weekends, which means you're in good time for the succulent Shakshuka (eggs poached in spicy tomato sauce with feta and lamb sausage). Wash it down with a Topless in Church, a perky choc-orange cocktail.

❷ Peranakan Perfection

Between Jln Besar and Sturdee Rd on Petain St is a row of lavishly decorated double-storey **terraces** dating back to the 1920s. The ornate decoration is typical of the so-called Late Shophouse Style.

❸ Cool Hunting

Behind its canary-yellow entrance, **Konzepp** (shop.konzepp.com; 129 Tyrwhitt Rd; ⊙noon-8pm Tue-Sun; Ⓜ Lavender) peddles impressive edits of independent fashion and design. The mostly men's selection of threads spans subversive Singaporean tees, cute French sweaters and playful Australian swimwear. Style hunters of both genders will go gaga over accessories like locally designed jewellery, leathergoods and Konzepp's own Hyper Grand watches.

❹ Coffee in a Hardware Store

A former hardware store provides the setting for **Chye Seng Huat Hardware** (www.cshhcoffee.com; 150 Tyrwhitt Rd; ⊙9am-7pm Tue-Fri, to 10pm Sat & Sun; Ⓜ Lavender), Singapore's hottest cafe and roastery. Slurp a glass of Nitro Black Matter, a malty, cold-brew coffee infused with CO_2 and served on tap, or book ahead for an on-site class

Getting crafty at Tyrwhitt General Company

in espresso, brewing or latte art (www.
papapalheta.com/education/classes).

⑤ Local Design
Right above Chye Seng Huat Hardware
lies **Tyrwhitt General Company** (http://
tyrwhittgeneralcompany.com; 150A Tyrwhitt
Rd; ⊙11am-7pm Tue-Sun; ⓂLavender), a
shop-cum-workshop peddling handmade
jewellery, art and knickknacks. Most of the
stock is local, including totes and colourful *kuih*- (candy-) shaped rings inspired by
childhood memories. Check the website
for upcoming workshops, which often
include leather craft.

⑥ Sweet Pie Finale
Expect childhood flashbacks at pie-
peddling **Windowsill Pies** (Map p210;
☑9004 7827; http://windowsillpies.sg; 78
Horne Rd; pie slices $7-8; ⊙11am-9.30pm
Tue-Thu, 11am-10.30pm Fri, 10am-10.30pm
Sat, 10am-9.30pm Sun; ⓂLavender), where
Scandi aesthetics merge with fake pine
trees and a giant, picnicking teddy bear.
You're here for a sweet slice of pie, from
seasonal winners like pumpkin pie with
Bourbon whip, to classic knockouts like
raspberry and lemon pie topped with
velvety meringue.

BIAN'S CAFE   CHINESE OPERA
Map p210 (www.singopera.com.sg; 01-27 Sultan
Plaza, 100 Jln Sultan; admission $10; ⊙11am-
7pm Mon-Fri; ⓂBugis) Visit this quaint cafe
between between 3pm and 6pm on Thursday afternoon (admission $10) and you'll
be treated to short bursts of Beijing Opera
tunes. You may even be able to have a go
yourself; Chinese Opera karaoke, anyone?
The site is also home to the grandly named
Singapore Chinese Opera Museum (Map
p210; 100 Jln Sultan; admission $5; ⊙11am-7pm
Tue-Sun), which documents the history and
development of the art form in Singapore.

☆ Bugis

BUGIS+   MALL
Map p210 (www.bugis-plus.com.sg; 201 Victoria St; ⓂBugis) This futuristic, Gen-Y mall
packs a virtual punch with its screen-
centric thrills and spills. Join gaming geeks
at **St Games** (Map p210; www.stgamescafe.
com; 03-16/17 Bugis+; ⊙11.30am-9.30pm Sun-
Thu, to midnight Fri & Sat) or the epic **Garena
Stadium** (Map p210; http://stadium.garena.
com; 03-19, Bugis+), or get nostalgic at amuse-
ment parlour **Arcadia** (Map p210; 05-04/05
Bugis+; ⊙11am-11pm Sun-Thu, to 1am Fri & Sat).
Alternatively, channel your inner Lorde in
one of the themed karaoke lounges at **K
Suites** (Map p210; www.ksuites.com.sg; 03-18
Bugis+). Level 4 houses a plethora of funky,
food-court-style eateries.

HOOD   LIVE MUSIC
Map p210 (www.hoodbarandcafe.com; 201 Victoria St, 05-07 Bugis+; ⊙5pm-1am Mon & Tue,
to 3am Wed-Fri, noon-3am Sat, noon-1am Sun;
ⓂBugis, City Hall) Inside the Bugis+ mall,
Hood's street-art interior sets a youthful
scene for nightly music jams from acts like
Rush Hour and Smells like Last Friday. If
it's undiscovered talent you're after, head in
for the weekly 'Saturday Original Sessions',
a showcase for budding musos itching to
share their singer-songwriter skills.

SINGAPORE DANCE THEATRE   DANCE
Map p210 (☑6338 0611; www.singaporedanceth-
eatre.com; 07-02/03, 201 Victoria Street; ⓂBugis)
This is the HQ of Singapore's premier dance
company, which keeps fans swooning with
its repertoire of classic ballets and contemporary works, many of which are performed
at Esplanade – Theatres on the Bay (p63).
The true highlight is the group's Ballet

THEGENERALCO.SG ©

HAJI LANE HIP

Running parallel to old-school Arab St, narrow, pastel **Haji Lane** (Map p210; Haji Lane; MBugis) is a go-to for one-off boutiques, bolthole cafes and people-watching. While shops can be a little hit or miss, **Dulcetfig** (Map p210; www.dulcetfig.com; 41 Haji Lane; ⊙noon-9pm Mon-Thu, to 10pm Fri & Sat, noon-8pm Sun; MBugis) drives female fashion bloggers wild with its genuinely cool local and foreign frocks and accessories, which include high-end vintage bags and jewellery. For a killer cup of Joe, squeeze into bright blue, art-pimped **CAD Cafe** (Map p210; http://cad.sg; 24 Haji Lane; ⊙8am-10pm Tue & Wed, to midnight Thu & Fri, 10am-midnight Sat, 10am-10pm Sun; MBugis), its name an acronym for Coffee, Art and Design. Be kind to yourself and order one of the pastries, straight from the oven of cultishly popular artisanal bakery the Bread Project.

under the Stars season at Fort Canning Park (p53), which usually runs for a limited season in July. See the website for programme details.

🛍 SHOPPING

Little India's streets are a browser's delight, laced with art, antiques, textiles, food and music. Quieter and more relaxed, Kampong Glam is even more eclectic – shop Arab St for textiles, rugs and bespoke perfumes, or Haji and Bali Lanes for independent fashion, records and hipster-approved accessories.

🛍 Little India

TEKKA CENTRE   CLOTHING
Map p210 (cnr Serangoon & Buffalo Rds; ⊙10am-10pm; MLittle India) One floor up from Tekka Centre's raucous hawker centre and wet market are a rainbow-coloured sea of Indian sari and textile stores and a small battalion of tailors. This is probably the cheapest place to pick up an Indian outfit, and while prices are labelled, well-mannered bargaining is always worth a try.

NALLI   CLOTHING
Map p210 (www.nallisingapore.com.sg; 10 Buffalo Rd; ⊙10am-9.30pm Mon-Sat, to 7.30pm Sun; MLittle India) For better quality cotton and silk saris, try this small, industrious shop on Buffalo Rd. Cotton saris go for as little as $30. The beautiful silk versions, most of which are upstairs, go for between $100 and $1000.

SIM LIM SQUARE   ELECTRONICS, MALL
Map p210 (www.simlimsquare.com.sg; 1 Rochor Canal Rd; ⊙11am-8pm; MBugis) A byword for all that is cut-price and geeky, Sim Lim is jammed with stalls selling motherboards, soundcards, games consoles, laptops and cameras. If you know what you're doing there are some deals to be had, but the untutored are more likely to be taken for a ride. Hard bargaining is essential.

MUSTAFA CENTRE   DEPARTMENT STORE
Map p210 (www.mustafa.com.sg; 145 Syed Alwi Rd; ⊙24hr; MFarrer Park) Little India's bustling 24-hour Mustafa Centre is a magnet for budget shoppers, most of them from the subcontinent. It's a sprawling place, peddling everything from electronics and garish gold jewellery, to shoes, bags, luggage and beauty products. There's also a large supermarket with a great range of Indian foodstuffs. If you can't handle crowds, avoid the place on Sunday.

🛍 Kampong Glam

⭐SIFR AROMATICS   PERFUME
Map p210 (www.sifr.sg; 42 Arab St; ⊙11am-8.30pm Mon-Sat, to 5pm Sun; MBugis) This Zen-like perfume laboratory belongs to third-generation perfumer Johari Kazura, whose exquisite creations include the heady East (50mL $140), a blend of oud, rose absolute, amber and neroli. Perfumes range from $85 to $300 for 50mL, while vintage perfume bottles range from $60 to $2000. Those after a custom-made fragrance should call a couple of days ahead before their visit.

TUCKSHOP & SUNDRY SUPPLIES   FASHION, ACCESSORIES
Map p210 (25 Bali Lane; ⊙11am-9pm Mon-Sat, noon-6pm Sun; MBugis) A vintage-inspired ode to Americana working-class culture, this

supercool menswear store offers a clued-in selection of rugged threads and accessories, including designer eyewear, grooming products and made-in-house leathergoods. Stock up on plaid shirts, sweat tops and harder-to-find denim from brands like Japan's Iron Heart and China's Red Cloud.

LITTLE SHOPHOUSE HANDICRAFTS
Map p210 (43 Bussorah St; ⊗10am-5pm; MBugis) Traditional Peranakan beadwork is a dying art, but it's kept very much alive in this quaint shop-cum-workshop. Starting at around $300, the shop's colourful slippers are designed by craftsman Robert Sng and hand-beaded by his sister, Irene. While they're not cheap, each pair takes a painstaking two months to complete. Beadwork aside, you'll also find Peranakan-style tea sets, crockery, vases, handbags and jewellery.

STRAITS RECORDS MUSIC
Map p210 (24A Bali Lane; ⊗3-10pm Mon-Fri, 2-10pm Sat, 2-8pm Sun; MBugis) Hiding up a set of stairs, Straits Records is one of the few alternative music stores in Singapore. Stock includes hip hop, hardcore and reggae CDs, as well as some old vinyl, T-shirts and books. CDs from local bands start at around $10.

🏠 Bugis

BUGIS STREET MARKET MARKET
Map p210 (www.bugis-street.com; Victoria St; ⊗11am-10pm; MBugis) What was once Singapore's most infamous sleaze pit – packed with foreign servicemen on R&R, gambling dens and 'sisters' (transvestites) – is now its most famous undercover street market, crammed with cheap clothes, shoes, accessories, manicurists, food stalls and, in a nod to its past, a sex shop.

One standout upstairs is the tiny **Good Old Days** (Map p210; Shop CSL/D4, Level 2; ⊗noon-10pm), which stocks '60s to '90s vintage frocks, handbags, jewellery and retro odds and ends.

BUGIS JUNCTION MALL
Map p210 (200 Victoria St; ⊗10am-10pm; MBugis) Featuring two streets of glassed-in, air-conditioned shophouse recreations, Bugis Junction lures teens and 20-somethings with its fast fashion, costume jewellery, *kawaii* (cute Japanese) collectables, and street-smart backpacks and courier bags. Global brands include concept store **Muji** and a small branch of bookstore **Kinokuniya**.

🏃 ACTIVITIES

🏃 Little India

AMRITA AYURVEDIC CENTRE MASSAGE
Map p210 (☑6299 0642; www.amrita.com.sg; 11 Upper Dickson Rd; 30min massage from $35; ⊗9am-9pm Mon-Sat, 8am-3pm Sun; MLittle India) If Little India's hyperactive energy leaves you frazzled, revive the Indian way with an Ayurvedic (traditional Indian medicine) massage at this modest, friendly massage joint. Treatments include Udvarthanam (using a paste of herbs and grains to cleanse the skin and improve circulation) and the highly popular Abhyangam (synchronised massage using medicated oils).

🏃 Kampong Glam

HOUNDS OF THE BASKERVILLES BARBER, TATTOO PARLOUR
Map p210 (☑6299 1197; 24 Bali Lane; buzz cut/full cut/shave $15/38/35; ⊗11am-10pm Mon-Sat; MBugis) Inked hipsters, antique cabinets bursting with clippers, and a hissing espresso machine: no place screams new-school Singapore like this old-school-inspired barber-cum-tattoo parlour. Get clippered or snipped (walk-ins only), or pimp your skin with a striking new tatt. The top-dog artist here is Rosman, a Javanese dude famed for his batik designs.

Orchard Road

Neighbourhood Top Five

1 Shopping the new-millennium way at **ION Orchard Mall** (p100), Singapore's sleekest, sharpest, mega mall, and the epitome of retail escapism.

2 Hunting for Indian antiques, bartering for an oriental rug or poring over ancient maps of Asia in culturally savvy **Tanglin Shopping Centre** (p100).

3 Slowing down your shopping spree with a leisurely stroll along heritage heavyweight **Emerald Hill Road** (p96).

4 Treating your palate to a tasting menu at **Iggy's** (p98), one of Singapore's most exalted restaurants.

5 Coming back down to earth with a traditional Singaporean breakfast of *kaya* (coconut jam) toast and *kopi* at **Killiney Kopitiam** (p96), the original locals' coffeeshop.

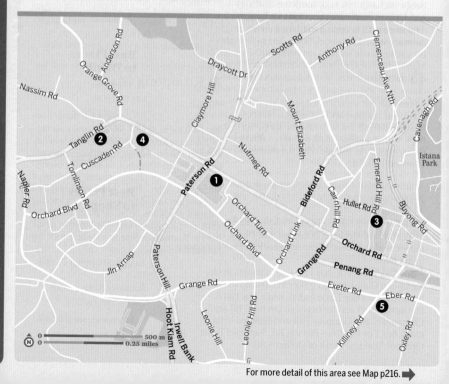

For more detail of this area see Map p216.

Explore Orchard Road

You would need the best part of a week to explore every floor of every mall in the Orchard Rd area, so do some shopping-mall homework before you go – keep reading.

Most malls don't open until 10am, but if you arrive early, fear not: you have the perfect excuse to charge up with breakfast and a powerful cup of Joe, either the old-school, Singaporean way at Killiney Kopitiam (p96), or the trendy, new-school way at the Providore (p98), Wild Honey (p98) or Kith Cafe (p97).

Whichever malls you trawl, it won't be long before your pins will yearn for a well-earned break. Spoil them with a quick foot rub at Lucky Plaza (p101) or go all out with some luxe pampering at one of the area's top-tier hotel spas.

Come 5pm, it's time to toast to your purchases with cut-price, happy-hour drinks, on Orchard Rd itself or just off it on historic beauty Emerald Hill Rd.

Local Life

→**Crowds** Shopping is Singapore's national sport, and the malls on Orchard Rd can get exceedingly busy. That can be half the fun, but if you prefer your shopping sans the hordes, head in as they open (usually around 10am) and browse bustle-free for about an hour or so.

→**Food courts** Shopping mall food courts might be culinary wastelands back home, but in Singapore, they're fantastic spots to eat fresh, authentic grub at very digestible prices. They're practically hawker centres with air-con, offering no shortage of local classics, as well as flavours from across the continent.

→**Fresh air** Air-conditioned malls are all well and good, but the time will come for a blast of good old-fashioned fresh air. So when the shopping is done, kick back with a cooling drink above the madness at Bar Canary (p99), or mingle with the postwork crowd on Emerald Hill Rd.

Getting There & Away

→**MRT** Orchard Rd is served by no less than three MRT stations: Orchard, Somerset and Dhoby Ghaut, so there's really no need to use any other form of transport to get here.

→**Bus** Bus 7 links Orchard Rd with Victoria St (for Kampong Glam), bus 65 links Orchard Rd with Serangoon Rd (for Little India), while bus 190 is the most direct service between Orchard Rd and Chinatown. For Dempsey Hill and Holland Village, catch bus 7 or 106 from Penang Rd, Somerset Rd or Orchard Blvd just south of Orchard Rd.

Lonely Planet's Top Tip

It's hard to believe it as you walk from mall to mall, but there is a rainforest within 2km of Orchard Rd, inside the grounds of the wonderful **Botanic Gardens** (Map p218). So, if you fancy a green escape from the concrete jungle, hop on bus 7 or 174 from the Orchard MRT exit on Orchard Blvd, and you'll be there in 10 to 20 minutes.

✖ Best Places to Eat

→ Iggy's (p98)
→ Takashimaya Food Village (p97)
→ Paradise Dynasty (p97)
→ Buona Terra (p98)
→ StraitsKitchen (p98)

For reviews, see p96.➡

▸ Best Places to Drink

→ Ice Cold Beer (p99)
→ Néktar (p99)
→ Bar Canary (p99)
→ KPO (p99)
→ Providore (p98)

For reviews, see p98.➡

▸ Best Places to Shop

→ ION Orchard Mall (p100)
→ Robinsons (p100)
→ Tanglin Shopping Centre (p100)
→ Reckless Shop (p100)
→ On Pedder (p100)

For reviews, see p100.➡

ORCHARD ROAD

⊙ SIGHTS

EMERALD HILL ROAD   NEIGHBOURHOOD
Map p216 (ⓂSomerset) Take time out from your shopping to wander up frangipani-scented Emerald Hill Rd, graced with some of Singapore's finest terrace houses. Special mentions go to No 56 (built in 1902, and one of the earliest buildings here), Nos 39 to 45 (with unusually wide frontages and a grand Chinese-style entrance gate), and Nos 120 to 130 (with art-deco features dating from around 1925). At the Orchard Rd end of the hill is a cluster of popular bars housed in beautiful shophouse renovations.

ISTANA   PALACE
Map p216 (www.istana.gov.sg; Orchard Rd; grounds & palace $2; ⊙8.30am-6pm, open days only; ⓂDhoby Ghaut) The grand, white-washed, neoclassical home of Singapore's president, set in 16 hectares of grounds, was built by the British between 1867 and 1869 as Government House, and is open to visitors five times a year: on Labour Day (1 May), National Day (7 August), Chinese New Year (January or February), Diwali (October or November) and Hari Raya Puasa (or Eid-ul Fitr, the festival marking the end of Ramadan; dates vary).

Only on these days will you get the chance to stroll past the nine-hole golf course, through the beautiful terraced gardens and into some of the reception rooms. The rest of the time, the closest you'll get are the heavily guarded **gates** on Orchard Rd.

CATHAY GALLERY   MUSEUM
Map p216 (www.thecathaygallery.com.sg; 2nd fl, The Cathay, 2 Handy Rd; ⊙11am-7pm Mon-Sat; ⓂDhoby Ghaut) **FREE** Film and nostalgia buffs will appreciate this pocket-sized silver-screen museum, housed in Singapore's first high-rise building. The displays trace the history of the Loke family, early pioneers in film production and distribution in Singapore and founders of the Cathay Organisation. Highlights include old movie posters, cameras and programs that capture the golden age of local cinema.

TAN YEOK NEE HOUSE   NOTABLE BUILDING
Map p216 (101 Penang Rd; ⓂDhoby Ghaut) Singapore's sole surviving example of a traditional Chinese mansion, elegant Tan Yeok Nee House was built in 1885 as the townhouse of a prosperous merchant. Today it's part of the Asian campus of the University of Chicago Booth School of Business. While it's not open to the public, you can still admire its fine roof decoration from outside, not to mention peek at its tranquil courtyard from the entrance.

✗ EATING

KILLINEY KOPITIAM   COFFEESHOP $
Map p216 (67 Killiney Rd; dishes $2-7; ⊙6am-11pm Mon & Wed-Sat, to 6pm Tue & Sun; ⓂSomerset) White wall tiles, fluorescent lights and endearingly lame laminated jokes: this old-school coffee joint is still *the* place for a Singaporean breakfast of *kaya* (coconut jam) toast, soft-boiled eggs and sucker-punch coffee. Post-breakfast, chow down staples like chicken curry, laksa or *nasi lemak* (coconut rice, dried anchovies and spices wrapped in a banana leaf) before sampling one of the sweet-dumpling desserts.

MUSTARD INCIDENT   AMERICAN $
Map p216 (B1 Tangs Orchard, 310 Orchard Rd; hot dogs $9-10; ⊙10.30am-9.30pm Mon-Thu & Sat, to 11pm Fri, 11am-8.30pm Sun; ⓂOrchard) Lurking in the basement of Tangs department store, this hole-in-the-wall hot-dog vendor makes all its sausages, condiments and sauces from scratch. Bust your jaw on the epic Frankenstein (pork and beef sausage, streaky bacon, chilli, garlic sauce and hot sauce) or go lighter with the satisfying Chicago dog, topped with fresh diced tomato.

Libations include a handful of American and European craft beers, with seating limited to a few stainless-steel benches.

GELATERIA ITALIA   ICE CREAM $
Map p216 (B4-K1 ION Orchard, 2 Orchard Turn; ice cream from $5.40; ⊙11am-10.30pm; ⓂOrchard) Lick yourself silly at this mouthwatering gelato stall, deep within the bowels of ION Orchard Mall. Free of nasty chemicals, preservatives and artificial colours or flavours, its luscious offerings include an obscenely rich dark truffle chocolate and a pistachio that – wait for it – actually tastes like pistachio!

★TIM HO WAN   CHINESE $$
Map p216 (01-29A/52 Plaza Singapura, 68 Orchard Rd; dishes from $3.80; ⊙10am-10pm Mon-Fri, 9am-10pm Sat & Sun; ⓂDhoby Ghaut) Hong Kong's Michelin-starred dumpling peddler

FOOD COURT FAVOURITES

Burrow into the basement of most malls on Orchard Rd and you'll find a food court with stall upon stall selling cheap, freshly cooked dishes from all over the world. These are the best two:

Takashimaya Food Village (Map p216; B2 Takashimaya Department Store, Ngee Ann City, 391 Orchard Rd; snacks from $1; ☺10am-11pm; Ⓜ Orchard) Slick, sprawling and heavenly scented, Takashimaya's basement food hall serves up a *Who's Who* of Japanese, Korean and other Asian culinary classics. Look out for *soon kueh* (steamed dumplings stuffed with bamboo shoots, yam, dried mushroom, carrot and dried prawn), and don't miss a fragrant bowl of noodles from the Tsuru-koshi stand.

Food Republic (Map p216; Level 4, Wisma Atria, 435 Orchard Rd; dishes $6-10; ☺10am-10pm Sun-Thu, to 11pm Fri & Sat; Ⓜ Orchard) OK, so this one is not actually in the basement, but the formula remains the same – lip-smacking food, a plethora of choices and democratic prices. Food Republic offers traditional hawker classics, as well as Korean, Japanese, Indian, Thai and Indonesian. Muck in with the rest of the crowd for seats before joining the longest queues. Roving 'aunties' push around trolleys filled with drinks and dim sum.

is now steaming in Singapore, with the same queues (head in after 8.30pm) and tick-the-boxes order form. While nothing compares to the original (the Singapore branches need to import many of the raw ingredients), the recipes are the same and the results still pretty spectacular. Must-tries include the sugary baked buns with barbecue pork and the plump prawn dumplings.

PARADISE DYNASTY
CHINESE $$

Map p216 (www.paradisegroup.com.sg; 2 Orchard Turn, 04-12A ION Orchard; dishes $7-23; ☺11am-9.30pm Mon-Fri, from 10am Sat & Sun; Ⓜ Orchard) Preened staffers in headsets whisk you into this svelte dumpling den, passing a glassed-in kitchen where Chinese chefs stretch their noodles and steam their buns. Skip the novelty flavoured *xiao long bao* (soup dumplings) for the original version, which arguably beat those from legendary competitor Din Tai Fung. Beyond these wobbly, silky marvels, standouts include *la mian* (hand-pulled noodles) with buttery, braised pork belly.

KITH CAFE
CAFE $$

Map p216 (☑6338 8611; kith.com.sg; 9 Penang Rd; dishes $6-24; ☺8am-10pm Tue-Sun; ☎🖉; Ⓜ Dhoby Ghaut;☎) Kith kicks butt on several levels. It opens when many Singapore cafes are still snoozing, it offers free wi-fi and cool magazines, the coffee is good (it has soy!), and the grub fresh and tasty. All-day breakfast items span virtuous muesli to cheeky egg-based slap-ups, and both the

salads and sandwiches pique interest with their gourmet combos.

The only downside is the dull roar of traffic, just beyond the shaded outdoor patio.

TAMBUAH MAS
INDONESIAN $$

Map p216 (☑6733 2220; www.tambuahmas.com.sg; B1-44 Paragon, 290 Orchard Rd; mains $7-25; ☺11am-10pm; ☎; Ⓜ Somerset) Hiding shyly in a corner of the Paragon's food-packed basement, Tambuah Mas is where Indonesian expats head for a taste of home. Bright, modern and good value for Orchard Rd, it proudly makes much of what it serves from scratch, a fact well evident in what could possibly be Singapore's best beef *rendang* (spicy coconut curry). No reservations, so head in early if dining Thursday to Saturday.

WASABI TEI
JAPANESE $$

Map p216 (05-70 Far East Plaza, 14 Scotts Rd; meals $10-28; ☺12.30-3pm & 5.30-9.30pm Mon-Fri, 12.30-4.30pm & 5.30-9.30pm Sat; Ⓜ Orchard) Channelling 1972 with its Laminex countertop and wooden wall panels, this tiny, cash-only sushi bar feels like a scrumptious local secret. Stake a spot at the counter and watch the Chinese chef prove that you don't have to be Japanese to make raw fish sing with flavour. Note: the newer sibling restaurant next door is no substitute for the original.

BODEGA Y TAPAS
TAPAS $$

Map p216 (esmirada.com; 442 Orchard Rd; tapas $7-19, mains $22-44; ☺noon-1am Mon-Sat, to midnight Sun; Ⓜ Orchard) At the busy junction of Orchard, Tanglin and Orange Grove

ORCHARD ROAD EATING

Rds, this contemporary bar-bistro channels España with breezy guitar riffs, splashes of Spanish red and beautiful tapas. Portions are generous (three tapas per person should suffice) and flavours simple and satisfying. The Iberico ham croquettes are velvety perfection, while the sizzling garlic prawns come with a welcome baguette to mop up all that oily, garlicky goodness.

Rotating, all-day drink specials add appeal, while mains branch out to include Italian, French and Hellenic influences.

PROVIDORE · CAFE $$

Map p216 (☑6732 1565; www.theprovidore.com; 02-05 Mandarin Gallery, 333A Orchard Rd; dishes $8.50-26.50; ☺9am-10.30pm; ☏; ⓂSomerset) Waiting for you at the top of the Mandarin Gallery's outdoor escalator is the Providore, a cool, upbeat cafe pimped with white tiles, industrial details and shelves neatly stocked with gourmet pantry fillers. Sip a full-bodied latte or scan the menu for an all-bases list of options, from breakfast-friendly organic muesli and pancakes, to gourmet salads and sandwiches, to a carbalicious lobster mac and cheese.

Weekend brunch is especially popular (head in before 11am).

WILD HONEY · CAFE $$

Map p216 (www.wildhoney.com.sg; 03-02 Mandarin Gallery, 333A Orchard Rd; breakfast $12-24; ☺9am-9pm, to 10pm Fri & Sat; ☏; ⓂSomerset) Paging Tribeca with its faux brickwork and exposed plumbing, Wild Honey peddles scrumptious, all-day breakfasts from around the world, from the tofu-laced Californian to the *shakshouka*-spiced Tunisian. Other options include muffins and cakes, gourmet sandwiches and freshly roasted coffee. Get there before 9.30am on weekends or prepare to wait. You'll find a second, larger branch inside Scotts Square mall, just off Orchard Rd.

DIN TAI FUNG · CHINESE $$

Map p216 (www.dintaifung.com.sg; B1-03/06 Paragon, 290 Orchard Rd; buns from $1.20, dumplings from $7.30; ☺10am-11pm; ⓂSomerset) This outlet of the prolific Taiwanese chain was the first to open in Singapore. Years later, its mere mention still leaves dumpling diehards in a drooling mess. Scan the menu and tick your choices, which should include the cult-status *xiao long bao* (soup dumplings) and the shrimp and pork wonton soup. The free-flow jasmine tea is a welcome touch.

★IGGY'S · INTERNATIONAL $$$

Map p216 (☑6732 2234; www.iggys.com.sg; Level 3, Hilton Hotel, 581 Orchard Rd; 3-course lunch $85, set dinner menus $195-275; ☺noon-1.30pm Mon-Fri & 7-9.30pm Mon-Sat; ☏; ⓂOrchard) Iggy's dark, luxe design promises something special, and head chef Akmal Anuar delivers with his arresting Italo-Japanese creations. As beautiful to look at as they are to eat, you might see burrata cheese paired with ginger, or soft angel-hair pasta set off against crunchy sakura prawns. Mere mortals don't eat like this every day, so treat yourself.

BUONA TERRA · ITALIAN $$$

Map p216 (☑6733 0209; www.scotts29.com/buonaterra; 29 Scotts Rd; 3/4/5/6 courses $88/108/128/148; ☺6-10.15pm Mon-Sat; ⓂNewton) You'll find no more than 10 linen-lined tables at this good-looking Italian. In the kitchen, young Lombard chef Denis Lucchi turns exceptional ingredients into elegant, modern dishes like house-made pappardelle pasta with wagyu short ribs, morel and Fontina cream. Lucchi's right-hand man is Emilian sommelier Gabriele Rizzardi, whose wine list, though expensive, is extraordinary; the Feudi del Pisciotto's 2011 L'eterno Pinot Noir blew us away. Always book ahead on Fridays and Saturdays.

STRAITSKITCHEN · HAWKER CENTRE $$$

Map p216 (☑6738 1234; www.singapore.grand.hyattrestaurants.com/straitskitchen; Grand Hyatt, 10 Scotts Rd; buffet lunch/dinner $45/55; ☺noon-2.30pm & 6.30-10.30pm Mon-Fri, 12.30-3pm & 6.30-10.30pm Sat & Sun; ⓂOrchard) The hawker centre goes glam at the Grand Hyatt's highly regarded buffet, as popular with locals as it is with out-of-towners. It's a perfect introduction to the region's classic dishes, from satay, laksa and *char kway teow*, to *rendang* and *murtabak*. Come early and with an empty stomach to get value for money, and stick to the drinks included in the price (add-ons can be exorbitant).

It's a good idea to book ahead if heading in for dinner later in the week.

🍺 DRINKING & NIGHTLIFE

Shopping is thirsty work. Thankfully, there's a string of places on or near Orchard Rd in which to refuel. You won't find bargain beer prices (with one

DRINKS ON THE HILL

Car-free Emerald Hill Rd offers a refreshing antidote to Orchard Rd's megamalls and chains. Its cluster of bars – housed in century-old Peranakan shophouses – are popular with the after-work crowd, who kick back with beers and vino at atmospheric, alfresco tables until 10pm, when revellers are obliged to head inside to appease the neighbours.

While we love **Que Pasa** (Map p216; www.quepasa.com.sg; 7 Emerald Hill Rd; ⊙1.30pm-2am Mon-Thu, to 3am Fri & Sat, 5.30pm-2am Sun; MSomerset) for its Iberian vibe, tapas and wine list, top billing goes to neon-pimped **Ice Cold Beer** (Map p216; 9 Emerald Hill Rd; ⊙5pm-2am Sun-Thu, to 3am Fri & Sat; MSomerset), a raucous, boozy dive bar with dart boards, pool table, and tongue-in-cheek soft-core pin-ups on the wall. It's a come-as-you-are kind of place where you don't have to be 20- or 30-something to have a rocking good time. Happy-hour deals run from 5pm to 9pm, and it's especially kicking on Friday nights.

notable exception), but you will find cool cafes and some good happy-hour deals. Of course, you can always grab a cheap beer at many of the shopping mall food courts.

NÉKTAR   BAR

Map p216 (nektar.com.sg; 31 Scotts Rd; ⊙5pm-1am Mon-Fri, to 2am Sat; MNewton) Think Néktar and think well-crafted cocktails in an intimate, colonial setting. Sink into a wicker chair on the back patio with a Cointreau-spiked, bitter chocolate martini. Admittedly, the drinks are pricier than at many comparable venues, but the romantic setting makes for a blissful escape from Orchard Rd's overstimulation.

Beers include a few obscure options, and you're welcome to order food from the Songs of India restaurant next door.

BAR CANARY   BAR

Map p216 (www.parkhotelgroup.com/orchard/dining/bar-canary; Park Hotel Orchard, 270 Orchard Rd; ⊙noon-1am Sun-Thu, to 2am Fri & Sat; MSomerset) Canary yellow sofas, tropical foliage and the evening sound of humming traffic and screeching birds – alfresco Bar Canary hovers high above the Orchard Rd madness. It's a chic, moody spot for an evening tipple, with attentive staff and well-positioned fans. Book six weeks ahead for its legendary Wednesday Ladies' Night deal: $35 for free-flow Veuve from 7.30pm to 9pm, followed by half-priced drinks all night. Entry is on Bideford Rd.

KPO   BAR

Map p216 (www.imaginings.com.sg; 1 Killiney Rd; ⊙4pm-1am Mon-Thu, to 2am Fri, 6pm-2am Sat; MSomerset) It may no longer be such a see-

and-be-seen place, but KPO remains a solid spot to kick back with a beer, especially on the rooftop terrace. It's a contemporary, tropical space, with concrete walls, timber detailing and no shortage of greenery. It's also the only bar in town with an attached post office.

Prices are reasonable for Orchard Rd; among the better options is the chicken *karaage* (Japanese-style deep fried).

CUSCADEN PATIO   BAR

Map p216 (B1-11 Ming Arcade, 21 Cuscaden Rd; ⊙3pm-1am Mon, Wed & Thu, to 2am Tue, to 3am Fri & Sat; MOrchard) This rundown basement bar with a small, open-air patio shouldn't be any good, but extra-friendly staff and extra-cheap drinks ensure it's as popular as any of the shiny bars around Orchard Rd. Cut-price beer deals mean you can sink a mug of San Miguel for as little as $5.90. On Tuesday nights, jugs of beer are yours for $13. Bargain. Soak up the savings with a serve of the disturbingly good chicken wings.

TWG TEA   CAFE

Map p216 (www.twgtea.com; 02-21 ION Orchard, 2 Orchard Turn; ⊙10am-10pm; MOrchard) Posh tea purveyor TWG peddles over 800 single-estate teas and blends from around the world, from English Breakfast to Rolls Royce varieties like Da Hong Pao from Fujian. Savour the flavour with a few tea-infused macaroons – the *bain de roses* is divine. There's a second outlet one floor down.

BAR ON 5   BAR

Map p216 (Mandarin Orchard, 333 Orchard Rd; ⊙11am-1am Sun-Thu, to 2am Fri & Sat; MSomerset) This slinky hotel bar has one of the best happy-hour deals in town: smooth, well-crafted martinis for under $10. Purists should forego the flavoured versions on the menu and request a classic dry instead. Drink specials 5pm to 9pm, accompanied by a largely middle-management crowd and eclectic tunes spanning ABBA to Rihanna.

🛍 SHOPPING

ION ORCHARD MALL   MALL

Map p216 (www.ionorchard.com; 2 Orchard Turn; ⊙10am-10pm; Ⓜ Orchard) Futuristic ION is the cream of Orchard Rd malls. Rising above Orchard MRT Station, its floors are busy without feeling packed. Basement floors focus on high-street labels like Zara and Uniqlo, while upper floor tenants read like the index of *Vogue*. Dining options span food-court bites to posher nosh, and the attached 56-storey tower offers a top-floor viewing gallery, **ION Sky** (www.ionsky.com.sg; ticket counter level 4; adult/child $16/8; ⊙10am-noon & 2-8pm).

PARAGON   MALL

Map p216 (www.paragon.com.sg; 290 Orchard Rd; ⊙10am-9pm; Ⓜ Somerset) Even if you don't have a Gold Amex, strike a pose inside this Maserati of Orchard Rd malls. Status labels include Burberry, Hermès, Jimmy Choo, and Singapore's own **Raoul** (www.raoul.com; 02-49 Paragon; ⊙10am-9pm), which offers sharp, detailed men's threads and crisp, invigorating womenswear, from classic cropped trousers to sassy cocktail frocks. High-street brands include Banana Republic, G-Star Raw and Miss Selfridge.

TANGLIN SHOPPING CENTRE   MALL

Map p216 (www.tanglinsc.com; 19 Tanglin Rd; ⊙9.30am-9pm; Ⓜ Orchard) A one-of-a-kind for the Orchard Rd area, this retro mall specialises in Asian art and is *the* place to come for quality rugs, carvings, ornaments, jewellery, paintings, furniture and the like. Top billing goes to **Antiques of the Orient** (www.aoto.com.sg; 02-40 Tanglin Shopping Centre; ⊙10am-6pm Mon-Sat, 11am-4pm Sun), a veritable treasure chest of original and reproduction prints, photographs and maps of Singapore and Asia. Especially beautiful are the richly hued botanical drawings commissioned by British colonist William Farquhar.

ROBINSONS   DEPARTMENT STORE

Map p216 (www.robinsons.com.sg; 260 Orchard Rd; ⊙10.30am-10pm; Ⓜ Somerset) Robinsons' arresting, light-filled flagship should be high on any fashionista's hit list. The department store's fashion edits are sharp and inspired, pairing well-known It labels like Chloe, Coach and Dior with lesser-known cognoscenti brands such as South Korea's Brownbreath, Denmark's Vito and Italy's MSGM. Clothes and kicks aside, you'll find anything from Claus Porto soaps to classic Danish design.

RECKLESS SHOP   FASHION

Map p216 (www.recklessericka.com; 02-08/09 Orchard Central, 181 Orchard Rd; ⊙11am-9.30pm; Ⓜ Somerset) Young, talented local designer Afton Chan thrills fashion fiends with her highly creative, affordable creations. There are three labels. Entry-level Odds focuses on street-chic womenswear, while midrange Still delivers svelte, professional pieces for working women. Most impressive, however, is main label Reckless Ericka, which melds classic tailoring with fantastical, fashion-forward aesthetics inspired by themes as diverse as photography and Japanese anime.

ON PEDDER   SHOES, ACCESSORIES

Map p216 (www.onpedder.com; Scotts Square, 6 Scotts Rd; ⊙10am-10pm; Ⓜ Orchard) Even if you're not in the market for high-end heels and bags, On Pedder thrills with its creative, whimsical items. The store hand picks only the most unique pieces from leading designers, whether it's ice-cream-cone stilettos from Charlotte Olympia, or embroided, book-shaped clutches from Olympia Le-Tan. Accessories include statement jewellery fit for a modern gallery.

There's a second branch at **Ngee Ann City** (Map p216; ☑6835 1307; 02-12 P/Q, Ngee Ann City, 391 Orchard Rd; ⊙10am-9.30pm; Ⓜ Orchard).

ROCKSTAR   FASHION

Map p216 (www.rockstarsingapore.blogspot.com. au; 22 Orchard Rd; ⊙11.30am-9.30pm; Ⓜ Dhoby Ghaut) You'll find both major and independent labels at Rockstar, well-known for its fun, youthful showcase of threads, shoes and accessories. Men's items span quirky shirts to statement espadrilles, with the bigger women's collection ranging from whimsical party frocks and little black dresses, to statement swimwear, candy-coloured sneakers and detail-focussed jewellery. There's a second branch at **Cathay Cineleisure** (Map p216; 03-08, Cathay Cineleisure Orchard, 8 Grange Rd; ⊙noon-10pm; Ⓜ Somerset).

POST-SHOP PAMPERING
....

When the relentless crowds, hulking bags, and buyers' remorse get too much, de-stress at one of the area's top pampering retreats. High-end spas recommend book-ing a few day in advance, though it's always worth trying your luck if you're already in the area.

➡ For cheap(ish) and cheerful, head straight to **Tomi Foot Reflexology** (Map p216; B1-114, Lucky Plaza, 304 Orchard Rd; 30min foot reflexology $30; ⊗10am-10pm; Ⓜ Orchard), in the basement of '80s throwback mall Lucky Plaza. Yes, that's Sting in the photo; even he knows just how good these acupressure rubs can be.

➡ Up several notches is **Spa Esprit** (Map p216; www.spa-esprit.com; 05-10, Paragon, 290 Orchard Rd; 1hr massage from $118; ⊗10am-9pm; Ⓜ Somerset), a hip apothecary-cum-spa inside Paragon. Freshly picked ingredients and CPTG (Certified Pure Therapeutic Grade) essential oils feature in treatments like the sublime Back to Balance body massage (90 minutes, $235).

➡ Around the corner from Orchard Rd at the St Regis Hotel, **Remède Spa** (Map p216; ☑6506 6896; www.remedespasingapore.com; St Regis Hotel, 29 Tanglin Rd; 1hr massage from $180; ⊗9am-10pm; Ⓜ Orchard) is reputed to have the best masseuses in town. The Wet Lounge – a marbled wonderland of steam room, sauna, ice foun-tains and jacuzzis – makes for a perfect prelude to standout treatments like the 90-minute Warm Jade Stone Massage ($290).

➡ Ladies who lunch swear by the facials at the Grand Hyatt's **Damai Spa** (Map p216; ☑6416 7156; www.singapore.grand.hyatt.com/hyatt/pure/spas; Grand Hyatt, 10 Scotts Rd; 1hr facial from $160, 1hr massage from $150; ⊗10am-10pm; Ⓜ Orchard). Choose from custom treatments based on skin type (60 minutes, $160), the sig-nature Damai Orchid Facial (90 minutes, $220), or celebrity-standard anti-aging options using high-tech serums and oxygen (60 minutes from $240).

NGEE ANN CITY　　　　MALL

Map p216 (www.ngeeanncity.com.sg; 391 Orchard Rd; ⊗10am-9.30pm; Ⓜ Orchard) It might look like a foreboding mausoleum, but this mar-ble-and-granite behemoth promises retail giddiness on its seven floors of stores. Inter-national luxury brands compete for space with bookworm-nirvana **Kinokuniya** (www.kinokuniya.com.sg; 03-10/15 Ngee Ann City; ⊗10am-9.30pm) (southeast Asia's second-largest bookstore) and the Japanese depart-ment store **Takashimaya** (www.takashimaya-sin.com; Ngee Ann City; ⊗10am-9.30pm), home to Takashimaya Food Village, one of the strip's best food courts.

WISMA ATRIA　　　　MALL

Map p216 (www.wismaonline.com; 435 Orchard Rd; ⊗10am-10pm; Ⓜ Orchard) With close to 100 stores over five floors, Wisma Atria's notables include Singapore's flagship stores for Coach and TAG Heuer, and a sprawling branch of Japanese department store Isetan. Cool hunters shop at **i.t** (www.itlabels.com.sg; 435 Orchard Rd, 03-15, Wisma Atria; ⊗10.30am-10pm), a Hong Kong concept store stocking high-end, avant-garde street-wear labels for women and men. Excellent food options in-clude Food Republic (p97) and a branch of Din Tai Fung.

The mall is linked via underground walkway to ION Orchard shopping mall and, in turn, Orchard MRT station.

313@SOMERSET　　　　MALL

Map p216 (www.313somerset.com.sg; 313 Or-chard Rd; Ⓜ Somerset) Right above Somerset MRT, young and vibrant 313 Somerset de-livers affordable, popular fashion and life-style brands, including Uniqlo, Zara, Cotton On, Aldo and Muji. It's also home to ever-busy Apple shop, EpiCentre, as well as cafes and restaurants.

WHEELOCK PLACE　　　　MALL

Map p216 (www.wheelockplace.com; 501 Orchard Rd; ⊗10am-10pm; Ⓜ Orchard) Linked to ION Orchard and the MRT by an underground walkway, Wheelock Place is more than just spas and laser clinics. Dapper gents head to **Benjamin Barker** (www.benjaminbarker.com.au; 02-11 Wheelock Place; ⊗11am-9.30pm) for sharp shirts, suits and accessories, while fellow Melbourne brand **Crumpler** (02-06, Wheelock Place; ⊗10.30am-9pm) is known globally for its funky, durable laptop, courier

MALL GUIDE 101

Which malls should you raid? That depends on what you're looking for. Scan the following quick-glance guide for an overview of which malls are best for you.

SHOPPING FOCUS	BEST MALLS
High-End Fashion	ION Orchard, Hilton Shopping Gallery, Paragon, Ngee Ann City, **Mandarin Gallery** (Map p216; www.mandaringallery.com.sg; 333A Orchard Rd; ☏; ⓂSomerset, Orchard)
High-Street Fashion	313@Somerset, ION Orchard, Wisma Atria
Youth Fashion	**Cathay Cineleisure Orchard** (Map p216; www.cineleisure.com.sg; 8 Grange Rd; ⓂSomerset), **The Cathay** (Map p216; 2 Handy Rd; ⓂDhoby Ghaut), **313@Somerset, Orchard Central** (Map p216; www.orchardcentral.com.sg; cnr Orchard & Killiney Rds; ◷11am-11pm; ⓂSomerset), **Far East Shopping Centre** (Map p216; 545 Orchard Rd; ⓂOrchard)
Kidswear	Forum, Paragon
Shoes	**Scotts Square** (Map p216; 6 Scotts Rd), Wisma Atria, **Far East Plaza** (Map p216; www.fareast-plaza.com; 14 Scotts Rd; ◷10am-10pm; ⓂOrchard)
Beauty & Grooming	Ngee Ann City, ION Orchard
Jewellery & Watches	ION Orchard, Mandarin Gallery, Wisma Atria, Paragon
Antiques, Crafts & Furnishings	Tanglin Shopping Centre, **Park Mall** (Map p216; 9 Penang Rd; ⓂDhoby Ghaut)
Books	Ngee Ann City

and travel bags. For edgy, asymmetrical threads for women, hit homegrown **Saturday** (B2-04, Wheelock Place; ◷10am-10pm).

PLAZA SINGAPURA
MALL

Map p216 (www.plazasingapura.com.sg; 68 Orchard Rd; ◷10am-10pm; ⓂDhoby Ghaut) Sprawling Plaza Singapura offers a slew of midrange options, among them British department store Marks & Spencer, New York grooming label Kiehl's, and playful Australian stationery store Smiggle. Dining options include a branch of legendary Hong Kong dumpling restaurant Tim Ho Wan (p96), while the cinema complex and string of toy and comic book stores are a hit with local teens.

HILTON SHOPPING GALLERY
MALL

Map p216 (www.hiltonshoppinggallery.com; 581 Orchard Rd; ◷10am-7.30pm Mon-Sat, 10.30am-6pm Sun; ⓂOrchard) Names, names, names, sweetie! This two-level concourse of aspiration reads like a VIP list at Paris Fashion Week. Drool, dream or drop a lot of coin at the likes of Rolex, Alexander Wang, Stella McCartney, Issey Miyake, Lanvin and 3.1 Phillip Lim.

FORUM
MALL

Map p216 (www.forumtheshoppingmall.com.sg; 583 Orchard Rd; ◷10am-10pm; ⓂOrchard) Peaceful, light-filled Forum eschews obvious brands for more discerning offerings. Women score playful, progressive pieces at **Tsumori Chisato** (www.tsumorichisato.com; 01-30-34 Forum), while guys and girls bag hip threads and footwear at **Club 21** (www.club-21global.com; 01-07/09 Forum; ◷10am-7.30pm Mon-Sat, to 6pm Sun). One floor up are designer kids' clothing and quality toys.

EXOTIC TATTOO
TATTOOS

Map p216 (☏6834 0558; www.exotictattoopiercing.com; 04-11, Far East Plaza, 14 Scotts Rd; ◷noon-8pm Mon-Sat, to 6pm Sun; ⓂOrchard) Visitors looking for a tattoo shop with a pedigree should know about this place: it's here that you can get exquisite work from Sumithra Debi (aka Su). One of the few female tattoo artists in Singapore, Sumithra is the granddaughter of Johnny Two-Thumbs, arguably Singapore's most legendary tattoo artist. In addition to ink work, the staff are deft at piercing.

Eastern Singapore

GEYLANG | KATONG/JOO CHIAT | EAST COAST PARK | CHANGI & PASIR RIS

Neighbourhood Top Five

❶ Riding a bicycle or rollerblading along **East Coast Park** (p106) before plonking yourself down to rest, watching the ships in the strait and soaking up the atmosphere.

❷ Eyeing-up the exuberant architectural candy of Katong's **Peranakan Terrace Houses** (p105), with their pastel-pretty exteriors and intricate stucco work.

❸ Tackling your own gastronomic walking tour around the numerous food joints in **Katong/Joo Chiat.**

❹ Delving into rich Peranakan culture at **Katong Antique House** (p106).

❺ Indulging in night-time white-pepper crab and people-watching at Geylang's iconic **No Signboard Seafood** (p108).

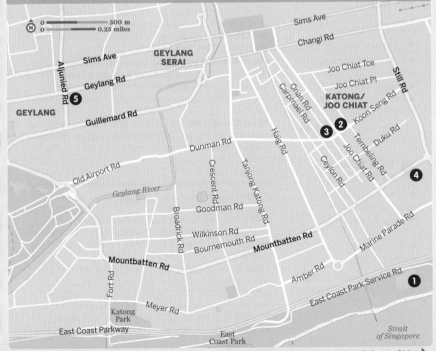

For more detail of this area see Map p213 and p214.

Lonely Planet's Top Tip

The problem with Katong and Geylang being culinary centres of Singapore is that restaurants can very quickly come and go. Find out about the latest and greatest with a web search for local food blogs.

Best Sights

➡ Changi Museum & Chapel (p106)

➡ Peranakan Terrace Houses (p105)

➡ Sri Senpaga Vinayagar Temple (p105)

➡ Katong Antique House (p106)

For reviews, see p105.➡

Best Places to Eat

➡ No Signboard Seafood (p108)

➡ Smokey's BBQ (p110)

➡ East Coast Lagoon Food Village (p110)

➡ Long Phuong (p110)

➡ Chin Mee Chin Confectionery (p108)

For reviews, see p108.➡

Best Places to Drink

➡ Sunset Bay Garden Beach Bar (p111)

➡ Coastal Settlement (p111)

➡ Coachman Inn (p107)

➡ Cider Pit (p111)

For reviews, see p111.➡

Explore Eastern Singapore

Though comprising a fair swath of the island, the neighbourhoods of the east receive far less attention from tourists than do those of the city centre. It's a shame, really, because these neighbourhoods are vibrant, alive and, on the whole, more reflective of Singapore culture. Closest to the city is the Geylang district, at once notorious as a red-light district, yet spiritual with myriad temples and mosques. The staggering amount of food outlets here is also a big draw.

Further east is Katong (also known as Joo Chiat), a picturesque neighbourhood of restored multicoloured shophouses that in recent years has come into its own as the spiritual heartland of Singapore's Peranakan people. Bordering Katong, and stretching for several kilometres along the seafront from the city right up to Tanah Merah, is East Coast Park.

Don't discount a visit to Changi and Pasir Ris, the city's easternmost regions. Here's where you'll find the moving Changi Museum and Chapel, a water theme park for kids, and the launching point for bumboats to the bucolic, bike-friendly oasis that is Pulau Ubin.

Local Life

➡**Food where it counts** Katong is Singapore's culinary heart, with everything from Singaporean laksa, to Vietnamese, Mexican, even American barbecue. Locals also raise their chopsticks in Geylang, a neighbourhood famed for its frog porridge.

➡**People watching people** Locals flock to Geylang for its fantastic food, true, but just as many go there to gawk at the sex workers trawling the streets. A swirl of neon and screaming scooters, it's Singapore's wilder side.

➡**East Coast Park** This is the East Coasters' communal backyard. Join them for beachside barbecues, cycling, sea sports and (more) great grub under the coconut palms.

Getting There & Away

➡**MRT** The east isn't well served by the MRT. Aljunied is Geylang's closest station; Paya Lebar and Eunos take you to the north end of Joo Chiat. Pasir Ris has its own station.

➡**Bus** Buses 33 and 16 go to the centre of Joo Chiat, passing through Geylang; 14 goes from Orchard Rd to East Coast Rd. Bus 12 goes to East Coast Rd from Victoria St; bus 36 gets there from Bras Basah Rd. Bus 2 from Tanah Merah MRT goes to Changi Village.

➡**Taxi** Best for East Coast Park.

◉ SIGHTS

◉ Geylang

AMITABHA BUDDHIST CENTRE
BUDDHIST CENTRE

(☑6745 8547; www.fpmtabc.org; 44 Lorong 25A; ☺10.30am-6pm Tue-Sun; Ⓜ Aljunied) Seek inner peace at this seven-storey Tibetan Buddhist centre, which holds classes on dharma and meditation (check its website for the schedule), as well as events during religious festivals. The upstairs meditation hall, swathed in red-and-gold cloth, is open to the public and filled with beautiful statues and other objects of devotion. If you're after prayer flags, spinning wheels and other spiritual items, you'll find them in the store on level 4.

PU JI SI BUDDHIST RESEARCH CENTRE
BUDDHIST CENTRE

(☑6746 6211; www.pujisi.org.sg; 39, Lorong 12; Ⓜ Aljunied) Part educational facility, part house of worship, this five-storey spiritual sanctuary includes meditation halls, a Buddhist library, and a seemingly endless well of serenity. Take the elevator up for a seat by the wishing fountain in the rooftop garden and ponder the eternal.

◉ Katong/Joo Chiat

PERANAKAN TERRACE HOUSES
NOTABLE BUILDINGS

Map p214 (Koon Seng Rd & Joo Chiat Pl; ☐16, 33, Ⓜ Eunos) Just off Joo Chiat Rd, these two streets feature Singapore's most extraordinary Peranakan terrace houses, joyously decorated with stucco dragons, birds, crabs and brilliantly glazed tiles. *Pintu pagar* (swinging doors) at the front of the houses are another typical feature, allowing cross breezes while retaining privacy. After falling into disrepair in the 1980s, the government designated them heritage buildings, heralding restoration work and skyrocketing their value to around $2.5 million each.

SRI SENPAGA VINAYAGAR TEMPLE
TEMPLE

Map p214 (19 Ceylon Rd; ☺6.30am-1.30pm & 6.30-9pm; ☐10, 12, 14, 32, 40) Easily among the most beautiful Hindu temples in Singapore, Sri Senpaga Vinayagar's interior is adorned with wonderfully colourful devotional art, all labelled in various languages. Another feature is the temple's *kamala paatham,* a specially sculptured granite footstone found in certain ancient Hindu temples. Topping it all off, literally, is the roof of the inner sanctum sanctorum, lavishly covered in gold.

GEYLANG: RED LIGHTS, SACRED SITES

All those nasty rumours about Geylang being an open-air meat market packed with brothels, girly bars, dubious hotels and alley after alley lined with prostitutes from all over Southeast Asia are absolutely true. Pound its pavements at night and it's easy to think you're on the heady streets of Bangkok's Patpong.

Yet strange as it may seem, Geylang is also one of the Lion City's spiritual hubs, with huge temples and mosques, and picturesque alleys dotted with religious schools, shrines and temples. A daytime stroll through the *lorongs* (alleys) that run north to south between Sims Ave and Geylang Rd offers unexpected charm for those who take the time to look.

Several fetching side streets well worth checking out include tree-lined **Lorong 27**, a small street chock-a-block with colourful shrines and temples. Chanting is a common sound on **Lorong 24A** – many of its renovated shophouses are home to smaller Buddhist associations. Gorgeous **Lorong 34** boasts both restored and unrestored shophouses painted in varying hues, as well as a number of colourful shrines and braziers for burning incense.

Geylang's other blessing is its food scene. Both Geylang Rd and Sims Ave heave with cheap, tasty, unceremonious local eateries, so round off your wander with the sort of local steam your mother would approve of.

Take an MRT to Aljunied station and head south along Aljunied Rd. Once you get to Geylang Rd, head either east or west. All the *lorongs* snake out from Geylang Rd.

KATONG ANTIQUE HOUSE — MUSEUM

Map p214 (☑6345 8544; 208 East Coast Rd; ☺11am-6.30pm by appointment only; ☐10, 12, 14, 32, 40) Part shop, part museum, the Katong Antique House is a labour of love for owner Peter Wee, a fourth-generation Baba Peranakan. A noted expert on Peranakan history and culture, Peter will happily regale you with tales as you browse an intriguing collection of Peranakan antiques, artefacts and other objets d'art. By appointment only, though it's sometimes open to the public (try your luck).

GEYLANG SERAI NEW MARKET — MARKET

Map p214 (1 Geylang Serai; ☺8am-10pm, individual stalls vary; ⓜPaya Lebar) Suitably inspired by *kampong* (village) architecture, this bustling market lies at the heart of Singapore's Malay community. The 1st floor is crammed with stalls selling everything from tropical fruits to Malay CDs, fabrics and skullcaps. Upstairs lies the popular hawker centre. Lined with great Malay and Indian stalls, it's a good spot for a fix of *pisang goreng* (banana fritters) and *bandung* (milk with rose cordial syrup).

◉ East Coast Park

EAST COAST PARK — PARK

This 15km stretch of seafront park is where Singaporeans come to swim, windsurf, wakeboard, kayak, picnic, bicycle, rollerblade, skateboard, and, of course, eat. You'll find swaying coconut palms, patches of bushland, a lagoon, sea sports clubs, and some excellent eateries.

Renting a bike from kiosks like **CycleMax** (Map p214; www.facebook.com/cyclemax.sg; 01-03, 1018 East Coast Parkway; 2hr bike hire $6; ☺9am-9pm Mon-Fri, to 10pm Sat, 8am-9pm Sun), enjoying the sea breezes, watching the veritable city of container ships out in the strait, and capping it all off with a beachfront meal is one of the most pleasant ways to spend a Singapore afternoon.

East Coast Park starts at the end of Tanjong Katong Rd in Katong and ends at the National Sailing Centre in Bedok, which is actually closer to the Tanah Merah MRT station. It's connected to Changi Beach Park by the Coastal Park Connector Network (PCN), an 8km park connector running along Changi Coast Rd, beside the airport

---

◉ TOP SIGHT
CHANGI MUSEUM & CHAPEL

Although shifted from the original Changi Prison site in 2001, the Changi Museum and Chapel remains a powerful ode to the WWII Allied POWs who suffered horrifically at the hands of the invading Japanese. Stories are told through photographs, letters, drawings and other fascinating artefacts. The tattered shoes of a civilian prisoner prove unexpectedly moving, while a tiny Morse code transmitter hidden inside a matchbox is a testament to the prisoners' ingenuity.

The museum is home to full-sized replicas of the famous Changi Murals painted by POW Stanley in the old POW hospital, the originals of which are off limits in Block 151 of the nearby Changi Army Camp. The museum's centrepiece is a replica of the original Changi Chapel built by inmates as a focus for worship and as a sign of solidarity. Tucked into the walls behind the altar, its cross made of ammunition casings, are mementos left by visitors – white crosses, red poppies, handwritten notes and colourful paper cranes.

Bus 2 from Victoria St or Tanah Merah MRT will take you past the museum on its way to Changi Village. Alight at bus stop 97201, also labelled 'opp. Changi Chapel Museum'.

DON'T MISS
➡ Audio guide
➡ Historic artefacts
➡ Changi Murals
➡ Replica chapel

PRACTICALITIES
➡ Map p213
➡ ☑6214 2451
➡ www.changimuseum. com
➡ 1000 Upper Changi Rd N
➡ admission free, audio guide adult/child $8/4, guided tour $12/8
➡ ☺9.30am-5pm, last entry 4.30pm

WORTH A DETOUR

FAR EAST: CHANGI VILLAGE

On the far northeast coast, **Changi Village** (Map p213; 🚌2, then Ⓜ Tanah Merah) is a refreshing escape from the hubbub of the city. A wander around the area offers a window into a more relaxed side of Singapore, where vests, bermuda shorts and flip-flops (the quintessential heartlander uniform) is the look, and people are slightly less accustomed to seeing *ang moh* (Europeans) in their midst. The atmosphere is almost villagelike, and a browse around the area will turn up cheap clothes, batik, Indian textiles and electronics.

Getting here is relatively easy. You can catch the East–West MRT to Tanah Merah station, from where bus 2 will whisk you right into the heart of Changi Village, passing en route interesting old black-and-white colonial bungalows along Loyang Ave before terminating beside the lively, renowned Changi Village Hawker Centre (p111).

Alternatively, grab a bike from one of the rental kiosks in East Coast Park and pedal the flat, 18km route, which will take you east through tranquil coastal parkland, north along Changi Coast Rd (heaven for plane spotters), and finally west along Changi Beach, where thousands of Singaporean civilians were executed during WWII.

Changi Beach is lapped by the polluted waters of the Strait of Johor and lousy for swimming, but there's a good stretch of sand for a romantic stroll. It's popular for weekend picnics and barbecues, but almost deserted during the week.

Next to the bus terminal and just up from Changi Beach is the Changi Point Ferry Terminal (p183), where you can catch bumboats to nostalgic Pulau Ubin – Singapore's most outstanding day trip. Just beyond the ferry terminal is the starting point of the Changi Point Coastal Walk, a relaxing, 2.2km-long boardwalk that straddles mangroves, a sandy beach, and the verdant grounds of government holiday villas.

The walk leads to the private Changi Sailing Club, whose public restaurant-bar **Coachman Inn** (Map p213; www.csc.org.sg; 32 Netheravon Rd, Changi Sailing Club; ⊘10am-10pm) is a wonderful spot to polish off a couple of beers while gazing out at bobbing yachts and Pulau Ubin. From the sailing club, it's an easy 750m up Netheravon Rd to the Coastal Settlement (p111) and its great coffee, food and lush garden locale.

If riding, a return trip from CycleMax in East Coast Park to Changi Village, with a lazy lunch thrown in, will take around four hours.

---

runway. At the western end of the park, the bicycle track continues right through to Katong, ending at the Kallang River.

On weekends only, bus 401 from Bedok Bus Interchange, outside Bedok MRT, takes you directly to East Coast Park. On weekdays, take bus 197 from Bedok and stop along Marine Pde Rd (ask the bus driver where to get off). Walk 250m south to an underpass, which will take you into the park.

⊙ Changi & Pasir Ris

PASIR RIS PARK   PARK
Map p213 (Pasir Ris Dr 3; Ⓜ Pasir Ris) Stretching along a couple of kilometres of the northeast coast, a short walk from Pasir Ris MRT station, this peaceful, 71-hectare waterside park has no shortage of family-friendly activities. Rent a bike or in-line skates to get around, or hoof it and explore the 6-hectare

mangrove boardwalk – go during low tide to see little crabs scurrying in the mud. Speaking of hooves, kids will love the pony rides at **Gallop Stables** (Map p213; ✆6583 9665; www.gallopstable.com; 61 Pasir Ris Green; 20min ride $45; ⊘9.30-11.30am & 2.30-6.30pm Tue-Sun), which need to be booked ahead.

Flanking the eastern side of the park, **Downtown East** (Map p213; www.downtowneast.com.sg; cnr Pasir Ris Dr 3 & Pasir Ris Close; ⊘10am-10pm; Ⓜ Pasir Ris) mall is a handy spot to grab a bite. Alternatively, look out for the several bars within the park.

LOYANG TUA PEK KONG TEMPLE   TEMPLE
Map p213 (20 Loyang Way; Ⓜ Bedok, then 🚌9) Adorned with large wooden carvings, swirling dragons, and hundreds of colourful effigies of deities, gods and saints, this modern temple embodies the Singaporean approach to spirituality, hosting three religions – Hinduism, Buddhism and Taoism – under one

vast roof. There's even a shrine devoted to Datuk Kung, a saint of Malay mysticism and Chinese Taoist practices. Off the beaten path, it's worth the trip if you're en route to Changi Village. Get off bus 9 at the Loyang Valley condominium and walk in.

✖ EATING

Eastern Singapore is not only rich in history, culture and architecture, it's home to some exceptional food, from the multicultural delights of Katong/ Joo Chiat to the superb seafood along East Coast Park. Hardier souls might brave the nightly, never-sleeping sleaze of Geylang, where some great food lurks among the prostitutes and punters. Look out for durian stalls along the way.

✖ Geylang

SHI SHENG FROG PORRIDGE   CHINESE $
(235 Geylang Rd; ⊙11.45am-3.45am; ☐2, 51, ⓂKallang) Although its numerous competitors are catching up in the popularity stakes, this hawker-style classic remains *the* place to tuck into classic frog porridge. The Cantonese-style porridge is beautifully smooth and gooey, and the trademark *kung bao* sauce is richly flavoured and available in three levels of spiciness. Best of all, only live frogs are used here, ensuring meat that's always super fresh.

126 EATING HOUSE   CHINESE $
(126 Sims Ave; dishes $3-15; ⊙24hr; ☐2, ⓂAljunied) Plastic stools, '70s wall tiles and thumping beats from the girlie bar next door: this round-the-clock classic is the quintessential Geylang experience. While the menu can be a little hit and miss, solid choices include the dumplings, cuttlefish sambal prawns, braised pork belly, and a delicious *otak-otak* (grilled fish cake) that's chunkier than the usual paste-like version.

ROCHOR BEANCURD   DESSERT $
(745 Geylang Rd; dough sticks $1, bean curd from $1.20; ⊙24hr; ✐; ⓂPaya Lebar) End on a sweet note at Rochor Beancurd, a tiny bolt-hole with an epic reputation. People head here from all over the city for a bowl of its obscenely fresh, silky beancurd (opt for it warm). Order a side of deep-fried dough

sticks and dip to your heart's content. Oh, and did we mention the egg tarts?

★NO SIGNBOARD SEAFOOD   SEAFOOD $$
(www.nosignboardseafood.com; 414 Geylang Rd; dishes from $15, crab per kg around $60; ⊙noon-1am; ⓂAljunied) Madam Ong Kim Hoi famously started out with an unnamed hawker stall (hence 'No Signboard'), but the popularity of her seafood made her a rich woman, with six restaurants and counting. Principally famous for its white-pepper crab, No Signboard also dishes up delightful lobster, abalone and less familiar dishes such as bullfrog.

Other Singapore branches are at East Coast Seafood Centre, Esplanade – Theatres on the Bay, and VivoCity.

✖ Katong/Joo Chiat

CHIN MEE CHIN CONFECTIONERY   BAKERY $
Map p214 (204 East Coast Rd; 2 pieces of kaya toast & coffee $3; ⊙8am-4.30pm Tue-Sun; ✐; ☐10, 12, 14, 32, 40) A nostalgia trip for many older Singaporeans, old-style bakeries like Chin Mee Chin are a dying breed, with their geometric floors, wooden chairs and industrious aunties pouring suckerpunch *kopi* (coffee). One of the few Singaporean breakfast joints that still makes its own *kaya* (coconut jam), it's also a good spot to pick up some pastries to go.

MARINE PARADE FOOD CENTRE   HAWKER CENTRE $
Map p214 (Block 84, Marine Parade Central; dishes from $3; ⊙individual stalls vary; ☐15, 31, 36, 196, 197) You'll probably end up spending more time deciding what to eat than on the meal itself at this long-standing hawker centre. The star stall is **Mr Wong's Seremban Beef Noodles** (Map p214; stall 01-184; noodles from $3.50; ⊙noon-7pm), whose Malaysian-style dish of thick gravy, *bee hoon* noodles, sliced beef, salted vegetables and crunchy roasted peanuts is an intense, spicy-sour rush. Order the dry version and add a dash of chilli sauce for extra kick.

328 KATONG LAKSA   PERANAKAN $
Map p214 (www.328katonglaksa.com.sg; 51/53 East Coast Rd; laksa from $4.50; ⊙8am-10pm; ☐10, 14) Of the numerous laksa stalls along this stretch, this is arguably the best. The namesake dish is a bowl of thin rice noodles in a light curry broth made with coco-

nut milk and Vietnamese coriander, topped with shrimps and cockles, and served by gruff staff. Order a side of *otak-otak* and prepare to lick those lips.

There's another branch at 216/218 East Coast Rd.

PENNY UNIVERSITY
CAFE **$**

Map p214 (www.pennyuni.com; 402 East Coast Rd; dishes $4.50-15; ⊙8.30am-6pm Tue-Thu, to midnight Fri & Sat, to 9pm Sun; 🛜✏; 🚍10, 14, 155, 196) Coffee snobs will appreciate this buzzing, laid-back new-schooler, one of very few speciality coffee shops on the East Coast. Anchor yourself at a booth or at the communal table, sip a latte and scan the clipboard menu for fresh, modern grub like vanilla-infused Greek yoghurt with granola or fantastic Turkish eggs (poached eggs on whipped yoghurt, topped with spicy Moroccan harissa sauce and oregano).

Staff are friendly and there's a shelf with stylish reads like *Monocle* magazine.

TIAN TIAN CHICKEN RICE
CHINESE **$**

Map p214 (www.tiantianchickenrice.com; 443 Joo Chiat Rd; dishes from $4; ⊙10.30am-9.30pm Tue-Sun; 🚍16, 33) Fans of the original branch at Maxwell Rd will inevitably scoff and put it down, but this eastern outpost of Singapore's most famous Hainanese chicken rice stall is actually good – tender boiled chicken served over fragrant rice with the best chilli sauce around. Save room because you need to order the Hainanese pork chop too.

LE CHASSEUR
CHINESE **$**

Map p214 (Block 27, Eunos Rd 2; dishes from $5, claypot rice from $11; ⊙11.30am-3pm & 5.30-9.30pm; 🚇Eunos) Think you're in for escargot? Think again. Set inside an airy, super-local hawker centre, low-frills Le Chasseur is one of Singapore's best bets for claypot chicken rice. Their version has a beautiful smokiness, weight and texture, and no added MSG, preservatives or pigment. Claypot rice aside, other winners include crispy pork knuckle and succulent barbecue cuttlefish.

Exit the north side of Eunos MRT station, head north up Eunos Cres and turn left at Eunos Ave 5. Turn left on Eunos Rd 2 and the hawker centre is 80m to your right. Alternatively, cut straight through the Eunos Court housing complex on Eunos Cres.

112 KATONG
FOOD COURT **$**

Map p214 (www.112katong.com.sg; 112 East Coast Rd; hawker dishes $3-10; ⊙10am-10pm; 🚍10, 14, 16, 32, 40) The top floor of this contemporary mall is home to excellent food court chain Food Republic, where you can chow down hawker classics like *popiah* (spring rolls), *char kway teow* (stir-fried rice noodles) and fish ball soup in air-conditioned comfort. The mall is also home to an outlet of cult-status dumpling restaurant **Din Tai Fung** (Map p214; 112 East Coast Rd, Stall 01-04, 112 Katong; dumplings from $7.30), best known for its heavenly *xiao long bao* (soup dumplings).

EASTERN SINGAPORE EATING

LOCAL KNOWLEDGE

DURIAN: THE KING OF (SMELLY) FRUITS

Durians get a bad rap in Singapore. They're banned from pretty much all forms of public transport, most notably from the MRT, few hotels will allow you to bring one through their front doors, and any shopping mall worth its salt will enforce a 'no durians' policy. Why? It's simple: they stink. Even before the formidable thorn-covered husk is removed, they stink. And once you've opened it: poo-whee! And yet durians are still known throughout Southeast Asia as the King of Fruits (largely because of their enormous size and those crownlike thorns) and are still loved by so many Singaporeans that you really should give one a go. Aficionados say the flavour of the soft, mushy flesh is like custard with a hint of almond. Others are less complimentary.

Tucking into a durian is a sticky affair, usually best attempted beside an oversized paper bag, used to dispose of as much of the mess as possible. If the smell of durian lingers on your hands, try soaking your fingers in a glass of Coca-Cola: apparently it conquers the stench.

You can buy durians from markets and street stalls around Singapore, but if you're looking for somewhere to eat the thing too, drop into the flagship store of **Durian Culture** (www.durianculture.com; 77 Sims Ave; ⊙24hr; 🚍2, 13, 67, 🚇Kallang). Located in Geylang, its manager, Wei Sang (who can tell the quality of a durian from simply looking at it) will happily advise you on what to pick and how to eat it. Too easy.

★ SMOKEY'S BBQ
AMERICAN **$$**

Map p214 (☑6345 6914; www.smokeysbbq.com.sg; 73 Joo Chiat Pl; mains $17-35; ☺2-11.30pm Tue-Thu & Sun, to midnight Fri & Sat, food from 4.30pm; 🛜; ⓑ16, 33, ⓜEunos) You'll be dreaming of sweet home Alabama at this breezy, all-American barbecue legend. The Californian owner makes all the dry rubs using secret recipes and the meats are smoked using hickory woodchips straight from the USA. Start with the spicy buffalo wings (the blue-cheese dressing is insane), then stick to slow-roasted, smoked meats like ridiculously tender, fall-off-the-bone ribs.

Portions are typically huge, so come hungry, and skip the oily, handcut fries for the standard variety. Grub aside, you'll also find a solid selection of interesting beers and ciders. Book ahead for dinner on weekends.

LOWER EAST SIDE
MEXICAN **$$**

Map p214 (☑6348 1302; 19 East Coast Rd; quesadillas & burritos $10-15, three tacos $18; ☺noon-11pm; ⓑ10, 12, 14, 32, 40) Chairs hanging from the ceiling, recycled timber tables and sexy Latino beats: this cool, casual taco shack packs in a diverse crowd, all here for a little south-of-the-border action. Dig into flavour-packed tacos like the standout *tilapia* (fish fillet, tomato, onion, coriander, red peppers and caper berries) or opt for firm, juicy burritos. One-for-one happy-hour deals run until 8pm.

From Friday to Sunday, head in before 7pm for dinner or book ahead.

LONG PHUONG
VIETNAMESE **$$**

Map p214 (159 Joo Chiat Rd; dishes $6-22; ☺11am-11pm; ⓑ33, ⓜEunos) Yellow plastic chairs, easy-wipe tables and staff shouting out orders: down-to-earth Long Phuong serves up Singapore's best Vietnamese food. The *pho* (Vietnamese noodle soup) is simply gorgeous, its fragrant broth featuring just the right amount of sweetness. Beyond it is a mouthwatering choice of classics, including mango salad and a very popular *sò huyet xào sa te* (cockles with satay). Cash only.

ROLAND RESTAURANT
SEAFOOD **$$**

Map p214 (☑6440 8205; www.rolandrestaurant.com.sg; Block 89, 06-750 Marine Parade Central; dishes from $10, crab per kg around $60; ☺11.30am-2.15pm & 6-10.15pm; ⓑ15, 31, 36, 196, 197) According to Roland, it was his mum, Mrs Lim, who invented Singapore's iconic chilli crab back in the 1950s. Decades on, Roland has his own giant restaurant, with a chilli crab that lures former prime minister Goh Chok Tong on National Day. The crabs are fleshy and sweet and the gravy milder than many of its competitors: good news if you're not a big spice fan.

Kick start your meal with an order of the delicious steamed golden beancurd – tender beancurd filled with crab and shrimp paste and topped with salted egg yolk. The restaurant is tucked away at the top of a carpark.

ENG SENG RESTAURANT
SEAFOOD **$$**

Map p214 (247-249 Joo Chiat Pl; dishes from $15; ☺4.30-9pm Thu-Tue; ⓜEunos) The black-pepper crab is so good here that locals are (1) willing to queue over an hour to order and (2) happy to be rudely told how many crabs they can order by the proprietor. The sticky, honeylike peppery sauce makes it worth arriving at 4.30pm for an early dinner. Order a side of the stir-fried Chinese broccoli, which delivers satisfying crunch and flavour.

FATBOY'S THE BURGER BAR
AMERICAN **$$**

Map p214 (www.fatboys.sg; 465 Joo Chiat Rd; burgers $12-20; ☺4pm-midnight Mon-Thu, noon-midnight Fri-Sun; ⓑ10, 14, 16, 32, 40) Standouts at this top burger joint include the Royale with Cheese and the vegetarian Big Bello, a juicy combo of grilled portobello mushroom and peppers, pineapple, caramelised onions, Monterey Jack cheese and smoked chipotle sauce. You can customise your own burgers, and the malt shakes come in flavours like peanut butter, crushed Oreo and adults-only Kahlua or Baileys. Bliss.

✗ East Coast Park

EAST COAST LAGOON FOOD VILLAGE
HAWKER CENTRE **$**

Map p214 (1220 East Coast Parkway; dishes from $3; ☺8am-9pm; ⓑ10, 196) There are few hawker centres with a better location. Tramp barefoot off the beach and order up some satay, crab or the uniquely Singaporean *satay bee hoon* from **Meng Kee** at stall 17. Expect to queue. Cheap beer and wine (!) available.

LONG BEACH
SEAFOOD **$$$**

Map p214 (☑6445 8833; www.longbeachseafood.com.sg; East Coast Seafood Centre, 1018 East Coast Parkway; dishes $10-80; ☺11am-3pm & 5pm-midnight Sun-Fri, to 1am Sat; ⓑ401, 13, 16) This renowned nosh spot is famous across the island for its black-pepper crab. Order it with a side of the fried *yu-tiao* (deep-fried pastry) with minced crab meat and prawn, and some *sambal kang kong* (spicy water spinach).

✖ Changi & Pasir Ris

CHANGI VILLAGE HAWKER CENTRE
HAWKER CENTRE $

Map p213 (2 Changi Village Rd; dishes from $3; ⏱10.30am-11.30pm; Ⓜ️Tanah Merah, then 🚌2) This is the most Malay of Singapore's food centres, with locals heading here for one thing – the *nasi lemak* (fragrant coconut rice topped with fried chicken or fish, fried anchovies and sambal chilli). While food bloggers never cease arguing about which stall does it best, the original **International Nasi Lemak** (Stall 01-03; nasi lemak $3-4.50) gets the most loving.

End on a sweet note at **Mei Xiang Goreng Pisang** (Stall 01-51; snacks from $0.70; ⏱10am-9pm), famed for its beautifully crisp, golden banana fritters.

COASTAL SETTLEMENT
CAFE $$

Map p213 (📞6475 0200; www.thecoastalsettlement.com; 200 Netheravon Rd; mains $16-24, pizzas $21-23; ⏱10.30am-midnight Tue-Sun, last food order 9.30pm; 🚌29) In a black-and-white colonial bungalow on verdant grounds, this cafe-bar-restaurant hybrid is ideal for long, lazy idling. It's like a hipster op shop, packed with Modernist furniture, the odd Vespa and cabinets filled with retro gizmos. Solid food options cover most bases, from thin-crust pizzas and *rendang* (spicy coconut curry) to a lip-smacking wagyu beef 'Cheese Burger'. Vegetarian options, however, are few.

The fresh juices are delicious and the coffee top notch. Busy Friday to Sunday, it's otherwise a relatively quiet, peaceful oasis.

CHARLIE'S CORNER
INTERNATIONAL $$

Map p213 (01-70 Changi Village Hawker Centre, 2 Changi Village Rd; dishes $6-32; ⏱11.30am-midnight Tue-Sun; Ⓜ️Tanah Merah, then 🚌2) It may have moved stalls, but Charlie's remains an institution. There's an endless variety of beers, not to mention a long list of comfort standbys, including the celebrated fish and chips, chilli dog and moniker Charlie's Burger. The prices are a little high for a hawker-centre stall, but it's a handy spot if you're heading back from a day on Pulau Ubin.

🍷 DRINKING & NIGHTLIFE

CIDER PIT
BAR

Map p214 (382 Joo Chiat Rd; ⏱5pm-1am Mon-Fri, 1pm-1am Sat & Sun; 📶; 🚌16, 33) Wedged in a nondescript concrete structure, Cider Pit is easy to miss. Don't. The watering hole peddles a great range of ciders, including Pipsqueak Brothers (try its Toffee Apple) and speciality beers like Singapore's Jungle and Australia's Little Creatures. It's a low-frills, unfussed kind of place, ideal for an easy-going drinking session.

SUNSET BAY GARDEN BEACH BAR
BAR

Map p214 (Car Park F2, 1300 East Coast Park; ⏱5pm-midnight Mon-Thu, 5pm-1am Fri, 11am-1am Sat, 11am-midnight Sun; 🚌10, 13, 14, 43, 48) What could be finer than relaxing with cocktails or a pint at a beachside bar surrounded by brilliant bougainvillea? While the night away to the far-off thrumming of cargo ships moored just off Singapore's southern shore. The food here is average, so chow down at the nearby East Coast Lagoon Food Village then head across for some Strait-side R&R.

☆ ENTERTAINMENT

NECESSARY STAGE
THEATRE

Map p214 (📞6440 8115; www.necessary.org; B1-02 Marine Parade Community Bldg, 278 Marine Parade Rd; 🚌12, 16, 36, 196) Since the theatre's inception in 1987, current artistic director Alvin Tan has collaborated with resident playwright Haresh Sharma to produce over 60 original works. Innovative, indigenous and often controversial, the Necessary Stage is one of Singapore's best-known theatre groups.

🛍 SHOPPING

KIM CHOO KUEH CHANG
FOOD, HANDICRAFTS

Map p214 (www.kimchoo.com; 109 East Coast Rd; ⏱10am-9.30pm; 🚌10, 14, 16, 32) Joo Chiat is stuffed with bakeries and dessert shops, but few equal old-school Kim Choo. Pick up traditional pineapple tarts and other brightly coloured Peranakan *kueh* (bite-sized snacks), and pit stop at the adjoining boutique for colourful Peranakan ceramics and clothing. If Peranakan beading takes

your fancy, fashion designer Raymond Wong runs four-session courses ($350).

RUMAH BEBE
CLOTHING, HANDICRAFTS

Map p214 (113 East Coast Rd; ⊙9.30am-6.30pm Tue-Sat; ▣10, 14, 16, 32) Bebe Seet is the owner of this 1928 shophouse and purveyor of all things Peranakan. She sells traditional *kebayas* (Nonya-style blouses with decorative lace) with contemporary twists and beautifully beaded shoes. If you've got time and the inclination, you can take beading classes run by Bebe, which include a two-session beginner's course in bookmark beading and a three-session course in 3D relief beading (both $160).

JOO CHIAT COMPLEX
MALL

Map p214 (1 Joo Chiat Rd; ⊙11am-10pm; Ⓜ Paya Lebar) An old-school shopping mall packed with Malay textiles, crafts, jewellery and traditional clothing, Joo Chiat Complex gets especially busy during Hari Raya, a celebration marking the end of the fasting month of Ramadan. You'll also find Peranakan *kebayas*, Malay and Indonesian foodstuffs, as well as tailors for any post-purchase adjustments.

ISAN GALLERY
HANDICRAFTS

(✆6442 4278; www.isangallery.com.sg; 42 Jln Kembangan; ⊙by appointment only; Ⓜ Kembangan) The home gallery of Percy Vatsaloo showcases intricately crafted and exquisitely beautiful textiles made by tribal craftspeople of Isan in northeast Thailand. Visitors are welcome by appointment, and most of the items on display are also for sale. Percy works closely with the craftspeople themselves, and half of the sale price goes directly to them.

TAMPINES MALL
MALL

Map p213 (www.tampinesmall.com.sg; 4 Tampines Central 5; ⊙10am-10pm; Ⓜ Tampines) One of Singapore's largest and most-crowded suburban shopping centres, conveniently located right next to the Tampines MRT station. Aimed at middle-class heartlanders, you'll find a branch of the Isetan department store, a cinema and several bookshops inside this bottle-green monster. There are two smaller malls next door: **Century Square** and **Tampines 1**. The latter has chain and independent clothing stores targeted at young people.

GEYLANG THIAN HUAT SIANG JOSS PAPER
JOSS PAPER

(503 Geylang Rd; ⊙8am-9.30pm; Ⓜ Aljunied) While you hopefully won't be needing offerings to burn at any funeral wake, this traditional purveyor of paper offerings is worth a peek if you find yourself on the streets of Geylang. It has everything from giant cash registers, yachts and houses, to lifelike shoes and piles of cash, all thrown into the fire to ensure a comfortable afterlife for the deceased.

🏃 SPORTS & ACTIVITIES

SKI360°
WATER SPORTS

Map p213 (www.ski360degree.com; 1206A East Coast Parkway; first hour weekdays/weekends $38/50, each subsequent hour $16/22; ⊙10am-7pm Mon, Tue & Thu, noon-9pm Wed & Fri, 9am-10pm Sat & Sun) What better way to cool off than by strapping on some waterskis, a kneeboard or a wakeboard and getting dragged around a lagoon on the end of a cable? OK, you could just go swimming, but where's the fun in that? Best visited on weekday mornings, when there's usually hardly anyone there. The poseur quotient goes through the roof at weekends, when it's just as entertaining sitting around hoping someone will come a cropper on the ramps.

On weekends, take bus 401 from Bedok MRT. On weekdays, you can take bus 197, stop along Marine Pde Rd and walk through an underpass.

WILD WILD WET
THEME PARK

Map p213 (www.wildwildwet.com; cnr Pasir Ris Dr 3 & Pasir Ris Close, Downtown East; adult/child/family $19/14/60; ⊙1-7pm Mon & Wed-Fri, 10am-7pm Sat & Sun; Ⓜ Pasir Ris) Get splash happy at this water-themed fun park, its eight 'rides' including twisting waterslides, a wave pool and a giant, giddy water ramp. If you're after a serious thrill, hit the Torpedo, which will hurtle you from an 18m-high capsule for a freefall you won't forget in a hurry. Thankfully, there's a jacuzzi to sooth frazzled nerves.

A free shuttle bus runs between Pasir Ris MRT and the theme park.

Northern & Central Singapore

Neighbourhood Top Five

1 Trekking through Singapore's steamy heart of darkness in **Bukit Timah Nature Reserve** (p117), a listed Asean Heritage Park and home to one of the largest surviving tracts of primary rainforest on the island.

2 Treating your kids to breakfast with orang-utans at the lush, engaging, utterly inspired **Singapore Zoo** (p115).

3 Spotting leopards and dodging bats as you give the tram tour the slip and roam around the **Night Safari** (p116).

4 Seeing the forest from a dizzying new angle on the 25m-high Treetops Walk at soul-tonic **MacRitchie Reservoir** (p116).

5 Travelling back to humbler island days at **Lorong Buangkok** (p117), Singapore's last surviving *kampong* (village).

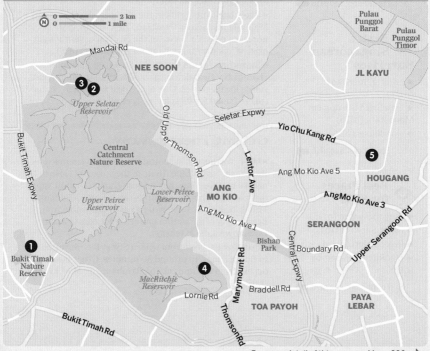

For more detail of this area see Map p209.

Lonely Planet's Top Tip

Places like Bukit Timah and MacRitchie Reservoir are by no means remote, but they can get exceedingly hot and humid, and once you're out on those walking trails there's nowhere to buy anything. So as well as remembering to don a hat and slap on some mosquito repellent, make sure you carry plenty of water, and perhaps a few snacks to keep you going.

⊙ Best Places for Adventure

➡ Bukit Timah Nature Reserve (p117)

➡ MacRitchie Reservoir (p116)

➡ Night Safari (p116)

➡ Green Corridor (p118)

For reviews, see p116.➡

⊙ Best Singaporean Surprises

➡ Lorong Buangkok (p117)

➡ Lian Shan Shuang Lin Monastery (p116)

➡ Handlebar (p119)

For reviews, see p116.➡

⊙ Best Places for Kids

➡ Singapore Zoo (p115)

➡ Night Safari (p116)

➡ River Safari (p118)

➡ MacRitchie Reservoir (p116)

For reviews, see p116.➡

Explore Northern & Central Singapore

This wonderfully wild and gloriously green part of Singapore is packed with sights and activities that take time to see and do, so unless you're here for an extended stay you're going to have to pick and choose carefully among the main attractions.

If you fancy taking advantage of the excellent walking trails, try to get your hiking done early in the morning. The weather will be cooler, and it will leave you most of the rest of the day to do other sightseeing.

The zoo and the night safari are both crammed with restaurants and cafes, but if you're visiting the other local sights, you might have to do some preplanning around meal times. Eat before you set off, bring some food with you (especially if you're planning to trek round MacRitchie Reservoir), or grab some grub at one of the MRT stations you'll be passing through.

Local Life

➡**Green Corridor** Join local joggers, nature enthusiasts, foragers, cyclists and curious squirrels on a stretch of Singapore's Green Corridor, an impromptu nature reserve and verdant escape running along the old Singapore–Malaysia rail route.

➡**Biker bar** Guitar riffs in the air, open sky above, and Malaysia just across the Strait. Trek to Singapore's northern edge for a slice of the city you never thought existed at sultry biker hangout Handlebar (p119).

➡**Suburban feasts** Get sticky fingers in Singapore's HDB-heavy Heartlands, packed with in-the-know, cult-status local eateries. One of the best is Mellben Seafood (p119), famed for its spicy, eggy chilli crab.

Getting There & Away

➡**MRT** Northern and central Singapore is encircled by the North–South Line. None of the stops are close to the nature reserves, but they're close enough to limit your taxi costs, or shorten your bus rides. From 2016, Bukit Timah Nature Reserve will be easily accessible from Beauty City MRT station on the under-construction Downtown Line extension.

➡**Bus** Bus 170 goes from Queen Street Bus Terminal to Bukit Timah in around 50 minutes. Other buses depart from the hubs at Toa Payoh or Ang Mo Kio MRT stations.

LONELY PLANET IMAGES / GETTY IMAGES ©

TOP SIGHT
SINGAPORE ZOO

One of the world's best, Singapore Zoo is a refreshing mix of spacious, naturalistic enclosures, freely roaming animals and interactive attractions. And then there's the setting: 28 soothing hectares on a lush peninsula jutting out into the waters of the Upper Seletar Reservoir. Don't miss it.

Animal Encounters

Get up close to Singapore's most famous gingers – the Singapore Zoo **orang-utans**. Tackle a scrumptious buffet breakfast in their company at the popular **Jungle Breakfast with Wildlife** (adult/child $33/23; ⊘9-10.30am) or get your photo taken with them during the **feeding sessions** at 11am and 3.30pm.

Further close encounters await at the **Fragile Forest**, a giant biodome that replicates the stratas of a rainforest. Cross paths with free-roaming butterflies, lories, Malayan flying foxes and ring-tailed lemurs. The pathway leads up to the forest canopy and the dome's most chilled-out locals, the two-toed sloths.

Complete with cliffs and a waterfall, the evocative **Great Rift Valley** exhibit is home to hamadryas baboons, Nubian ibexes, banded mongooses, black-backed jackals and rock hyraxes. You'll also find replica Ethiopian village huts, which offer insight into the area's unforgiving living conditions.

Fun for the Kids

Let your own little critters go wild at **Rainforest Kidzworld**, a sprawl of slides, swings, pulling boats and carousel. Kids can also ride ponies, feed farmyard animals and splash in the wet-play area.

DON'T MISS
➡ The orang-utans
➡ Fragile Forest
➡ Great Rift Valley
➡ Rainforest Kidzworld

PRACTICALITIES
➡ Map p209
➡ ☎6269 3411
➡ www.zoo.com.sg
➡ 80 Mandai Lake Rd
➡ adult/child $28/18
➡ ⊘8.30am-6pm
➡ Ⓜ Ang Mo Kio then ☐138

⊙ SIGHTS

SINGAPORE ZOO
ZOO

See p115.

MACRITCHIE RESERVOIR
PARK

Map p209 (☑1800 471 7300; www.nparks.gov.sg; Lornie Rd; ☺7am-7pm, Treetop Walk 9am-5pm Tue-Fri, 8.30am-5pm Sat & Sun; ⓂToa Payoh, then ᮁ157) Though not quite as wild as Bukit Timah, MacRitchie Reservoir remains an evocative escape. Walking trails skirt the water's edge and snake through a jungle spotted with long-tailed macaques and huge monitor lizards. You can rent kayaks at the **Paddle Lodge** (☑6344 6337; www.scf.org.sg; per hr $15; ☺9am-noon & 2-6pm Tue-Sun, last hire 4.30pm; ⓂStadium), but the highlight is the excellent 11km walking trail – and its various well-signposted off-shoots. Aim for the **Treetop Walk** (☺9am-5pm Tue-Fri, 8.30am-5pm Sat & Sun), the highlight of which is traversing a 250m-long suspension bridge, perched 25m up in the forest canopy.

Trails then continue along, through the forest and around the reservoir, sometimes on dirt tracks, sometimes on wooden boardwalks.

ⓘ COMBO TICKETS

If you plan on visiting the Singapore Zoo, Night Safari, River Safari or Jurong Bird Park, save money by buying one of the 'Park Hopper' combo tickets. Of the four attractions, the best two by far are the Singapore Zoo and Night Safari, for which a combined ticket costs $64 for adults and $41 for children. Tickets are valid for 30 days. Book online to avoid the queues.

It takes three to four hours to complete the main circuit. From the **service centre** (Map p209), which has changing facilities and a small cafe, near where bus 157 drops you off, start walking off to your right (anti-clockwise around the lake) and you'll soon reach the Paddle Lodge. Treetop Walk is about 3km or 4km beyond this.

LIAN SHAN SHUANG LIN MONASTERY
TEMPLE

Map p209 (184E Jln Toa Payoh; ☺7am-5pm; ⓂToa Payoh) Also known as the Siong Lim Temple, this breathtaking monastery was established in 1898 and inspired by the Xi

---

⊙ TOP SIGHT
NIGHT SAFARI

Next door to the zoo, but completely separate, Singapore's acclaimed Night Safari offers a very different type of nightlife. Home to over 120 species of animals, the park's moats and barriers seem to melt away in the darkness, giving you the feeling of travelling through a jungle filled with the likes of leopards, tigers and alligators. It's an atmosphere further heightened by the herds of strolling antelopes, often passing within inches of the electric shuttle trams that quietly cart you around.

The 45-minute tram tour comes with a guide whose commentary is a good introduction to the park. Alight at the East Lodge Trail and hit the atmospheric walking trails, which lead to enclosures inaccessible by tram. Among them is the deliciously creepy Giant Flying Squirrel walk-through aviary. Kids will love the entertaining, intelligent 20-minute **Creatures of the Night** (☺7.30pm, 8.30pm & 9.30pm, plus 10.30pm Fri & Sat) show.

When returning from the safari, you'll need to catch a bus at around 10.35pm to make the last MRT train departing Ang Mo Kio at 11.35pm. Otherwise, there's a taxi stand out front – expect to pay around $20 for a trip back to the CBD.

DON'T MISS...

➡ Electric Tram Tour
➡ East Lodge Walking Trail
➡ Creatures of the Night

PRACTICALITIES

➡ Map p209
➡ www.nightsafari.com.sg
➡ 80 Mandai Lake Rd
➡ adult/child $39/25
➡ ☺7.30pm-midnight, restaurants & shops from 5.30pm
➡ ⓂAng Mo Kio then ᮁ138

Chang Shi temple in Fuzhou, China. Two majestic gates frame the entrance, while further to the right is a seven-storey pagoda adorned with carvings. Inside the complex, shaded pathways lead from bonsai-filled courtyards to the monastery's three main halls, of which the Mahavira Hall is the most spectacular.

To the left of the monastery stands the weathered **Cheng Huang Temple** (Map p209; ⊘9am-5pm), dedicated to the Town God, administrator of justice in the netherworld. The main hall was built in 1912, its thick beams stained from decades of incense smoke.

The monastery and temple are about 1km east of Toa Payoh MRT station – follow the signs down Kim Keat Link, off Lorong 6 Toa Payoh, or take bus 238 three stops.

LORONG BUANGKOK VILLAGE
Map p209 (Lorong Buangkok; MAng Mo Kio, then ☐88) This wonderfully ramshackle *kampong* (village) seems willed into existence from an old black-and-white photograph. Chickens roam past colourful wooden houses, crickets hum in the background, and the 27 families here seem to have carefree sensibilities uncommon in the general populace (the $10 per month rent probably helps). This is mainland Singapore's last blip of resistance against the tide of modern development, and a wonderfully evocative way to experience what life was like for many Singaporeans before the development frenzy following independence.

Although the area is slated for redevelopment, the bulldozers have so far stayed away.

Take bus 88 from Ang Mo Kio MRT station in the direction of Pasir Ris, and get off on Ang Mo Kio Ave 5 (10 minutes), just after Yio Chu Kang Rd. Walk north up Yio Chu Kang Rd and, after about 50m, turn right onto Gerald Dr. After about 200m, turn right into Lorong Buangkok. Fifty metres later you'll see a dirt track on your left that leads to the village.

MEMORIES AT OLD FORD FACTORY MUSEUM
Map p221 (✆6462 6724; 351 Upper Bukit Timah Rd; adult/child $3/2.50; ⊘9am-5.30pm Mon-Sat, noon-5.30pm Sun; ☐170) This former Ford Motors assembly plant is most remembered as the place where the British surrendered Singapore to the Japanese on 15 February 1942. Through photographs, ration books, diaries, prisoner drawings and a large

NORTHERN & CENTRAL SINGAPORE SIGHTS

TOP SIGHT
BUKIT TIMAH NATURE RESERVE

This luxurious pocket of primary forest is just a short bus ride from the centre, and while you won't see any tigers, you'll still find plenty of long-tailed macaques and dozens of bird species.

The 163-hectare sprawl offers five well-established walking trails (35 minutes to two hours return), plus a popular 6km mountain-bike trail. Maps of all the colour-coded routes can be found on wooden signboards.

The quickest, most popular hike is the one leading straight up to the summit of Bukit Timah (163m), Singapore's highest peak. The down-and-dirty Rock Path is worth a try, too.

Due to metro construction works and general maintenance, the reserve is scheduled to reopen in early 2015, with limited access until 2016 – check the website for updates.

The quickest way here is on bus 174: alight at the first stop on Jln Jurong Kechil as the bus turns into it from Bukit Timah Rd. Walk in the opposite direction of the bus on Jln Jurong Kechil (which becomes BT Timah Link) and turn left at Jln Anak Bukit. The first street on your right is Hindhede Dr.

DON'T MISS...
➡ Bukit Timah summit
➡ Rock Path
➡ Long-tailed macaques

PRACTICALITIES
➡ Map p209
➡ ✆1800 471 7300
➡ www.nparks.gov.sg
➡ 177 Hindhede Dr
➡ ⊘6am-7pm, visitor-centre exhibition 8.30am-5pm
➡ ☐170, 174

interactive map, the museum charts Singapore's three dark years of Japanese occupation during WWII. Bus 170 stops here, just after Bukit Timah Nature Reserve.

SUN YAT SEN NANYANG MEMORIAL HALL
MUSEUM

Map p209 (www.sysnmh.org.sg; 12 Tai Gin Rd; adult/child $4/2; ⊙10am-5pm Tue-Sun; MⓉToa Payoh then ⓆⒷ145) Built in the 1880s, this national monument was the headquarters of Dr Sun Yat Sen's Chinese Revolutionary Alliance in Southeast Asia, which led to the overthrow of the Qing dynasty and the creation of the first Chinese republic. Dr Sun Yat Sen briefly stayed in the house while touring Asia to whip up support for the cause. It's a fine example of a colonial Victorian villa and houses a museum with items pertaining to Dr Sun's life and work.

Next door is the **Sasanaramsi Burmese Buddhist Temple** (Map p209; 14 Tai Gin Rd; ⊙6am-9pm), a towering building guarded by two *chinthes* (lionlike figures) and housing a beautiful white-marble Buddha statue, decorated somewhat bizarrely with a 'halo' of different-coloured LED lights.

RIVER SAFARI
NATURE RESERVE

Map p209 (www.riversafari.com.sg; 80 Mandai Lake Rd; adult/child $25/16, boat ride adult/child $5/3; ⊙9am-6pm; MⒶAng Mo Kio then ⓆⒷ138) Right beside the Singapore Zoo and Night Safari, this new blockbuster wildlife park recreates the habitats of seven world-famous rivers. While most are underwhelming, the **Mekong River** and **Amazon Flooded Forest** exhibits are impressive, their epic aquariums rippling with giant catfish and stingrays, electric eels, red-bellied piranhas, manatees and sea cows.

Another highlight is the **Giant Panda Forest** enclosure, home to rare red pandas and the park's famous black-and-whiters, KaiKai and JiaJia.

Young kids will enjoy the 10-minute **Amazon River Quest Boat Ride**, a tranquil, theme-park style tour past roaming monkeys, wild cats and exotic birdlife. The ride begins with a big splash, so if you're sitting in the front row, keep feet and bags off the floor. Boat ride time slots often fill by 1pm, so go early or purchase tickets online to secure a tour time that suits.

✕ EATING

LOONG FATT TAU SAR PIAH
BAKERY $

Map p209 (☑6253 4584; 639 Balestier Rd; pastries from $1.50; ⊙8am-4.30pm Mon-Sat; ⓆⒷ131, 166, 167, 851) Balestier Rd is famous for

---

GREEN CORRIDOR

The Green Corridor is to Singapore what the High Line is to New York – a disused rail route transformed into an unlikely urban oasis. Unlike the High Line, however, Singapore's Green Corridor is a relatively wild creature – a grassy track cutting through suburbs, secondary forest, grasslands, small farms and mudflats on its way from the old railway station of Tanjong Pagar in the south to the Malaysian border in the north.

The track follows the old Singapore–Malaysia rail route. Constructed in the early 1900s to transport tin and rubber from the Malay Peninsula to Singapore's port, the land remained in Malaysian hands until 2010, when a land swap was sealed and the terminus of the Malaysian railway moved to Woodlands in Singapore's north. That development-driven Singapore suddenly found itself with a cross-country oasis prompted a grassroots campaign to preserve it. Overwhelming public support prompted the government to listen, and it now seems that the corridor will remain a verdant spine running down the island.

Given Singapore's heat and the Green Corridor's current lack of facilities and signage, only the most intrepid would attempt walking or cycling the entire route. For most people, a leisurely stroll along a small section is a satisfying, invigorating experience. An especially interesting stretch runs from old Bukit Timah Railway Station (accessed from a dirt path beside the old rail bridge crossing Bukit Timah Rd at Rifle Range Rd) north to Hillview Rd. It's an easy 3km, dotted with old cast-iron railway bridges and skirting the dense jungle greenery of Bukit Timah Nature Reserve. You can download maps of the Green Corridor at www.thegreencorridor.org.

bakeries that peddle *tau sar piah,* a snack-friendly, Hokkien-style pastry filled with salty or sweet bean paste. Loong Fatt is the oldest and fairest of them all, a place that still makes its *tau sar piah* by hand and that bakes them in old-fashioned ovens. The pastry is gorgeously flaky and buttery, and the fillings dense and moist.

MELLBEN SEAFOOD
SEAFOOD **$$**

Map p209 (Stall 01-1222, 232 Ang Mo Kio Ave 3; chilli crab for 2 around $40; ⊙5-10pm; ⓂAng Mo Kio) When it comes to chart-topping chilli crab, no shortage of locals will direct you to Mellben, a modern, breezy, hawker-style set-up at the bottom of a nondescript HDB block. The crabs here yield gorgeous chunks of sweet, fresh meat, while the gravy is spicy and distinctly eggy. Tables can only be reserved if dining before 7pm.

If this is too early, head in midweek to avoid the longest queues. Service can sometimes be slow, so come with a little patience.

PASARBELLA
@ THE GRANDSTAND
MARKET **$$**

Map p209 (www.pasarbella.com; 200 Turf Club Rd; ⊙varies, generally stalls 9.30am-7pm, restaurants 10am-10pm; ⍰; ⍰67, 77, 170, 174, 961, 970) Set in a racecourse grandstand, this trendy, indoor farmers market is packed with eateries and artisanal food stalls. Tuck into *al granchio* (crabmeat) pasta at **Da Paolo** (www.dapaolo.com.sg; Stall 02-06 K30/31/32; sandwiches from $8.50, pasta from $13; ⊙9.30am-8.30pm Mon-Thu, to 9.30pm Fri-Sun), or grab a cheese platter at the **Cheese Ark** (⍰9830 3368; Stall 02-K28; 2-person cheese platter $20-25; ⊙10am-8.30pm Mon-Thu, to 9pm Fri-Sun) fromagerie, which stocks rare cheeses from small-scale producers.

For Third Wave coffee, hit **Dutch Colony Coffee Co** (⍰6467 0255; www.dutchcolony.sg; Stall 02-K67/K68; ⊙9.30am-7pm Sun-Thu, to 9pm Fri & Sat).

Not technically part of PasarBella but still at the Grandstand is **VeganBurg** (www.veganburg.com; Stall 01-32; burgers from $5.90; ⊙11.45am-9.30pm Mon-Fri, 10.30am-9.45pm Sat & Sun; ⍰), famed for its mouthwatering vegan burgers.

WORTH A DETOUR

BIKER BAR HIDEOUT

It might be an effort to get to, but once you make it, you'll be happily lingering a while. **Handlebar** (⍰6475 9571; www.handlebaroriginal.com; 57 Jln Menpurong; ⊙5pm-1am Tue-Thu, 5pm-2am Fri, 3pm-2am Sat, 3pm-1am Sun; ⍰Sembawang, then bus 882) is Singapore's only 'biker bar', hidden away at the end of a narrow, jungle-fringed road on the island's northern edge. Started by two free-wheeling rev heads, it's an offbeat ode to hitting the road, with scooter-panel bar stools, Mustang-turned–pool table and hardcore daiquiris made using petrol-engine blenders. The crowd is super-chilled and mixed, with everyone from motor heads, factory workers, hipsters and expat families enjoying the well-priced pints and alfresco patio, and getting messy with Americana 'cocaine wings' (barbecue hot chicken wings) and chilli cheese fries.

🍺 DRINKING & NIGHTLIFE

MIDDLE ROCK
BAR

Map p209 (1382 Ang Mo Kio Avenue 1, Bishan Park; ⊙5pm-1am Mon-Fri, to 2am Sat, to midnight Sun; ⍰133, ⓂAng Mo Kio) Swaying palms, flickering lights, and snug nooks and gazebos – no, you're not in Phuket, you're at one of Singapore's best-kept secrets, a languid garden bar right in Bishan Park. It's a grown-up, relaxing hideout, with music soft enough for audible conversation and a generous Sunday happy hour that runs from noon to 8pm.

BAR BAR BLACK SHEEP
PUB

Map p209 (www.bbbs.com.sg; 879 Cherry Ave; ⊙noon-midnight; ⍰67, 77, 170, 174, 961, 970) Swirling fans, dangling lanterns and a mostly 30- and 40-something crowd downing beers in flip-flops: Bar Bar Black Sheep is a curious hybrid, an open-air, cash-only pub with a trio of hawker stalls peddling North Indian, Western and Thai grub (go for the latter). Of the four branches around town, locals will tell you that this one's the best.

Holland Village, Dempsey Hill & the Botanic Gardens

HOLLAND VILLAGE | DEMPSEY HILL | BOTANIC GARDENS

Neighbourhood Top Five

1 Taking deep, blissful breaths in Singapore's lush and velvety **Botanic Gardens** (p122). Picnicking on the lawns, slipping into ancient rainforest and exploring a string of tranquil themed gardens.

2 Marvelling at the beauty, diversity and sheer quantity of orchids on display at the **National Orchid Garden** (p122), set snugly in the Botanic Gardens.

3 Shopping for unique homewares in the relaxed **antique shops and galleries** of Dempsey Hill.

4 Escaping to Ubud without ever leaving town at intoxicating Balinese restaurant **Blue Bali** (p124).

5 Channelling your past colonial life with elegant dim sum and cocktails at fan-swirling, jungle-fringed **Chopsuey** (p123).

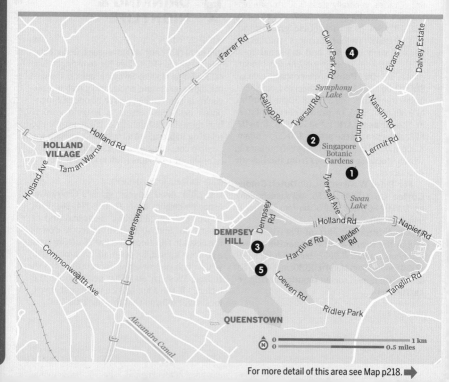

For more detail of this area see Map p218.

Explore Holland Village, Dempsey Hill & the Botanic Gardens

The must-see sight here is the Botanic Gardens (p122) and you'd do well to set aside half a day to fully soak up its charms.

Making a picnic out of your visit can be fun, especially if you have kids in tow. Stock up on picnic goodies at the gourmet delis in upmarket Holland Village or leafy Dempsey Hill. Alternatively, browse for antiques in Dempsey Hill and lunch there as well, at either Chopsuey (p123) or PS Cafe (p123), before heading across to the Botanic Gardens. For a dirt-cheap hawker feed by the gardens, make a beeline for leafy Food Canopy (p124).

Come evening, it's an easy stroll to Blue Bali (p124) if you feel like staying put for sunset drinks and dinner. If not, head to livelier Holland Village to wine and dine with a largely well-heeled expat crowd.

Local Life

→ **Jogging** If you've brought a pair of trainers with you on your travels, do as many Singapore residents do and work that city smog out of your lungs with a brisk jog around the Botanic Gardens. Early morning is best, when the air is still cool, or else just before sunset.

→ **Shopping** If the high energy, same-same shopping malls of nearby Orchard Rd begin to bore you, shift down a gear or two and amble over to Dempsey Hill or Holland Village and their booty of small, independent shops and boutiques.

→ **Gourmet** It's not just the expats who lap up the Western food offerings in Holland Village and Dempsey. Follow moneyed Singaporeans also through the doors of cute cafes and well-stocked delicatessens to get your fix of comfort food.

Getting There & Away

→ **MRT** The Botanic Gardens and Holland Village both have their own MRT stations.

→ **Bus** Dempsey Hill isn't connected to the MRT. You can walk here from the Botanic Gardens, or else catch a bus (7, 75, 77, 105, 106, 123 or 174) from behind Orchard MRT, on Orchard Blvd. Get off two stops after the Botanic Gardens then walk up to your left. Buses 75 and 106 are two of several linking Holland Village with Dempsey Hill. It's just under 2km to walk between the two, but the walk is an unpleasant one along busy Holland Rd.

Lonely Planet's Top Tip

Check the Botanic Gardens website (www.sbg.org.sg) for details of upcoming concerts, which are staged for free by Symphony Lake. Also keep an eye out for free guided tours of the gardens. At the time of writing they were running on Saturday mornings, but always check for updates.

✕ Best Places to Eat

→ Chopsuey (p123)

→ PS Cafe (p123)

→ Blue Bali (p124)

→ Halia (p124)

For reviews, see p123.➡

☙ Best Places to Drink

→ PS Cafe (p123)

→ Park (p124)

→ RedDot Brewhouse (p125)

For reviews, see p124.➡

⌂ Best Places for Browsing

→ Dempsey Hill Antiques Shops (p125)

→ Holland Village Shopping Centre (p125)

For reviews, see p125.➡

HOLLAND VILLAGE, DEMPSEY HILL & THE BOTANIC GARDENS

TOP SIGHT
SINGAPORE BOTANIC GARDENS

For instant stress relief, take a dose of the Singapore Botanic Gardens. Suddenly the world is a tranquil, verdant paradise of rolling lawns, themed gardens and glassy lakes. Free, themed guided tours run on Saturdays (check the website), and if you're lucky enough to be in town when opera is scheduled by Symphony Lake, go.

Orchid & Ginger Gardens

The Botanic Gardens' now famous orchid breeding began in 1928 and its legacy is the **National Orchid Garden**. Its 3 hectares are home to over 1000 species and 2000 hybrids, around 600 of which are on display – the largest showcase of tropical orchids on earth.

Next to the orchid garden, the 1-hectare **Ginger Garden** contains over 250 members of the Zingiberaceae family. It's also where you'll find Halia (p124), which, alongside Blue Bali (p124) just outside the Gardens, offers one of Singapore's most memorable dining experiences.

Ancient Rainforest & Swan Lake

Hit the boardwalk and escape into this rare patch of dense primeval **rainforest**, older than the Botanic Gardens themselves. Of the rainforest's 314 species of vegetation, over half are now considered rare in Singapore.

For a touch of romanticism, it's hard to beat **Swan Lake**. One of three lakes in the gardens, it boasts a tiny island cluttered with nibong palms. Look out for the mute swans, imported from Amsterdam.

DON'T MISS...

➡ National Orchid Garden
➡ Rainforest
➡ Ginger Garden
➡ Swan Lake

PRACTICALITIES

➡ Map p218
➡ ☏6471 7361
➡ www.sbg.org.sg
➡ 1 Cluny Rd
➡ garden admission free, National Orchid Garden adult/child $5/free
➡ ⊘5am–midnight, National Orchid Garden 8.30am–7pm, last entry 6pm, Healing Garden 5am–7.30pm Wed–Mon, Jacob Ballas Children's Garden 8am–7pm, last entry 6.30pm Tue–Sun
➡ ☐7, 105, 123, 174, Ⓜ Botanic Gardens

 SIGHTS

SINGAPORE BOTANIC GARDENS   GARDENS
See p122.

**SRI MUNEESWARAN
HINDU TEMPLE**   TEMPLE

(3 Commonwealth Dr; ⒨Commonwealth) This is believed to be Southeast Asia's largest shrine for Sri Muneeswaran, completed in 1998 after the original hut-and-shrine – built by Indian railway workers in 1932 – became a victim of Queensway's widening. Interestingly, the building has no central pillars in the inner sanctum, allowing devotees full view of rituals. Free **hatha yoga classes** are held on Sundays and Mondays (6pm to 7pm and 7pm to 8pm), with a dedicated class for children on Sundays (5.30pm to 7pm).

✗ EATING

Expat-heavy Holland Village is home to a host of restaurants and cafes serving predominantly Western food. Over in fellow expat-staple Dempsey Hill, the location is less city-residential and more colonial hill station – this was once an army barracks, after all.

✗ Holland Village

**HOLLAND VILLAGE
MARKET & FOOD CENTRE**   HAWKER CENTRE $

Map p218 (Lor Mambong; dishes from $3; ⊘10am-late; ⒨Holland Village) Avoid the run-of-the-mill restaurants across the street and join the locals for cheap, scrumptious Singapore grub. A small clutch of stalls sell chicken rice, prawn noodles and other hawker staples. If you're new to the hawker food scene, there's a handy signboard outside that gives the lowdown on the most popular dishes.

DA PAOLO PIZZA BAR   ITALIAN $$

Map p218 (www.dapaolo.com.sg; 44 Jln Merah Saga; pizzas $19-29, pasta $22-28; ⊘noon-2.30pm & 5.30-10.30pm Mon-Fri, 11am-10.30pm Sat & Sun; ⒨Holland Village) The successful Da Paolo chain has two outlets on this street alone: a deli-cafe (at No 43) and this polished bistro with terrace seating. Under a cowhide ceiling, svelte expats nosh on delicious thin-crust pizzas, competent pastas and a

showstopping warm peanut butter caramel chocolate brownie. There's a good-value set lunch ($23) and a two-for-one happy hour from noon to 2.30pm and 5.30pm to 7.30pm.

ORIGINAL SIN   VEGETARIAN $$

Map p218 (☑6475 5605; www.originalsin.com.sg; Stall 01-62, 43 Jln Merah Saga; mains $24-28; ⊘11.30am-2.30pm & 6-10.30pm; ✗; ⒨Holland Village) Vibrant textiles, crisp linen and beautiful stemware set a smart, upbeat scene for sophisticated, flesh-free dishes like spicy, quinoa-stuffed roasted capsicum, and chargrilled eggplant moussaka. The restaurant is on a residential street dotted with eateries; book an outdoor table if possible.

2AM DESSERT BAR   DESSERT $$

Map p218 (www.2amdessertbar.com; 21A Lorong Liput; dishes $15-20; ⊘6pm-2am Mon-Sat; ⒨Holland Village) Posh desserts with wine and cocktail pairings is the deal at this swanky hideout. While the menu includes savoury grub like burgers and beef-cheek croquettes, you're here for Janice Wong's sweet showstoppers, from basil white chocolate to purple potato puree with blackberry parfait, leather, lavender marshmallows and fruits of the forest sorbet. Book ahead if heading in Thursday to Saturday night.

✗ Dempsey Hill

★PS CAFE   INTERNATIONAL $$

Map p218 (☑9070 8782; www.pscafe.com; 28B Harding Rd; mains $23-36; ⊘11.30am-3.30pm & 6.30-10.30pm; ✗; ☐7, 75, 77, 105, 106, 123, 174) A chic, light-filled tropical oasis of wooden floorboards, floor-to-ceiling windows and patio tables facing thick tropical foliage. From brunch to dinner, edibles are beautiful and healthy, whether it's fish croquette Benedict or a 'Morocco miracle stack' of roasted portobello mushroom, grilled vegetables, smoked eggplant and couscous. The weekend brunch is a no-bookings affair, so head in by 10.30am to avoid the longest queues.

★CHOPSUEY   CHINESE $$

Map p218 (☑9224 6611; www.chopsueycafe.com; Block 10, Dempsey Rd; dim sum $7-15; ⊘11.30am-4pm & 6.30-10.30pm Mon-Fri, 9.30am-4pm & 6.30-10.30pm Sat & Sun, bar to 11pm Sun-Thu, to 1am Fri & Sat; ☐7, 75, 77, 105, 106, 123, 174) Swirling ceiling fans, crackly 1930s tunes and preened ladies on rattan chairs – Chopsuey has colonial chic down pat. Peddling revamped versions of retro American-Chinese dishes, the real highlight here is the lunchtime yum cha, with standouts including Schezuan tofu, prawn dumplings and *san choi bao* (spicy minced meat wrapped in lettuce leaves). The marble bar is perfect for solo diners.

LONG BEACH SEAFOOD
SEAFOOD $$$

Map p218 (☑6323 2222; www.longbeachseafood. com.sg; 25 Dempsey Rd, 01-01; crab per kg around $60; ⊘11am-3pm & 5.30pm-1.30am; ☑7, 75, 77, 105, 106, 123, 174) One of Singapore's top seafood restaurant chains. Settle in on the verandah, gaze out at thick forest and tackle the cult-status black-pepper crab. The original Long Beach lays claim to inventing the iconic dish, and the version here is fantastically peppery and earthy.

✕ Botanic Gardens

FOOD CANOPY
HAWKER CENTRE $

(1J Cluny Rd; dishes from $3; ⊘7am-8pm; ⓜBotanic Gardens) This breezy collection of hawker stalls sits outside the Botanic Gardens' Healing Garden. There's lots of favourites, from *kaya* (coconut jam) toast and *kopi*, to roasted duck, Ginseng chicken soup, Korean *bibimbap* and Indian *rojak*. The Tom Yam Fried Fish Bee Hoon from the Handmade Noodles stall is especially good. If coming by taxi, tell the driver it's next to the Raffles Building.

★BLUE BALI
INDONESIAN $$

(☑6733 0185; www.bluebali.sg; 1D Cluny Rd; tapas $8-20, mains $16-32; ⊘3pm-midnight Tue-Sun; ☏; ⓜBotanic Gardens) Skirting the Botanic Gardens, Blue Bali is an enchanting dreamscape of Balinese wooden pavilions, cabanas over water and sarong-wrapped staff. Head in for a romantic sundowner and tapas-style bites like Javanese satay, fried homemade tofu or chilli-spiked pumpkin prawns, all of which better suit the low tables than the mains. Great happy-hour deals run from 5pm to 8pm.

CASA VERDE
INTERNATIONAL $$

Map p218 (Singapore Botanic Gardens, 1 Cluny Rd; lunch $9-18, pizzas $21-25, dinner mains $25-30; ⊘7.30am-9.30pm; ☝; ⓜBotanic Gardens) The most accessible and family-friendly restaurant in the Botanic Gardens, 'Green House' serves up decent Western grub – pasta, salads, sandwiches – plus woodfired pizzas and a smattering of local dishes.

HALIA
FUSION $$$

Map p218 (☑6476 6711; www.halia.com.sg; Singapore Botanic Gardens, 1 Cluny Rd; mains $28-68, dinner set menu $88-98, English tea $28; ⊘noon-4pm & 6-10pm Mon-Fri, 10am-5pm & 6-10pm Sat & Sun; ☏; ⓜBotanic Gardens) Atmospheric Halia is surrounded by the Botanic Gardens' ginger plants, a fact echoed in a number of unusual ginger-based dishes. Menus are a competent, fusion affair (think chilli crab spaghettini or Parmesan and almond-crusted stingray), and the weekday set lunch (two/three courses $28/32) is especially good value. There's a dedicated vegetarian dinner menu, and at weekends you can also come for brunch (10am to 4pm) or English tea (3pm to 5pm).

🍷⚓ DRINKING & NIGHTLIFE

Lorong Mambong in Holland Village is pedestrianised in the evenings and transforms from a quiet street into a Kuta-style throng of bars and eateries. Discerning drinkers have since moved on to the new wave of bars in Chinatown and Tanjong Pagar, so the only real reason to head here is for the good after-work happy-hour deals. In contrast, Dempsey is more upmarket and sedate, and better for supping than sipping. That said, you will find a few cafe-bar options if you fancy a post-meal tipple.

PARK
BAR

Map p218 (Stall 01-01, 281 Holland Ave; ⊘10am-midnight Tue-Thu & Sun, to 2am Fri & Sat; ☏; ⓜHolland Village) Holland Village's coolest dig sits in converted shipping containers at the top of Holland Ave. Industrial yellow tables, shophouse tiles and filament bulbs deliver a suitably hip fit-out, with outdoor patio seating and well-priced pints for this part of town. Order a side of Spam chips (thinly sliced, deep-fried Spam), one of life's unexpected surprises.

WALA WALA CAFÉ BAR
BAR

Map p218 (www.walawala.sg; 31 Lorong Mambong; ⊘4pm-1am Mon-Thu, 4pm-2am Fri, 3pm-2am Sat, 3pm-1am Sun; ⓜHolland Village) Perennially packed at weekends (and on most evenings, in fact), Wala Wala's main draw is its live music on the 2nd floor, with warm-up acts Monday to Friday from 7pm and main acts nightly from 9.30pm. Downstairs it pulls in

DEMPSEY HILL ANTIQUES

Many of Dempsey Hill's former British Army barrack buildings are home to long-established art and antique shops, peddling anything from teak furniture to landscaping ornaments and ancient temple artefacts. Aside from these listed, there are more than a dozen other similar shops, with most open daily from around 10am to 6pm. See www.dempseyhill.com for a complete rundown.

Shang Antique (Map p218; www.shangantique.com.sg; 18D Dempsey Rd; ⊗10.30am-7pm; 🚍7, 75, 77, 105, 106, 123, 174) Specialises in Southeast Asian objects, some of them around 2000 years old, with price tags to match. Those with more style than savings can pick up anything from old opium pots to beautiful table runners for under $30.

Pasardina Fine Living (Map p218; 13 Dempsey Rd; ⊗9.30am-6.30pm; 🚍7, 75, 77, 105, 106, 123, 174) Has just about everything decorative and Asian for the home (and can also customise furniture).

Asiatique (Map p218; 14A Dempsey Rd; ⊗11am-7pm; 🚍7, 75, 77, 105, 106, 123, 174) Stocks unique, statement furniture, some made using petrified wood.

football fans with its large sports screens. Like most of the places here, tables spill out onto the street in the evenings.

REDDOT BREWHOUSE   MICROBREWERY
Map p218 (www.reddotbrewhouse.com.sg; 25A Dempsey Rd; ⊗noon-midnight Mon-Thu, noon-2am Fri & Sat, 10am-midnight Sun; 🚍7, 75, 77, 105, 106, 123, 174) In a quiet spot in Dempsey Hill, RedDot Brewhouse has been pouring its own microbrews for years. Ditch the average food and focus on the suds, sipped to the sound of screeching parrots. There are nine beers on tap (from $6 for a half-pint), including an eye-catching, spirulina-spiked green pilsner. Happy hour runs from noon to 7pm, with $4 half-pints and $8 pints.

🛍 SHOPPING

EM GALLERY   FASHION, HOMEWARES
Map p218 (📞6475 6941; www.emtradedesign.com; Block 16, 01-04/05 Dempsey Rd; ⊗10am-7pm Mon-Fri, 11am-7pm Sat & Sun; 🚍7, 75, 77, 105, 106, 123, 174) Singapore-based Japanese designer Emiko Nakamura keeps Dempsey's lunching ladies looking fab in her light, sculptural creations. Emiko also collaborates with hilltribes in northern Laos to create naturally dyed handwoven handicrafts, such as bags and cushions. Other homewares might include limited-edition (and reasonably priced) Khmer pottery from Cambodia or handmade Thai dinner sets.

HOLLAND VILLAGE
SHOPPING CENTRE   MALL
Map p218 (211 Holland Ave; ⊗10am-8.30pm; Ⓜ Holland Village) Holland Village Shopping Centre remains a magnet for expats seeking art, handicrafts, homewares and offbeat fashion. Dive into **Lim's Arts & Living** (Map p218; 211 Holland Ave, 02-01, Holland Village Shopping Centre; ⊗10am-8.30pm), where tacky giftware sits alongside some genuinely good finds, from Peranakan-style ceramics to cheongsam frocks. Shopped out? Hit the nail spas on Level 3.

West & Southwest Singapore

SOUTHWEST SINGAPORE | WEST SINGAPORE

Neighbourhood Top Five

1 Stretching your legs for a park-to-park walk along the **Southern Ridges** (p128) to Mt Faber, then hopping onto the cable car for gob-smacking views of the city, port and Sentosa Island.

2 Kickstarting your Sunday with a scrumptious Thai brunch at jungle hideaway **Tamarind Hill** (p131).

3 Landing a peckish, rainbow-coloured parrot on your arm at family-friendly **Jurong Bird Park** (p129).

4 Joining serious twitchers for a spot of birdwatching in the mangroves of **Sungei Buloh Wetland Reserve** (p129).

5 Reliving a little 1950s tourism at the wonderfully quirky and offbeat theme park **Haw Par Villa** (p129).

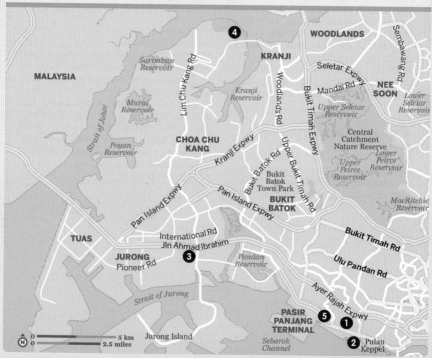

For more detail of this area see Map p220 and p221. ➡

Explore West & Southwest Singapore

This vast area is packed with sights that together would take a number of days to see. But you don't need to visit them all – none are absolute must-see attractions, most are quirky or somewhat specialist – so pick and choose what best suits you to plan your foray into western Singapore without wasting too much travel time.

Bundling sights together into one trip makes sense. The Science Centre, Omni-Theatre and Snow City stand side by side, while a number of sights in the northwest are accessed via Kranji MRT station.

Consider timing your visit to Mt Faber to coincide with sunset, so as the sun goes down you can either be on the cable car or at a restaurant or bar on the summit. It's then easy to get back to your hotel via the Harbour-Front MRT station.

Local Life

→**Deals** Don't forget to look into the combined ticket deals for the Science Centre, the Omni-Theatre and Snow City. Likewise, Jurong Bird Park is part of a possible three-in-one ticket deal with Singapore Zoo and the Night Safari. You can also get various Sentosa Island deals if you're travelling there by cable car.

→**University treasures** Western Singapore's universities harbour some lesser-known cultural diversions. The National University of Singapore is home to three museums in one, its collection including important works by Singaporean artistic heavyweight Ng Eng Teng. Further afield, Nanyang Techonological University is where you'll find the Chinese Heritage Centre, a tranquil museum exploring the Chinese diaspora.

→**Sun-kissed** The west and southwest are full of parks, hills and nature reserves. They're wonderful places for strolling around, but don't underestimate the strength of the Singapore sun. Slop on the sunscreen, slap on a hat, and pack those water bottles.

Getting There & Away

→**MRT** This vast area is actually served pretty well by the MRT. Some attractions have their namesake stations. Otherwise, HarbourFront, Jurong East, Boon Lay, Chinese Garden, Pioneer and Kranji are all useful stations that are either walking distance to sights or have bus connections to them.

→**Bus** For the more out-of-the-way sights you'll need to combine MRT trips with a bus ride. We list all the options with each review. The Kranji Express is a handy minibus service you can use to visit the farms in the northwest.

Lonely Planet's Top Tip

Western Singapore is home to two outstanding public swimming complexes at Jurong East and Jurong West. Consider spending half the day sightseeing and the other half cooling off by the pool or soothing tired muscles in the jacuzzi. Both are family-friendly affairs, with top-notch facilities for visitors of all ages, and both are amazingly cheap.

Best Places to Eat

➡ Tamarind Hill (p131)
➡ Faber Peak (p132)
➡ PeraMakan (p131)

For reviews, see p131.➡

Best for Kids

➡ Jurong Bird Park (p129)
➡ Snow City (p133)
➡ Jurong Swimming Pools (p133)
➡ Singapore Science Centre (p130)

For reviews, see p128.➡

Best Natural Escapes

➡ Southern Ridges (p128)
➡ Sungei Buloh Wetland Reserve (p129)
➡ Labrador Nature Reserve (p129)
➡ Kranji Farms (p130)

For reviews, see p128.➡

WEST & SOUTHWEST SINGAPORE

 **SIGHTS**

Southwest Singapore

MT FABER PARK & CABLE CAR
PARK

(Map p220; www.faberpeaksingapore.com; ⊙park 8.45am-10pm; MHarbourFront) **Mt Faber** (116m) is the centrepiece of Mt Faber Park and the climax to the Southern Ridges nature walk. The most spectacular way to get here is via the **cable car** (www.singaporecablecar.com.sg; adult/child return $29/18; ⊙8.45am-9.45pm), which connects Mt Faber to HarbourFront and Sentosa – frustratingly, only return tickets are sold. Alternatively, you can walk. It's a short but steep climb through secondary rainforest, dotted with lookout posts and some splendid colonial-era black-and-white bungalows.

If you're hiking up here, don't forget some water for the journey.

REFLECTIONS AT BUKIT CHANDU
MUSEUM

Map p220 (www.nhb.gov.sg; 31K Pepys Rd; adult/child $2/1; ⊙9am-5.30pm Tue-Sun; MPasir Panjang) Atop Bukit Chandu (Opium Hill) and housed in a renovated colonial-era villa, this modest WWII interpretive centre combines first-hand accounts, personal artefacts, maps and historical footage to recount the brutal fall of Singapore. The focus is on the 1st and 2nd Battalions of the Malay Regiment who bravely but unsuccessfully attempted to defend the hill in the Battle of Pasir Panjang when the Japanese invaded in 1942.

To reach the museum, alight at Pasir Panjang MRT station, cross the main road and walk uphill along Pepys Rd for about 15 minutes. Beside the museum is the entrance to Kent Ridge Park and the Southern Ridges walk.

NUS MUSEUM
MUSEUM

Map p221 (www.nus.edu.sg/museum; University Cultural Centre, 50 Kent Ridge Cres; ⊙10am-

---

WALKING THE SOUTHERN RIDGES

Mt Faber is connected to Kent Ridge Park via a series of parks and hills known as the **Southern Ridges** (Map p220; www.nparks.gov.sg; MPasir Panjang). It's a wonderfully accessible area to walk in, and much less testing than the hikes around Bukit Timah or MacRitchie Reservoir. The entire network of trails stretches for 9km, though the direct route from Kent Ridge Park to Mt Faber is a manageable 4km. And while the walking itself isn't tough, Singapore's hot, humid weather makes it important to pack plenty of water.

Start at **Kent Ridge Park** (Map p220; Vigilante Dr; ⊙24hr), located a brief walk beyond wartime-museum Reflections at Bukit Chandu. Hit the short **canopy walk**, before strolling downhill to **HortPark** (Map p220; 33 Hyderabad Rd; ⊙24hr), which includes a children's playground and themed gardens with winding pathways and stepping stones crossing trickling streams. The prototype **glasshouses**, not open to the public, were used to test building materials, cooling systems, temperatures and humidity for the giant conservatories at Gardens by the Bay (p52).

From HortPark, a leaflike bridge crosses over Alexandra Rd to the stunning Forest Walk, which offers eye-level views of the jungle canopy blanketing Telok Blangah Hill. The walkway eventually leads to **Telok Blangah Hill Park** (Map p220) with its flower-filled **Terrace Garden**, and further along to **Henderson Waves**, an undulating sculptural pedestrian walkway suspended 36m above the forest floor. The shardlike towers soaring in the distance are part of Reflections at Keppel Bay, a residential development designed by starchitect Daniel Libeskind.

The final 500m to the summit of **Mt Faber** is a short but reasonably steep climb that's rewarded with fine views, restaurants and the option of a cable car ride back down the hill to HarbourFront mall and MRT station, or further on to Sentosa Island. It's easy to walk down to HarbourFront from here, on a pathway that descends the forested hillside.

To get to Kent Ridge Park, take the MRT to Pasir Panjang, cross the main road then walk about 15 minutes up Pepys Rd to Reflections at Bukit Chandu. If you go this way, you can grab a bite to eat at Eng Lock Koo (p131).

7.30pm Tue-Sat, to 6pm Sun; Ⓜ Kent Ridge then ⊞A2 university shuttle bus) **FREE** Located on the campus of the **National University of Singapore (NUS)**, this trio of small art museums holds some remarkably fine collections. Ancient Chinese ceramics and bronzes dominate the ground-floor **Lee Kong Chian Art Museum**, while one floor up, the **South and Southeast Asian Gallery** showcases paintings, sculpture and textiles from the region. Above it, the **Ng Eng Teng Gallery** is dedicated to Ng Eng Teng (1934–2001), one of Singapore's foremost artists, best known for his figurative sculptures.

At the time of writing, the **Lee Kong Chian Natural History Museum** (Map p221; http://lkcnhm.nus.edu.sg; 2 Conservatory Dr; Ⓜ Kent Ridge then ⊞A2 university shuttle bus), formerly the Raffles Museum of Biodiversity Research, was due to re-open in its striking, purpose-built building in early 2015. The museum is directly opposite the NUS Museum.

LABRADOR NATURE RESERVE   HISTORIC PARK

Map p220 (www.nparks.gov.sg; Labrador Villa Rd; ⊙24hr; ⊞408, Ⓜ Labrador Park) Combining forest trails rich in birdlife and a beachfront park, Labrador Park is scattered with evocative **war relics**, only rediscovered in the 1980s. Look out for old gun emplacements mounted on moss-covered concrete casements as well as remains of the entrance to the old fort that stood guard on this hill. The Labrador Secret Tunnels – a fascinating series of storage and armament bunkers – were closed indefinitely at the time of writing.

HAW PAR VILLA   MUSEUM

Map p220 (☑6872 2780; 262 Pasir Panjang Rd; ⊙9am-7pm, Ten Courts of Hell exhibit 9am-6pm; Ⓜ Haw Par Villa) **FREE** The refreshingly weird and kitsch Haw Par Villa was the brainchild of Aw Boon Haw, the creator of the medicinal salve Tiger Balm. After building a villa here in 1937 for his beloved brother and business partner, Aw Boon Par, the siblings began building a Chinese mythology theme park within the grounds. The result is a curious garden of garish statues and dioramas, each recounting Chinese folk stories and fables.

Top billing goes to the Ten Courts of Hell, a walk-through exhibit depicting the gruesome torments awaiting sinners in the underworld.

⊙ West Singapore

JURONG BIRD PARK   WILDLIFE RESERVE

Map p221 (www.birdpark.com.sg; 2 Jurong Hill; adult/child $25/16; ⊙8.30am-6pm; Ⓜ Boon Lay then ⊞194 or 251) Jurong Bird Park may be a little more neglected than higher profile siblings Singapore Zoo, Night Safari and River Safari, but it remains a great place for young kids. Home to some 600 species of feathered friends – including spectacular macaws – its highlights include the interactive High Flyers (11am and 3pm) and Kings of the Skies (10am and 4pm), as well as the wonderful Lory Loft forest enclosure, where you can feed colourful lories and lorikeets.

Young ones can splash about at the Birdz of Play (11am to 5.30pm weekdays, 9am to 5.30pm weekends), a wet-and-dry play area with an on-site shop selling swimwear, and there's a guided tram to cart you around the park when energy levels are low.

SUNGEI BULOH WETLAND RESERVE   WILDLIFE RESERVE

Map p221 (☑6794 1401; www.sbwr.org.sg; 301 Neo Tiew Cres; ⊙7.30am-7pm; Ⓜ to Kranji then ⊞925) **FREE** This raw sweep of mudflats, ponds and secondary forest is a birdspotter's paradise, with migratory birds including egrets, sandpipers and plovers joining locals like herons, bitterns, coucals and kingfishers. It's also the best place to see monitor lizards. Free guided tours run every Saturday at 9.30am.

The reserve is one of the few remaining mangrove areas in Singapore, and its three walking trails (from 3km to 7km) are dotted with bird-viewing huts and lookouts. The trails will double to six by late 2014: part of a major extension that will also include a new visitors centre, cafe, and a second entrance on Kranji Way. Don't forget the mosquito repellant!

KRANJI WAR MEMORIAL   MEMORIAL

Map p221 (☑6269 6158; 9 Woodlands Rd; ⊙7am-6pm; Ⓜ Kranji then ⊞160, 170, 960 or 961) **FREE** The austere white structures and rolling hillside of the Kranji War Memorial contain the WWII graves of thousands of Allied troops. Headstones, many of which are inscribed simply with the words: 'a soldier of the 1939–1945 war', are lined in neat rows across manicured lawns. Walls are inscribed with the names of over 25,000 men and women who lost their lives in Southeast Asia, and registers are available for inspection. The memorial is a 1km walk from Kranji MRT station.

SINGAPORE SCIENCE CENTRE   MUSEUM
Map p221 (www.science.edu.sg; 15 Science Centre Rd; adult/child $12/8; ⊙10am-6pm; MJurong East) Packed with all types of push-pull-twist-and-turn gadgets, Singapore's endearingly geeky science museum electrifies curious little minds. It's as absorbing as it is educational, covering subjects as varied as the human body, aviation, optical illusions, ecosystems, the universe and robotics.

To reach it, alight at Jurong East MRT station, turn left along the covered walkway, cross the road and continue past a covered row of stalls before crossing Jurong Town Hall Rd.

TIGER BREWERY   BREWERY
Map p221 (☑6860 3005; www.tigerbrewery-tour.com.sg; 459 Jln Ahmad Ibrahim; adult/child $18/12; ⊙10am, 11am, 1pm, 2pm, 4pm & 5pm Mon-Fri; MBoon Lay then ☒182) You've been drinking its beers all holiday, so you might as well see how they're made. Visits to the Tiger Brewery are divided into two parts: the first is a 45-minute tour of the place, including the brew house and the packaging hall; the second is the real highlight – 45 minutes of free beer tasting in the wood-and-leather Tiger Tavern. Tours must be booked in advance.

CHINESE GARDEN   PARK
Map p221 (1 Chinese Garden Rd; ⊙6am-11pm; MChinese Garden) Flanking Jurong Lake, this garden offers 13.5 hectares of landscaped tranquillity – perfect for an afternoon stroll, though not worth the trek from the city alone. The garden features numerous pavilions, a seven-storey pagoda (open 8am to 7pm), an impressive display of *penjing* (Chinese bonsai; open 9am to 5pm), and a Japanese Garden (6am to 7pm). The rundown turtle and tortoise museum is best avoided.

CHINESE HERITAGE CENTRE   MUSEUM
Map p221 (☑6790 6176; http://chc.ntu.edu.sg; Nanyang Technological University, 12 Nanyang Dr;

VISITING SINGAPORE'S FARMS

Few visitors to Singapore realise that there's a small but thriving farming industry in northwest Singapore. We're not talking rolling fields of grazing cows: in Singapore, limited space calls for farms that specialise in organic vegetables, goat's milk, or plants, flowers and herbs. They offer a refreshingly different take on Singaporean life.

The **Kranji Countryside Association** (www.kranjicountryside.com) is a farm collective helping to promote the industry. It runs a daily minibus service, the **Kranji Express** (Kranji MRT station; adult/child $3/1; ⊙9am-6pm, every 75min) that does a loop from the Kranji MRT station, visiting many of the best farms en route, including ones where you can buy goat's milk, sample frog meat, see fish, grab a coffee, have lunch or even spend the night. You can hop off the bus whenever you see a farm you like the look of, then hop back on again when the bus next comes around. The scheduled stops change from time to time, but usually include the following:

GardenAsia (www.gardenasia.com; 240 Neo Tiew Cres; ⊙bistro 11am-6pm Wed & Thu, to 11pm Fri & Sat, 10am-6pm Sun) A large, well-stocked garden centre with a lovely waterside bistro.

D'Kranji Farm Resort (www.dkranji.com.sg; 10 Neo Tiew Lane 2; ⊙restaurant 11am-2.30pm & 5.30-11pm; beer garden 4pm-1am) Smart villa-style accommodation, plus a restaurant and beer garden.

Bollywood Veggies (www.bollywoodveggies.com; 100 Neo Tiew Rd; admission $2, Kranji Express passengers free; ⊙9am-6.30pm Wed-Fri, 8am-6.30pm Sat & Sun) A very popular place to stop and amble through the rustic garden with its cashew, papaya and starfruit trees, and nosh on beautiful, healthy grub at the bistro.

Hay Dairies Goat Farm (Map p221; ☑6792 0931; www.haydairies.com.sg; 3 Lim Chu Kang Lane 4; ⊙9am-4pm) Here you can buy fresh goat's milk and other snacks.

Jurong Frog Farm (Map p221; ☑6791 7229; www.jurongfrogfarm.com.sg; 56 Lim Chu Kang Lane 6; ⊙9am-5.30pm Sat & Sun, by appointment only Tue-Fri) A bit run down, but visitors can sample frog meat here.

WORTH A DETOUR

GILLMAN BARRACKS

Where soldiers once stomped, curators now roam. Built in 1936 as a British military encampment, **Gillman Barracks** (Map p220; www.gillmanbarracks.com; 9 Lock Rd; ⊙individual galleries vary, generally 11am-7pm Tue-Sat, to 6pm Sun; Ⓜ Labrador Park) is now a rambling art outpost, with 15 commercial galleries studding verdant grounds. It's a civilised way to spend a late afternoon, browsing free temporary exhibitions of painting, sculpture and photography from some of the world's most coveted creatives.

Among the galleries is the Manila-based **Drawing Room** (www.drawingroomgallery. com; 01-06 Gillman Barracks ; ⊙11am-7pm Tue-Sat, to 6pm Sun), which showcases most contemporary Filipino artists. Next door, New York's **Sundaram Tagore** (www.sundaramtagore.com; 01-05, Gillman Barracks; ⊙11am-7pm Tue-Sat, to 6pm Sun) takes a more global approach, its stable of artists including award-winning photographers Edward Burtynsky and Annie Leibovitz. Across the street, Italy's **Partners & Mucciaccia** (www.partnersandmucciaccia.net; 02-10 Gillman Barracks; ⊙noon-7pm Tue-Fri, 11am-7pm Sat, 11am-6pm Sun) profiles mostly modern and contemporary Italian artists, with the odd retrospective featuring the likes of Marc Chagall and Pablo Picasso. Further up the hill, Berlin-based **ARNDT** (www.arndtberlin.com; 01-35 Gillman Barracks; ⊙11am-7pm Wed-Sat, to 6pm Sun) represents a mix of European and Asian artists, among them influential Indonesian painter and sculptor Jumaldi Alfi.

Plan ahead and book a table at Gillman's **Naked Finn** (Map p220; www.nakedfinn. com; 01-13 Gillman Barracks; ⊙noon-2pm & 6-10pm Mon-Fri, noon-3pm & 6-10.30pm Sat), a hip eatery/cocktail joint with an ever-changing menu of phenomenally fresh seafood (if it's on the menu, don't pass up the beautifully grilled Atlantic scallop). If you don't have a booking, try your luck – walk-ins are welcome, but space is limited.

If heading in on the MRT, alight at Labrador Park station and walk north up Alexandra Rd for 800m; the entry to Gillman Barracks is on your right. A one-way taxi fare from the CBD is around $10.

⊙9.30am-5pm Mon-Fri, 10am-5pm Sat; Ⓜ Pioneer then 🚌179) **FREE** It's no must-see, but this small museum at Nanyang Technological University is worth a visit if you're seeking some off-the-radar culture. Of its three exhibitions, 'Chinese More or Less' and 'From Danmaxi to Xinjiapo: Ceramic and the Chinese in Singapore' are the most interesting. The former focuses on the Chinese diaspora, including representations of Chinese people in popular Western culture, while the latter showcases archaeological artefacts found in and around Singapore, some dating back to the 14th century.

✕ EATING

In addition to the restaurants listed here, some of the bigger attractions in this part of Singapore have their own dining facilities. Jurong East MRT station is connected to two major malls with fantastic food options, and Kranji MRT station also has some eateries.

ENG LOCK KOO HAWKER CENTRE $
Map p220 (114 Pasir Panjang Rd, cnr Pepys Rd; mains from $3; ⊙individual stalls vary, generally 5am-3pm; Ⓜ Pasir Panjang) Handy for breakfast or lunch if you're on your way to either Reflections at Bukit Chandu or Kent Ridge Park for the Southern Ridges walk, this small collection of stalls inside an airy corner-shop premises does tea and coffee, not to mention hawker favourites like chicken rice and *nasi goreng* (fried rice).

PERAMAKAN PERANAKAN $$
Map p220 (www.peramakan.com; L3 Keppel Club, 10 Bukit Chermin Rd; mains $10-24; ⊙11.30am-2.30pm & 6-9.30pm; ☎; Ⓜ Telok Blangah) Run by a genial couple of cooking enthusiasts, this paragon of homestyle Baba-Nonya cuisine migrated from its spiritual Joo Chiat home. Thankfully, classics such as *sambal* (chilli, onions and prawn paste) squid and *rendang* (spicy coconut curry) remain as good as ever. One dish not worth missing is *ayam buah keluak* (chicken in rich spicy sauce served with Indonesian black-nut pulp).

FABER PEAK   INTERNATIONAL $$

Map p220 (☑6377 9688; www.faberpeaksinga-pore.com; 109 Mt Faber Rd; ⓜHarbourFront, cable car Mt Faber) The Mt Faber cable car terminal is home to a trio of eateries, all with bird's-eye views. Top billing goes to yakitori-focussed, patio-graced Japanese restaurant **Moonstone** (www.epicurean.com.sg; 109 Mt Faber Rd; dishes $4-20; ⊙4pm-12.30am Sun-Thu, to 2am Fri & Sat). Cross-cultural dishes and patio dining define **Faber Bistro** (☑6377 9688; www.mountfaber.com.sg; 101 Mt Faber Rd; mains $13-15; ⊙3-11pm Mon-Thu, to 2am Fri, 11am-2am Sat, 11am-11pm Sun; ⓜHarbourFront), while super-casual family-friendly **Spuds & Aprons** (☑6377 9688; 109 Mt Faber Rd; mains $16-38; ⊙11am-11pm Sun-Wed, to 12:30am Thu, to 2am Fri & Sat) is another global affair, with a mix of local noodle and rice dishes, grilled sandwiches and mains like juicy pork belly.

On weekends bus 409 runs up here from HarbourFront MRT station. At other times you'll have to take a taxi, ride the cable car or walk up yourself.

★TAMARIND HILL   THAI $$$

Map p220 (☑6278 6364; www.tamarindrestaurants.com; 30 Labrador Villa Rd; mains $20-59, Sun brunch $60; ⊙noon-3pm & 6.30-10.30pm; ☐408, ⓜLabrador Park) In a colonial bungalow in lush Labrador Park, Tamarind Hill sets an elegant scene for exceptional Thai. The highlight here is the Sunday brunch (noon to 3pm), which offers a buffet of beautiful cold dishes and salads, and also as many dishes off the a la carte menu as you like (the sauteed squid is sublime). Book ahead.

🍺 DRINKING & NIGHTLIFE

★COLBAR   BAR

Map p220 (☑6779 4859; 9A Whitchurch Rd; ⊙11am-midnight Tue-Sun, kitchen closes 8.30pm; ☐191) Raffish Colbar is a former British officers' mess turned drinking spot. It's still 1930-something here: money is kept in a drawer, football team photos hang on the wall and locals linger with beers and well-priced ciders on the spacious verandah.

The old, stained menu has no shortage of hangover-friendly colonial classics, including a standout chicken curry with diced vegetables and proper old-school chips, all made by the venerable Mrs Tan.

☆ ENTERTAINMENT

ST JAMES POWER STATION   CLUB, LIVE MUSIC

Map p220 (www.stjamespowerstation.com; 3 Sentosa Gateway; ⊙hours vary, generally 5pm-late; ⓜHarbourFront) This 1920s power station is now a multivenue entertainment hub. Popular with a mostly local crowd, its bars and clubs include lush bar **Peppermint Park** (⊙5pm-3am Mon-Thu, to 4am Fri & Sat), thumping Thai club/live-music hybrid **Neverland II** (⊙9.30pm-6am), and karaoke bar **Mono** (⊙6pm-5am Sun-Thu, to 6am Fri & Sat). Minimum age at Mono is 18; at Neverland II it's 21 for women and 23 for men.

SINGAPORE TURF CLUB   HORSE RACING

Map p209 (www.turfclub.com.sg; 1 Turf Club Ave; Level 1 Grandstand & Level 2 Gallop $6, Owners' Lounge $30; ⓜKranji) Although not quite as manic as the Hong Kong races, a trip to Singapore Turf Club is nevertheless a hugely popular day out (bring your passport!). Races usually run on Fridays (6.20pm to 10.50pm) and Sundays (12.50pm to 6.30pm) and a dress code is enforced: no jogging shorts or singlets in the public grandstand; no shorts, collarless T-shirts or sandals in the Owners' Lounge.

OMNI-THEATRE   CINEMA

Map p221 (www.omnitheatre.com.sg; 21 Jurong Town Hall Rd; adult/child $12/10; ⊙vary according to showtimes, usually noon-6pm; ⓜJurong East) Next door to the Science Centre and Snow City, this IMAX cinema is home to Asia's largest seamless dome screen and shows stunning 45-minute documentary films.

🛍 SHOPPING

VIVOCITY   MALL

Map p220 (www.vivocity.com.sg; 1 HarbourFront Walk; ⊙10am-10pm; ⓜHarbourFront) Not just Singapore's largest shopping mall, VivoCity offers that rare commodity, open space. There's an outdoor kids' playground on level 2 and a rooftop 'skypark' where little ones can splash about in free-to-use paddling pools. The retail mix is mostly midrange, and there's a large Golden Village cineplex.

JEM   MALL

Map p221 (www.jem.sg; 50 Jurong Gateway Rd; ⊙10am-10pm; ⓜJurong East) Jem is located in booming Jurong East, an area planned to become a major shopping hub. Tenants include

MAKING A PUBLIC SPLASH
· ·
Singapore has some seriously impressive public pools which, at a couple of dollars or less, are among the island's best bargains. The following are among the best:

Jurong East Sports & Cultural Centre (Map p221; ☑6563 5052; 21 Jurong East St 31; adult/child $2/1; ☺8am-9.30pm Tue, Thu & Fri, 6.30am-9.30pm Wed & Sat, 2.30-9.30pm Sun; ⓂChinese Garden) A wow-inducing combo of giant wave pool, lazy river, waterslides, wading pool, jacuzzi and Olympic-sized pool. Expect huge crowds on weekends. It's a 600m walk from Chinese Garden MRT; walk west along Boon Lay Way and turn right into Jurong East St 31.

Jurong West Sports & Recreation Centre (Map p221; ☑6515 5332; 20 Jurong West Street 93; adult/child $2/1; ☺8am-9.30pm Wed-Mon ; ⓂPioneer) Thinner crowds is the trade off at this aquatic park in Singapore's far-flung west. It too features a lazy river, alongside a waterslide, wet-play area for young kids, jacuzzi and two 50-metre pools, one sheltered. From Pioneer MRT, walk west for 350m.

Pasir Ris Sports & Recreation Centre (Map p213; ☑6583 5523; 120 Pasir Ris; adult/child $1.50/1; ☺8am-9.30pm Thu-Tue; ⓂPasir Ris) Across in Singapore's northeast, this $40-million showstopper comes with two waterslides, wading and learner pools, jacuzzi and a 50m pool. It's also packed on weekends. You'll find it 300m north of Pasir Ris MRT on Pasir Ris Central.

Toa Payoh Swimming Complex (Map p209; ☑6752 5513; 301 Toa Payoh Lorong 6; adult/child $1.30/0.70; ☺6.30am-9.30pm Mon & Wed-Sun, 2.30-9.30pm Tue; ⓂToa Payoh) A simple, satisfying combo of wading pool and two 50m pools. Separate diving and competition pools are used for elite training by Singapore's national water polo, diving and synchronised swimming teams. It's 300m west of Toa Payoh MRT.

Most pools let you pay using EZ Link transport card. Bring your own towel, and check opening times, as pools sometimes close for maintenance. See www.myactivesg.com.

Uniqlo and H&M, Japanese bookstore chain Kinokunya, and local department store Robinsons. There's a booty of kids' clothing stores on level 4, state-of-the-art cinemas on level 6, and a funky food court in between.

Jem is attached to fellow newcomer **Westgate** (Map p221; westgate.com.sg; Gateway Dr; ☺10am-10pm; ⓂJurong East), home to Japanese department store Isetan and its fantastic basemant food hall. On level 4, **Westgate Wonderland** is a 1020-sq-metre adventure playground for kids, with both dry and wet areas, and a 10m-tall tree house.

🏃 SPORTS & ACTIVITIES

SNOW CITY   SNOW SPORTS
Map p221 (www.snowcity.com.sg; 21 Jurong Town Hall Rd; adult/child per 2hr $28/23, combined 1hr snow access & Science Centre ticket $18/16; ☺10am-6pm; ⓂJurong East) A hangar-sized deep freeze chilled to a numbing -5°C, Snow City features a slope three storeys high and 70m long, accessed via a silvery Star Trek–style airlock. Each session gives you an hour to throw yourself at high speed down the slope on a black inner tube. All visitors must be wearing long trousers (which can be rented) and socks (which can be bought). Ski jackets and boots are provided.

RINK   ICE SKATING
Map p221 (www.therink.sg; JCube, 2 Jurong East Central 1; adult/child $14/12, with rental skate boots, gloves & socks $21.50/19.50; ☺10am-9.30pm Mon-Thu & Sun, to 11.45pm Fri & Sat; ⓂJurong East) Singapore's first Olympic-sized ice rink is located on the third level of youthful mall JCube. Between 9.45pm and 11.45pm on Fridays and Saturdays, disco bunnies get their skates on for the weekly 'Disco on Ice'.

Sentosa Island

Neighbourhood Top Five

1 Indulging your inner child at Singapore's blockbuster theme park, **Universal Studios** (p136), home to warrior mummies, bad-tempered dinosaurs and the world's tallest duelling roller coasters.

2 Exploring the adorable, curious and deadly at the world's largest aquarium, **S.E.A. Aquarium** (p137).

3 Grabbing a board and riding some artificial waves at beachside **Wave House** (p139).

4 Sliding on your shades and brunching by docked yachts at trendy **Kith Cafe** (p138).

5 Cranking up the romance with an elegant dinner at tropical-chic **Cliff** (p138).

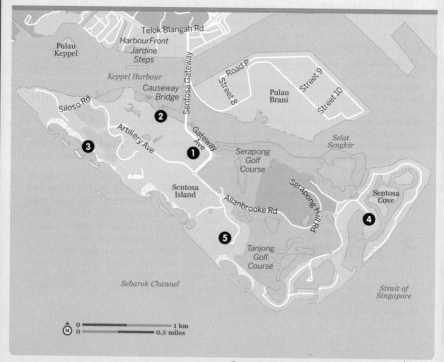

For more detail of this area see Map p222

Explore Sentosa Island

Epitomised by its star attraction, Universal Studios, Sentosa is essentially one giant theme park. And as such, kids love it. Packed with rides, activities and shows, most of which cost extra, it's very easy for a family to rack up a huge bill in one day spent here. And that's not counting visits to the casino. The beaches, of course, are completely free and very popular with locals and tourists alike.

You need at least a full day to experience everything Sentosa has to offer (and a very large wallet), but it's quite possible to just come here for a morning or afternoon on the beach. In fact, some people just come here for a drink in the evening. There are certainly worse ways to watch the sunset than at a beach bar on Sentosa, gin and tonic in hand.

Local Life

➡ **Weekend Brunch** Join clued-in locals and expats for a see-and-be-seen weekend brunch at Sentosa Cove, an upmarket residential and restaurant precinct in Sentosa's far east. The choice spot is Kith Cafe (p138), where both the coffee and grub are excellent.

➡ **Pool Party** Hang with Singapore's sun-kissed party people at Endless Summer (p139), W Singapore's monthly pool party. It's a fun, chilled-out session with no shortage of eye candy downing drinks, scanning the crowd, and cooling off in the hotel's to-die-for swimming pool.

Getting There & Away

➡ **Cable car** Ride the cable car to Sentosa from Mt Faber or the HarbourFront Centre.

➡ **Monorail** The Sentosa Express (7am to midnight) goes from VivoCity to three stations on Sentosa: Waterfront, Imbiah and Beach. VivoCity is directly connected to HarbourFront MRT station.

➡ **Walk** Simply walk across the Sentosa Boardwalk from VivoCity.

➡ **Bus** On Sentosa, a 'beach tram' (an electric bus) shuttles the length of all three beaches, running from 9am to 10pm Sunday to Friday, and from 9am to 11.30pm Saturday. Three colour-coded bus routes link the main attractions. Bus 1 runs from 7am to 10.30pm Sunday to Friday (to midnight Saturday), bus 2 runs from 9am to 10.30pm daily, and bus 3 runs from 8am to 10.30pm daily. All routes depart from the bus stop just east of Beach monorail station. The monorail, tram and buses are free.

Lonely Planet's Top Tip

Sentosa can get oppressively busy on weekends and public holidays. Queues and waiting times are generally shorter earlier in the week. Where possible, consider purchasing tickets online to save time as well. And be sure to pick up the handy *Sentosa Island* map leaflet, available at booths as you enter the island.

Best Thrills

➡ Universal Studios (p136)
➡ iFly (p139)
➡ Wave House (p139)

For reviews, see p137.➡

Best Places to Eat

➡ Cliff (p138)
➡ Mykonos on the Bay (p137)
➡ Malaysian Food Street (p137)
➡ Kith Cafe (p138)

For reviews, see p137.➡

Best for Families

➡ Universal Studios (p136)
➡ Adventure Cove Waterpark (p138)
➡ Songs of the Sea (p138)
➡ Skyline Luge Sentosa (p139)

For reviews, see p137.➡

UNIVERSAL STUDIOS SINGAPORE, RESORTS WORLD SENTOSA ©

 TOP SIGHT
UNIVERSAL STUDIOS

The top-draw attraction at Resorts World, Universal Studios offers a booty of rides, shows, shops and restaurants, all neatly packaged into themes based on your favourite Hollywood films. Attractions span the toddler-friendly to the seriously gut wrenching.

Rides & Rollercoasters

Transformers the Ride, an exhilarating, next-generation motion thrill ride, deploys high-definition 3D animation to transport you to a dark, urban otherworld where you'll be battling giant robots, engaging in high-speed chases, and even plunging off the edge of a soaring skyscraper. It's an incredibly realistic, adrenalin-pumping experience.

If you're a hardcore thrill-seeker, strap yourself onto **Battlestar Galactica**, the world's tallest duelling roller coasters. Choose between the sit-down HUMAN roller-coaster or the CYLON, an inverted rollercoaster with multiple loops and flips. If you can pull your attention away from screaming, make sure to enjoy the bird's eye view.

Roller-coaster thrills of the indoor kind are what you'll get on **Revenge of the Mummy**. The main attraction of the park's Ancient Egypt section, the ride will have you twisting, dipping and hopping in darkness on your search for the Book of the Living. Contrary to Hollywood convention, your journey ends with a surprising, fiery twist.

WaterWorld

Gripping stunts, fiery explosions and ridiculously fit eye candy is what you get at WaterWorld, a spectacular live show based on the Kevin Costner flick. Head here at least 20 minutes before show time if you want a decent seat. Those wanting a drenching should sit in the soak zone, right at the front.

DON'T MISS

➡ Transformers the Ride
➡ Battlestar Galactica
➡ Revenge of the Mummy
➡ WaterWorld

PRACTICALITIES

➡ Map p222
➡ www.rwsentosa.com
➡ Resorts World
➡ adult/child/senior $74/54/36
➡ ⊙10am-7pm
➡ monorail Waterfront

SIGHTS

UNIVERSAL STUDIOS THEME PARK
See p136.

★ S.E.A. AQUARIUM AQUARIUM
Map p222 (www.rwsentosa.com; Resorts World; adult/child incl entry to Maritime Experiential Museum $38/28; ☺10am-7pm; monorail Waterfront) You'll be gawking at over 800 species of aquatic creatures at the world's biggest aquarium. It's a sprawling, state-of-the-art complex that recreates 49 aquatic habitats found between Southeast Asia, Australia and Africa. The Open Ocean habitat is especially spectacular, its 36m-long, 8.3m-high viewing panel the world's largest.

Adjoining the aquarium is the interactive **Maritime Experiential Museum**, which explores the history of the maritime Silk Route.

FORT SILOSO MUSEUM
Map p222 (www.sentosa.com.sg; Siloso Point; adult/child $12/9; ☺10am-6pm, free guided tours 12.40pm & 3.40pm Fri-Sun; cable car Sentosa) Dating from the 1880s, when Sentosa was called Pulau Blakang Mati (Malay for 'the island behind which lies death'), this British coastal fort proved famously useless during the Japanese invasion of 1942. Documentaries, artefacts, animatronics and recreated historical scenes talk visitors through the fort's history, and the underground tunnels are fun to explore.

Designed to repel a maritime assault from the south, Siloso's heavy guns had to be turned around when the Japanese invaded from the Malaya mainland in WWII. The British surrender soon followed, with the fort later used as a POW camp by the Japanese.

IMAGES OF SINGAPORE MUSEUM
Map p222 (www.sentosa.com.sg; Imbiah Lookout; adult/child $10/7; ☺9am-7pm; monorail Beach) This interactive museum uses wax dummies, film footage and dramatic light-and-sound effects to traverse seven centuries of Singapore history. Kicking off with Singapore's Malay sultanate days, exhibits weave their way through its consolidation as a port and trading centre, WWII and the subsequent Japanese surrender.

BUTTERFLY PARK & INSECT KINGDOM WILDLIFE RESERVE
Map p222 (www.sentosa.com.sg; Imbiah Lookout, 51 Imbiah Rd; adult/child $16/10; ☺9.30am-7pm;

SENTOSA ISLAND SIGHTS

> **ⓘ SENTOSA ISLAND ENTRANCE FEE**
>
> Sentosa Island charges a small entry fee, based on the form of transport you take. If you walk across from VivoCity, the fee is $1. If you ride the Sentosa Express monorail, it's $4, which you can pay using your EZ Link or Nets transport card. Ride the cable car (p128) and the entrance fee is included in the price of your cable car ticket.

monorail Imbiah) A tropical rainforest in miniature, the Butterfly Park claims over 50 species of butterflies, many of which are endangered and nearly all of which have been bred in the park itself. Critters at the Insect Kingdom include thousands of mounted butterflies, rhino beetles, Hercules beetles (the world's largest) and scorpions.

EATING

As well as the places reviewed below, don't forget that the beach bars we list in our Drinking & Nightlife section all do food as well as drinks. And there are dozens of restaurants and cafes in Resorts World. Most attractions have at least a snack stall by the entrance, if not a full-blown cafe-restaurant.

MALAYSIAN FOOD STREET HAWKER CENTRE $
Map p222 (www.rwsentosa.com; Resorts World; snacks from $1, dishes from $3; ☺11am-10pm Mon-Thu, 9am-11pm Fri & Sat, 9am-10pm Sun; monorail Waterfront) With its faux Malaysian streetscape, this indoor hawker centre beside Universal Studios feels a bit fake. Thankfully, there's nothing fake about the food, cooked by some of Malaysia's best hawker vendors.

MYKONOS ON THE BAY GREEK $$
Map p222 (☏6334 3818; www.mykonosonthebay.com; 01-10 Quayside Isle, 31 Ocean Way, Sentosa Cove; tapas $9-27, mains $23-45; ☺6.30-10.30pm Mon-Wed, noon-2.30pm & 6.30-10.30pm Thu & Fri, noon-10.30pm Sat & Sun; ⏱; monorail Beach then ⌫3) At Sentosa Cove, this slick, marina-flanking taverna serves up Hellenic flavours that could make your *papou* weep. Sit alfresco and tuck into perfectly charred, marinated octopus, aubergine salad and

housemade *giaourtlou* (spicy lamb sausage). Book ahead later in the week.

KITH CAFE
CAFE **$$**

Map p222 (www.kith.com.sg; 31 Ocean Way, Sentosa Cove; ⊙8am-10pm Wed-Mon; ✆; monorail Beach then ▣3) This is the best of Kith's trio of outlets, set beside million-dollar yachts at salubrious Sentosa Cove. Grab a copy of Kinfolk, scan the crowd and tuck into fantastic cafe grub like Blackstone Eggs (English muffins with poached eggs, roasted tomatoes, bacon, grilled asparagus and hollandaise sauce).

SAMUNDAR
INDIAN **$$**

Map p222 (www.samundar.com.sg; 85 Palawan Beach Walk; mains $8-26; ⊙10.30am-9pm; ✆; monorail Beach then Sentosa Beach Tram) Grab an outdoor table and a few beers and order up big from the tandoor menu at this beachside beauty. Herbivores can rejoice, with no less than 14 mains, while the set meals (available until 5pm) are good value, priced similarly to the mains.

CLIFF
INTERNATIONAL **$$$**

Map p222 (✆6371 1425; www.sentosadining. com.sg; Sentosa Resort, 2 Bukit Manis Rd; mains $28-98; ⊙6.30-10pm; monorail Beach then ▣3) Perched high above Palawan Beach (although tree cover obscures some of the view), fine-dining Cliff is set by the dreamy swimming-pool area of luxury hotel Sentosa Resort. Book two weeks ahead to secure a coveted table by the balcony's edge – an especially evocative spot to savour artful dishes with predominantly French and Italian influences. Vegetarian options are few and far between.

🍷 DRINKING & NIGHTLIFE

WOOBAR
BAR

Map p222 (www.wsingaporesentosacove.com; W Singapore Sentosa Cove, 21 Ocean Way; ⊙8am-midnight Mon-Thu, to 2am Fri-Sun; monorail Beach then ▣3) The W Singapore's hotel bar is glam and camp, with suspended egg-shaped pods, gold footrests and floor-to-ceiling windows looking out at palms and pool. The afternoon 'high tea' (from $58 for two, excluding tax) is served in dainty bird-cages, while the weekly Wednesday Ladies' Night ($36 before tax) comes with free-pour

champagne between 7.30pm and 9pm, followed by half-price drinks until midnight.

COASTES
BAR

Map p222 (Siloso Beach; ⊙9am-11pm Sun-Thu, to 1am Fri & Sat; monorail Beach) More family-friendly than many of the other beach venues, Coastes has picnic tables on the sand and sun lounges ($20) by the water. If you're peckish, there's a comprehensive menu of decent standard offerings, including burgers, pasta and salads.

TANJONG BEACH CLUB
BAR

Map p222 (✆6270 1355; www.tanjongbeachclub. com; Tanjong Beach; ⊙11am-11pm Tue-Fri, 10am-midnight Sat & Sun; monorail Beach then Sentosa Beach Tram) Generally quieter than the bars on Siloso beach (except during the busy Sunday brunch session), Tanjong Beach Club is an evocative spot, with evening torches on the sand, a small, stylish pool for guests, and a sultry lounge-and-funk soundtrack.

⭐ ENTERTAINMENT

SONGS OF THE SEA
THEATRE

Map p222 (www.sentosa.com.sg; Siloso Beach; standard/premium seats $15/18; ⊙shows 7.40pm & 8.40pm; monorail Beach) Set around a replica Malay fishing village, this ambitious show fuses Lloyd Webber–esque theatricality with an awe-inspiring sound, light and laser extravaganza worth a hefty $4 million. Prepare to gasp, swoon and (occasionally) cringe.

🏃 SPORTS & ACTIVITIES

ADVENTURE COVE WATERPARK
SWIMMING

Map p222 (www.rwsentosa.com; Resorts World Sentosa; adult/child $36/26; ⊙10am-6pm; monorail Waterfront) The choice of rides at this water park are somewhat limited and better suited to kids and families. That said, adult thrill seekers will appreciate the Riptide Rocket (Southeast Asia's first hydro-magnetic coaster), Pipeline Plunge, and Bluewater Bay, a wave pool with serious gusto.

Rainbow Reef sees you snorkelling among 20,000 fish, while for an extra charge, you can wade with stingrays at the aptly named Ray Bay. The popular Dolphin Island attraction, also charged separately, allows visitors to interact with Indo-Pacific dolphins in a pool. Despite the popularity of this activity, it has received criticism by animal welfare groups who claim the captivity of marine life is debilitating and stressful for the animals, and that this is exacerbated by human interaction.

Adventure Cove Waterpark gets especially crowded on weekends and on holidays, so consider visiting outside these peak periods.

WAVE HOUSE SURFING

Map p222 (www.wavehousesentosa.com; Siloso Beach; 30min surf session from $35; ⏱10.30am-10.30pm, Double Flowrider 11am-10pm, FlowBarrel 1-10pm Mon, Tue, Thu & Fri, 11am-10pm Wed, Sat & Sun; monorail Beach) Two specially designed wave pools allow surf dudes and dudettes to practise their gashes and their cutbacks at ever-popular Wave House. The non-curling Double Flowrider is good for beginners, while the 3m FlowBarrel is more challenging. Wave House also includes beachside eating and drinking options.

SWIMMING SWIMMING

Sentosa has three artificial, family-friendly beaches with enough swaying palms to indulge those tropical daydreams. **Siloso Beach** (Map p222; cable car Sentosa, monorail Beach) is the most popular, jam-packed with activities, eateries and bars. With its free paddling pools, **Palawan Beach** (Map p222; monorail Beach) is great for younger kids, while **Tanjong Beach** (Map p222; monorail Beach) is the quietest of the three. Three bars on Siloso Beach and one on Tanjong Beach offer small swimming pools for customers.

Always stick to the designated swimming zones.

IFLY INDOOR SKYDIVING

Map p222 (www.iflysingapore.com; Cable Car Rd; adult/child from $79/70; ⏱10.30am-10pm Thu-Tue, noon-10pm Wed; monorail Beach) If you fancy freefalling from 3600m to 900m *without* leaping out of a plane, leap into this indoor skydiving centre. The price includes an hour's instruction followed by two short but thrilling skydives in a vertical wind chamber. Check the website for off-peak times, which offer the cheapest rates.

SKYLINE LUGE SENTOSA THRILL RIDING

Map p222 (www.sentosa.com.sg; luge & skyride combo from $15; ⏱10am-9.30pm; monorail

W IS FOR POOL PARTY

W Singapore's jaw-dropping pool is the setting for the hotel's hugely popular pool party **Endless Summer** (Map p222; www.wsingaporesentosacove.com; W Singapore Sentosa Cove, 21 Ocean Way; incl one drink $35; ⏱2-8pm, first Sun of month). Usually held on the first Sunday of the month, it draws a diverse crowd of locals, expats and hotel guests, both straight and gay, young and not so young. It's a fabulous way to spend a lazy, boozy, tropical afternoon, with DJ sets, live music, and no shortage of oversized sunglasses, bikinis and six-packs. Food for sale includes hot dogs, popcorn and decent satay. Visit the hotel website for dates and to book.

Beach) Take the skyride chairlift from Siloso Beach to Imbiah Lookout, then hop onto your luge (think go-cart meets toboggan) and race family and friends through hairpin bends and bone-shaking straights carved through the forest (helmets are provided and mandatory!). Young kids will love this.

MEGAZIP ZIP LINING

Map p222 (www.megazip.com.sg; Siloso Beach; zip line ride $39; ⏱11am-7pm; monorail Beach) Check out this 450m-long, 75m-tall zipline from Imbiah Lookout to a tiny island off Siloso Beach. An electric cart is on hand to shuttle riders up from the beach to the start point, where there's also a small adventure park with a climbing wall ($19) and other activities.

GOGREEN SEGWAY ECO ADVENTURE TOUR

Map p222 (☎9825 4066; www.segway-sentosa.com; fun ride $12, 30min eco adventure $38; ⏱10am-8pm; monorail Beach) These two-wheeled transporters will have you zipping around a 10-minute 'fun ride' circuit or, if you prefer, exploring the beachfront on a guided Eco Adventure trip. Equally futuristic are the electric bikes, yours to hire for $12 an hour. Eco Adventure riders must be at least 10 years old.

Islands & Day Trips

Pulau Ubin p141

An unkempt jungle of an island, Pulau Ubin offers a forest full of weird and wonderful creatures, dusty village streets and, best of all, the chance to explore it all by bicycle.

Southern Islands p143

Located just off the southeast coast of Sentosa, this trio of islands is tailor made for beachside picnics and lazy tropical lounging. Head across for a quick, soothing getaway.

Pulau Bintan p144

Expats and moneyed Singaporeans lap up the all-inclusive resorts in the north, but exploring Bintan's south offers an altogether more authentic taste of Indonesian island life.

Johor Bahru p147

Just under an hour away by bus from Singapore, the Malaysian city of Johor Bahru, or JB, is popular for cheap food, cheap-ish shopping, lively streets and a Lego theme park.

Pulau Ubin

Explore

It may be just a 10-minute bumboat ride from Changi Village, but Ubin seems worlds apart from mainland Singapore, and is the perfect city getaway for those who love the outdoors; particularly cycling.

Singaporeans like to wax nostalgic about Ubin's *kampong* (village) atmosphere, and it remains a rural, unkempt expanse of jungle full, of fast-moving lizards, strange shrines and cacophonic birdlife. Tin-roofed buildings bake in the sun, chickens squawk and panting dogs slump in the dust, while in the forest, families of wild pigs run for cover as visitors pedal past on squeaky rented bicycles. Set aside a full day if you can. It takes a couple of hours just to get here and, once you arrive, you won't want to be rushed.

The Best...
➡**Sight** Chek Jawa Wetlands
➡**Place to Eat** Pulau Ubin Village
➡**Activity** Cycling

Top Tip
To help reduce litter, maps are no longer given out on Pulau Ubin. However, you will find maps of the island drawn on wooden signboards that you can photograph and use for navigation.

Getting There & Away
Getting to Pulau Ubin is half the fun. First catch bus 2 from Tanah Merah MRT station (30 minutes) to the terminus bus stop at Changi Point Ferry Terminal. From there it's a 10-minute chug-along bumboat ride to Ubin (one-way $2.50, bicycle surcharge $2; 6am to 9pm). The small wooden boats seat 12 passengers, and only leave when full, but you rarely have to wait long. No tickets are issued. You just pay the boathand once you're on board.

◎ SIGHTS

PULAU UBIN VILLAGE   VILLAGE
Although not really a tourist sight, Pulau Ubin's only village of note is a ramshackle time capsule of Singapore's past and an interesting place to wander round. Fish traps and the skeletal remains of abandoned jetties poke out of the muddy water, stray cats prowl for birds, and docile dogs laze around on the sleepy streets. It's also the gateway to the island; home to the ferry terminal, bike-hire shops and the island's only restaurants.

CHEK JAWA WETLANDS   NATURE RESERVE
(⊙8.30am-6pm) **FREE** If you only have time for one part of the island, make it this part. Skirting the island's southeast, Chek Jawa Wetlands features a 1km **coastal boardwalk** that will have you strolling over the sea and through protected mangrove swamp to the 20m-high **Jejawi Tower**.

CYCLING AROUND UBIN

Apart from walking (which isn't a bad option at all) cycling is the only way to get around Ubin. Those heading for the Ketam Mountain Bike Park tend to bring their own better-quality bikes with them, but for the rest of us there are plenty of places in Pulau Ubin Village that rent perfectly adequate bikes for the day, from around $5 to $12. The bikes are pretty much identical, although some vendors seem to change prices on a whim. Cheapest and fairest of the lot is **shop 31**, which rents adult bikes for $5 to $8, and kids bikes for $5. Vendors should throw in a basket, a bike lock and a helmet if you ask.

You can't get maps of the island, but there are maps on signboards dotted around the place, so you can follow them. Because of the large swamp area in the central northern region of the island, you can't do a complete loop so if you want to explore the east and the west (note: the far west is off limits) you'll have to do a bit of back-tracking, but distances here are small so it hardly matters.

Although it looks like you can on the signboard maps, you can't in fact cross Sungai Mamam swamp for a shortcut between Noordin Campsite and Mamam Campsite. You have to go back via the main road.

Pulau Ubin

Pulau Ubin

Climb it for sweeping coastal and jungle views. You can't bring your bikes into the reserve so rent one with a bike lock and secure it to the bike stands at the entrance.

GERMAN GIRL SHRINE   TAOIST TEMPLE
Housed in a yellow hut beside an Assam tree, this shrine is one of the island's quirkier sights. Legend has it that the young German daughter of a plantation manager was fleeing British troops who had come to arrest her parents in WWI and fell fatally into a quarry. Somewhere along the way, this daughter of a Roman Catholic family became a Taoist deity, whose help some Chinese believers seek for good health and fortune.

The shrine is now filled with all manner of toys, offerings, folded lottery tickets, a medium's red table and chair, burning candles and joss paper. One hopes the little girl approves; her ghost is said to haunt the area to this day.

WEI TUO FA GONG TEMPLE   BUDDHIST TEMPLE
Sitting on small hillock overlooking a pond filled with carp and turtles, this 80-year-old temple contains a number of shrines surrounded by a huge variety of statuettes and iconography. They don't get too many visitors out this way, so chances are you'll be invited to stay for a cup of tea.

✖ EATING & DRINKING

The only place to have a meal is in **Pulau Ubin Village**. Get off the boat and turn left. There are half a dozen or so places here, most housed in *kampong* huts with tin roofs. They all serve similar fare, with noodles and rice dishes featuring alongside lots of seafood (naturally). Chilli crab is a favourite – expect to pay around $20 per person. Wash it down with a Tiger beer – what else?

There are a couple of **drinks stalls** along Jln Endul Senin; there are snacks, too.

SPORTS & ACTIVITIES

KETAM MOUNTAIN BIKE PARK   CYCLING

A series of trails of varying difficulty leads around Ketam Quarry and through some of the surrounding area. While it's not the most hardcore bike park on the planet, you really need to be more than just a beginner to deal with the steep slopes, sharp corners and relatively poor traction at various points on most of the trails.

There's a small bike-skills zone off to your left as you enter the area, and the German Girl Shrine is also close by.

Southern Islands

Explore

Three other islands popular for local escapes are bite-sized St John's, Lazarus and Kusu. Just south of Sentosa, they're ideal for fishing, swimming or just relaxing. While mildly crowded on weekends, they're almost deserted on weekdays – unless your visit (unluckily) coincides with a school camp.

Facilities are almost nonexistent but there are toilets on St John's and Kusu. Staying overnight in a bungalow is possible on St John's.

The Best...

→ **Sight** Kusu Kramats
→ **Place for a picnic** Kusu Island
→ **Activity** Beach bumming on Lazarus Island (p144)

Top Tip

Consider visiting on a Sunday, when the ferry service operates longer hours. Also, stock up on food and drinks before going as there are no shops or eateries on the Islands. You'll find a provisions shop and small eatery at Marina South Pier.

Getting There & Away

The **Southern Islands Ferry** (Map p205; www.islandcruise.com.sg; 31 Marina Coastal Dr;

adult/child return $18/12; ☺10am & 2pm Mon-Fri, 9am, midday & 3pm Sat, 9am, 11am, 1pm, 3pm & 5pm Sun) stops first at St John's (30 minutes), hangs around for about an hour, then sails on to Kusu (15 minutes). You can hop off one and catch the next with your return ticket, though there aren't many services (two on weekdays, three on Saturday, five on Sunday). Coming back, the last ferry leaves Kusu at 4pm Monday to Friday, at 4.30pm on Saturday and at 6.15pm on Sunday. Always check the schedule on the ferry company website before heading to the terminal. To get to Marina South Pier, take the MRT to Marina Bay, then take bus 402.

SIGHTS & ACTIVITIES

KUSU ISLAND   ISLAND

(www.islandcruise.com.sg) By far the smallest of the three islands, Kusu is also the most pleasant. Step off the boat and into an area of picnic-friendly landscaped gardens, home to a small **turtle sanctuary** and the colourful Taoist **Tua Pek Kong Temple**. Further on is the **beach**, its shallow water ideal for young kids. All of this, though, is on reclaimed flat land, which surrounds the original piece of Kusu – a forest-covered rock topped by the **Kusu Kramats**, three 19th-century Malay shrines.

You can visit the shrines, all painted a bright canary yellow, by climbing the 152 steps up through the trees to the top. Chances are you'll find devotees in the middle of prayer, their requests ranging from wealth, harmony and health, to marital bliss and (in the case of childless couples) the pitter patter of little feet.

ST JOHN'S ISLAND   ISLAND

(www.islandcruise.com.sg) Spooky St John's has a chequered past: it was a quarantine for immigrants in the 1930s before becoming a political prison and later a rehabilitation centre for opium addicts. A prison-like feel still lingers, barbed-wire fences and watch towers dotting the landscape. There's a small **beach** where some people picnic and a tiny tin-roofed **mosque** used by maintenance workers, but most visitors head here for a quiet spot of **fishing**.

The island has one self-contained, three-bedroom **bungalow** (per night from $53.50). For more information, click onto www.

sentosa.com.sg and follow the 'Nature' link. Camping is not allowed on St John's, although people occasionally flout the rules.

LAZARUS ISLAND   ISLAND

(www.islandcruise.com.sg) Almost entirely undeveloped, with little more than a bit of jungle and a sweeping **beach**, Lazarus Island is connected to St John's via a concrete walkway. The beach is a gorgeous, sandy affair – dotted with the odd posh yacht and (unfortunately) rubbish swept up by the tides. That said, it's as perfect a beach as you can expect in Singapore, and a fabulous spot to roll out your beach towel and soak up some rays.

Pulau Bintan

Explore

While the all-inclusive resorts in Bintan's north are a popular quick escape from Singapore, few venture to the island's rawer south. It's here that you'll find Bintan's cultural heart and biggest town, Tanjung Pinang – a gritty, ramshackle place of noisy, dusty, potholed streets that are utterly Indonesian. Dodge mopeds and rickshaws as you fight through the busy back-alleys to a local coffeeshop to get your bearings.

Rested, explore the market alleyways at the northeastern end of Jln Merdeka (between Jln Plantar and Jln Gambir), then head to the small jetties where you can board bumboats to either Senggarang (home to a Chinatown on stilts) or Penyengat, a small, rural island with royal tombs, palaces and a beautiful mosque.

The Best...

➡**Sight** Masjid Raya Sultan Riao
➡**Dish** *Ikan bakar* at Penyengat
➡**Place to Eat** Pinang Citywalk (p146)

Top Tip

It's cheaper and far less hassle to change money at moneychangers than in a bank. There are loads on Jln Merdeka (turn left out of the ferry terminal).

Getting There & Away

Ferries leave for Tanjung Pinang (1½ hours) from Singapore's Tanah Merah Ferry Terminal (bus 35 from Bedok MRT station). A seven-day, single-entry tourist visa for Indonesia ($17 or US$10, cash only) can be bought on arrival at Tanjung Pinang. The 13,000Rp departure tax must be paid in local currency when you leave.

Ferry companies include the following:

Falcon (⊡Singapore 6542 6786; www.indofalcon.com.sg; adult/child 1-way $28/23, return $50/40)

Sindo Ferries (p183)

Wave Master (⊡Singapore 6786 9959; www.streetdirectory.com/berlian-ferries; 1-way/return $40/50)

Need to Know

➡**Area Code** ⊡+62 771
➡**Location** 60km from Singapore

◉ SIGHTS

◉ Tanjung Pinang

Bintan's capital is a historic port town and trade centre with a still-thriving market culture and plenty of hustle and bustle. Touts swarm all over you as you get off the ferry. Ignore them all. Unfortunately, the tourist office (left as you leave the ferry terminal complex) had closed down on our last visit.

CETIYA BODHI SASANA   BUDDHIST TEMPLE

(Jln Plantar 2) This small, dockside Buddhist temple is the starting point for frenetic dragon boat races, held annually during the Dragon Boat Festival (fifth day of the fifth lunar month). If you're lucky, you might catch a Chinese opera at the open-air stage facing the temple. To get here, turn left out of the ferry terminal, walk about 500m down the main road, and turn left down Jln Pasar Baru (which becomes Jln Plantar). Just before reaching the water, turn left to the temple. On your way, explore the fascinating maze of alleyways and market stalls between Jln Plantar and Jln Gambir.

SLEEPING ON BINTAN

Tanjung Pinang is best tackled as a day trip from Singapore. The town's hotels range from spartan to utterly depressing. If you insist on staying overnight, book one of the better-quality resorts in the island's north.

Bintan Resort Ferries (p183) runs five direct services each way between Tanah Merah Ferry terminal and Bandar Bentan Telani on the north coast (six to seven each way on weekends). Most resorts organise shuttle services to and from the harbour as part of their package price.

Beyond the two slumber options listed below, you'll find a comprehensive list of resorts at www.bintan-resorts.com.

Mayang Sari Beach Resort (☑0770 692 505; http://mayang.nirwanagardens.com; Jln Panglima Pantar, Lagoi; r from US$114; ❇☎) A friendly, good-value spot featuring 50 thatched-roof, Balinese-style chalets, each with its own verandah. The property sits on a pleasant sandy beach, and has its own spa.

Banyan Tree Bintan (☑0770 693 100; www.banyantree.com; r incl breakfast from US$450; ❇☎☀) The lush and privileged Banyan Tree has famed spa facilities, a long beach and airy, elevated guest villas with traditional Indonesian accents and private relaxation pools.

VIHARA BHATRA SASANA   BUDDHIST TEMPLE

(Jln Merdeka) Dragons adorn the beautifully painted upturned eaves on the roof of this Chinese temple. A statue of Kuan Yin (Guanyin), the goddess of mercy, stands at the central altar. Turn left out of the ferry terminal and keep walking to the end of the road. The temple is on your right, on the corner with Jln Ketapang.

SULTAN SULAIMAN
BADRUL ALAMSYAH   MUSEUM

(Jln Ketapang; ⏱8.30am-2.30pm Tue-Thu, Sat & Sun, 8.30-11.30am Fri) Housed in a handsome building built by the Dutch in 1918, this petite museum houses mostly Chinese artefacts – coins, pottery, musical instruments, clothing, jewellery – but lacks English captions. Look out for the old *caping,* a type of chastity belt. To get here, turn right at Vihara Bhatra Sasana and it's soon on your left.

⊙ Penyengat

Once the heart of the Riao-Johor sultanate and the cultural hub of the Malay empire, the tiny island of Penyengat grew in the 16th century when the Malay sultanate fled here after being defeated by the Portuguese in Malacca. It's now home to Indo-Malaysians and Hakka Chinese immigrants who live either in stilt houses on the coastline or in brightly painted bungalows in the island's lush interior.

It's a 10-minute boat ride from Tanjung Pinang (per person one-way 6000Rp). The

15-man boats only leave when full so you sometimes have to wait a while. To get to the jetty, turn left out of the main ferry terminal, left at the first crossroads and then walk straight down the alleyway in front of you, which leads to the jetty.

MASJID RAYA SULTAN RIAO   MOSQUE

Its minarets topped with tall conical spires, this yellow-and-green fairytale of a mosque dates back to 1832. It's an active place of worship and although visitors are welcomed, they are expected to wear appropriate clothing; cover yourself up, or else admire the building from afar.

TOMBS & PALACES   HISTORICAL SITE

Penyengat was the royal capital of the Riao-Johor sultanate, and the island is dotted with the ruins of the palaces and tombs of these Malay rulers. Ones to look out for on your wanders include the ruined yet still-imposing palace **Istana Kantor**, straight on from the mosque, and the **tomb of Raja Hamidah**, off to the left of the mosque. There are many others that you'll stumble across as you walk around the island.

FORT   HISTORICAL SITE

At the far west of the island are the ruins of an impressive stone fort, built by the sultan Raja Haji in the 18th century to fend off Dutch attacks. Ironically, the **cannons** you see here are Dutch made. Raja Haji, incidentally, was the author of the first Malay grammar book, a reminder that this island

BECAK TOURS

Penyengat is small enough to walk around, but a fun alternative is to take a tour in a **becak** (pronounced 'beerchuk'; one-hour tour around 30,000Rp), a motorcycle rickshaw with a sidecar. Before jumping on board, make sure you agree on the price and clearly state that you want to see the entire island, including the fort.

was once a hotbed of intellectual and religious minds, and at one time was home to more than 9000 people.

◉ Senggarang

This predominantly Chinese village on the other side of the bay from Tanjung Pinang is reached by small wooden boats (per person one-way 6000Rp, 10 minutes), which are taken from the jetty called Plantar 1. To get to Plantar 1, continue past the alleyway that leads down to the jetty for boats to Penyengat and take the next left.

CHINATOWN VILLAGE

Boats to Senggarang will drop you at the jetty used to access Senggarang's so-called Chinatown. Far removed from Singapore's Chinatown, this one is residential rather than commercial, its many houses built on stilts above (thickly littered) sea water. The locals are mostly Teochew Chinese, believed to have been here since the 18th century. Look out for the private shrines that decorate the entranceway of many homes.

VIHARA DHARMA SASANA BUDDHIST TEMPLES

A decorative Chinese archway leads to this trio of temples, which look out to sea. The first two approached are also the oldest. Thought to be between 200 and 300 years old, their roof carvings are particularly ornate. Behind them is a more modern temple and two huge, colourful Buddha statues.

Walking away from Senggarang jetty, take the first left, continue to the end of the boardwalk, then turn right and keep walking until you hit dry land. From there you'll see the archway entrance to the complex.

BANYAN TREE TEMPLE BUDDHIST TEMPLE

If you walk out of the Vihara Dharma Sasana temple complex and keep going

straight, you'll soon reach a small village where, off to the right of the main road, you'll find a particularly unusual temple, housed in a building believed to date from 1811. Originally the house of a wealthy Chinese man, believed to be buried here, the building has, over the years, been swallowed up by the roots of a large banyan tree.

You can get back to the jetty from here without returning to the temple complex by taking the first left on your way back.

✖ EATING

If you're planning to catch an early morning ferry from Singapore, Tanah Merah Ferry Terminal has a branch of the excellent coffeeshop chain Killiney Kopitiam, where you can enjoy a Singaporean breakfast of *kaya* toast, runny eggs and *kopi*. They do plenty of main dishes too and, if you don't like *kopi*, they also do fresh Western-style coffee.

✖ Tanjung Pinang

Turn left out of the ferry terminal and you'll soon find a few *kedai kopi* (locals coffeeshops), where you can grab a drink, a snack or a bowl of *goreng* (noodles). In the evening, you'll find several food stalls scattered around town selling *mie bangka*, a Hakka-style dumpling soup. Other delicacies to look out for include *gong gong*, snails eaten with a toothpick, and *otak-otak*, small fishcakes barbecued in strips of banana leaves.

PINANG CITYWALK HAWKER CENTRE $

(Jln Teuku Umar; dishes 5000-13,000Rp; ⊗7am-2am, individual stalls vary) One of the cleaner places to eat in town is this modern, airy hawker centre, complete with a stage for bands. The large selection of stalls sell everything from fresh seafood, to *ayam penyat* (smashed fried chicken with spicy sambal) and *nasi lemak* (coconut rice). The beer here is refrigerated, which means there's no need for dodgy ice.

Pinang Citwalk is located behind the Vihara Bhatra Sasana temple. Enter from Jln Teuku Umar or Jln Ketapang.

✖ Penyengat

The jetty you walk along as you arrive on the island has a few small restaurants with outdoor seating. Look out for *ikan bakar,* delicious barbecued fish eaten with a side salad, a sweet-chilli dip and plain rice. Expect to pay around 35,000Rp per serving. Do as the locals do and eat it with your fingers. The teapots on the table are hand-washing water.

✘ Senggarang

Some locals open up the front of their stilt houses as small restaurants. Expect only the most basic of dishes, and little choice. Otherwise, you can grab snacks at small shops in the village near the Banyan Tree Temple.

Johor Bahru

Explore

Easy to visit in a day from Singapore, JB (no one calls it Johor Bahru) is determined to shake off its 'Wild West' reputation. New developments such as Puteri Harbour and Legoland to the west of the centre offer a glimpse of the region's shiny future, while central JB itself continues to offer a raffish antidote to Singapore's near-perfection.

Legoland aside, JB isn't known for any major tourist attractions. The main reason to visit is to experience a city more laid-back and gritty than its southern cousin.

Arrive in the morning and head to a coffeeshop like Restoran Huamui in the Heritage District for a leisurely breakfast. Wander the colourful lanes nearby, see a couple of the area's temples or (once it reopens) the Royal Abu Bakar Museum, then catch a bus or taxi to either Legoland or Johor Premium Outlets. By the time you read this, you should be able to dine at Puteri Harbour before catching a ferry directly from here to HarbourFront, Singapore.

Alternatively, head back to the Heritage District for a bite and a drink in a funky back-alley bar before making your way back across the border on the bus.

The Best...

➡**Sight** Royal Abu Bakar Museum
➡**Place to Eat** Kam Long Fishead Curry (p149)
➡**Place to Drink** Roost Juice Bar (p150)

Top Tip

Immigration checkpoints, for people coming back into Singapore, can be hellishly busy on weekend evenings. Try to avoid coming back at this time if you can.

Getting There & Away

Bus Getting to JB by bus takes about an hour. The easiest way is to catch the **Causeway Link** (www.causewaylink.com.my; 1-way $2.50/RM2.60; ⊘every 15min to 30min, roughly 6am-11.30pm). There are several routes, of which CW2 (departing from Queen Street Bus Terminal) and CW5 (departing from the Newton Food Centre car park on Clemenceau Ave N) are the most convenient.

Buy your ticket at the bus stop using the correct change. You will need to disembark at the Singapore immigration checkpoint to clear immigration, then reboard any Causeway Link bus route across to JB (don't lose your ticket!), where you will need to clear Malaysian immigration.

The Malaysian immigration checkpoint is in the heart of JB, and buses to KSL City Mall (bus IM17), Puteri Harbour (bus LM1) and Legoland (bus LM1) depart from the adjoining JB Sentral bus station at street level. If heading to Legoland, ignore the uniformed touts at the bus station; buy your bus ticket (one way RM4.50) on the bus, and your Legoland ticket online or at the park itself.

Taxi A taxi from central Singapore to central JB will cost you around $40. You can also pay for a seat in a shared taxi from Queen Street Bus Terminal for $10 per person. Shared taxis leave when full.

◉ SIGHTS

ROYAL ABU BAKAR MUSEUM   MUSEUM
(☏07-223 0555; Jln Ibrahim; adult/child US$7/3; ⊘9am-5pm Sat-Thu) The marvellous Istana Besar, once the Johor royal family's principal

---

ⓘ MALAYSIA VISAS

Most foreigners do not need a Malaysian visa for short-term stays, but check before you leave. Border formalities are pretty straightforward, although weekends can get very busy. Don't forget your passport!

Johor Bahru

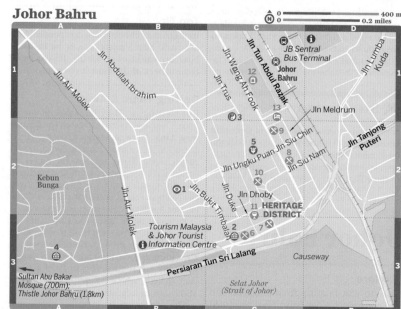

Johor Bahru

palace, was built in Victorian style by Anglophile sultan Abu Bakar in 1866. It was opened as a museum to the public in 1990 and displays the incredible wealth of the sultans. It's now the finest museum of its kind in Malaysia, and the 53-hectare palace grounds (free entry) are beautifully manicured.

In mid-2014 the museum was being extensively remodelled and was yet to be reopened.

ROUFO GUMIAO   TAOIST TEMPLE
(Jln Trus; ◷7.30am-5.30pm) Once the centre of JB's Chinese immigrant community, and used by five different ethnic groups to worship five different Chinese gods, this small but atmospheric temple is more than 130 years old. Little remains of its original ma-

sonry after major renovations in 1995, but it does house some genuine antiques.

SULTAN ABU BAKAR MOSQUE   MOSQUE
(Jln Gertak Merah) With stunning whitewashed walls and blue-tiled roofing, this mosque features a mix of architectural influences, including Victorian. Built between 1892 and 1900, it's hailed as one of the most magnificent mosques in the area. Sadly, non-Muslims cannot enter the building.

CHINESE HERITAGE MUSEUM   MUSEUM
(42 Jln Ibrahim; RM10; ◷9am-5pm Tue-Sun) Well laid-out exhibits document the history of Chinese immigrants in the region. Learn how the Cantonese brought their carpen-

try skills here, while the Hakkas traded in Chinese medicines and the Hainanese kickstarted a trend in coffeeshops, a legacy which lasts to this day.

SRI RAJA MARIAMMAN DEVASTHANAM
HINDU TEMPLE

(www.rajamariammanjb.com; 4 Jln Ungku Puan) Adorned with ornate carvings, devotional artwork and a commanding, brightly painted *gopuram* (tower), this beautiful Hindu temple is the heart of JB's Hindu community.

BANGUNAN SULTAN IBRAHIM
LANDMARK

(State Secretariat Bldg, Bukit Timbalan) Sitting magnificently atop Bukit Timbalan, designed by Palmer & Turner architects, the Bangunan Sultan Ibrahim is a mighty melange of colonial pomp, Islamic motifs and indigenous design. Completed in 1942, the city landmark was used as a fortress by the Japanese as they prepared to attack Singapore.

✗ EATING & DRINKING

KAM LONG FISHHEAD CURRY
SEAFOOD $

(Jln Wong Ah Fook; curry from RM19; ⏰8am-4pm) Old-school tiles, swirling fans and regular queues: coffeeshop-style Kam Long enjoys celebrity status for one thing and one thing alone: rich, bubbling fishhead curry. The fish is always wonderfully fresh, the gravy packed with flavour, and the topping of *taukee* (fried beancurd skins) a fantastic, textured twist. You may have to wait for (or share) a table, but with food this good, who's complaining?

HIAP JOO BAKERY & BISCUIT FACTORY
BAKERY $

(13 Jln Tan Hiok Nee; buns from RM2.50; ⏰7am-5.30pm Tue-Sat) For over 80 years this little bakery has baked delicious buns, cakes and biscuits in a charcoal oven just as the founder had done before in his native Hainan, China. Join the queue for its famous coconut buns (filled with sweet, moist desiccated coconut) and the legendary banana cake (available Tuesday to Saturday), both great snacks for roaming explorers.

NIGHT MARKET
MALAY $

(off Jln Siu Chin; dishes from RM4; ⏰3.30pm-midnight) Open-air stalls selling all manner of local dishes line the T-shaped alleyway here, which links Jln Siu Chin, Jln Meldrum and Jln Wong Ah Fook. Come early evening, the place heaves with hungry customers, and while there's no shortage of tasty noodle and rice dishes, our favourite is the *sup kambing*, a slightly spicy mutton soup mopped up with chunks of French bread.

ISLANDS & DAY TRIPS JOHOR BAHRU

SLEEPING IN & AROUND JOHOR BAHRU

Thistle Johor Bahru (☎07-222 9234; www.thistle.com; Jln Sungai Chat; r from RM325; P ❄ @ 🛜 🏊) The sleekest option in Johor Bahru itself, with marble bathrooms, curvaceous swimming pool and a light, crisp, contemporary ambience. Overlooking the Strait of Johor, the hotel is located 4km from central JB, just off the main road, Jln Lingkaran.

Traders Hotel (☎07-560 8888; www.shangri-la.com/johor/traders; Persiaran Puteri Selatan, Puteri Harbour, Nusajaya; rm from RM380; @ 🛜 🏊; 🚌LM1) Located in up-and-coming Puteri Harbour, 33km west of central Johor Bahru, this new, 238-room hotel is the best in the region, with an in-house spa, infinity pool looking out over the marina, and stylish rooms with designer furniture and marble bathrooms. The suitelike Premier Rooms feature a separate lounge area. Free shuttle bus to Legoland.

Legoland Hotel (☎07-597 8888; www.legoland.com.my/Hotel; 7 Jln Legoland, Bandar Medini Iskandar; r from RM850; 🛜 🏊; 🚌LM1) Flanking the Legoland theme park – a 33km trip west of central Johor Bahru – the 249-room, family-focussed Legoland Hotel rightfully looks like a giant Lego castle. There are dedicated adult and kids pools, disco lights in the lifts, and three room themes: Pirate, Adventure and Kingdom. The more expensive Premium Rooms face Legoland itself.

Citrus Hotel (☎07-222 2888; www.citrushoteljb.com; 16 Jln Station; d/f from RM150/209; ❄ 🛜) If you insist on sleeping in the city centre, Citrus Hotel is one of the better options. Rooms are small but brightly accented, and staff are friendly. On the downside, the building is not very well sound proofed and the wi-fi signal can be frustratingly weak.

ISKANDAR MALAYSIA: BACK TO THE FUTURE

Peninsular Malaysia's southernmost city has some very ambitious plans. Upon completion in 2025, Iskandar Malaysia – a development region which includes Johor Bahru and stretches from Pasir Gudang in the east to Tanjung Pelepas in the west – is set to radically transform the area into a cutting-edge metropolis and liberal trading port.

Its new, Moorish-inspired administrative centre, Kota Iskandar, has been built from scratch, 33km west of central Johor Bahru, in Nusajaya. This district is also home to Puteri Harbour, a burgeoning marina district that's home to the luxe Traders Hotel, shops, cafes and waterfront restaurants such as Indian standout **Olive** (07-509 6617; Puteri Harbour, Nusajaya, Level LG; mains RM12-35; 11am-11pm; ; LM1), which peddles fantastic *Lahori seekh* (spiced lamb kebab) and prawn biryani.

Four kilometres west of Puteri Harbour is Iskandar's first theme park, **Legoland Malaysia Resort** (www.legoland.com.my; 7 Jln Legoland, Bandar Medini Iskandar; Legoland & Legoland Water Park adult/child RM150/120; varies, generally 10am-6pm; ; LM1). The resort incorporates the rides, rollercoasters and giant Lego replicas of Legoland, the waterslides and pools of Legoland Water Park, as well as the Legoland Hotel, which makes for a fun one-night base if you're travelling with young kids. If you don't have kids, neither of the parks is really worth going out of your way for.

At the time of research, direct ferry services (adult/child RM58/43 return) between HarbourFront in Singapore and Puteri Harbour were scheduled to commence in 2014. Visit www.ridaa.com.my or http://iskandar.asia for updates.

Bus LM1 connects JB Sentral to Puteri Harbour (35 minutes) and Legoland (45 minutes) via the Larkin Bus Terminal. A taxi from central Johor Bahru to Legoland will cost around RM70 to RM80 – use only the trusted blue-coloured 'Executive Taxis'.

Many of the stalls are Muslim-run, so don't expect to sink a beer with your meal. Wash it down with a fresh coconut instead.

RESTORAN HUAMUI — COFFEESHOP $
(131 Jln Trus; mains RM6-9; 8am-6pm) This airy, fan-cooled coffeeshop with delightful mosaic-tiled flooring is also very popular with locals. The menu is a mix of Malay, Indonesian and Chinese. We loved the *kampong* (village) fried rice. Also does *kaya*-toast set breakfasts.

ANNALAKSHMI — INDIAN $
(07-227 7400; 39 Jln Ibraham; set meals by donation; 11am-3pm Mon-Sat;) An authentic vegetarian Indian restaurant run by volunteers of the Temple of Fine Arts, with the motto of 'eat what you want and give as you feel'. Meals are a set and the ambience is somewhat refined.

ROOST JUICE BAR — BAR
(9 Jln Dhoby; noon-4pm & 6pm-midnight Mon-Sat, 6pm-midnight Sun) A trendy back-alley bar with retro furniture and laid-back staff, this is the coolest hangout in the colonial district. Beer is half the price you'd pay in Singapore, and the fresh-fruit smoothies (served in mini seaside buckets!) are delicious.

🛍 SHOPPING

Recent price rises mean shopping in JB is not the bargain it once was. Prices are still slightly cheaper than Singapore, but quality is poorer.

JOHOR BAHRU CITY SQUARE — MALL
(Jln Wong Ah Fook; 10am-10pm) In the city centre, slick and shiny City Square houses over 200 retailers, with local and global fashion labels, cinemas and decent food options.

KSL MALL — MALL
(www.kslcity.com.my; 33 Jln Seladang; 10am-10pm) With around 500 retailers, KSL is JB's biggest mall. Expect high-street brands, food, bars, a Tesco and cinemas. To get here, catch bus IM17 from JB Sentral bus station.

JOHOR PREMIUM OUTLETS — MALL
(www.premiumoutlets.com.my; Indahpura, Kulaijaya; 10am-10pm) Expect 20% to 60% off premium brands at this top-notch outlet mall. Stores include Aigner, Coach, Ermenegildo Zegna, Furla, Polo, Ralph Lauren and Tumi. There's no shortage of food options, including a food court. Catch bus JPO1 from the JB Sentral bus station (around one hour). From Puteri Harbour or Legoland, catch JBO (45 minutes).

Sleeping

Staying in Singapore is expensive. Budget travellers have it best, as hostel rooms can be had for $20 a night. Newer midrange hotels are lifting the game with better facilities and good, regular online deals. Luxury digs are expensive but plentiful and among the world's best, with options from colonial and romantic, to architecturally cutting-edge.

Hostels

A recent wave of 'flashpacker' hostels in and around Chinatown and Little India have smartened up the budget slumber scene. Dorms may still be on the smaller side, but new bunks, coupled with stylish communal bathrooms and lounge areas are making for an altogether more appealing scenario. Note that hostels tend to get booked up on weekends, especially the (limited) private rooms, so book in advance. Little India remains the place with the most budget beds.

Hotels

Singapore offers a thrilling collection of hotels, from luxe colonial digs like the Raffles Hotel and Fullerton Hotel, to hip, idiosyncratic boutique spots like Wanderlust, Naumi and the New Majestic. Standards are high, but then so are the prices – check web offers for bargains. Central business hotels like Carlton City can be great value on weekends, while other midrange options like Ramada Singapore at Zhongshan Park counter their not-so-central location with lower prices and top-notch facilities.

Serviced Apartments

For medium- to long-term stays, Singapore has a number of serviced apartments. It is also possible to rent rooms in private flats or whole private apartments; visit www.airbnb.com for an extensive choice. Rents are high, regardless of how near or far from the city centre you are.

Probably the best place to start looking for long-term rental in Singapore is **Singapore Expats** (www.singaporeexpats.com), which has detailed information on the different districts, outlines the whole rental procedure and carries an apartment search engine. The Singapore section of www.craigslist.org is also a good place to look.

Actual Prices May Vary

In Singapore's midrange and top-end hotels, room rates are about supply and demand, fluctuating daily. Travellers planning a trip to Singapore need to keep this in mind, especially if you're planning to come here during a major event. For example, room prices *triple* during the Formula One night race.

Be aware that top hotels usually add a 'plus plus' (++) after the rate they quote you. Ignore this at your peril. The two plusses are service charge and GST, which together amounts to a breezy 17% on top of your bill. All prices quoted in our listings are from the day of our visit inclusive of the ++ tax; your own price may vary.

Accommodation Websites

Apart from booking directly on the hotel's website listed in our reviews, you can also book rooms on these websites.
➡ **Asiarooms** (www.asiarooms.com)
➡ **Booking.com** (www.booking.com) User-friendly hotel booking site.
➡ **Lonely Planet** (http://hotels.lonelyplanet.com) Book rooms on Lonely Planet's website.
➡ **HotelsCombined** (www.hotelscombined.com)
➡ **Kayak** (www.kayak.com)

NEED TO KNOW

Price Ranges
$ under $100
$$ $100 to $250
$$$ over $250

Reservations
Book way in advance during peak periods, which include the Formula One race. Even average hostels tend to be booked up over the weekends.

Tipping
Tipping isn't expected in hostels. It's good form to tip hotel porters and cleaning staff a dollar or two.

Checking In & Out
Check-in time is usually 2pm, check out at 11am. If the hotel isn't full, you can usually extend these hours out by an hour or two if you ask nicely. Similarly, your room may be ready for check-in before the official time. If not, you should be able to leave you luggage at the hotel until your room is ready.

Breakfast
Hostels often include a simple breakfast (toast with spreads and coffee/tea). Midrange and top-end hotels may include breakfast, depending on the deal or room type. This is usually indicated when booking online. If breakfast is not included in the price, it is often offered as an add-on.

Air-Conditioning
Air-conditioning is standard in most hotels and hostels. Properties with air-conditioning are indicated with an air-con icon in our reviews.

Lonely Planet's Top Choices

Fullerton Bay Hotel (p154) What's not to love about a luxe hotel where every handsome room is waterside?

Parkroyal on Pickering (p154) A lush, vertical jungle designed by one of Singapore's hottest architect studios.

Raffles Hotel (p154) Legend and romance still linger at Singapore's most famous slumber pad.

W Singapore – Sentosa Cove (p162) Luxury meets youthful verve at this chic, playful retreat on hedonistic Sentosa Island.

Best by Budget

$
Bunc@Radius (p158) Our favourite flashpacker hostel delivers cheap chic in the backpacker heartland of Little India.

5footway.inn Project Boat Quay (p154) Another new-school hostel, with local art and a killer location right on Boat Quay.

Checkers Inn (p158) A backpacker classic, packed with colour, savvy and spunk.

$$
Wanderlust (p159) Idiosyncratic rooms packed with imagination, quirkiness and designer twists in intriguing Little India.

Park Regis (p154) Attentive service, modern rooms and a fantastic pool just a stone's throw from Chinatown and the Quays.

Holiday Inn Express (p159) A fresh, new, good-value option just a block from Orchard Rd.

$$$
Fullerton Bay Hotel (p154) Elegant, light-filled luxury perched right on Marina Bay.

Parkroyal on Pickering (p154) Striking architecture, hanging gardens and a stunning infinity pool.

Capella Singapore (p162) Cascading pools, lush jungle gardens and svelte, chic interiors on Sentosa.

Best for History

Raffles Hotel (p154) A rambling, colonial icon with a long list of illustrious guests

Fullerton Hotel (p154) Soaring columns and historical anecdotes grace a former GPO.

Hotel Fort Canning (p155) An elegant, park-fringed oasis.

Best for Kids

Marina Bay Sands (p155) Home to the world's most celebrated rooftop pool.

Shangri-La's Rasa Sentosa Resort (p162) Kid-centric poolside fun surrounded by Sentosa's theme parks and attractions.

W Singapore – Sentosa Cove (p162) Whimsical rooms and an epic pool at Sentosa's discerning end.

Best Views

Marina Bay Sands (p155) Ego-boosting views of downtown skyscrapers or sci-fi Gardens by the Bay.

Fullerton Hotel (p154) Romantic river panoramas and views of Marina Bay Sands' light-and-laser spectacular.

Ritz-Carlton Millenia Singapore (p155) Survey burgeoning skyline and Marina Bay from this uber-luxe retreat.

Where to Stay

Neighbourhood	For	Against
Colonial District, Marina Bay & the Quays	Very central, with good transport options. Variety of accommodation, from flashpacker hostel to iconic luxury hotels.	Cheap hotel accommodation is generally of poor to average quality, and usually in noisy areas.
Chinatown & the CBD	A stone's throw from great eateries, bars and nightlife. Culturally rich, good transport links and an excellent range of accommodation, many in restored shophouses.	Too touristy for some.
Little India & Kampong Glam	Backpacker Central, with the largest choice of cheap accommodation in Singapore. Has some lovely higher-end boutique hotels. Also has a unique atmosphere that is unlike any other district of Singapore. Fabulous food and good transport links.	Too grotty for some. Streets can get very noisy in the evenings, especially at weekends. Not much in the way of quality, international-standard hotels.
Orchard Road	On the doorstep of Singapore's shopping mecca. Fine choice of quality hotels, including top-name international chains.	Slim pickings for budget travellers. Hotlist eateries and bars thin on the ground.
Eastern Singapore	Quiet (a relative concept in Singapore), close to the cooling breeze of East Coast Park, close to the airport.	The MRT service doesn't run to this area; sights in the east are quite spread out so there's no real central location to stay in.
Northern & Central Singapore	Competitively priced hotels offering more bang for your buck. A local neighbourhood vibe, great local eateries and good transport links.	Reliance on transport to reach the city centre and major sights. Lack of hotlist restaurants, bars and clubs within walking distance.
Sentosa & Other Islands	Ideal for families, with a resort-like vibe and easy access to kid-friendly attractions, beaches and sporting activities. Quieter, basic options can be found on St John's Island and Pulau Ubin.	Synthetic Sentosa lacks character, and getting into the city centre is a slight hassle; this becomes more of an issue from the other islands.

SLEEPING

🛏 Colonial District, Marina Bay & the Quays

5FOOTWAY.INN PROJECT
BOAT QUAY   HOSTEL $

Map p202 (www.5footwayinn.com; 76 Boat Quay; dm from $22, tw incl breakfast $76; ❄@🛜; MClarke Quay) Right on Boat Quay, this 66-room, new-school hostel is the best of 5.footway.inn's four Singapore branches. White-washed dorms come in two-, three- and four-bed configurations, and though rooms are small (superior rooms have windows), they're modern and comfortable, with white wooden bunks and handy bedside power sockets. Bathrooms are modern, reception operates round-the-clock, and the cheap-chic breakfast lounge comes with river-view balcony seating.

There's no communal kitchen, though Chinatown's cheap eats are an MRT stop away.

★ PARK REGIS   HOTEL $$

(☎6818 8888; www.parkregissingapore.com; 23 Merchant Rd; r from $200; ❄@🛜🏊; MClarke Quay) The Park Regis' regular deals are fantastic value, offering central, higher-end midrange accommodation at very accessible prices. Rooms are smallish but modern and light-filled, with window seating and warm, amber accents. The gym is small but adequate, and overlooks the hotel's fabulous terrace pool, which comes with a cascading waterfall feature and bar.

Staff are wonderfully helpful, and the hotel is an easy walk from both the Quays and Chinatown.

PARK VIEW HOTEL   HOTEL $$

(☎6338 8558; www.parkview.com.sg; 81 Beach Rd; r incl breakfast from $152; ❄@; MBugis) This midrange hotel is centrally located to the Bugis shopping area, though where the park is we can't say. Though all rooms have bathtubs, some of the cheaper rooms are windowless. Don't expect anything beyond dull shades of white, beige and brown in the rooms here – the real value is in the location.

★ FULLERTON BAY HOTEL   HOTEL $$$

Map p202 (☎6333 8388; www.fullertonbayhotel. com; 80 Collyer Quay; r from $550; ❄@🛜🏊; MRaffles Place) The Fullerton Hotel's luxe, contemporary sibling sits right on Marina Bay. It's a light-filled, heavenly scented, deco-inspired number. Rooms are suitably plush and stylish, with high ceilings, wood and marble flooring, and warm, subdued hues. The marble bathrooms feature Bulgari amenities and a glass panel looking into the room and at Marina Bay and beyond. Some rooms face Customs House, so ensure to request one facing Marina Bay directly.

The hotel's rooftop bar and pool are stunning, and the hotel's afternoon high tea arguably the finest in town.

★ PARKROYAL ON PICKERING   HOTEL $$$

Map p208 (☎6809 8888; www.parkroyalhotels.com; 3 Upper Pickering St; r from $350; ❄@🛜🏊; MChinatown) Dramatic, cascading gardens; bird-cage cabanas right on the infinity pool; and a striking design evocative of terraced paddy fields. This outstanding newcomer is the work of local architect firm Woha, who designed everything down to the wastepaper baskets. Rooms are light, crisp and contemporary, with natural wood and soothing green hues, high ceilings and heavenly mattresses.

Desks are generously sized, and stylish bathrooms feature sliding panels and amenities from the on-site St Gregory Spa.

★ RAFFLES HOTEL   HOTEL $$$

Map p202 (☎6337 1886; www.raffleshotel.com; 1 Beach Rd; r from $745; ❄@🛜🏊; MCity Hall) The grand old dame of Singapore's Colonial District has seen many a famous visitor in her time, from Somerset Maugham to Michael Jackson. It's a beautiful place of white colonial architecture, lush pockets of green, and historic bars. Rooms are suitably Old World and elegant, with spacious parlours, polished wooden furniture and floorboards, verandahs and lazily swirling ceiling fans.

Then there's the location, right in the heart of the Colonial District and within easy reach of most of the must-see neighbourhoods.

FULLERTON HOTEL   HOTEL $$$

Map p202 (☎6733 8388; www.fullertonhotel. com; 1 Fullerton Sq; r from $400; ❄@🛜🏊; MRaffles Place) Occupying what was once Singapore's magnificent, Palladian-style general post office, the grand old Fullerton offers classically elegant rooms in muted tones. Entry-level rooms look 'out' into the inner atrium, so consider spending a little

BOOKING ON THE FLY

If you arrive in Singapore without a hotel booking, don't despair. The efficient **Singapore Hotel Association** (www.sha.org.sg) has desks at Changi airport, one at each terminal's arrival hall.

There are dozens of hotels on its lists, ranging from budget options right up to Raffles Hotel. There's no charge for the service, and promotional or discounted rates, when available, are passed on to you. You can also book the hotels over the internet on the association's website.

If you've made it as far as Orchard Rd and still don't have a hotel room (and don't fancy sleeping in the park), **Singapore Visitors Centre @ Orchard** (Map p216; ☑1800 736 2000; www.yoursingapore.com; cnr Cairnhill & Orchard Rds; ☺ 9.30am-10.30pm, hotel reservations until 9pm daily) works with hotels in the local area and can help visitors get the best available rates.

more to gain access to the hotel's private Straits Club (complimentary breakfast and evening cocktails) and upgrade to the more inspiring river- or marina-view rooms.

The 25m terrace pool is a swoon-worthy showpiece, complete with river and skyline views.

HOTEL FORT CANNING   LUXURY HOTEL $$$
Map p202 (☑6559 6770; www.hfcsingapore.com; 11 Canning Walk; r from $550; ❄@☎☒; ⓂDhoby Ghaut) What was once British military headquarters is now a luxury hideaway, surrounded by the greenery of Fort Canning Park. While we love the three swimming pools, exceptional gym and complimentary evening aperitifs and canapes, the rooms are the star attraction. Graced with high ceilings and parquetry flooring, they make for gorgeous retreats, each with Poltrona Frau chaise longue, Jim Thompson silk bedheads, and soothing botanical colours.

Original French windows and see-through glass separate room and bathroom, the latter a white marble wonder with soaking tub and large window looking out over the park or city.

NAUMI   BOUTIQUE HOTEL $$$
Map p202 (☑6403 6000; www.naumihotel.com; 41 Seah St; r incl breakfast from $400; ❄@☎☒; ⓂCity Hall, Esplanade) Slinky, revamped Naumi comes with commissioned artwork, playful quotes and a rooftop infinity pool with skyline views. Standard rooms are relatively small but cleverly configured, with chic, neutral hues, 400 thread-count Egyptian cotton, Nespresso machine and complimentary minibar. Shower panels turn opaque at the flick of a switch, with a dramatically lit, stand-alone 'beauty bar'

(bathroom counter) in the room itself. Ninth-floor rooms come with city views.

Suites are decadent and utterly extraordinary. Choose from a classic Coco Chanel-inspired design or a bold, colourful Andy Warhol number, the latter with a stand-alone round tub slap bang in the middle of your room.

RITZ-CARLTON MILLENIA SINGAPORE   LUXURY HOTEL $$$
Map p202 (☑6337 8888; www.ritzcarlton.com/singapore; 7 Raffles Ave; r from $420; ❄@☎☒; ⓂPromenade) No expense was spared, no feng shui geomancer went unconsulted and no animals were harmed in the building of this luxe, five-star establishment. Its recently refreshed rooms are light, plush and beige, with good-sized work spaces, high-end linen and unimpaired city or Marina Bay views. The hotel's multimillion-dollar art collection features works by Hockney, Warhol, Stella and Chihuly, and its afternoon high tea is exceptional.

MARINA BAY SANDS   HOTEL $$$
Map p205 (☑6688 8888; www.marinabaysands.com; 10 Bayfront Ave; r from $420; ❄@☎☒; ⓂBayfront) Part of the ambitious Marina Bay Sands casino/retail complex, the Sands hotel is famed for its amazing rooftop infinity pool, which straddles the roofs of the three hotel buildings. Hotel rooms are spacious, modern and comfortable, though admittedly cookie-cutter in style. A good choice for casino and mall fans, check online for the best deals.

SOMERSET BENCOOLEN   APARTMENTS $$$
Map p216 (☑6849 4688; www.somerset.com; 51 Bencoolen St; 1-bed apt from $320; ❄@☒;

SLEEPING COLONIAL DISTRICT, MARINA BAY & THE QUAYS

Ⓜ Dhoby Ghaut) If you're going to live large in Singapore, the Somerset Bencoolen might be the place to do it. The fully furnished serviced apartments are big and beautiful, with floor-to-ceiling windows offering spectacular views. The rooftop pool is an especially nice touch, as are the guided floorlights in the lobby, presumably to help get you to your room after a big night. Book well in advance or prepare to be waitlisted.

🛏 Chinatown & the CBD

Riding the shophouse restoration wave, Chinatown has some particularly fine mid- to top-range boutique hotels. There's also a growing band of good-value, centrally located hostels.

RUCKSACK INN   HOSTEL $
Map p206 (☑6438 5146; www.rucksackinn. com; 52 Temple St; dm incl breakfast from $22; ✳@☎; Ⓜ Chinatown) Travellers' messages are lovingly scrawled all over the streetside columns of this friendly, two-level hostel. Decked out in white metal bunk beds and quirky wall murals, the dorms come in six-, eight- and 12-bed configurations, with one six-bed female-only room. All are clean,

modern and cosy, and the communal showers feature rain shower heads. Perks include iMac computers, Xbox and Wii consoles, and 24-hour breakfast.

5FOOTWAY.INN
PROJECT CHINATOWN 1   HOSTEL $
Map p206 (www.5footwayinn.com; 63 Pagoda St; dm from $22, tw incl breakfast $76; ✳@☎; Ⓜ Chinatown) Yet another branch of flashpacker hostel 5footway.inn, occupying three locations along Pagoda St in buzzing Chinatown. Concrete floors, iMac computers and colourful art keep things looking cool, though the scuffed walls could use a lick of paint. Rooms are comfy though small (book a window room if you insist on natural light), with a female-only dorm available, as well as a small outdoor terrace for alfresco downtime.

FERNLOFT   HOSTEL $
Map p206 (☑6323 3221; www.fernloft.com; Unit 92, 2nd fl, 5 Banda St; dm incl breakfast from $22; ✳@☎; Ⓜ Chinatown) Located in a housing block overlooking the Buddha Tooth Relic Temple, this compact branch of the excellent Fernloft hostel chain is run by the charismatic Auntie Aini. As with many hostels in Singapore, the dorms (which include a

---

HISTORIC HOTELS

It's not just Raffles (p154) that has an illustrious past. Goodwood Park Hotel (p160), dating from 1900 and designed to resemble a Rhine castle, served as the base for the Teutonia Club, a social club for Singapore's German community, until 1914 when it was seized by the government as part of 'enemy property'. In 1918 the building was auctioned off and renamed Club Goodwood Hall, before it morphed again into the Goodwood Park Hotel in 1929, and fast became one of the finest hotels in Asia.

During WWII it accommodated the Japanese high command, some of whom returned here at the war's end to be tried for war crimes in a tent erected in the hotel grounds. By 1947 the hotel was back in business with a $2.5 million renovation programme bringing it back to its former glory by the early 1960s. Further improvements in the 1970s have left the hotel as it is today.

The Fullerton Hotel (p154) occupies the magnificent colonnaded Fullerton Building, named after Robert Fullerton, the first governor of the Straits Settlements. Upon opening in 1928, the $4 million building was the largest in Singapore. The General Post Office, which occupied three floors, was said to have the longest counter (100m) in the world at the time. Above the GPO was the exclusive Singapore Club, in which Governor Sir Shenton Thomas and General Percival discussed surrendering Singapore to the Japanese.

In 1958 a revolving lighthouse beacon was added to the roof; its beams could be seen up to 29km away. By 1996 the GPO had moved out and the entire building underwent a multimillion-dollar renovation and reopened in 2001 to general acclaim, receiving the prestigious Urban Redevelopment Authority Architectural Award the same year.

four-bed female-only room) are window-less, though everything is kept clean and tidy.

Best of all, you're within walking distance of Chinatown and Tanjong Pagar's booming restaurant and bar scenes.

BEARY GOOD HOSTEL HOSTEL $

Map p206 (☑6222 4955; www.abearygoodhostel.com; 66 Pagoda St; dm incl breakfast from $27, tw incl breakfast $78; ✳@☎✉; ⓂChinatown) While Beary Good Hostel and its Smith St sibling Beary Nice Hostel only offer dorms, the bigger Beary Best Hostel (also nearby on Upper Cross Rd) delivers two-bed private rooms for privacy seekers. Whichever Beary branch you choose, you can expect fun, brightly painted spaces, free local calls, separate bathrooms for boys and girls, and 24/7 reception.

PILLOWS & TOAST HOSTEL $

Map p206 (☑6220 4653; www.pillowsntoast.com; 40 Mosque St; dm incl breakfast from $28; ✳@☎; ⓂChinatown) It's dorm beds only at this super-friendly, centrally located hostel. Although the wooden bunks are looking a little worn, rooms are clean (the hostel has a shoes-off policy). Common areas are small but treated with TLC.

BLISS HOTEL BOUTIQUE HOTEL $$

Map p206 (☑6438 1088; www.blisshotel.com.sg; 62 Upper Cross St; s/d from $120/140; ✳☎; ⓂChinatown) Budget, boutique Bliss has an enviable location right across the street from the Chinatown MRT station. Rooms are contemporary and smart, with comfortable beds and modern fixtures. Be aware that some rooms come with see-through glass toilet and shower, which makes for awkward moments if you have company. Sound-proofing is not a strong point; light sleepers should bring ear plugs just in case.

Service is professional and courteous.

★AMOY BOUTIQUE HOTEL $$$

Map p206 (☑6580 2888; www.stayfareast.com; 76 Telok Ayer St; s/d incl breakfast from $318/368; ✳@☎; ⓂTelok Ayer) Not many hotels are accessed through a historic Chinese temple, but then the Amoy is no ordinary slumber pad. History inspires this contemporary belle, from the lobby feature wall displaying old Singaporean Chinese surnames, to custom-made opium beds in the cleverly configured 'Cosy Single' rooms. Plush doubles include grilled wall motifs and Ming-style porcelain basins, and all rooms feature designer bathroom, Nespresso machine and complimentary minibar.

The generosity continues with free limousine pickup from the airport.

NEW MAJESTIC HOTEL BOUTIQUE HOTEL $$$

Map p206 (☑6347 1927; www.newmajestichotel.com; 31-37 Bukit Pasoh Rd; r from $248; ✳@☎✉; ⓂOutram Park) Still one of the best boutique hotels in Chinatown, offering 30 unique rooms done up in a mix of vintage and designer furniture, each designed by a different Singaporean artist. Among the highlights are the private garden suite, attic rooms with loft beds and 6m-high ceilings, and the fabulous aquarium room with a glass-encased bathtub as its central feature.

Rooms come with a Nespresso coffee machine, and discounts can bring rates down to less than $300. Topping it off is a small but fetching mosaic pool, and a pop-up shop in the lobby selling local design wares and cool Singapore tomes.

SCARLET BOUTIQUE HOTEL $$$

Map p206 (☑6511 3333; www.thescarlethotel.com; 33 Erskine Rd; r from $255; ✳@☎; ⓂOutram Park) The revamped Scarlet offers great service and stylish rooms just around the corner from trendy, bar-packed Ann Siang Rd and Club St. In colour schemes of teal blue or gold and bronze, the chic rooms feature silky wallpaper, dark Oriental furniture and firm mattresses. The 1st-floor Premium rooms are especially plush and fun, complete with velvety chaise longues.

Although rooms on the 1st floor don't have windows, high ceilings and skylights render them far from gloomy. Check the hotel website, as discounts of 20% are commonly available.

HOTEL 1929 BOUTIQUE HOTEL $$$

Map p206 (☑6347 1929; www.hotel1929.com; 50 Keong Saik Rd; s/d from $199/219; ✳@☎; ⓂOutram Park) Owned by the same people behind nearby New Majestic, 1929 is also pretty slick, although not in the same class as its big brother. Rooms are tight, but good use is made of limited space, and interiors are cheerily festooned with vintage designer furniture (look out for reproduction Eames and Jacobson) and Technicolor mosaics.

Rooftop suites have private terraces, and discounts mean you can snag some rooms for less than $200. iPads are also available for loan.

CARLTON CITY
HOTEL $$$

Map p208 (✆6632 8888; carltoncity.sg; 1 Gopeng St; r from $280; ✳@☎❄; MTanjong Pagar) A soaring, polished business hotel in booming Tanjong Pagar, the 386-room Carlton City delivers smart, generic rooms in muted grey, cocoa and red. Although small, bathrooms are contemporary, with most offering both shower and bathtub. On-site facilities include an outdoor pool and jacuzzi, small gym with modern equipment, and funky 'sky bar' looking out over the port and Sentosa.

CLUB
BOUTIQUE HOTEL $$$

Map p206 (✆6808 2188; www.theclub.com.sg; 28 Ann Siang Rd; r from $470; ✳☎; MChinatown) Behind its crisp, white, colonial-era facade, the Club keeps things svelte and light with 28 spacious, minimalist, white-and-black rooms spiked with coloured mood lighting and low-rise beds. In-house hangouts include rooftop bar Ying Yang and designer whiskey bar B28, though most punters seem to prefer toasting and flirting further along Ann Siang Hill and Club St.

🛏 Little India, Kampong Glam & Jalan Besar

Little India is the heart of the backpacker scene, with a raffish charm and vibrant street life. Northeast of Little India, Jalan Besar is pulling cool hunters with its string of Third Wave cafes, of-the-moment eateries and small design shops.

★ BUNC@RADIUS
HOSTEL $

Map p210 (✆6262 2862; www.bunchostel.com; 15 Upper Weld Rd; dm incl breakfast from $20; ✳@☎; MBugis, Little India) Fresh, clean, new-school Bunc@Radius is the coolest flashpacker hostel in town. Concrete floor, art installations and a choice of both iMac and PC computers give the spacious lobby are hip, boutique feel. Dorms – in six-, eight-, 10- and 12-bed configurations – offer both single and double beds, with each thick mattress wrapped in a hygiene cover (no bed bugs!).

There's a female-only floor, private rooms with flatscreen TV, an outdoor movie deck with bean bags, and a fabulous, semialfresco kitchen that will make you want to cook.

HIVE
HOSTEL $

(✆6341 5041; www.thehivebackpackers.com; 269A Lavender St; dm/s/tw incl breakfast from $21/40/60; ✳@☎; MBoon Keng) On the edge of up-and-coming hipster 'hood Jalan Besar, ever-friendly Hive is looking fresh after a recent renovation. Dorms are a cooling, contemporary combo of white-washed walls, metal bunks and concrete floors, while the modern bathrooms feature rain showers. The private rooms are great value, and the communal lounge/dining area is a comfy spot to nibble on your free breakfast.

Five minutes' walk south of Boon Keng MRT Station.

B88 HOSTEL
HOSTEL $

Map p210 (✆6298 0015; www.b88hostel. com; 134 Jln Besar; dm incl breakfast from $26; ✳@☎; MBugis, Little India) Within walking distance of Little India, Kampong Glam and emerging hipster 'hood Jalan Besar, this five-floor hostel serves up both mixed and female-only dorms. All feature open-ended 'pod-like' beds, with two dorms offering queen-size mattresses. Only one dorm comes with windows, though this is also the noisiest.

Communal bathrooms are modern, and the kitchen-lounge combo is a funky, boho-chic affair, with patchwork armchairs and a mural celebrating Singaporean food and coffee.

CHECKERS INN
HOSTEL $

Map p210 (✆6392 0693; www.checkersinn.com. sg; 46-50 Campbell Lane; dm incl breakfast from $25; ✳@☎; MLittle India) Bright, spacious and fabulously funky, Checkers Inn has no shortage of fans. From the feature walls to the bed sheets, dorms are splashed with colour, and there are female-only dorms available. The modern, communal kitchen is capped with a striking Technicolor ceiling, while the smart, modern lounge area is more boutique chic than budget pit.

FOOTPRINTS
HOSTEL $

Map p210 (✆6295 5134; www.footprintshostel. com.sg; 25A Perak Rd; dm incl breakfast from $25; ✳@☎; MLittle India) A cheap and friendly hostel in Little India. Dorms – which come in beds of six, 10 and 12 – are narrow but bright and clean, with female-only dorms available to boot. The communal bathrooms are modern, while the communal living area recalls the set of a bad Hong Kong movie – think chunky leather couches, pastel hues and a chandelier that could make royalty blush.

★ WANDERLUST   BOUTIQUE HOTEL **$$**

Map p210 (☑6396 3322; www.wanderlusthotel.com; 2 Dickson Rd; r from $170; ✳@☎; ⓜBugis) Wanderlust delivers wow factor with its highly imaginative, individually designed rooms, from monochromatic 'Pantone' numbers and comic-book 'mono' rooms, to 'whimsical' rooms with themes like 'tree' and 'space'. Extra perks include excellent service, free breakfast, complimentary iPad use and a hip bar and French noshery.

ALBERT COURT VILLAGE HOTEL   HOTEL **$$**

Map p210 (☑6339 3939; www.stayfareast.com; 180 Albert St; r from $200; ✳@☎; ⓜLittle India) A short walk south of Little India, this is a splendid, colonial-era hotel in a shophouse redevelopment that now shoots up eight storeys. Rooms are classic and spacious, with carved wooden furniture, smallish but spotless bathrooms, and a choice of fan or aircon. Service is top-notch and there's wi-fi throughout. As is the case for most hotels in Singapore, you'll find the best deals online.

IBIS SINGAPORE ON BENCOOLEN   HOTEL **$$**

Map p210 (☑6593 2888; www.ibishotel.com; 170 Bencoolen St; r from $200; ✳@☎; ⓜBugis) Ibis offers sensible, low-frills comfort, from a generic lobby sexed up with colourful modular furniture, to smallish, spotless, cookie-cutter rooms with crisp sheets, light wood and peachy hues. Bathrooms are small, clean and modern, and guests have complimentary access to a California Fitness gym nearby. Thoughtful extras include a free shuttle bus to Sentosa. See the website for regular discounts.

KAM LENG HOTEL   BOUTIQUE HOTEL **$$**

(☑6239 9399; www.kamleng.com; 383 Jln Besar; r from $90; ✳☎; ⓠ65, 145, 857, ⓜFarrer Park) Hipster meets heritage at Kam Leng, a revamped retro hotel in the up-and-coming Jalan Besar district. Common areas are studiously raw, with distressed walls, faded Chinese signage, colourful wall tiles and Modernist furniture. Rooms are tiny and simple, yet cool, with old-school terrazzo flooring and pastel colour accents. A word of warning: rooms facing Jln Besar can get rather noisy.

Kam Leng is also home to Suprette (p90), one of the neighbourhood's hottest eateries.

PERAK HOTEL   HOTEL **$$**

Map p210 (☑6299 7733; www.peraklodge.net; 12 Perak Rd; r from $150; ✳@☎; ⓜLittle India) Located on a quiet side street in the heart of Little India, the Perak features a fetching, whitewashed colonial exterior. Inside, it's a case of Eastern accents (think Buddha statue), helpful staff, and clean, small rooms with functional furniture, classic decor and bathrooms whose grouting could use a decent scrubbing. Wi-fi is free but only available in the lobby.

MAYO INN   HOTEL **$$**

Map p210 (☑6295 6631; www.mayoinn.com; 9 Jln Besar; r from $100; ✳☎; ⓜBugis) A no-frills, midrange hotel with courteous staff and basic, IKEA-fitted rooms with sparkling bathrooms. More expensive rooms ($140 to $200) come with their own small roof terrace. Breakfast is not available.

🛏 Orchard Road

HOLIDAY INN EXPRESS   HOTEL **$$**

Map p216 (☑6690 3199; www.ihg.com; 20 Bideford Rd; r incl breakfast from $200; ✳@☎; ⓜSomerset) Just around the corner from Orchard Rd, this newcomer is crisp, fresh and good value. The light-filled lobby is upbeat and contemporary, pimped with funky furniture and iMac computers. Rooms are bright and tasteful, with neutral hues, bold yellow lounge chairs, iPod docking stations and small bathrooms with decent-sized showers. Communal washing machines and dryers are a handy touch. Lowest rates usually run Friday to Sunday.

SLEEP LOCAL

While the legality of short-term accommodation rentals in Singapore remains a bit of a grey area, sites like **Airbnb** (www.airbnb.com) offer a great range of privately-owned rooms and apartments to rent. Centrally located private rooms usually start at around $60 per night, while whole studio apartments with kitchen can go for under $150 per night. Find one within walking distance of an MRT station and you've saved money for shopping, drinks and a few extra massages.

YORK HOTEL
HOTEL $$

Map p216 (☎6737 0511; www.yorkhotel.com.
sg; 21 Mount Elizabeth; r from $200; ❄@🖥≋;
MOrchard) The big, bustling York hotel
comes with a gleaming lobby, sprawling
restaurant and variations on white and
beige. Rooms are pleasant and classically
furnished, their smallish, clean bathrooms
equipped with small bathtubs. The sell-
ing point here is the spaciousness of the
rooms, and the proximity to Orchard Rd.
Hotel facilities include a small gym, and a
palm-fringed outdoor pool and jacuzzi that
screams '80s resort.

RENDEZVOUS HOTEL
HOTEL $$

Map p216 (☎6336 0220; www.stayfareast.com; 9
Bras Basah Rd; r from $200; ❄@🖥≋; MBras
Basah, Dhoby Ghaut) A good midrange option
near Orchard Rd, the Rendezvous features
dramatic sculptures in its svelte lobby, a nod
to its ambition to become an 'art hotel'. Admittedly, the beige-and-brown rooms aren't
quite as sexy, although all are refurbished
and comfortable, with firm mattresses and
marble bathrooms with rain shower heads.
Both the gym and pool are small, though
the latter is nonetheless inviting.

Best of all, the location is handy for Orchard Rd and the MRT interchange station
of Dhoby Ghaut.

ST REGIS
HOTEL $$$

Map p216 (☎6506 6888; www.stregis.com; 29
Tanglin Rd; r from $400; ❄@🖥≋; MOrchard)
One of the newer additions to Orchard Rd's
five-star hotel scene, St Regis doesn't disap-
point, from its striking facade to its classic,
French-inspired decadence and impeccable
service. Rooms are enormous, with lavish
textiles, tasteful art and marble bathrooms
with free-standing soaking tubs. Each room
comes with 24-hour butler service to boot.

The in-house spa is one of the city's best,
and the hotel also offers an indoor tennis
court (at an additional fee).

GOODWOOD PARK HOTEL
HOTEL $$$

Map p216 (☎6737 7411; www.goodwoodparkho-
tel.com; 22 Scotts Rd; r from $240; ❄@🖥≋;
MOrchard) Dating back to 1900, this wonderful heritage hotel feels like an elegant,
Old World retreat. Deluxe rooms in the
main building are impressively spacious;
the kind of place you just want to hang out
in, sinking into a plush sofa with a good
book. Rooms in the newer wing are newly
renovated but smaller. The property boasts

two beautiful swimming pools, not to mention gracious service.

SHANGRI-LA HOTEL
LUXURY HOTEL $$$

Map p216 (☎6737 3644; www.shangri-la.com/
singapore/shangrila; 22 Orange Grove Rd; r from
$320; ❄@🖥≋; MOrchard) Announced by
the grandest of lobbies, this vast, opulent
hotel nestles in the leafy lanes surround-
ing the west end of Orchard. Six hectares of
tropical gardens set a lush, soothing mood,
with the low-rise, bougainvillea-laced Gar-
den Wing radiating an almost resortlike
vibe. Rooms are spacious and elegant, al-
though those in the Tower Wing could use
an update.

On-site highlights include a high-end spa
and huge, curvaceous pool.

QUINCY
BOUTIQUE HOTEL $$$

Map p216 (☎6738 5888; www.quincy.com.sg; 22
Mount Elizabeth; s/d from $295/355; ❄@🖥≋;
MOrchard) Smart, slimline Quincy offers svelte, Armani-chic rooms, with light
grey walls and high ceilings with fetching back-lighting. TVs are flat, mattresses
soft, and charcoal-tiled bathrooms stocked
with Molton Brown amenities. Minibar is
complimentary, and guests are entitled to
two free laundry items per day. The glass-
enclosed balcony pool is fabulous, and most
online deals include breakfast.

FOUR SEASONS HOTEL
HOTEL $$$

Map p216 (☎6734 1110; www.fourseasons.
com/singapore; 190 Orchard Blvd; r from $400;
❄@🖥≋; MOrchard) In a quiet street just
above Orchard Rd, the Four Seasons de-
livers the coveted combo of centrality and
retreatlike tranquillity. Common areas are
softly lit and elegant, with antique-style
furniture and mosaic-lined lifts. Rooms
are spacious and subdued, with sublimely
comfortable mattresses, fabulous art, and
marble bathrooms with deep-soaking tubs
and separate shower. On the lower floors,
rooms facing Cuscaden Rd are the quietest.

The hotel also has four tennis courts
(two indoor), a spa and well-equipped gym,
as well as two (somewhat dated-looking)
pools.

SINGAPORE MARRIOTT
HOTEL $$$

Map p216 (☎6735 5800; www.marriott.com/
sindt; 320 Orchard Rd; r from $400; ❄@🖥≋;
MOrchard) A fabulously central location
makes this a popular high-end choice.
Rooms are stylish and well sized, with

marble-topped writing desk, sofa, and marble bathroom with spacious shower. Poolside rooms come with a terrace overlooking the hotel's gorgeous pool, though these can get noisy during the day. Wi-fi is free for Marriott loyalty program members (it's free to join).

🛏 Eastern Singapore

Eastern Singapore basically covers everything east of the Kallang MRT station. It's a good place to stay for those seeking a different perspective of the Lion City, with easy access to East Coast Park and its off-shore breezes, and the airport.

BETEL BOX   HOSTEL $

Map p214 (✆6247 7340; www.betelbox.com; 200 Joo Chiat Rd; dm $20-25, d $80; @🛜; Ⓜ Paya Lebar) Although somewhat cramped, Betel Box has its perks, among them walking access to Joo Chiat's plethora of top local eateries and reasonably easy access to East Coast Park. The air-conditioned communal area features cheap beer, TV, DVDs, video games, computers and a pool table, as well as a book-exchange and tons of travel guides. The hostel also hosts some fantastic cycling and eating tours.

GRAND MERCURE ROXY   HOTEL $$

Map p214 (✆6344 8000; www.mercure.com; 50 East Coast Rd; r incl breakfast from $195; ✳@🛜🏊; 🚌36) This popular hotel (the entrance is on Marine Parade Rd) has a great location close to both Katong and the East Coast Park and is a mere 9km from the airport. Rooms are neutrally hued and contemporary, and the hotel pool and gym are welcome extras. Bonus! Free airport shuttle. Wi-fi is chargeable.

VENUE HOTEL   HOTEL $$

Map p214 (✆6346 3131; www.venuehotel.sg; 305 Joo Chiat Rd; r from $99; ✳@🛜; 🚌16, 33) Right in the heart of Katong, low-cost Venue gives a striking first impression with its dark, slinky, sculptural lobby. Rooms are small, simple and modern, with boldly coloured feature walls, contemporary bathrooms, and a choice of standard or low-rise beds. Premium rooms come with a decadent soaking tub at the foot of the bed. There's no breakfast, pool or gym, but with rates like these, who's complaining?

VILLAGE HOTEL CHANGI   HOTEL $$

Map p213 (✆6379 7111; www.changivillage.com.sg; 1 Netheravon Rd; r from $180; ✳@🛜🏊; 🚌2) With its free shuttle, this smart if somewhat generic hotel is a great choice if you want to be near Changi Airport. It's nestled among gorgeous gardens, with superb views across to Malaysia and Pulau Ubin from its beautiful rooftop pool. Close to the Changi Golf Course, the sailing club, beach park and the gentle pace of Changi Village, it offers a chilled-out slice of Singapore life.

🛏 Northern & Central Singapore

RAMADA SINGAPORE AT ZHONGSHAN PARK   HOTEL $$

Map p209 (✆6808 6888; www.ramada.com; 16 Ah Hood Rd; r from $180; ✳@🛜🏊; 🚌130, 131, 145, 851, Ⓜ Novena) This slick new Ramada makes up for its slighty inconvenient location with great rates. In reality, it's well serviced by buses and an easy 1km walk from Novena MRT station, from where Orchard Rd is two stops away. Rooms are simple yet sophisticated, with warm earthy hues, Singapore-themed artwork, comfortable beds and modern bathrooms. The light-filled gym features modern equipment and the pool is contemporary and stunning.

DAYS HOTEL SINGAPORE AT ZHONGSHAN PARK   HOTEL $$

Map p209 (✆6808 6838; www.dayshotelsingapore.com; 1 Jln Rajah; r from $160; 🚌, Ⓜ Novena) This brand new three star delivers small, comfortable rooms, each painted in bright, bold colours, with funky, striped carpet, 81cm LED TV and small but modern bathroom. There's a small gym with new equipment, and communal areas that are sharp and of-the-moment. Buses on Balestier Rd offer easy access to Little India and the Colonial District, and Novena MRT is a 1km walk south.

Check online for deals, which sometimes see room rates plummet to around $112 per night.

🛏 Sentosa & Other Islands

As well as the places listed below, the garish Resorts World complex (www.rwsentosa.com) on Sentosa Island has seven hotels and

STUCK AT THE AIRPORT?

If you're only in Singapore for a short time or have an endless wait between connections, try the **Ambassador Transit Hotel** (Map p213; ☑Terminal 1, 6542 5538, Terminal 2, 6542 8122, Terminal 3, 6507 9788; www.harilelahospitality.com; s/d/tr $77/92/115; ☒). Rates quoted are for the first six hours and each additional hour block thereafter is around $16.50; rooms don't have windows and there are budget singles ($47, with each subsequent hour charged at $14) with shared bathrooms. The Terminal 1 branch has an outdoor pool, while both the Terminal 1 and 2 branches offer a gym.

The only swish option at Changi Airport is the **Crowne Plaza** (Map p213; ☑6823 5300; www.ihg.com; 75 Airport Blvd, Changi Airport; r from $265; ☒@� ☒). It's a svelte, business-orientated place, with an in-house spa and lush, palm-studded pool. A skybridge connects the hotel to Terminal 3, with Terminals 1 and 2 accessible by SkyTrain. Unfortunately, the lack of competition means hiked-up prices.

suite complexes to choose from. Handy to fall back on if the others we've listed are full.

MAMAM BEACH — CAMPGROUND
Map p142 (Pulau Ubin) FREE Pulau Ubin offers two free campsites: Noordin Beach (currently closed due to erosion) and Mamam Beach. Neither is particularly idyllic, but Mamam is the nicer of the two, and does at least have toilets and nonpotable running water (BYO drinking water), although no showers. Register at the police post (to your right as you step off the boat) if you intend to camp on Ubin.

ST JOHN'S HOLIDAY BUNGALOW — CHALET $
(www.sentosa.com.sg/en/nature/southern-islands/st-johns-island; St John's Island; bungalow Tue-Thu $53.50, Fri-Mon $107; ⊙Sentosa Information Centre 9am-8pm) This three-bedroom bungalow on St John's Island can accommodate up to 10 people and comes with a basic kitchen and cooking utensils. You can only book it by going in person to the **Sentosa Information Centre** on the 3rd floor of VivoCity and reservations are only available two months in advance from the month of visit. Rates double during the school holidays.

Keep in mind that there are no dining and retail outlets on the island, so you'll need to bring your own food and drinks.

★CAPELLA SINGAPORE — RESORT $$$
Map p222 (☑6591 5000; www.capellahotels.com/singapore; 1 The Knolls, Sentosa Island; r from $710, villas from $1200; ☒@� ☒; monorail Beach) The Capella is one of Singapore's A-list slumber numbers, an arresting melange of colonial and contemporary architecture, elegant spa, restaurants, bar and three cascading swimming pools in lush, landscaped gardens. The beautifully appointed rooms are spacious and chic, with king-size bed; earthy, subdued hues; and striking contemporary bathrooms. The villas are even more decadent, each with its own private plunge pool.

Service is stellar. Check the website for 'Advance Purchase' discounts.

★W SINGAPORE – SENTOSA COVE — LUXURY HOTEL $$$
Map p222 (☑6808 7288; www.wsingapore-sentosacove.com; 21 Ocean Way, Sentosa Cove, Sentosa Island; r from $390; ☒@� ☒; monorail Beach) Brand-spanking new, the 240-room W is one of Singapore's hottest slumber spots. Rooms are playful, whimsical and spacious, with a choice of mood lighting, botanical motifs and good-sized bathrooms. Of the 10 room categories, the spa-themed 'Away Rooms' are especially fabulous, each with its own private plunge pool. The hotel's huge, 24-hour pool is one of Singapore's best, complete with wet bar and underwater speakers.

Extra perks include an of-the-moment gym and a high-tech, luxury spa.

SHANGRI-LA'S RASA SENTOSA RESORT & SPA — RESORT $$$
Map p222 (☑6275 0100; www.shangri-la.com; 101 Siloso Rd, Sentosa Island; r from $400; ☒@� ☒; monorail Beach) Singapore's only true beachfront resort is ideal for a short family break. Rooms are light, chic and tropical, in calming hues of cream and pistachio green. Service is top-notch, and the huge kid-friendly pool area, which has children's water slides and leads down towards Siloso Beach, is extremely inviting.

The resort has no less than five restaurants, and the free shuttle bus into central Singapore is especially handy.

Understand Singapore

Singapore Today

Eco-friendly architectural wonders, a billion-dollar super park and a swell of world-class bars and eateries... Singapore has never looked or felt so sexy. Yet the city state's ascent from regional nerd to global 'It' kid is not without its challenges. Driven by an influx of foreign workers, massive population growth is straining infrastructure, affordability and the patience of many Singaporeans. Simultaneously, the reported local exploitation of poorer foreign workers is threatening to tarnish the Red Dot's sparkling new look.

Best on Film

Ilo Ilo (Anthony Chen, 2013) A touching story about a troubled Chinese-Singaporean boy and his Filipino maid. The film won the Caméra d'Or award at the 2013 Cannes Film Festival.

12 Storeys (Eric Khoo, 1997) A dark comedy about the lives of separate individuals living in the same public-housing apartment block.

881 (Royston Tan, 2007) Musical comedy about the *getai* (stage singing) aspirations of two friends. Colourful, campy and touches on a fading Singapore art form.

Best in Print

Singapore Story (Lee Kuan Yew; 1999) To get the official story on the Singapore Miracle, go straight to the source – the man who masterminded the whole thing.

Singapore: A Biography (Mark Ravinder Frost and Yu-Mei Balamsingchow; 2010) Staid title aside, this is a well-written and handsomely illustrated history of Singapore across 450 riveting pages.

Little Ironies: Short Stories of Singapore (Catherine Lim; 1978) The doyenne of Singapore fiction has published numerous short-story collections and novels. This is her first collection.

Sustainable City

With the opening of Gardens by the Bay in 2012, Singapore moved another step closer towards its vision of becoming a 'City in a Garden', a cutting-edge role model of urban sustainability and biodiversity. A planned 35% improvement in energy efficiency between 2005 and 2030 led the government to introduce a sustainability rating system for buildings – the so-called Green Mark. Since 2008, all construction projects greater than 2000 sq metres (both new and retrofitted) are obliged to meet the Green Mark's minimum standards.

At present, Green Mark–certified buildings account for more than 20% of Singapore's gross floor space, and generous incentive schemes have encouraged an ever-growing number of buildings to incorporate sustainable design features, among them sun-shading exteriors, extensive overhangs, sky gardens, efficient water systems and computer systems capable of monitoring carbon emissions.

Among the best role models is Orchard Rd mall 313@Somerset. Its credentials include the use of non-potable water for 81% of its total water consumption, the recycling of cooking oil, and energy-saving escalators and elevators. Even more impressive is the newly built, award-winning Parkroyal on Pickering hotel, where the design incorporates rainwater harvesting and dramatic, cooling overhanging gardens.

Foreign Frustration

Singapore's population more than doubled from 2.4 million in 1980 to almost 5.5 million in 2014, an increase driven in no small part by waves of foreign workers. Indeed, non-Singaporeans now constitute almost half of the nation's headcount. According to the ruling People's Action Party (PAP), large-scale immigration has been essential to the country's economic growth.

For a growing number of Singaporeans, however, it's seen as the cause of numerous woes, from overcrowded transport to rising living costs. In 2014 the Economist Intelligence Unit declared Singapore the world's most expensive city in which to live.

Tension between Singaporeans and imported workers has increased. Perceived government preference for 'foreign talent' is a common social-media theme, as is criticism of those at the lower end of the foreign-worker chain. Dubbed 'PRCs', mainland Chinese labourers are commonly ridiculed for an apparent lack of social graces, and a perceived poor grasp of English. Among the biggest critics are the Singaporean Chinese.

Filipinos can also be the targets of local prejudice. In June 2014 the Philippines asked the Singaporean authorities to take action against a local blog called 'Filipino infestation in Singapore – five-point guide to showing displeasure without breaking the law'. Four months earlier, social media comments posted by British banker Anton Casey referring to MRT commuters as 'poor' provoked a massive backlash, with Casey receiving death threats, losing his job and fleeing Singapore. Given that many locals blame the influx of foreign workers on their own soaring living costs, Casey's class-based sneer struck a particularly raw nerve.

Maid to Order

Singapore's foreign workers include 215,000 domestic maids. It's a multimillion-dollar industry accused of exploitation in a 2014 report by broadcaster Al Jazeera. The report described scenes of maids being sold under signs such as 'Filipino and Indon Maids: No Off Day Lowest Pay and Fee'. Some agencies reportedly displayed workers in various mock work scenarios, and accusations of racial stereotyping in the marketing of maids also surfaced.

Domestic workers – many of whom hail from the Philippines, Indonesia and Myanmar – commonly find themselves trapped in a cycle of debt created by their agencies' high placement fees. It's a similar scenario for many of Singapore's 300,000-plus foreign construction workers, for whom the absence of a minimum wage, paired with agent fees and kickbacks demanded by more unscrupulous employers, creates a cycle of exploitation.

According to many international observers, the riot that rocked Little India on 8 December 2013, involving an estimated 400 foreign workers from mainly India and Bangladesh, was fuelled in part by the workers' growing resentment. The government denies the claim – its inquiry into the incident concluded that the treatment of migrant workers played no part in the riot.

if Singapore were 100 people

74 are Chinese
13 are Malay
9 are Indian
4 are others (Eurasians, Westerners etc)

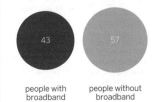

broadband access
(% of population)

43

57

people with broadband

people without broadband

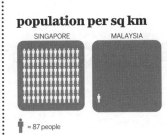

population per sq km

SINGAPORE   MALAYSIA

≈ 87 people

History

Celebrating 50 years of independence in 2015, the Lion City is the quintessential success story. In less than an average human lifespan, Asia's Little Red Dot has metamorphosed from a dusty, developing nation into one of the world's most stable, safe and prosperous countries. The story of Singapore is one of vision, planning and unrelenting determination.

Precolonial Singapore

Pretty much every museum you'll see in Singapore is devoted to postcolonial history, simply because there is not a great deal of undisputed precolonial history. Malay legend has it that long ago a Sumatran prince visiting the island of Temasek saw a strange animal he believed to be a lion. The good omen prompted the prince to found a city on the spot of the sighting. He called it Singapura (Lion City).

In 1703 English trader Andrew Hamilton described the island as a place where 'the soil is black and fat, and the woods abound in good masts for shipping, and timber for building'. The Sultan of Johor, Abdu'l Jajlil Ri'ayat Shah, had offered Hamilton the island, but he refused.

Chinese traders en route to India had plied the waters around what is now Singapore from at least the 5th century AD, though records of Chinese sailors as early as the 3rd century refer to an island called Pu Luo Chung, which may have been Singapore, while others claim there was a settlement in the 2nd century.

Between the 7th and 10th centuries, Srivijaya, a seafaring Buddhist kingdom centred at Palembang in Sumatra, held sway over the Strait of Malacca (now Melaka). Raids by rival kingdoms and the arrival of Islam brought the eclipse of Srivijaya by the 13th century. Based mainly on the thriving pirate trade, the sultanate of Melaka quickly acquired the commercial power that was once wielded by Srivijaya.

The Portuguese took Melaka in 1511, sparking off a wave of colonialism. The equally ambitious Dutch founded Batavia (now Jakarta) to undermine Melaka's position, finally wresting the city from their European competitors in 1641. In the late 18th century the British began looking for a harbour in the Strait of Melaka to secure lines of trade between China, the Malay world and their own interests in India. Renewed war in Europe led, in 1795, to the French annexation of Holland, which prompted the British to seize Dutch possessions in Southeast Asia, including Melaka.

TIMELINE	AD 300	1200s	1390s
	Chinese seafarers mark the island on maps, labelling it Pu Luo Chung, believed to have come from the Malay name Pulau Ujong, meaning 'island at the end'.	A Sumatran Srivijayan prince founds a settlement on the island and calls it Singapura (Lion City), having reputedly seen a lion there. Later named Temasek (Sea Town).	Srivijayan prince Parameswara flees Sumatra to Temasek after being deposed. He later founds the Sultanate of Malacca, under which Temasek is an important trading post.

After the end of the Napoleonic Wars, the British agreed to restore Dutch possessions in 1818, but there were those who were bitterly disappointed at the failure of the dream of British imperial expansion in Southeast Asia. One such figure was Sir Stamford Raffles, lieutenant-governor of Java.

The Raffles Era

For someone who spent a limited amount of time in Singapore, Sir Stamford Raffles had an extraordinary influence on its development. His name appears everywhere in the modern city, but his impact extends far beyond civic commemoration.

The streets you walk along in the city centre still largely follow the original plans Raffles drew. The ethnic districts still evident today, particularly in the case of Little India, were demarcated by him. Even the classic shophouse design – built of brick, with a continuous covered verandah known as a 'five-foot way' and a central courtyard for light, ventilation and water collection – has been attributed to him. More importantly, Singapore's very existence as one of the world's great ports is a direct consequence of Raffles' vision of creating a British-controlled entrepôt to counter Dutch power in the region.

When Raffles landed at Singapore in early 1819, the empire of Johor was divided. When the old sultan had died in 1812, his younger son's accession to power had been engineered while an elder son, Hussein, was away. The Dutch had a treaty with the young sultan, but Raffles threw his support behind Hussein, proclaiming him sultan and installing him in residence in Singapore.

In Raffles' plans the sultan wielded no actual power but he did serve to legitimise British claims on the island. Raffles also signed a treaty with the more eminent *temenggong* (senior judge) of Johor and set him up with an estate on the Singapore River. Thus, Raffles acquired the use of Singapore in exchange for modest annual allowances to Sultan Hussein and the *temenggong*. This exchange ended with a cash buyout of the pair in 1824 and the transfer of Singapore's ownership to Britain's East India Company.

Along with Penang and Melaka, Singapore formed a triumvirate of powerful trading stations known as the Straits Settlements, which were controlled by the East India Company in Calcutta but administered from Singapore.

Raffles had hit upon the brilliant idea of turning a sparsely populated, tiger-infested malarial swamp with few natural resources into an economic powerhouse by luring in the ambitious and allowing them to unleash their entrepreneurial zeal. While it was to be many decades before

1613	1819	1823	1826
Portuguese attack the town on the island and burn it to the ground. Singapura never regains its former importance while the Portuguese rule Malacca, and it slides into obscurity.	Sir Stamford Raffles, seeking a site for a new port to cement British interests in the Malacca Strait, lands on Singapura and decides it's the ideal spot.	Raffles signs a treaty with the Sultan and *temenggong* (senior judge) of Johor, who hand control of most of the island to the British. Raffles returns to Britain and never sees Singapore again.	Penang, Melaka and Singapore are combined to form the Straits Settlements. Large waves of immigration wash over Singapore's free ports as merchants seek to avoid Dutch tariffs.

Singapore's anarchic social conditions were brought under control, the essential Rafflesian spirit still underpins the city's tireless drive to succeed.

Colonisation & Occupation

Singapore Under the British

Raffles' first and second visits to Singapore in 1819 were brief and he left instructions and operational authority with Colonel William Farquhar, former Resident (the chief British representative) in Melaka. When Raffles returned three years later, he found the colony thriving but chaotic.

It was then that he drew out his town plan that remains today, levelling one hill to form a new commercial district (now Raffles Pl) and erecting government buildings around another prominence called Forbidden Hill (now called Fort Canning Hill).

William Farquhar

Colonel William Farquhar was Singapore's first official resident and a keen naturalist. He commissioned local Chinese artists to paint a series of 477 startlingly vibrant images of local flora and fauna.

His plan also embraced the colonial practice, still in evidence, of administering the population according to neat racial categories. The city's trades, races and dialect groups were divided into zones: Europeans were granted land to the northeast of the government offices (today's Colonial District), though many soon moved out to sequestered garden estates in the western suburbs. The Chinese predominated around the mouth and the area southwest of the Singapore River, though many Indians lived there too (hence the large Hindu temple on South Bridge Rd). Hindu Indians were, and still are, largely centred in Kampong Kapor and Serangoon Rd; Gujarati and other Muslim merchants were housed in the Arab St area; Tamil Muslim traders and small businesses operated in the Market St area; and the Malay population mainly lived on the swampy northern fringes of the city. In time, of course, these zones became less well defined, as people decanted into other parts of the island.

Despite its wealth, the colony was a dissolute place, beset by crime, clan violence, appalling sanitation, opium addiction, rats, mosquitoes and tigers. Life for the majority was extremely harsh; the Chinatown Heritage Centre is probably the best place to appreciate just how harsh.

Raffles sought to cooperate with, and officially register, the various *kongsi* – clan organisations for mutual assistance, known variously as ritual brotherhoods, secret societies, triads and heaven-man-earth societies. (Many of them had their headquarters on Club St, and a couple still hold out against the area's rapid gentrification.) Labour and dialect-based *kongsi* would become increasingly important to Singapore's success in the 19th century, as overseas demand for Chinese-harvested products such as pepper, tin and rubber – all routed through Singapore from the Malay peninsula – grew enormously.

Singapore's access to *kongsi*-based economies in the region, however, depended largely on revenues from an East India Company product

1867	1877	1939	1942
Discontent at ineffectual administration persuades the British to declare the Straits Settlements a separate crown colony, no longer run from India.	Britain establishes a Chinese Protectorate in an effort to tackle the 'coolie trade' – the exploitative labour market system run by Chinese secret societies.	Britain completes a huge naval base for around $500 million, boasting the world's largest dry dock and enough fuel to run the British Navy for months. It's dubbed 'Fortress Singapore'.	Fortress Singapore is cruelly exposed when incomplete preparations for a northern invasion mean Japanese forces overrun the island. The Allies surrender on 15 February.

that came from India and was bound for China – opium. Farquhar had established Singapore's first opium farm for domestic consumption, and by the 1830s excise and sales revenues of opium accounted for nearly half the administration's income, a situation that continued for a century after Raffles' arrival. But the British Empire produced more than Chinese opium addicts; it also fostered the Western-oriented outlook of Straits-born Chinese.

In the 19th century, women were rarely permitted to leave China. Thus, Chinese men who headed for the Straits Settlements often married local women, eventually spawning a new, hybrid culture now known in Singapore as Peranakan.

Despite a massive fall in rubber prices in 1920, prosperity continued, immigration soared and millionaires were made almost overnight. In the 1930s and early '40s, politics dominated the intellectual scene. Indians looked to the subcontinent for signs of the end of colonial rule, while Kuomintang (Nationalist) and Communist Party struggles in the disintegrating Republic of China attracted passionate attention. Opposition to Japan's invasions of China in 1931 and 1937 was near universal in Singapore.

Singapore Under the Japanese

When General Yamashita Tomoyuki pushed his thinly stretched army into Singapore on 15 February 1942, it began a period Singapore regards as the blackest of its history. For the British, who had set up a naval base near the city in the 1920s, surrender was sudden and humiliating – and some historians have pinpointed the fall of Singapore as the moment when the myth of British impregnability was blown apart and the empire began its final decline.

The impact of the Japanese occupation on the collective political and social memory of Singapore cannot be underestimated, and it has partly inspired Singapore's modern preoccupation with security. Japanese rule was harsh. Yamashita had the Europeans and Allied POWs herded onto the Padang, from there they were marched away for internment. Many of them were taken to the infamous Changi prison, while others were herded up to Siam (Thailand) to work on the Death Railway.

The Japanese also launched Operation Sook Ching to eliminate Chinese opposition. Chinese Singaporeans were driven out of their homes, 'screened', then either given a 'chop' (a mark on the forehead meaning they had been cleared for release) or driven away to be imprisoned or executed (there's a memorial to one massacre at Changi Beach). Estimates of the number of Chinese killed vary – some sources put the number at 6000, others at more than 45,000.

> In WWII the British expected the Japanese to attack Singapore south from the sea. Instead they blitzed Singapore from the north, coming from Malaysia on foot and bicycle.

> **WWII Sites**
> ....
> Fort Siloso (Sentosa Island)
> ....
> Images of Singapore (Sentosa Island)
> ....
> Reflections at Bukit Chandu (southwest Singapore)
> ....
> Labrador Nature Reserve (southwest Singapore)
> ....
> Memories at Old Ford Factory (central Singapore)
> ....
> Kranji War Memorial (west Singapore)

1942–45	1945–59	1959	1963
Singapore is renamed Syonan by the Japanese. Many Chinese are massacred, Allied prisoners incarcerated at Changi or shipped off to the Death Railway. Economy collapses.	British resume control. Straits Settlements wound up in 1946. Until 1955 Singapore is run by part-elected legislative councils, then a semiautonomous government.	First full legislative elections held. People's Action Party (PAP), led by Lee Kuan Yew, wins. Aggressive economic development and social programmes are launched.	After strong campaigning from Lee Kuan Yew, Singapore joins Sabah and Sarawak in combining with Malaya to form the single state of Malaysia.

The Japanese renamed the island 'Syonan' (Light of the South), changed signs into Japanese, put clocks forward to Tokyo time and introduced a Japanese currency (known by contemptuous locals as 'banana money').

The war ended suddenly with Japan's surrender on 14 August 1945, and Singapore was passed back into British control. While the returning British troops were welcomed, the occupation had eroded the innate trust in the empire's protective embrace. New political forces were at work and the road to independence was paved.

The Lee Dynasty

Lee Kuan Yew famously cried on national television in 1965 after Singapore separated from Malaysia. The event (separation, not the tears) marked the birth of modern Singapore.

If one person can be considered responsible for the position Singapore finds itself in today, it is Lee Kuan Yew.

Born in 1923, this third-generation Straits-born Chinese was named Harry Lee, and brought up to be, in his own words, 'the equal of any Englishman'. His education at the elite Raffles Institution and Cambridge University equipped him well to deal with both colonial power and political opposition when Singapore took control of its own destiny in the 1960s.

The early years were not easy. Race riots in 1964 and ejection from the Malay Federation in 1965 made Lee's task even harder. Lee used tax incentives and strict new labour laws to attract foreign investment. This, combined with huge resources poured into developing an English-language education system that churned out a competent workforce, saw Singapore's economy rapidly industrialise.

Under Lee's rigidly paternal control, his People's Action Party (PAP) also set about eliminating any viable political opposition, banning critical publications and moulding the city into a disciplined, functional society built along Confucian ideals, which value the maintenance of hierarchy and social order above all things.

Lee was successful at containing what he evidently saw as the anarchic tendencies of Singapore's citizens, inspiring ever more ambitious attempts at social engineering. For example, a (now defunct) matchmaking club was established to pair off suitable couples – one of the dating clubs was restricted to graduates.

Lee's rapid industrialisation filled government coffers and enabled the PAP to pursue massive infrastructure, defence, health, education, pension and housing schemes, giving Singaporeans a level of prosperity and security that remains the envy of many countries in the region and around the world. Housing and urban renovation, in particular, have been the keys to the PAP's success. By the mid-1990s, Singapore had achieved the world's highest rate of home ownership.

1964	1965	1971	1975
Race rioting between Malays and Chinese sees 36 people killed and more than 500 injured, fuelling the already-testy relations between the PAP and the Malay ruling party UMNO.	Singapore expelled from federation after a unanimous vote in the Malaysian Parliament in Kuala Lumpur. Lee Kuan Yew cries as he announces the news. The Republic of Singapore is born.	British forces withdraw, sparking economic crisis. PAP mounts an election to win a mandate for tough laws curbing unions, luring foreign investment.	Singapore becomes the world's third-busiest port and third-largest oil refiner; also a rig- and drilling-platform manufacturer and a huge oil-storage centre.

Despite resigning as prime minister in 1990 after 31 years in the job, and handing over to the more avuncular but no less determined Goh Chok Tong, Lee still keeps an eye on proceedings and his comments on various issues frequently flag future government policy.

'Even from my sickbed,' said Lee in 1988, 'even if you are going to lower me into the grave and I feel that something is wrong, I'll get up.'

Recent Past & Impending Future

Lee Kuan Yew's son, Lee Hsien Loong, who was deputy Prime Minister and Defence Minister under Goh Chok Tong, took over the top job unopposed in 2004.

The challenges he has faced to date have been as great as those faced by his father, among them the Asian financial crisis starting in 1997, the SARS outbreak in 2003 and the global financial crisis of 2007, all of which had a major impact on the country's economy and its sense of vulnerability to forces beyond its control. Though economically and financially Singapore is in a strong position, the migration of its manufacturing base to cheaper competitors such as Vietnam and China has forced the government to embark on a radical makeover of the country in an attempt to ensure its success extends into the future.

Challenges have also presented themselves in the form of growing opposition to the ruling PAP. While the party won the expected majority in a landslide victory in 2006, its actual votes fell by 8.69%. Indeed, more than a third of the eligible electorate voted against the incumbent. The tone for the next election had been set.

The 2011 election reflected the expected appetite for change. This election had the highest proportion of contested seats (94.3%) since Singapore achieved its independence in 1965. Local media, often accused of being mouthpieces of the government, appeared to give more even coverage to the PAP and opposition parties. Social media, once banned in campaigning, played a huge part in dissemination of information. Even Prime Minister Lee Hsien Loong participated in an online chat (his first). Attendances at opposition rallies were off the charts.

The election results were telling. The PAP lost a further 6.46% of the electorate, gaining 60.14% of the votes and 81 out of 87 seats. The biggest gains went to the Worker's Party, with a political agenda focused on the everyday concerns of Singaporeans, from wages, the cost of living and healthcare, to housing affordability, public transport and the disproportionately high salaries of ministers. The election would prove to be a sobering wake-up call for the PAP. Post-election, a review of ministerial salaries was immediately mooted, and Senior Minister Goh Chok Tong and Minister Mentor Lee Kuan Yew both tendered their resignations.

Singapore's first national campaign was launched in August 1958, shortly after the People's Action Party (PAP) took power in the city council elections. The campaign aimed to curb spitting in public, a prevalent social habit at the time.

'Majulah Singapura' (Onward Singapore) is Singapore's national anthem. Its lyrics entirely in Bahasa Malay, the anthem was created in 1958 by Indonesian-born composer Zubir Said, who took a year to complete the music and lyrics.

1990	2004	2011	2015
Lee Kuan Yew steps down as Prime Minister, handing over reins to Goh Chok Tong. Lee becomes Senior Minister and retains oversight of government policy.	Prime Minister Goh Chok Tong steps down. He is replaced by Lee Kuan Yew's son, Lee Hsien Loong, who builds two casinos, reversing decades of government policy on casino gambling.	Watershed general election results see the ruling PAP party face its worst result ever, winning 60.14% of the vote, down 6.46% from 2006.	City Hall and the Old Supreme Court are reopened as the National Gallery Singapore, the nation's spectacular new ode to the visual arts.

People & Cultures of Singapore

Singapore is the ultimate melting pot. With no less than four official languages, it's a place where mosques sidle up against Hindu and Taoist temples, where European chefs experiment with Chinese spices, and where local English is peppered with Hokkien, Tamil and Malay words. Since Sir Stamford Raffles set up a free trading port on the island in 1819, the Little Red Dot has been defined and redefined by its wave of migrants, from early Chinese workers to modern-day expats seeking their corporate fortunes.

Chinese

A scarcity of farmland, as well as political and social unrest, drove many mainland Chinese to seek their fortunes elsewhere in the 19th century, including Raffles' fledgling settlement. By 1840, 50% of Singapore's population was Chinese, made up mainly of Hokkien, Teochew, Hainanese, Cantonese and Hakka Chinese from China's southeast provinces.

Raffles' demarcation of Chinatown based on ethnic lines merely reinforced the segregation of these different dialect groups, and each would become known for a particular set of skills in the colony. The Hokkien and Teochew were commonly associated with trade and agriculture, the Cantonese and Hakka with handicrafts and construction, and the Hainanese with cooking. That Hainanese chicken rice is Singapore's best-loved dish is a lasting legacy of this culinary reputation.

With the majority of the literate population bilingual, English and Mandarin are the most commonly used languages in daily life. While English is the main language taught in schools, children also learn their mother tongues to ensure they stay in touch with their traditional roots.

While Chinese dialects are still widely spoken in the Lion City, especially among older Chinese, the government's long-standing campaign to promote Mandarin, the main nondialectal Chinese language, has been very successful and increasing numbers of Singaporean Chinese now speak it at home.

Since 1921, Chinese have made up around three-quarters of the island's headcount, and their influence on Singaporean culture is dominant, from the influence of feng shui in the design of buildings such as Marina Bay Sands and Suntec City, to the Confucian principles underlying Singapore's paternalist system of government, a formula of benevolent sovereign and respectful subjects.

Malays

They may only count for 13% of the population, but the Malays – the island's original inhabitants – are Singapore's second-biggest ethnic group. From Singapore's national anthem to the names of Singaporean streets, neighbourhoods, reserves and islands, Malay culture has played a significant role in defining the modern nation.

While the majority of Malay Singaporeans originate from the Malay peninsula, the community is heterogeneous, with others tracing their roots back to the Riau Islands, Java, Sumatra and Sulawesi. A small number are the descendants of mixed marriages between local Malay women and Arab or Indian Muslim men, the latter migrating to Singapore in the late 19th and 20th centuries.

Language and faith unify Malay Singaporeans. Most are practising Sunni Muslims, a fact made evident by the number of bustling mosques in Malay enclaves such as Geylang Serai, not to mention the popularity of the *tudung* (head scarf) or the traditional *baju kurung* (a long-sleeved tunic worn over a sarong) among Malay-Singaporean women.

The community's historic heart is Kampong Glam, a district still packed with halal eateries serving Malay classics such as *nasi lemak* (a coconut rice dish) and *asam laksa* (a sour, spicy fish noodle dish), dishes that also define the greater Singaporean food repertoire. It's here that you'll also find the Malay Cultural Centre and iconic Sultan Mosque.

Despite its cultural influence, this minority has faced challenges over the years, including an over-representation at the lower end of the educational scale, negative stereotypes in the employment sector and under-representation in senior government, military and judicial positions.

Peranakans

In Singapore, Peranakan (locally born) people are descendants of immigrants who married local women who were mostly of Malay origin. The result of hundreds of years of immersion and the meeting of foreign and local customs has resulted in an intriguing hybrid culture that's recently experienced a revival.

It's acknowledged that the Peranakan fall into three broad categories: the Chitty Melaka and Jawi Peranakan are descended from early migrants from India, while the Straits Chinese Peranakan are of mainland Chinese origin. No matter which group, there's a fierce sense of roots and traditions within.

In Singapore, the largest group is the Straits Chinese, a reflection of the population breakdown at large. The term 'Straits Chinese' originated within communities in the former colonial Straits Settlements of Singapore, Penang and Melaka.

These days, Chinese and Peranakan culture tend to overlap and it's sometimes hard to distinguish between the two. Peranakan men, called Babas, and the women, Nonya, primarily speak a patois that mixes Bahasa Malay, Hokkien dialect and English, though that's changed over time, along with the education system in Singapore. Most of the current Peranakans speak English and Mandarin. Visually, Peranakan are indistinguishable from people of Han Chinese descent, but traditional families still cling to their customs and traditions and are proud of their heritage, evocatively showcased at both Singapore's Peranakan Museum and Baba House.

Indians

At just under 10% of the population, Indians are the third-largest ethnic group in Singapore. It might be a relatively small group in Singapore, but it's one of the biggest outside India, and its fidelity to the motherland's customs and traditions shines through in Little India's street life and the fervent celebration of Hindu festivals such as Thaipusam and Deepavali.

A number of Indians worked as *sepoys* (soldiers) for the British army, and Indian convict labour played a vital role in the early settlement's development, clearing jungle, filling swamps and constructing buildings that included St Andrew's Cathedral, the Istana palace and Sri Mariamman Temple. Upon completing their sentences, many stayed on in Singapore, finding work as labourers or setting up small businesses.

Must Reads

A Peranakan Legacy: The Heritage of the Straits Chinese (Peter Wee)

The Shrimp People (Rex Shelley)

Kebaya Tales: Of Matriarchs, Maidens, Mistresses and Matchmakers (Lee Su Kim)

The Singapore Grip (JG Farrell)

A traditional Peranakan wedding is an elaborate 12-day affair, heavily steeped in Chinese traditions from the Fujian province in China, mixed with some Malay customs. These days, such elaborate affairs are few and far between, though they have made a comeback, albeit in a severely truncated one-day form.

PEOPLE & CULTURES OF SINGAPORE PERANAKANS

Some became *dhobis* (laundry workers), a fact echoed in the name of Dhoby Ghaut MRT station. Many South Indians became well known as *chettiars* (moneylenders).

More than half of today's Indian Singaporeans are Tamils, hailing from the area now known as Tamil Nadu, a corner of southern India where Hindu traditions are strong. The remainder are mainly Muslim or Christian, with a minority of Sikhs, Jains, Buddhists and Zoroastrians. While a small, English-educated Indian elite has always played a prominent role in Singaporean society, a large percentage of the community remains working class.

Eurasians

If you meet a Singaporean whose surname is Clarke, de Souza or Hendricks, chances are they are Eurasian, a term used to describe people of mixed Asian and European descent. In the early colonial days, the majority of Eurasian migrants arrived from the Malaysian trading port of Malacca (Melaka), which alongside Goa, Macau and Ceylon (modern Sri Lanka) claimed notable mixed-race communities, a legacy of Portuguese, Dutch and British colonisers marrying local women.

Shared Christian beliefs and shared cultural traditions created a firm bond between Singapore's British ruling class and the island's Eurasian community, and many Eurasians enjoyed privileged posts in the civil service. The bond would erode after the opening of the Suez Canal, when an increase in European arrivals saw the 'half Europeans' sidelined. Ironically, Eurasians suffered great persecution during Singapore's Japanese occupation in WWII, in which they were branded 'British sympathisers'.

These days, Singapore is home to around 15,000 Eurasians, and the group features prominently in the media and entertainment industries. The Eurasians' mixed-race appearance is especially appealing to advertisers, who see it as conveniently encompassing Singapore's multiracial make-up. The majority of modern Singaporean Eurasians are of British descent, with English as their first language.

Each HDB (Housing Development Board) public housing complex is subject to ethnic-based quotas that accurately reflect Singapore's own demographic mix. These quotas are in place to help prevent the formation of 'ethnic enclaves'.

Architecture

Singapore is an architectural chocolate box, its assortment of treats spanning sugar-white colonial churches and technicolour shophouses, to gobsmacking contemporary icons. Despite the wrecking-ball rampage of the 1960s and '70s, the island nation managed to retain significant swaths of heritage buildings, and their contrast against an ever-evolving skyline is delicious and dramatic.

Colonial

Not long after the East India Company set up its trading port at the mouth of the Singapore River, migrants from across Asia began leaving their architectural mark. The Chinese built seaside temples such as Thian Hock Keng Temple, Indian Hindus added colour with the likes of Sri Mariamman Temple, and Chulia Muslims from India's south erected shrines such as Nagore Durgha. For the most part, these early structures faithfully reflected the architectural styles of each group's homeland.

Distant influences also underscored the work of the European colonisers. Irishman George Drumgoole Coleman – considered Singapore's pre-eminent colonial architect – found inspiration in the classical aesthetics of the Palladian style developed by 16th-century Italian architect Andrea Palladio. Coleman was a skilful adapter of the style, seamlessly pairing its proclivity for Doric columns, porticoes and rotundas with wide verandahs and overhanging eaves better suited to Singapore's tropical climate. The Colonial District is home to many of his works, among them Caldwell House in CHIJMES and Old Parliament House. His finest creation is arguably the Armenian Church, modelled after St Gregory's Church in Echmiadzin, the mother church in northern Armenia.

Coleman, who became Singapore's town surveyor and superintendent of public works in 1826, set a fine example for other colonial architects. Among these were Brother Lothaire and Father Charles Benedict Nain, who together designed the elegant St Joseph's Institution, now better known as the Singapore Art Museum. Nain would go on to design the chapel at CHIJMES, a sublimely elegant, Anglo-French Gothic affair.

As Singapore's wealth and importance increased through the 19th century, so did the grandeur of its buildings. Some of the finest are the work of Major John Frederick Adolphus McNair, among them the Empress Place Building (home to the Asian Civilisations Museum) and Singapore's former Government House, Istana, just off Orchard Rd. The popularity of all things classical held sway well into the first decades of the 20th century, as seen in the Fullerton Hotel and the old Supreme Court, the latter being the last example of British colonial architecture in Singapore. At time of research, City Hall and the old Supreme Court building were scheduled to reopen in 2015 as the National Gallery Singapore, the sombre-looking buildings to be connected by a striking yet harmonious glass-and-steel roof structure. The structure and gallery are the work of France's Studio Milou Architecture and Singapore's CPG Consultants.

Shophouses

Before HDB (Housing Development Board) flats, the definitive Singaporean building was the shophouse. Its long, narrow design was also a distinctive feature of other port cities such as Penang and Melaka.

Shophouses were designed to have a shop or business on the lower floor and accommodation upstairs. Often projecting over the footpath is a solid canopy, known as a five-foot way. The canopy was in use in southern China and parts of Southeast Asia and was mandated by Sir Stamford Raffles in 1822, when in a set of ordinances he stated that 'all houses constructed of brick or tiles have a common type of front each having an arcade of a certain depth open to all sides as a continuous and open passage'.

A considerate Raffles wanted to ensure pedestrians were protected from the sun and rain. But shopkeepers had other ideas and before long they all became extensions of the shops inside. Most five-foot ways are now clear of commerce, but walk along Buffalo Rd in Little India, or the northern end of Telok Ayer St in Chinatown, and you get an idea of how difficult it became for pedestrians to negotiate these passageways.

The load-bearing walls separating the buildings are heavy masonry, which was a departure from the traditional timber, and not only provided strength and privacy from neighbours, but also deterred the spread of fire.

The first shophouses dating from 1840 are plain, squat, two-storey buildings. These Early shophouses, in the vernacular, were followed by First Transitional, Late, Second Transitional and art-deco style. Classical elements such as columns are often used on the facades, along with beautiful tiles and bright paint – the Chinese, Peranakans and Malays all favoured lively colours. Some of the finest surviving examples grace Koon Seng Rd and Joo Chiat Pl in Katong, as well as Pertain Rd (between Jalan Besar and Sturdee Rd) near Little India.

Shophouses typically featured a central courtyard, which was often open to the sky, allowing natural light to penetrate the building and, in the early days, acting as a useful water collection method (the courtyards usually had open cisterns). In some designs, a high rear wall acted as a kind of wind deflector, diverting breezes downwards and channelling them through the house.

A peculiarly Singaporean variation was the 'chophouse' – re-created examples of which can be seen at the Chinatown Heritage Centre. Built to the same basic design as the shophouse, they were constructed to hold many dozens, sometimes hundreds of residents. Floors were divided into tiny, dark, miserable cubicles and the high concentration of people meant conditions were squalid in the extreme. A few chophouses remain in Little India, along Desker Rd for example, but most of them have been torn down.

The term 'shophouse' is a literal translation from Chinese ('tiam chu' in Hokkien, 'dian wu' in Mandarin). The most decorative of the various styles is the 'Late' shophouse style, in which even the wall space is commonly cut back by the presence of richly decorated windows, pilasters and other detailing.

HDB Flats

Only in Singapore could you walk safely through a tower-block estate at night and find a drink vending machine full, working and unvandalised. While public high-rise housing estates are being torn down elsewhere, in Singapore they work. They have to: land is limited, so the government had little choice but to build upwards. The state-run Housing Development Board (HDB) is locked into a mammoth construction project, erecting areas of well-built, well-maintained and affordable housing. So far, it's built over a million units.

HDB 'towns' such as Toa Payoh, Pasir Ris and Tampines provide homes for around 85% of the population. HDB developments have markets, schools, playgrounds, shops and hawker centres hardwired into

BUNGALOWS: THE BLACK & WHITES

Not the single-storey retirement homes of the West, Singapore's bungalows are named after Bangalore-style houses and are usually two storeys high, with large verandahs on the upper floor.

Most were built in the style now locally known as 'black and whites', after the mock-Tudor, exposed-beam look adopted between the late 19th century and WWII. The design itself was greatly influenced by the Arts and Crafts Movement. Originating in England in the 1860s, the movement placed renewed value on craftsmanship, a counter reaction to England's rapid industrialisation. By the 1930s, the mock-Tudor style made way for the so-called 'tropical art-deco' style, which favoured flat roofs, curved corners and a strong, streamlined horizontal design.

These 'black and whites' are much sought after by expatriates chasing colonialism's glory days of three generations ago, and you'll find many of them lurking in leafy residential areas off Orchard Rd, such as Nassim Rd and the stretch of Scotts Rd near the Sheraton Towers hotel. They also cluster in exclusive areas such as Alexandra Park and Ridley Park, where you can practically taste the gin slings and elegantly discreet liaisons.

Down at Mountbatten Rd in Kallang are examples of both the highly decorative Victorian bungalow and the concrete art-deco bungalows dating from the 1920s and '30s.

them. The older ones (from the 1960s and '70s) have mature trees keeping them shady and (relatively) attractive. Many blocks also have 'void decks', empty areas on the ground floor that allow a breeze to circulate, and where old men play chess in the shade.

Singapore's most striking HDB complex is the mammoth Pinnacle@Duxton, completed in 2009. Located on the corner of Cantonment Rd and Neil St, just south of Chinatown, the project consists of seven 50-storey apartment towers connected by two levels of sky bridges housing gardens and a jogging track. Height and scale aside, the complex is unique in that it offered residents an unprecedented choice of exterior facade treatments, from planter boxes to bay windows and balconies. The result is a highly differentiated facade that is one of modern Singapore's most eclectic.

The HDB is locked into a continuous renovation and upgrading programme, even though the majority of the flats are privately owned, making them perhaps unique among the world's public housing projects. Every few years, they get licks of paint and new features added.

The MRT system makes it simple to visit the HDB heartlands. Just jump on a train and pop up somewhere like Toa Payoh. You won't see stunning architecture, but you will get a glimpse of what life is like for most Singaporeans.

Modern & Contemporary

The Pinnacle@Duxton is one of an ever-growing number of bold architectural statements, many of them designed by world-renowned 'starchitects'. Among the earliest and most iconic is the 52-level OCBC Centre in the Central Business District (CBD). Designed by Chinese-American IM Pei and completed in 1976, it's a striking brutalist statement, its curved concrete core embedded with three panels of windows. The windows' keypadlike appearance and the building's slimline profile are behind its local nickname, 'the calculator'.

The OCBC's lofty neighbours include Japanese architect Kurokawa Kisho's 66-storey Republic Plaza and Tange Kenzo's 66-level UOB Plaza One and mini-me UOB Plaza Two. Tange also designed the URA Centre in Chinatown. The latter is home to the Singapore City Gallery, an

Feng shui influences the design of many buildings in Singapore, including Suntec City. Its five office towers symbolise the fingers of a left hand, including one squat tower as the thumb. In the hand lies the Fountain of Wealth, its water flowing downwards into the complex, accumulating positive *qi* (energy) and prosperity.

One of Singapore's most eclectic buildings is the granite-clad Parkview Square (2002) at 600 North Bridge Rd. Designed by American James Adam and local firm DP Architects, it's known as the 'Gotham Building' for its over-the-top art-deco-inspired motifs and ornamentation, at their most intense in the gilded, coffered-ceiling lobby.

interesting place to drop by if you want to learn more about the future of Singapore's built environment. This future includes the Tanjong Pagar Centre, a 64-storey office-and-residential tower designed by American architectural royalty Skidmore, Owings & Merrill (SOM). Once completed in 2016, the 290m-tall tower will become Singapore's tallest resident.

Israeli-Canadian Moshe Safdie, best known for his modular housing complex Habitat 67 in Montreal, is the creative force behind Marina Bay Sands, an integrated resort fronting Marina Bay. Completed in 2010, its three-tower hotel, topped by a curved, 340m-long cantilever, has arguably become Singapore's most internationally recognisable building.

Marina Bay, itself a functioning reservoir, is home to several outstanding examples of contemporary design. At its northern end is Esplanade – Theatres on the Bay, designed by Singapore's DP Architects and London-based Michael Wilford and Partners. The complex is most famous for the aluminium sunshades that clad its bulbous theatre and concert hall buildings. Their appearance has led to comparisons with durians and the eyes of flies. Behind Marina Bay Sands are Singapore's newest botanic gardens, Gardens by the Bay. The project's two giant glass-and-steel conservatories, designed by Wilkinson Eyre Architects, are the largest climate-controlled glasshouses in the world.

West of Marina Bay and the CBD is Polish-American architect Daniel Libeskind's award-winning Reflections at Keppel Bay, a high-end residential complex with undulating towers that offer constantly shifting perspectives.

French architect Jean Nouvel's newer Nouvel 18 is no less dramatic. Located directly opposite the Shangri-La Hotel, its towers are embedded with eight sky gardens, which break up the glass facades in a case of Jenga meets jungle. It's a concept echoed in Foster & Partners' brand new South Beach development. A striking mixed-use office, hotel and residential project opposite Raffles Hotel, its two curving towers are sliced with densely planted sky gardens. It's a change of style for Sir Norman Foster's firm, whose Supreme Court building and Expo MRT are famed for their UFO-like discs.

This 'building as garden' concept drives the Parkroyal on Pickering, a stunning 12-storey hotel where the lush hanging gardens, laced with gullies and waterfalls, seem to draw Hong Lim Park, located across the street, right up the building. Behind the project is WOHA. One of Singapore's most exciting architecture studios, its creations to date include the School of the Arts building (winner of the 2011 Jørn Utzon Award for International Architecture) and Stadium MRT station, the latter inspired in part by the work of minimalist sculptor Richard Serra and noted for its dramatic spatial composition. One of WOHA's latest projects is the Oasia Downtown hotel in Tanjong Pagar. The 30-storey building will feature a living green facade of creepers and flowering plants that will be one of the world's tallest vertical gardens.

Singlish: A Primer

Want to go to Chinatown see see walk walk? You sit this bus. Welcome to the colourful, sometimes confusing world of Singlish, the Singaporeans' very unique take on English. A local patois spiked with borrowed words from Hokkien, Tamil and Malay, it's the direct product of the island's multiracial, multilingual history. Love it or loathe it, knowing the basics can help avoid those lost-in-translation moments. So don't pray pray ah! Get into the Singlish swing.

Singlish

While there isn't a Singlish grammar as such, there are definite characteristics. Verb tenses tend to be nonexistent. Past, present and future are indicated instead by time indicators, so in Singlish it's 'I go tomorrow' or 'I go yesterday'. Long stress is placed on the last syllable of phrases, so that the standard English 'government' becomes 'guvva-men'.

Words ending in consonants are often syncopated and vowels are often distorted. A Chinese-speaking taxi driver might not immediately understand that you want to go to Perak Rd, since they know it as 'Pera Roh'.

A typical exchange might – confusingly – go something like this: '*Eh, this Sunday you going cheong* (party) *anot*? No *ah*? Why like that? Don't be so boring *lah*!' Prepositions and pronouns are dropped, word order is flipped, phrases are clipped short and stress and cadence are unconventional, to say the least.

The particle 'lah' is often tagged on to the end of sentences for emphasis, as in 'No good lah'. Requests or questions may be marked with a tag ending, since direct questioning can be rude. As a result, questions that are formed to be more polite often come across to Westerners as rude. 'Would you like a beer?' becomes 'You wan beer or not?'

While most Singaporeans love Singlish, the government does not. In 2000 it even launched a 'Speak Good English' campaign (www.goodenglish.org.sg) to improve the standard of English. The campaign includes its own downloadable app, 'Say It Right'.

Slanging Like a Local

a bit the	very; as in '*Wah! Your car a bit the slow one*'
ah beng	every country has them – boys with spiky gelled hair, loud clothes, the latest mobile phones and a choice line in gutter phrases
ahlian	the female version of the *ah beng* – large, moussed hair, garish outfits, armed with a vicious tongue; also known as *ah huay*
aiyo!	'oh, dear!'
alamak!	exclamation of disbelief or frustration, like 'oh my God!'
angmoh	common term for Westerner (Caucasian), with derogatory undertone; literally 'red-haired monkey' in Hokkien
ayam	Malay word for chicken; adjective for something inferior or weak
blur	slow or uninformed; popular phrase is '*blur like sotong*'
buaya	womaniser, from the Malay for crocodile
can?	'is that OK?'

can!	'yes! That's fine'
charbor	babe, woman
cheena	derogatory term for old-fashioned Chinese in dress or thinking
confirm	used to convey emphasis when describing something/someone, as in *'He confirm blur one'* (He's not very smart)
go stun	to reverse, as in *'Go stun the car'* (from the naval expression 'go astern')
heng	luck, good fortune (Hokkien)
hiao	vain
inggrish	English
kambing	foolish person, literally 'goat' (Malay)
kaypoh	busybody
kena	Malay word close to meaning of English word 'got', describing something that happened, as in *'He kena arrested for drunk driving'*
kena ketok	ripped off
kiasee	scared, literally 'afraid to die'; a coward
kiasu	literally 'afraid to lose'; selfish, pushy, always on the lookout for a bargain
kopitiam	coffeeshop
lah	generally an ending for any phrase or sentence; can translate as 'OK', but has no real meaning, added for emphasis to just about everything
lai dat	'like that'; used for emphasis, as in *'I so boring lai dat'* (I'm very bored)
looksee	take a look
minah	girlfriend
or not?	general suffix for questions, as in *'Can or not?'* (Can you or can't you?)
see first	wait and see what happens
shack	tired; often expressed as *'I damn shack sial'*
shiok	good, great, delicious
sotong	Malay for 'squid', used as an adjective meaning clumsy, or generally not switched on
steady lah	well done, excellent; an expression of praise
wah!	general exclamation of surprise or distress
ya ya	boastful, as in *'He always ya ya'*; also expressed *'He damn ya ya papaya'*

Survival Guide

Transport

ARRIVING IN SINGAPORE

Singapore is one of Asia's major air hubs, serviced by both full-service and budget airlines. The city-state has excellent and extensive regional and international connections. You can also catch trains and buses to Malaysia and Thailand. Book flights, tours and rail tickets online at lonelyplanet.com/bookings.

Changi Airport

Changi Airport (☏1800 542 4422; www.changiairport.com), 20km northeast of Singapore Central Business District (CBD), has three main terminals, with a fourth terminal scheduled to open in 2017. Regularly voted the world's best airport, Changi Airport is a major international gateway, with frequent flights to all corners of the globe. You'll find free internet, courtesy phones for local calls, foreign-exchange booths, medical centres, left-luggage, hotels, day spas, showers, a gym, swimming pool and no shortage of shops.

Taxi

Taxi lines at Changi are fast moving and efficient. The fare structure is complicated, but count on spending anywhere between $20 and $38 into the city centre,

depending on the time of travel. The most expensive time is between 5pm and 6am, when a whole raft of surcharges kick in.

A four-seater limousine taxi costs $55 to anywhere on the island, plus $15 surcharge for each additional stop. A seven-seater limousine taxi costs $60, plus $15 surcharge per additional stop. Enquire at the ground transport desk at the airport.

Train

The Mass Rapid Transit (MRT) is the best low-cost way to get into town. The station is located below terminals 2 and 3, the fare to Orchard Rd is $2.30 and the journey takes around 40 minutes. You have to change trains at Tanah Merah (just cross the platform). The first train leaves at 5.30am (6am Sundays) and the last goes at 11.18pm.

Bus

Public bus 36 runs from terminals 1, 2 and 3 to Orchard Rd and the Colonial District ($1.85, one hour). Buses leave roughly every five to 15 minutes, the first departing just after 6am and the last just before 11pm.

Faster and more convenient are the airport shuttle buses (adult/child $9/6, 20 to 40 minutes) that leave from the arrival halls at terminals 1, 2 and 3 and drop passengers at any hotel,

except those on Sentosa and in Changi Village. Waiting time is up to 15 minutes during peak hours (6am to 9am and 5pm to 1am) and up to 30 minutes at all other times. See the ground transport desk in the arrival halls.

Bus

If you are travelling beyond JB (Johor Bahru), Malaysia, the simplest option is to catch a bus straight from Singapore, though there are more options and lower fares travelling from JB.

Numerous private companies run comfortable bus services to Singapore from many destinations in Malaysia, including Melaka and Kuala Lumpur, as well as from destinations such as Hat Yai in Thailand. Many of these services terminate at **Golden Mile Complex** (5001 Beach Rd), close to Kampong Glam. Golden Mile Complex houses numerous bus agencies specialising in journeys between Singapore and Malaysia and Singapore and Thailand. You can book online at www.busonlineticket.com.

From Johor Bahru in Malaysia, **Causeway Link** (www.causewaylink.com.my; 1-way $2.50/RM2.60; ☺every 15 to 30 min, roughly 6am-11.30pm) commuter buses run regularly to various locations in Singapore, including Newton Circus, Jurong East

CLIMATE CHANGE & TRAVEL

Every form of transport that relies on carbon-based fuel generates CO_2, the main cause of human-induced climate change. Modern travel is dependent on aeroplanes, which might use less fuel per kilometre per person than most cars but travel much greater distances. The altitude at which aircraft emit gases (including CO_2) and particles also contributes to their climate change impact. Many websites offer 'carbon calculators' that allow people to estimate the carbon emissions generated by their journey and, for those who wish to do so, to offset the impact of the greenhouse gases emitted with contributions to portfolios of climate-friendly initiatives throughout the world. Lonely Planet offsets the carbon footprint of all staff and author travel.

Bus Terminal and Kranji MRT station. For details on catching a bus to JB, see p147.

Sea

There are plans to introduce direct ferry services between Puteri Harbour in Iskandar Malaysia and HarbourFront, Singapore – check www.ridaa.com.my and http://iskandar.asia for more information. Ferry services from Malaysia and Indonesia arrive at various ferry terminals in Singapore.

Changi Point Ferry Terminal (☑6546 8518; 51 Lorong Bekukong; Ⓜ Tanah Merah then bus 2)

HarbourFront Cruise & Ferry Terminal (☑6513 2200; www.singaporecruise.com; Ⓜ HarbourFront)

Tanah Merah Ferry Terminal (☑6513 2200; www.singaporecruise.com; Ⓜ Tanah Merah then bus 35)

Indonesia

Direct ferries run between the Riau Archipelago islands of Pulau Batam and Pulau Bintan and Singapore. The ferries are modern, fast and air-conditioned.

BatamFast (☑6270 0311; www.batamfast.com) Ferries from Batam Centre, Sekupang and Harbour Bay in Pulau Batam terminate at Harbour-Front Ferry Terminal. Ferries from Nongsapura, also in Pulau

Batam, terminate at the Tanah Merah Ferry Terminal.

Bintan Resort Ferries (☑6542 4369; www.brf.com.sg) Ferries from Bandar Bintan Telani in Pulau Bintan arrive at Tanah Merah Ferry Terminal.

Indo Falcon (☑6270 6778; www.indofalcon.com.sg) Ferries from Pulau Batam arrive at HarbourFront Ferry Terminal. Ferries from Tanjung Pinang in Pulau Bintan terminate at Tanah Merah Ferry Terminal.

Sindo Ferries (☑6542 7105; www.sindoferry.com.sg) Ferries from Batam Centre, Sekupang, WaterFront and Tanjung Balai arrive at HarbourFront Ferry Terminal. Ferries from Tanjung Pinang arrive at the Tanah Merah Ferry Terminal.

Wave Master (☑6272 0501; www.wavemaster.com.sg) Ferries from Batam Centre and Sekupang arrive at Harbour-Front Ferry Terminal. Ferries from Nongsapura and Tanjung Pinang in Pulau Bintan terminate at the Tanah Merah Ferry Terminal.

Train

Malaysia & Thailand

Singapore is the southern terminus for the Malaysian railway system, **Keretapi Tanah Malayu** (KTM; www.ktmb.com.my). KTM trains from Malaysia terminate at the **Woodlands Train Checkpoint** (11 Woodlands

Crossing; ☐170, Causeway Link from Queen St). Trains depart daily from Butterworth at 8am and Kuala Lumpur (KL) at 8.30am, 2pm and 10.30pm. Journey time is 14 hours from Butterworth and eight to 8½ hours from KL. You can book tickets either at the station or via the KTM website.

The luxurious **Eastern & Oriental Express** (☑6395 0678; www.belmond.com/eastern-and-oriental-express) departs Bangkok on the 42-hour, 1943km journey to Singapore – one of the world's great train journeys. Don your linen suit, sip a gin and tonic and dig deep for the fare: itineraries (including side tours) start from $3430 per person for four days/three nights.

GETTING AROUND

Singapore is the easiest city in Asia to get around. The TransitLink Guide – $2.80 from **Kinokuniya** (www.kinokuniya.com.sg; 391 Orchard Rd, 03-10/15, Ngee Ann City; ⊙10am-9.30pm) book shop – lists all MRT and bus routes and includes maps showing the surrounding area of all MRT stations.

For online bus information, including the useful IRIS service (which offers live next-bus departure times), see www.sbstransit.com.sg or download the 'SBS Transit iris' Smartphone app. For train information, see www.smrt.com.sg.

There's also a consolidated website at www.publictransport.sg.

Mass Rapid Transit

The efficient MRT subway system is the easiest, quickest and most comfortable way to get around Singapore. The system operates from 5.30am to midnight, with trains at peak times running every two to three minutes, and off-peak every five to seven minutes.

In the inner city, the MRT runs underground, emerging overground out towards the suburban housing estates. It consists of five colour-coded lines: North–South (red), North–East (purple), East–West (green), Circle Line (yellow) and Downtown (blue). Extensions of the Downtown line – known as Downtown 2 and Downtown 3 – are scheduled to open in 2016 and 2017 respectively.

You'll find a map of the network at www.smrt.com.sg.

Fares & Fare Cards

Single-trip tickets cost from $1.40 to $2.50 (plus a $1 refundable deposit), but if you're using the MRT a lot it can become a hassle buying and refunding tickets for every journey. A lot more convenient is the EZ-Link card. Alternatively, a **Singapore Tourist Pass** (www.thesingaporetouristpass.com.sg) offers unlimited train and bus travel ($10 plus a $10 refundable deposit) for one day.

Bus

Singapore's extensive bus service is clean, efficient and regular, reaching every corner of the island. The two main operators are **SBS Transit** (☎1800 287 2727; www.sbstransit.com.sg) and **SMRT** (www.smrt.com.sg). Both offer similar services.

For information and routes, check the websites.

Bus fares range from $1 to $2.10 (less with an EZ-Link card). When you board the bus, drop the exact money into the fare box (no change is given), or tap your EZ-Link card or Singapore Tourist Pass on the reader as you board, then again when you get off.

Train operator **SMRT** (www.smrt.com.sg) also runs late-night bus services between the city and various suburbs from 11.30pm to 2.30am on Fridays, Saturdays and the eve of public holidays. The flat rate per journey is $4.50. See the website for route details.

Taxi

You can flag down a taxi any time, but in the city centre taxis are technically not allowed to stop anywhere except at designated taxi stands.

Finding a taxi in the city at certain times is harder than it should be. These include during peak hours, at night, or when it's raining. Many cab drivers change shifts between 4pm and 5pm, making it notoriously difficult to score a taxi then.

The fare system is also complicated, but thankfully it's all metered, so there's no haggling over fares. The basic flagfall is $3 to $3.40 then $0.22 for every 400m.

There's a whole raft of surcharges to note, including the following:

➡ 50% of the metered fare from midnight to 6am.

➡ 25% of the metered fare between 6am and 9.30am Monday to Friday, and 6pm to midnight daily.

➡ $5 for airport trips from 5pm to midnight Friday to Sunday, and $3 at all other times.

➡ $3 city-area surcharge from 5pm to midnight.

➡ $2.30 to $8 for telephone bookings.

Payment by credit card incurs a 10% surcharge. You can also pay using your EZ-Link transport card. For a comprehensive list of fares and surcharges, visit www.taxisingapore.com.

Comfort Taxi and City-Cab (☎6552 1111)
Premier Taxis (☎6363 6888)
SMRT Taxis (☎6555 8888)

Bicycle

Avoid cycling on roads. Drivers are aggressive and the roads themselves uncomfortably hot. A much safer and more pleasant option for cyclists is Singapore's large network of parks and park

---

THE EZ-LINK AROUND TOWN

If you're staying in Singapore for more than a day or two, the easiest way to pay for travel on public transport is with the **EZ-Link card** (www.ezlink.com.sg). The card allows you to travel by train and bus by simply swiping it over sensors as you enter and leave a station or bus. EZ-Link cards can be purchased from the customer service counters at MRT stations for $12 (which includes a $5 nonrefundable deposit). The card can also be bought at 7-Elevens for $10 (which also includes a $5 nonrefundable deposit). Cards can be topped up with cash or by ATM cards at station ticket machines. The minimum top-up value is $10 while the maximum stored value allowed on your card is $100.

connectors, not to mention the dedicated mountain-biking areas at Bukit Timah Nature Reserve, Tampines and Pulau Ubin.

Other excellent places for cycling include East Coast Park, Sentosa, Pasir Ris Park and the route linking Mt Faber Park, Telok Blangah Hill Park and Kent Ridge Park.

Only fold-up bikes are allowed on trains and buses, and only during the following hours: 9.30am to 4pm and 8pm onwards Monday to Friday; all day Saturday, Sunday and public holidays.

Note that only *one* fold-up bike is allowed on buses at any time, so you might as well ride if you have to.

Hire

Bikes can be rented at several places along East Coast Park and on Sentosa Island and Pulau Ubin, with adult prices starting from $5 a day on Pulau Ubin and around $6 an hour elsewhere.

Boat

Visit the islands around Singapore from the Marina South Pier. There are regular ferry services from Changi Point Ferry Terminal to Pulau Ubin ($2). To get there, take bus 2 from Tanah Merah MRT.

Car & Motorcycle

Singaporeans drive on the left-hand side of the road and it is compulsory to wear seat belts in the front and back of the car. The *Mighty Minds Singapore Street Directory* ($12.90) is invaluable and

available from petrol stations, bookshops, FairPrice supermarkets and stationery stores.

Driving

If you plan on driving in Singapore, bring your current home driver's licence. Some car-hire companies may also require you to have an international driving permit.

While the roads themselves are immaculate, aggressive driving is common, speeding and tailgating endemic, use of signals rare and wild lane-changing universal.

In short, we don't recommend driving in Singapore, but if you do, practice extreme defensive driving and have your road rage under control.

Motorcycles are held in low esteem and some drivers display little regard for bike safety. Be alert.

Hire

If you want a car for local driving only, it's worth checking smaller operators, where the rates are often cheaper than the big global rental firms. If you're going into Malaysia, you're better off renting in Johor Bahru, where the rates are significantly lower (besides, Malaysian police are renowned for targeting Singapore licence plates).

Rates start from around $60 a day. Special deals may be available, especially for longer-term rental. Most rental companies require that drivers are at least 23 years old.

All major car-hire companies have booths at Changi Airport as well as in the city.

Avis (☑6737 1668; www. avis.com.sg; 01-07 Waterfront Plaza, 390A Havelock Rd)

Europcar (☑9186 9798; www.europcar.com; Changi Airport Terminal 1)

Hertz (☑6542 5300; www. hertz.com; Changi Airport Terminal 2 & 3)

Restricted Zone & Car Parking

At various times through the day, from Monday to Saturday, much of central Singapore is considered a restricted zone. Cars are allowed to enter but they must pay a toll. Vehicles are automatically tracked by sensors on overhead ERP (Electronic Road Pricing) gantries, so cars must be fitted with an in-vehicle unit, into which drivers must insert a cash card (available at petrol stations and 7-Elevens). The toll is extracted from the card. The same system is also in operation on certain expressways. Rental cars are subject to the same rules. Check www.onemotoring. com.sg for ERP rates and hours of operation.

Parking in the city centre is expensive, but fairly easy to find – almost every major mall has a car park. Outdoor car parks and street parking spaces are usually operated by the government – you can buy booklets of parking coupons, which must be displayed in the window, from petrol stations and 7-Elevens. Many car parks are now run using the same in-vehicle unit and cash card and ERP gantries instead of the coupon system.

Directory A–Z

Customs Regulations

You are not allowed to bring tobacco into Singapore unless you pay duty. You will be slapped with a hefty fine if you fail to declare and pay.

You are permitted 1L each of wine, beer and spirits duty free. Alternatively, you are allowed 2L of wine and 1L of beer, or 2L of beer and 1L of wine. You need to have been out of Singapore for more than 48 hours and to anywhere but Malaysia.

It's illegal to bring in chewing gum, firecrackers, obscene or seditious material, gun-shaped cigarette lighters, endangered species or their by-products and pirated recordings or publications.

Discount Cards

If you arrived on a Singapore Airlines or Silk Air flight, you can get discounts at shops,

restaurants and attractions by presenting your boarding pass. See www.singaporeair.com/boardingpass.

Electricity

230V/50Hz

PRACTICALITIES

➡ English daily newspapers in Singapore include the broadsheet *Straits Times*, the *Business Times* and the afternoon tabloid *New Paper*.

➡ Pornographic publications are strictly prohibited, but toned-down local editions of *Cosmopolitan* and lads' magazines such as *FHM* and *Maxim* are allowed.

➡ Singapore uses the metric system for weights and measures. Weights are in grams and kilograms and volume in millilitres and litres.

Emergency

Ambulance/Fire (☏995)
Police (☏999)

Gay & Lesbian Travellers

Sex between males is illegal in Singapore, carrying a minimum sentence of 10 years. In reality, nobody is ever likely to be prosecuted, but the ban remains as a symbol of the government's belief that the country is not ready for the open acceptance of 'alternative lifestyles'.

Despite that, Singapore has a string of popular LGBT bars. A good place to start looking for information is on the websites of **Travel Gay Asia** (www.travelgayasia.com), **PLUguide** (www.pluguide.com) or **Utopia** (www.utopia-asia.com), which provide coverage of venues and events.

Singaporeans are fairly conservative about public affection, though it's more common to see displays of familiarity among lesbian couples these days. A gay male couple doing the same would definitely draw negative attention.

Health

Hygiene in Singapore is strictly observed and the tap

water is safe to drink. However, hepatitis A does occasionally occur. You only need vaccinations if you come from a yellow-fever area. Singapore is not a malarial zone, though dengue fever is an increasing concern.

Dengue Fever

Singapore has suffered a sharp rise in cases of this nasty mosquito-borne disease in recent years. There is no vaccine so avoid mosquito bites. Peak biting periods are dawn and dusk, though it's best to use insect-avoidance measures at all times. Symptoms include high fever, severe headache and body ache. Some people develop a rash and diarrhoea. There is no specific treatment – just rest and paracetamol. Do not take aspirin. See a doctor to be diagnosed and monitored. For more information, visit www.dengue.gov.sg.

Prickly Heat

This is an itchy rash caused by excessive perspiration trapped under the skin. It usually strikes people who have just arrived in a hot climate. Keep cool, bathe often, dry the skin and use a mild talcum or prickly heat powder, or resort to air conditioning.

Internet Access

Most hotels offer internet access and will help get you set up if you bring your own laptop. Backpacker hostels all offer free internet access and wi-fi.

SingTel (http://info.singtel.com; cnr Exeter & Killiney Rds), StarHub (www.starhub.com; B2-17/18/18A, Plaza Singapura, 68 Orchard Rd) and M1 (www.m1.com.sg; B3-23, 313@ Somerset, 313 Orchard Rd) are local providers of broadband internet via USB modem dongles. Bring your own or buy one from them. You can get prepaid data SIM cards if you have your own dongle.

Legal Matters

Singapore's reputation for harsh laws is not undeserved: don't expect any special treatment for being a foreigner. Despite the surprisingly low-key police presence on the street, they appear pretty fast when something happens. Police have broad powers and you would be unwise to refuse any requests they make of you. If you are arrested, you will be entitled to legal counsel and contact with your embassy.

Don't even think about importing or exporting drugs. At best, you'll get long jail terms. At worse, you'll get the death penalty.

Medical Services

Singapore's medical institutions are first-rate and generally cheaper than private healthcare in the West. But needless to say, travel insurance is advisable. Check with insurance providers as to which treatments and procedures are covered before you leave home.

Clinics

Your hotel or hostel should be able to direct you to a local GP: there are plenty around.

Raffles Medical Clinic (✆6311 2233; www.rafflesmedicalgroup.com.sg; 585 North Bridge Rd; MBugis) A walk-in clinic at Raffles Hospital.

Singapore General Hospital (✆6321 4311; www.sgh.com.sg; Block 1, Outram Rd; MOutram Park). Also has an emergency room.

Emergency Rooms

There are several 24-hour emergency rooms.

Gleneagles Hospital (✆6473 7222; www.gleneagles.com.sg; 6A Napier Rd; ⊞7, 75, 77, 105, 106,123, 174)

Mount Elizabeth Hospital Novena (✆6653 8090; www.mountelizabeth.com.sg; 38 Irrawaddy Rd; MNovena)

Mount Elizabeth Hospital Orchard (✆6653 8089; www.mountelizabeth.com.sg; 3 Mt Elizabeth Rd; MOrchard)

Raffles Hospital (✆6311 1555; www.rafflesmedical-group.com.sg; 585 North Bridge Rd; MBugis) .

Money

The country's unit of currency is the Singapore dollar, locally referred to as the 'singdollar', which is made up of 100 cents. Singapore

WIRELESS@SG: FREE WI-FI ACCESS

Singapore has an ever-expanding network of around 1000 wireless hot spots – and most cafes, pubs, libraries and malls operate them. In Chinatown you'll find free wifi hot spots in Trengganu St, Pagoda St, Smith St, Sago St and Kreta Ayer Sq – simply choose the wireless@chinatown wifi network. While you don't need a local number to access Chinatown's free wifi, you will need a local number to access the free Wireless@SG hot spots throughout the city. Grab a SIM card from a convenience store or mobile-phone store (you will need to show your passport in order to buy one). A list of Wireless@SG hot spots can be found at www.ida.gov.sg (click on 'Infocomm' and then 'Infastructure').

uses 5¢, 10¢, 20¢, 50¢ and $1 coins, while notes come in denominations of $2, $5, $10, $50, $100, $500 and $1000. The Singapore dollar is a highly stable and freely convertible currency.

ATMs

Cirrus-enabled ATMs are widely available at malls, banks, MRT stations and commercial areas.

Changing Money

Banks can exchange money, but virtually nobody uses them for currency conversion because the rates are better at the moneychangers dotted all over the city. These tiny stalls can be found in just about every shopping centre (though not necessarily in the more modern malls). Rates can be haggled a little if you're changing amounts of $500 or more.

Credit Cards

Credit cards are widely accepted, except at local hawkers and food courts. Cases of smaller stores charging an extra 2% to 3% for credit-card payments have decreased in recent years.

Opening Hours

Opening hours can vary between individual businesses. General opening hours are as follows.

Banks Monday to Friday 9.30am to 4.30pm – some branches open at 10am and some close at 6pm or later; Saturday 9.30am to noon or later.

Government and Post Offices Monday to Friday between 8am and 9.30am to between 4pm and 6pm; Saturday between 8am and 9am to 11.30am and 1.30pm.

Restaurants Top restaurants generally open between noon and 2pm for lunch and 6pm till 10pm for dinner. Casual restaurants and food courts are open all day.

Shops 10am to 6pm, larger shops and department stores open till 9.30pm or 10pm. Some smaller shops in Chinatown and Arab St close on Sunday. It's busiest in Little India on Sunday.

Post

Postal delivery in Singapore is very efficient. Call ☑1605 to find the nearest branch or check www.singpost.com.sg.

The post offices on **Killiney Rd** (☑6734 7899; 1 Killiney Rd; ⊙9.30am-9pm Mon-Fri, to 4pm Sat, 10.30am-4pm Sun; Ⓜ Somerset) and **Orchard Rd** (B2-62 ION Orchard, 2 Orchard Turn; ⊙11am-7pm; Ⓜ Orchard) are open on Sundays. At Changi Airport, you'll find a **post office** (⊙8am-9.30pm) in the departure check-in hall of terminal 2.

Public Holidays

Listed here are public holidays in Singapore. For those days not based on the Western calendar, the months in which they are likely to fall are provided. The only holiday that has a major effect on the city is Chinese New Year, when virtually all shops shut down for two days.

New Year's Day 1 January

Chinese New Year Three days in January/February

Good Friday April

Labour Day 1 May

Vesak Day June

Hari Raya Puasa July

National Day 9 August

Hari Raya Haji September

Deepavali November

Christmas Day 25 December

Taxes & Refunds

As a visitor you are entitled to claim a refund of the 7% Goods and Services Tax on your purchases, provided you meet certain conditions (see p42).

Telephone

Country code (☑65)

➡ There are no area codes within Singapore; telephone numbers are eight digits unless you are calling toll-free (☑1800).

➡ You can make local and international calls from public phone booths. Most phone booths take phonecards.

➡ Singapore also has credit-card phones that can be used by running your card through the slot.

➡ Calls to Malaysia (from Singapore) are considered to be STD (trunk or long-distance) calls. Dial the access code ☑020, followed by the area code of the town in Malaysia that you wish to call (minus the leading zero) and then the phone number. Thus, for a call to ☑346 7890 in Kuala Lumpur (area code ☑03) you would dial ☑02-3-346 7890.

Mobile Phones

In Singapore, mobile-phone numbers start with 9 or 8.

You can buy a local SIM card for around $18 (including credit) from post offices, convenience stores and local telco stores – by law you must show your passport to get one.

M1 (www.m1.com.sg; B3-23, 313@Somerset, 313 Orchard Rd)

SingTel (http://info.singtel.com; cnr Exeter & Killiney Rds)

StarHub (www.starhub.com; B2-17/18/18A Plaza Singapura, 68 Orchard Rd)

Phonecards

Phonecards are popular among Singapore's migrant workers, so there are plenty on sale. There's a small phonecard stall outside the Centrepoint shopping centre on Orchard Rd, and plenty of retailers around Little India; check which countries they service before you buy.

Time

Singapore is eight hours ahead of GMT/UTC (London), two hours behind Australian Eastern Standard Time (Sydney and Melbourne), 13 hours ahead of American Eastern Standard Time (New York) and 16 hours ahead of American Pacific Standard Time (San Francisco and Los Angeles). So, when it is noon in Singapore, it is 8pm in Los Angeles and 11pm in New York the previous day, 4am in London and 2pm in Sydney.

Tourist Information

Before your trip, a good place to check for informa-tion is the website of the **Singapore Tourism Board** (STB; ☑1800 736 2000; www.yoursingapore.com).

In Singapore, there are several tourism centres offering a wide range of services, including tour bookings and event ticketing, plus a couple of electronic information kiosks.

Chinatown Visitor Centre (2 Banda St; ☺9am-9pm Mon-Fri, to 10pm Sat & Sun; ⓂChinatown) Aside from offering free maps of Chinatown and Singapore, Chinatown's very own visitor centre can book walking tours of the area and also sells a small range of quality souvenirs, including books of Singapore art, reproduction watercolours of Singapore street scenes, and T-shirts.

Singapore Visitors Centre @ ION Orchard (Level 1, ION Orchard Mall, 2 Orchard Turn; ☺10am-10pm; ⓂOrchard)

Singapore Visitors Centre @ Orchard (☑1800 736 2000; www.yoursingapore.com; cnr Orchard & Cairnhill Rds; ☺9.30am-10.30pm; ⓂSomerset) Brochures, maps, helpful staff.

Travellers with Disabilities

A large government campaign has seen ramps, lifts and other facilities progressively installed around the island. The footpaths in the city are nearly all immaculate, MRT stations all have lifts and there are some buses and taxis equipped with wheelchair-friendly equipment.

The **Disabled People's Association Singapore** (☑6791 1134; www.dpa.org.sg) can provide information on accessibility in Singapore.

Visas

Citizens of most countries are granted 90-day entry on arrival. Citizens of India, Myanmar, the Commonwealth of Independent States and most Middle Eastern countries must obtain a visa before arriving in Singapore. Visa extensions can be applied for at the **Immigration & Checkpoints Authority** (☑6391 6100; www.ica.gov.sg; 10 Kallang Rd; ⓂLavender).

Behind the Scenes

SEND US YOUR FEEDBACK

We love to hear from travellers – your comments keep us on our toes and help make our books better. Our well-travelled team reads every word on what you loved or loathed about this book. Although we cannot reply individually to your submissions, we always guarantee that your feedback goes straight to the appropriate authors, in time for the next edition. Each person who sends us information is thanked in the next edition – the most useful submissions are rewarded with a selection of digital PDF chapters.

Visit **lonelyplanet.com/contact** to submit your updates and suggestions or to ask for help. Our award-winning website also features inspirational travel stories, news and discussions.

Note: We may edit, reproduce and incorporate your comments in Lonely Planet products such as guidebooks, websites and digital products, so let us know if you don't want your comments reproduced or your name acknowledged. For a copy of our privacy policy visit lonelyplanet.com/privacy.

OUR READERS

Many thanks to the travellers who used the last edition and wrote to us with helpful hints, useful advice and interesting anecdotes:

Andrea Yvonne Leber, Andrew Hackett, Christian Proulx, Claudia Artz, Helen Edwards, Holger Lichau, Ken Westmoreland, Laura Cavatorta, Lisa Wilkie, Meike Herbers, Nguyen Truong Giang, Nico Bryant-Stevens, Peta Roberts, Prerana Jalla, Steve Hollins, Tatjana Gazibara, Thomas Sarosy, Walter Hirschle

AUTHOR THANKS

Cristian Bonetto

A heartfelt thank you to Helen Burge, Alistair Cook, Felix Haubold, Chris Edwards, Jonathan Choe, Guillaume D, Mary-Ann Gardner, Sara Egan, Myles Bascao Agunit, Benjamin Milton Hampe and Michael Dean. Many thanks also to Richie Raupe, Lim Wee Keong, my patient family, and all the Singaporeans and expats kind enough to share their own favourite bits of the Little Red Dot.

ACKNOWLEDGMENTS

Cover photograph: Supertrees at night, Gardens by the Bay, Brook Mitchell/4Corners

THIS BOOK

This 10th edition of Lonely Planet's *Singapore* guidebook was researched and written by Cristian Bonetto. The 9th edition was written by Shawn Low and Daniel McCrohan, and the 8th edition by Mat Oakley and Joshua Samuel Brown. This guidebook was commissioned in Lonely Planet's London office, and produced by the following:

Destination Editor Sarah Reid
Product Editors Elin Berglund, Bruce Evans
Senior Cartographer Julie Sheridan
Book Designer Katherine Marsh
Assisting Editors Andrew Bain, Kate Evans, Erin Richards, Saralinda Turner
Cartographer Rachel Imeson
Cover Researcher Naomi Parker
Thanks to Ryan Evans, Larissa Frost, Jouve India, Wayne Murphy, Claire Murphy, Karyn Noble, Samantha Tyson, Dora Whitaker

See also separate subindexes for:

✗ **EATING P194**

🍷 **DRINKING & NIGHTLIFE P195**

☆ **ENTERTAINMENT P196**

🛍 **SHOPPING P196**

🏃 **SPORTS & ACTIVITIES P197**

🛏 **SLEEPING P197**

Index

Singapore Maps

Sights
- Beach
- Bird Sanctuary
- Buddhist
- Castle/Palace
- Christian
- Confucian
- Hindu
- Islamic
- Jain
- Jewish
- Monument
- Museum/Gallery/Historic Building
- Ruin
- Sento Hot Baths/Onsen
- Shinto
- Sikh
- Taoist
- Winery/Vineyard
- Zoo/Wildlife Sanctuary
- Other Sight

Activities, Courses & Tours
- Bodysurfing
- Diving
- Canoeing/Kayaking
- Course/Tour
- Skiing
- Snorkelling
- Surfing
- Swimming/Pool
- Walking
- Windsurfing
- Other Activity

Sleeping
- Sleeping
- Camping

Eating
- Eating

Drinking & Nightlife
- Drinking & Nightlife
- Cafe

Entertainment
- Entertainment

Shopping
- Shopping

Information
- Bank
- Embassy/Consulate
- Hospital/Medical
- Internet
- Police
- Post Office
- Telephone
- Toilet
- Tourist Information
- Other Information

Geographic
- Beach
- Hut/Shelter
- Lighthouse
- Lookout
- Mountain/Volcano
- Oasis
- Park
- Pass
- Picnic Area
- Waterfall

Population
- Capital (National)
- Capital (State/Province)
- City/Large Town
- Town/Village

Transport
- Airport
- Border crossing
- Bus
- Cable car/Funicular
- Cycling
- Ferry
- MRT station
- Monorail
- Parking
- Petrol station
- Skytrain/Subway station
- Taxi
- Train station/Railway
- Tram
- Underground station
- Other Transport

Note: Not all symbols displayed above appear on the maps in this book

Routes
- Tollway
- Freeway
- Primary
- Secondary
- Tertiary
- Lane
- Unsealed road
- Road under construction
- Plaza/Mall
- Steps
- Tunnel
- Pedestrian overpass
- Walking Tour
- Walking Tour detour
- Path/Walking Trail

Boundaries
- International
- State/Province
- Disputed
- Regional/Suburb
- Marine Park
- Cliff
- Wall

Hydrography
- River, Creek
- Intermittent River
- Canal
- Water
- Dry/Salt/Intermittent Lake
- Reef

Areas
- Airport/Runway
- Beach/Desert
- Cemetery (Christian)
- Cemetery (Other)
- Glacier
- Mudflat
- Park/Forest
- Sight (Building)
- Sportsground
- Swamp/Mangrove

MAP INDEX

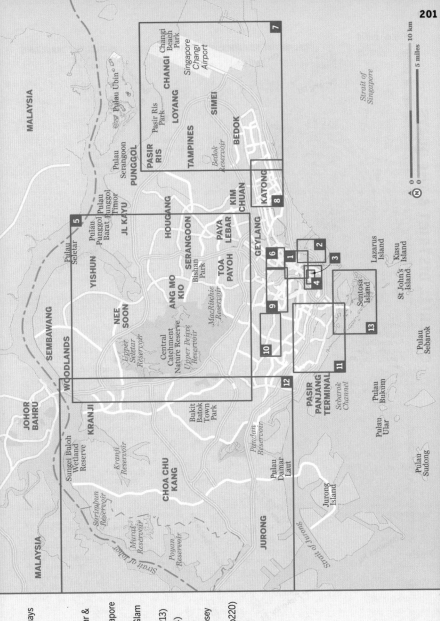

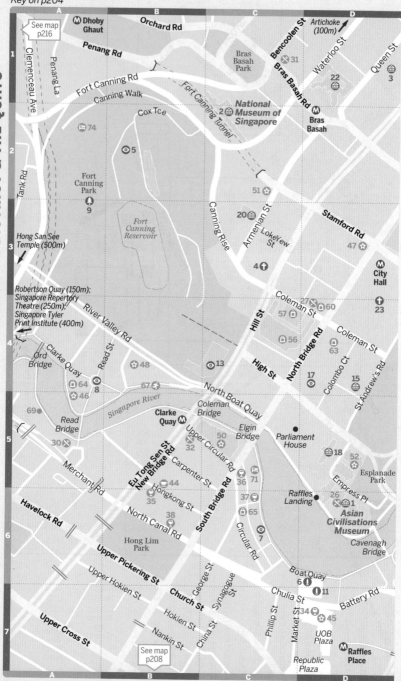

COLONIAL DISTRICT & THE QUAYS

Key on p204

See map p216

Ⓜ Dhoby Ghaut

Orchard Rd

Penang Rd

Bencoolen St

Artichoke (100m)

Bras Basah Park

31

Waterloo St

Queen St

22

3

Fort Canning Rd

Penang La

Clemenceau Ave

Canning Walk

Fort Canning Tunnel

National Museum of Singapore

2

Bras Basah Rd

Ⓜ Bras Basah

Cox Tce

74

5

Fort Canning Park

9

Fort Canning Reservoir

Tank Rd

Canning Rise

51

20

Armenian St

Loke Yew St

Stamford Rd

47

Ⓜ City Hall

4

23

Hong San See Temple (500m)

Robertson Quay (150m); Singapore Repertory Theatre (250m); Singapore Tyler Print Institute (400m)

River Valley Rd

Coleman St

27

60

57

56

Hill St

North Bridge Rd

Coleman St

63

Clarke Quay

Ord Bridge

64

8

48

67

13

High St

17

15

Colombo Ct

St Andrew's Rd

Read St

Singapore River

North Boat Quay

46

69

Read Bridge

Clarke Quay Ⓜ

Coleman Bridge

Elgin Bridge

Parliament House

18

52

Esplanade Park

30

Upper Circular Rd

50

32

Merchant Rd

Eu Tong Sen St New Bridge Rd

Carpenter St

36

71

Empress Pl

26

1

Raffles Landing

Asian Civilisations Museum

Hongkong St

44

35

37

65

Havelock Rd

North Canal Rd

38

South Bridge Rd

Circular Rd

7

Cavenagh Bridge

Hong Lim Park

Upper Pickering St

Boat Quay

6

11

Upper Hokien St

Church St

George St

Synagogue St

Chulia St

Battery Rd

Phillip St

Market St

34

45

Upper Cross St

Hokien St

China St

Nankin St

UOB Plaza

Ⓜ Raffles Place

Republic Plaza

See map p208

A B C D

1 2 3 4 5 6 7

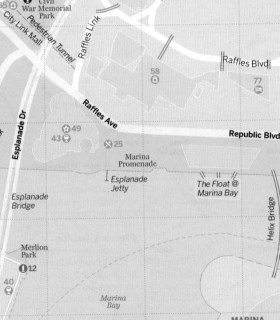

400 m
0.25 miles

See map p210

Tan Quee Lan St
Parkview Square
Liang Seah St
Beach Rd
Rochor Rd
Nicoll Hwy
Ophir Rd
Middle Rd
Victoria St
Bain St
16
North Bridge Rd
53 54
Cashin St
14 29
Purvis St 24
Seah St 33
75
41
21 62
76
Beach Rd
Bras Basah Rd
10
Temasek Ave
Rochor Rd
61 70
59
42
28
Civilian War Memorial
Esplanade
68
66
Temasek Blvd
Nicoll Hwy
M Promenade
55
Civil War Memorial Park
Pedestrian Tunnel
City Link Mall
Raffles Link
Singapore Flyer (200m)
58
Raffles Blvd
77
East Coast Parkway
The Padang
19
Connaught Dr
Esplanade Dr
Raffles Ave
Republic Blvd
43
49
25
Marina Promenade
Queen Elizabeth Walk
Esplanade Jetty
Esplanade Bridge
The Float @ Marina Bay
Helix Bridge
Anderson Bridge
Merlion Park
12
73
Fullerton Rd
40
Marina Bay
MARINA SOUTH
72
Collyer Quay
Marina Bay Sands
Marina Bay Sands Hotel

See map p205

39

COLONIAL DISTRICT & THE QUAYS *Map on p202*

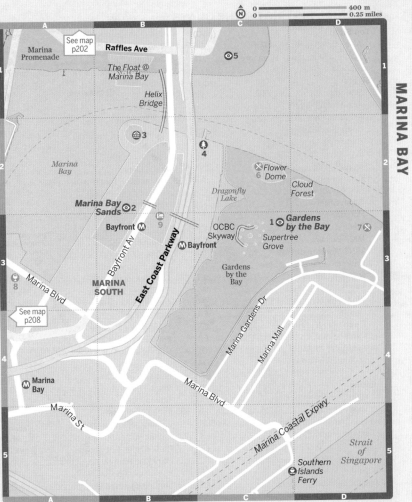

CHINATOWN

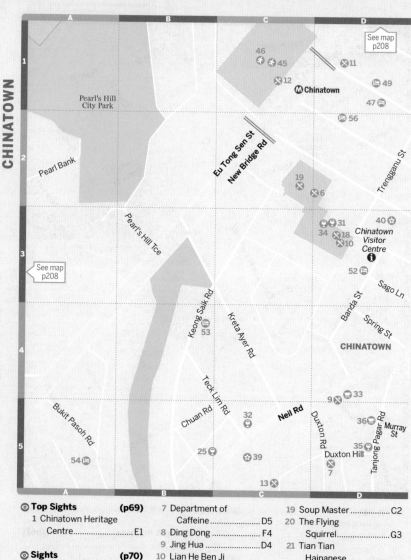

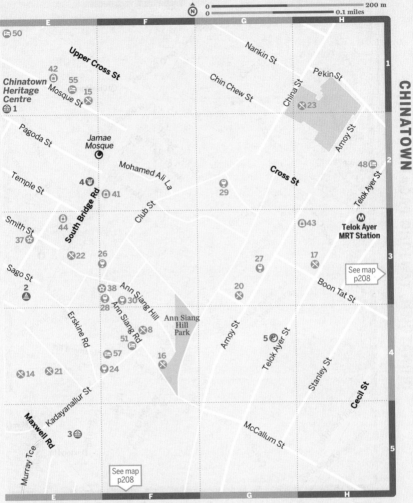

CHINATOWN, TANJONG PAGAR & THE CBD

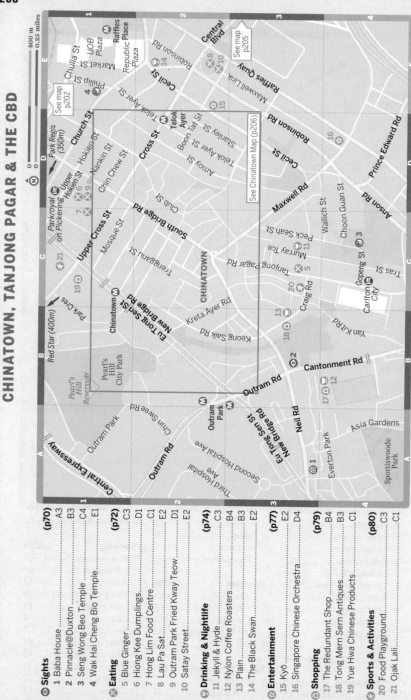

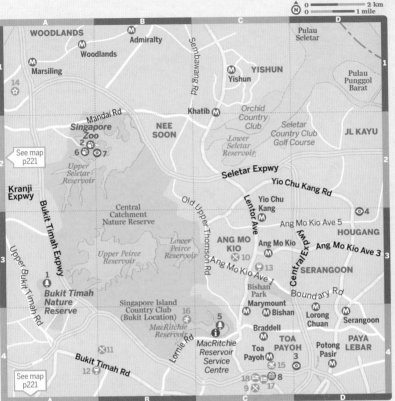

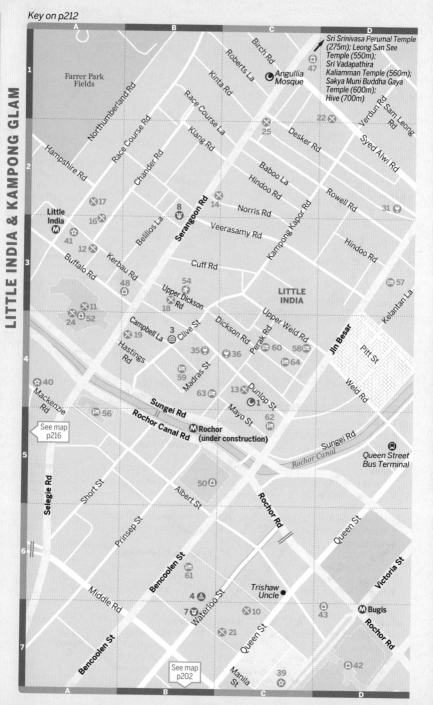

LITTLE INDIA & KAMPONG GLAM

Farrer Park Fields

Northumberland Rd

Hampshire Rd

Race Course Rd

Chander Rd

Klang Rd

Race Course La

Kinta Rd

Roberts La

Birch Rd

Angullia Mosque

Sri Srinivasa Perumal Temple (275m); Leong San See Temple (550m); Sri Vadapathira Kaliamman Temple (560m); Sakya Muni Buddha Gaya Temple (600m); Hive (700m)

47

22

25

Desker Rd

Verdun Rd

Sam Leong Rd

Syed Alwi Rd

Baboo La

Hindoo Rd

Rowell Rd

31

Serangoon Rd

8

14

Norris Rd

Veerasamy Rd

Kampong Kapor Rd

Hindoo Rd

Little India

41

17

16

Beilios La

12

Kerbau Rd

Buffalo Rd

48

Cuff Rd

LITTLE INDIA

57

Kelantan La

24

11

52

54

Upper Dickson Rd

18

Campbell La

19

3

Clive St

Dickson Rd

Upper Weld Rd

Perak Rd

60

58

Jln Besar

Pitt St

Hastings Rd

35

36

59

Madras St

64

Weld Rd

40

Mackenzie Rd

56

Sungei Rd

Rochor Canal Rd

63

13

1

Dunlop St

Mayo St

62

Sungei Rd

Rochor Canal

Queen Street Bus Terminal

See map p216

Rochor (under construction)

50

Short St

Albert St

Rochor Rd

Selegie Rd

Prinsep St

Queen St

61

Bencoolen St

Middle Rd

4

7

Waterloo St

Trishaw Uncle

10

43

Bugis

21

Queen St

Rochor Rd

Victoria St

Bencoolen St

See map p202

Manila St

39

42

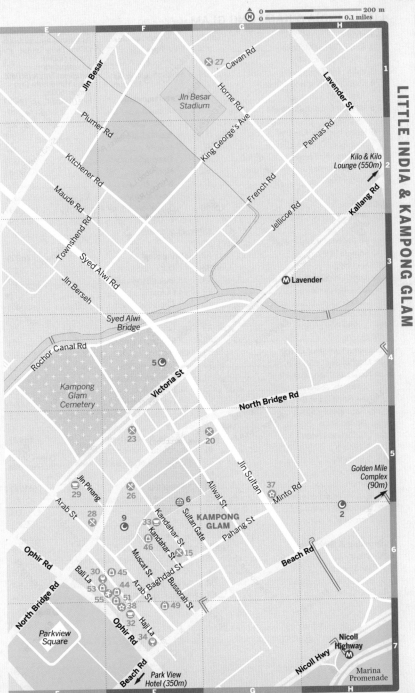

LITTLE INDIA & KAMPONG GLAM *Map on p210*

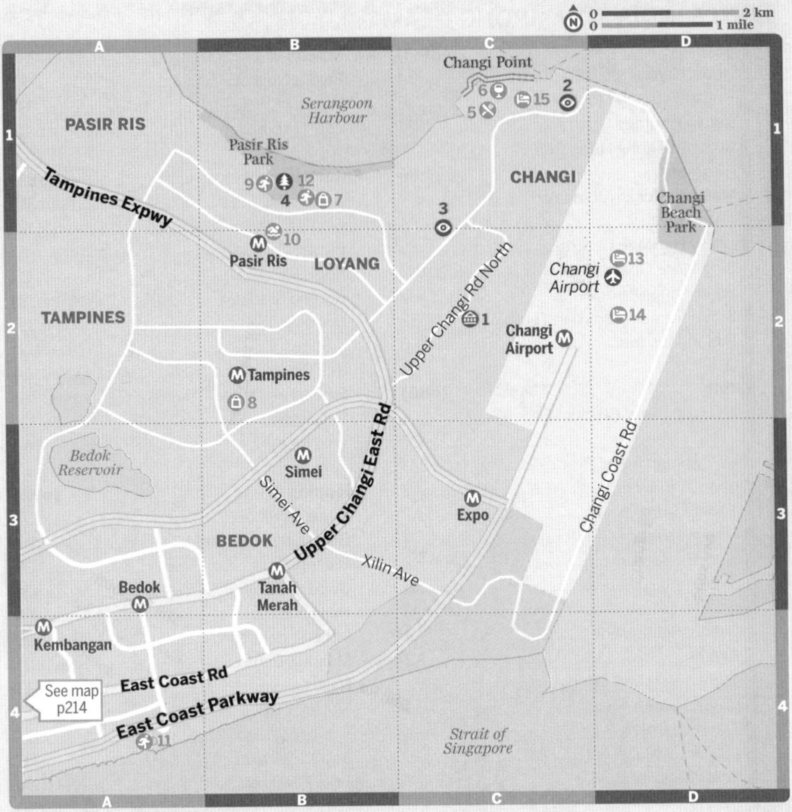

Sights **(p106)**
1 Changi Museum & Chapel....................C2
2 Changi Village....................C1
3 Loyang Tua Pek Kong Temple....................C1
4 Pasir Ris Park....................B1

Eating **(p111)**
Changi Village Hawker Centre....................(see 2)
Charlie's Corner....................(see 2)
5 Coastal Settlement....................C1
International Nasi Lemak....................(see 2)
Mei Xiang Goreng Pisang....................(see 2)

Drinking & Nightlife **(p107)**
6 Coachman Inn....................C1

Shopping **(p112)**
7 Downtown East....................B1
8 Tampines Mall....................B2

Sports & Activities **(p112)**
9 Gallop Stables....................B1
10 Pasir Ris Sports & Recreation Centre....................B2
11 Ski360°....................A4
12 Wild Wild Wet....................B1

Sleeping **(p161)**
13 Ambassador Transit Hotel....................D2
14 Crowne Plaza Changi Airport....................D2
15 Village Hotel Changi....................C1

EASTERN SINGAPORE

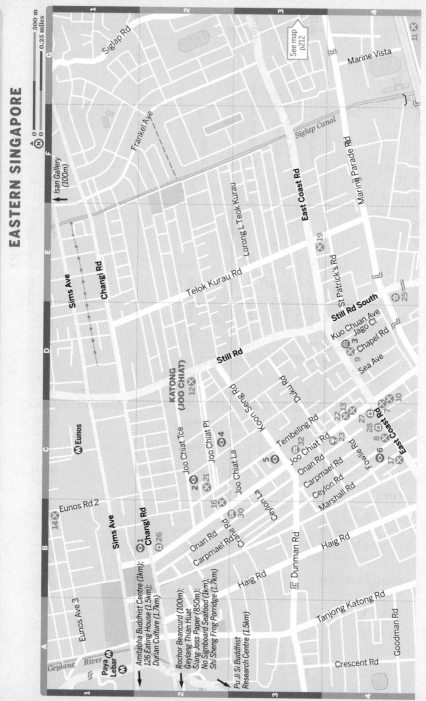

0 500 m
0 0.25 miles

See map p212

Siglap Rd

Frankel Ave

Marine Vista

Siglap Canal

Isan Gallery (100m)

Sims Ave

Changi Rd

East Coast Rd

Lorong L Teok Kurau

Marine Parade Rd

Telok Kurau Rd

Eunos

St Patrick's Rd

Still Rd South

Still Rd

Kuo Chuan Ave
Jago Cl

KATONG
(JOO CHIAT)

Chapel Rd

Sea Ave

Eunos Rd 2

Joo Chiat Tce

Joo Chiat Pl

Koon Seng Rd

Duku Rd

Tembeling Rd

Sims Ave

Changi Rd

Joo Chiat La

Joo Chiat Rd

Onan Rd

Fowlie Rd

East Coast Rd

Onan Rd

Carpmael Rd
Crane La

Ceylon La

Ceylon Rd

Carpmael Rd

Ceylon Rd

Marshall Rd

Eunos Ave 3

Dunman Rd

Haig Rd

Amitabha Buddhist Centre (1km);
126 Eating House (1.5km);
Durian Culture (1.7km)

Rochor Beancurd (100m);
Geylang Than Huat
Siang Joss Paper (850m);
No Signboard Seafood (1km);
Shi Sheng Frog Porridge (1.7km)

Haig Rd

Tanjong Katong Rd

Goodman Rd

Pu Ji Si Buddhist
Research Centre (1.5km)

Crescent Rd

Geylang River

Paya Lebar

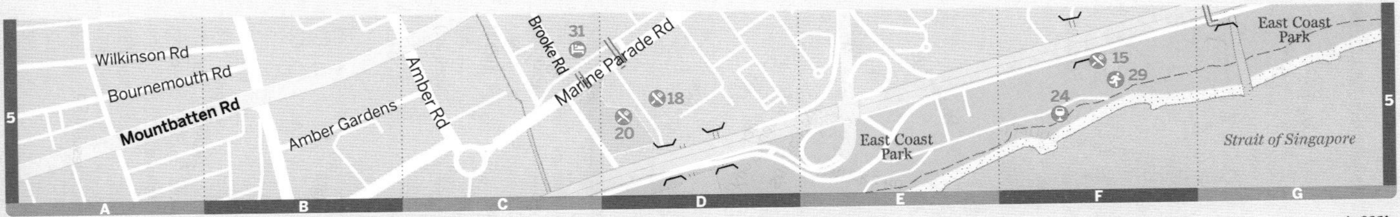

EASTERN SINGAPORE

East Coast Park

Strait of Singapore

East Coast Park

East Coast Park

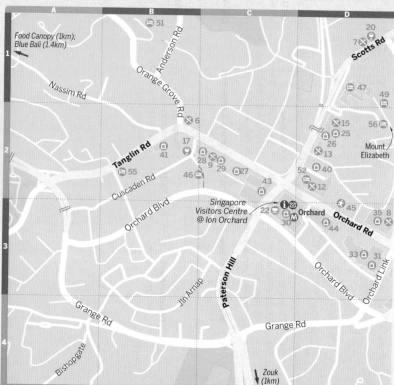

Food Canopy (1km);
Blue Bali (1.4km)

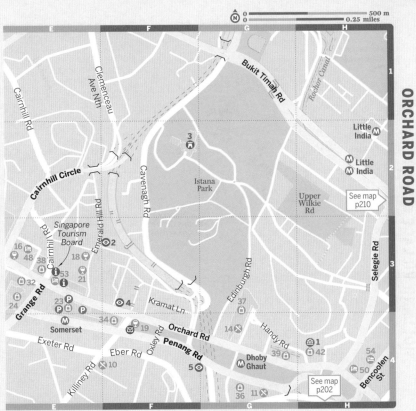

HOLLAND VILLAGE & DEMPSEY HILL

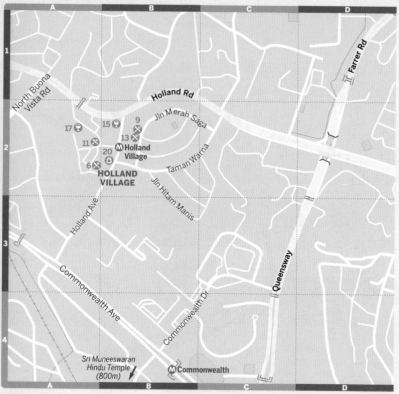

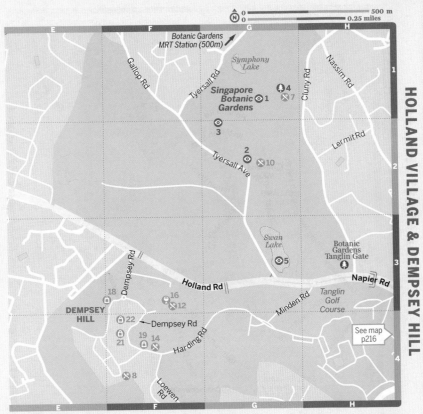

SOUTHWEST SINGAPORE

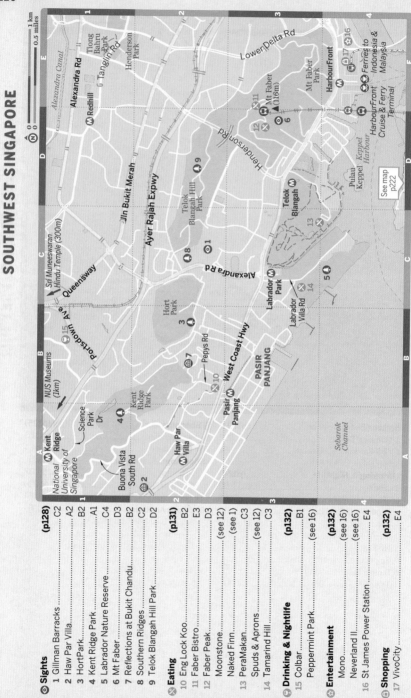

WEST SINGAPORE

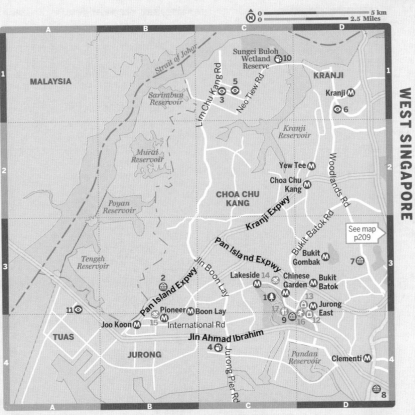

SENTOSA ISLAND

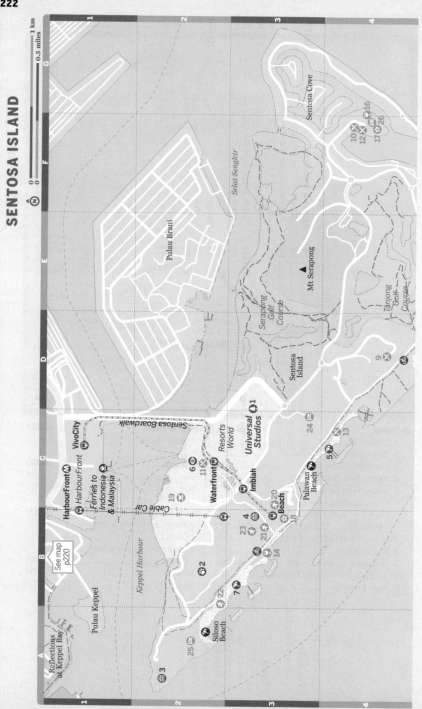

0 0.5 miles
0 1 km

A **B** **C** **D** **E** **F** **G** **H**

Reflections at Keppel Bay
Pulau Keppel
Keppel Harbour
See map p220
HarbourFront
HarbourFront
VivoCity
Ferries to Indonesia & Malaysia
Sentosa Boardwalk
Pulau Bruni
Selat Senghtr
Cable Car
Resorts World
Universal Studios
Waterfront
Imbiah
Beach
Palawan Beach
Siloso Beach
Serapong Golf Course
Mt Serapong
Sentosa Island
Sentosa Cove
Tanjong Golf Course

SENTOSA ISLAND

Strait of
Singapore

Our Story

A beat-up old car, a few dollars in the pocket and a sense of adventure. In 1972 that's all Tony and Maureen Wheeler needed for the trip of a lifetime – across Europe and Asia overland to Australia. It took several months, and at the end – broke but inspired – they sat at their kitchen table writing and stapling together their first travel guide, *Across Asia on the Cheap*. Within a week they'd sold 1500 copies. Lonely Planet was born. Today, Lonely Planet has offices in Franklin, London, Melbourne, Oakland, Beijing and Delhi, with more than 600 staff and writers. We share Tony's belief that 'a great guidebook should do three things: inform, educate and amuse'.

Our Writer

Cristian Bonetto

Cristian has been roaming Singapore's famous and lesser-known corners for years, and his addiction to the city's food, architecture and climate is yet to wane. Also the author of Lonely Planet's *Pocket Singapore*, the Australian-born writer majored in English and politics at the University of Melbourne before embarking on a career as a playwright and television scriptwriter. With a passion for cities and air miles, it was only a matter of time before he turned to travel writing. To date, Cristian has contributed to 13 Lonely Planet titles including New York City, Italy, Denmark and Sweden. His musings have also appeared in a string of other publications including the *Telegraph* (UK), *7X7* (San Francisco), and *Corriere del Mezzogiorno* (Italy). Follow Cristian on Twitter @cristianbonetto.

Published by Lonely Planet Publications Pty Ltd
ABN 36 005 607 983
10th edition – Feb 2015
ISBN 9781743210017
© Lonely Planet 2015   Photographs © as indicated 2015
10 9 8 7 6 5 4 3 2 1
Printed in China